C000286008

Mercia

The Rise and Fall of a Kingdom

Mercia

The Rise and Fall of a Kingdom

Annie Whitehead

AMBERLEY

First published 2018

Amberley Publishing
The Hill, Stroud
Gloucestershire, GL5 4EP

www.amberley-books.com

Copyright © Annie Whitehead 2018

The right of Annie Whitehead to be identified as the Author
of this work has been asserted in accordance with the
Copyrights, Designs and Patents Act 1988.

All rights reserved. No part of this book may be reprinted
or reproduced or utilised in any form or by any electronic,
mechanical or other means, now known or hereafter invented,
including photocopying and recording, or in any information
storage or retrieval system, without the permission in writing
from the Publishers.

All images author archives unless otherwise indicated.

British Library Cataloguing in Publication Data.
A catalogue record for this book is available from the British Library.

ISBN 978 1 4456 7652 4 (hardback)
ISBN 978 1 4456 7653 1 (ebook)

Typeset in 10.5pt on 13.5pt Sabon.
Typesetting and Origination by Amberley Publishing.
Printed in the UK.

Contents

Acknowledgements

Sitting in undergraduate lecture theatres, listening to the tales of Penda energetically riding up and down the country trying to protect his territory, and of Ælfhere, the blast of madness from the western territories, I was entranced. But it quickly occurred to me that these men were maligned. Even the course name – the Supremacy of Wessex – seemed to overlook the fact that Mercia once enjoyed its own supremacy. The very names of the Mercians were more appealing to me, more distinct; they were one-offs: Penda, Offa, Godiva, Eadric Streona … this latter one was perhaps not so maligned, but I remember the famous line uttered by Cnut, and retold to me in those lectures with such relish: 'Pay this man what we owe him …'

Thus, first on my list of people to thank must be my tutor, Ann Williams, who continues, all these years later, to educate and inspire me. I would also like to thank Richard Tearle for his kind permission to use his photographs, fellow Amberley author Sharon Bennett Connolly for her support and encouragement, and Andy and Margaret Austen who gave up their free time to show me round St Wystan's Church and its crypt. Chris Monk assisted me with translations, and Josh Desbottes helped collate many charter references.

The internet is a wonderful tool, not merely for research but for talking to people, and I am grateful to Marie Hilder, Alex Hibberts, Ian Andrews, Gerry Lyons and Jennifer Robinson for their insights and the fascinating discussions about Mercia and Anglo-Saxon England generally.

Finally, to my family: my husband Ian, and my 'kids', Adam, Lizzie and Imogen, for graciously giving me the space and time to complete this project.

Introduction

Mercia survives as a name only in titles of institutions. The constabulary of the West Mercia Police is responsible for the counties of Shropshire, Herefordshire and Worcestershire, which does at least give a clue about the location of part of this once powerful kingdom.

In reply to the question 'where is it?' it is usually enough to answer that it was a kingdom of the midlands, but the truth is that its borders changed many times as Mercian power waxed and waned, though its heart was the land either side of the River Trent.

At its zenith, it controlled the areas which even today can be recognised for their roles in the history of commerce and manufacturing: Birmingham and London. It is an erstwhile kingdom, but it is still the heart of England, and it is far from derelict.

Whilst people might not necessarily have heard of the kingdom of Mercia, they will, undoubtedly, have heard of some of the kings and queens who emerged from that territory, to make their mark as powerful rulers, or to become the stuff of legend: Penda, the pagan warrior, Offa the famous dyke-builder, Æthelflæd, Lady of the Mercians, Godiva riding through the centre of Coventry.

The record is in two halves, pre- and post-Viking, in the way it has been preserved. Pre-Viking, virtually all the source material was written by the victims, or perceived victims, of Mercian aggression and/or expansion. Post-Viking, the surviving documents tend to hail from places which weren't sacked or burned by those Vikings, i.e. Wessex, the traditional enemy of Mercia. Even that source material is scarce; William of Malmesbury, writing in the twelfth century, said that he would speak only briefly of the kingdom of the Mercians, because there was 'no great abundance' of materials.

In piecing together the history of this huge and hugely important kingdom, we are mostly reliant on what others had to say about it. This leads inevitably to two main problems: firstly, the bias that is concomitant with such a surviving body of written evidence, and secondly, the notion that they themselves were illiterate and uncultured – although, as we shall see, this was not the case. Add to this the fact that the Mercians were victims as well, in this case of the Vikings and that many land-books and charters were lost, presumed burned, and we find that almost all of what we know about the Mercians is written from the perspective of their enemies. The Mercians therefore tend to be seen firstly as aggressors, when in reality they were behaving no differently from those in other kingdoms, and secondly as a weak country, which did not withstand the onslaught of the Danish invaders.

Our tale begins with enmity and war between Mercia and Northumbria in the seventh century and ends with those two former kingdoms allied against the Godwines, the powerful family whose story is so inextricably linked with Hastings and 1066.

It is in the seventh century that Penda appears on the scene. At that time there were several kingdoms in England, traditionally known at the Heptarchy because it is usually stated that there were seven of them: Northumbria was originally two kingdoms, Deira, which centred around the city we now call York, and Bernicia to the north, centred around Bamburgh; the kingdom of the West Saxons, later to become known as Wessex, was in the southwest; in the east was the kingdom of the East Angles; there were also minor kingdoms of the East Saxons and the South Saxons; the kingdom of Kent; and – occupying the land in-between north and south – were the Mercians. Chapter Two will examine the origins of these people, and how their borders, like all the kingdoms of the Heptarchy, expanded and contracted over the centuries. Bede described the Mercians as the people who lived in the Trent Valley. Their fortunes fluctuated, as did their borders, but the salient point for the beginning of the history of the Mercians is that their northern border collided with that of Northumbria.

Of the 'Anglo-Saxons' themselves, the only contemporary uses of the term occur in the reigns of Alfred and his immediate successors who were kings both of 'Saxon' Wessex and 'Anglian' Mercia, and in Continental sources, where it was used to distinguish 'the Saxons of Britain' from 'the Saxons of Saxony'. In this period, the 'English' are different from the British – the Welsh and other peoples who were here before the Angles, Saxons and Jutes.

It is not the purpose of this book to examine, much less analyse, the reigns of Alfred the Great or Æthelred Unræd (the 'Unready') except insofar as the Mercian rulers had dealings with them. And speaking of the latter, since we have a king of Mercia named Æthelred, and an ealdorman of Mercia with the same name, he will be referred to as Æthelred Unræd throughout. The term 'Viking' is used to denote the invaders who, in the early days of the attacks, were almost all Danish. The book differentiates between Dane and Norse, both when they were campaigning and especially when they settled in England.

Conventionally it is considered that the history of Mercia ended with its absorption into the great kingdom of Wessex in the early tenth century, but that is to exclude some of the most powerful men of the tenth and eleventh centuries, so our story will go right up the point where the hopes of English resistance against the Normans faded.

This is the story of the Mercians, the kings, queens, saints, sinners, earls and warrior women who governed the kingdom and shaped its history.

Sources and Abbreviations

Anglo-Saxon names and their spellings are not easy on the eye, nor were they necessarily consistent, particularly when the later chroniclers were writing. In a history covering more than half a millennium many different people will be introduced, so, for ease and consistency, I have used the same spellings within the quotations, even if this is not how they were written in the original translations.

The main source we have for this period is a collection known as the *Anglo-Saxon Chronicle*. It is not one single record, but several different versions, including a distinct chronicle known as the *Mercian Register*, which survives for the period of Æthelflæd, Lady of the Mercians. When appropriate, the versions are referred to, but otherwise it is referred to as the *ASC*. I have used Dorothy Whitelock's translation in *English Historical Documents* (*EHD*) up to 1042 and then G.N. Garmonsway for the years 1043–1066.

The other 'national' chronicles are also composites. The Welsh Annals are referred to as *Annales Cambriae* (*AC*) but also refer to the *Brut y Tywysogion*. The Irish Annals used are the *Annals of Ulster*, the *Annals of Tigernach* and the '*Three Fragments*' – probably compiled in the eleventh century.

The other chroniclers and chronicles are:

Bede: a monk who wrote the *Historia Ecclesiastica* (*HE*). Based in Northumbria, he completed his chronicle of the *Ecclesiastical History of the English People* in 731.

Eddius Stephanus: a monk at Ripon, he wrote the *Life* of St Wilfrid (who died in 709) somewhere between 709 and 720.

Felix: a monk at Crowland who wrote the *Life* of St Guthlac (d. 714) between about 730 and 740.[1]

St Boniface: a West Saxon whose work took him to the Continent and who wrote several letters of interest. He died in 754.

Alcuin: originally from York, he spent most of his career in the court of Charlemagne. His letters contain valuable information and commentary. He died in 804.

Byrhtferth: a monk at Ramsey who wrote the *Lives* of St Ecgwine (d. 717) and St Oswald of Worcester (d. 992) and who lived *c.* 970 – *c.* 1020.

Nennius: a Welsh monk, credited with writing the *Historia Brittonum* in around 830.

Asser: a Welsh monk who wrote the *Life* of King Alfred the Great (d.899) in 893.

Æthelweard the Chronicler: an ealdorman, member of the royal house of Wessex, and an historian who wrote a history of England up to 975. The first three books borrow heavily from the *ASC*, but the fourth book differs in many details, providing an independent view of the tenth century, from one who lived through much of it. He died *c.* 998.

Encomium Emmæ Reginæ: this eleventh-century tract was written around 1041/2, in honour of Queen Emma, consort of Æthelred Unræd and then Cnut.

Goscelin of St Bertin: a Flemish monk writing in the mid- to late-eleventh century.

Hemming: a monk of Worcester who compiled Hemming's Cartulary, which incorporated the *Liber Wigorniensis*, a collection of charters and land-books. His record is primarily one of the spoliation of the Church of Worcester. It is uncertain when he died, but he was writing in the latter part of the eleventh century.

Florence of Worcester: a monk who died in 1118, and whose work *Chronicon ex chronicis* was either taken over, or actually written, by John of Worcester (d. *c.* 1140).[2]

Simeon of Durham: a Durham monk and chronicler who died *c.* 1129.

Orderic Vitalis: an Anglo-Norman Benedictine monk who wrote contemporary chronicles of the eleventh and twelfth centuries, he died in 1142.

William of Malmesbury: wrote a history of the English kings, and of the English Bishops (*Gesta Pont*); he died *c.* 1143.

Geoffrey of Monmouth: a Welshman who wrote a *History of the Kings of Britain* and died *c.* 1155.

Henry of Huntingdon: a twelfth-century Englishman who wrote the *Historia Anglorum*, he died *c.* 1157.[3]

Hugh Candidus: a monk at Peterborough who wrote a history of that foundation. He died *c.* 1160.

Liber Eliensis (*LE*): a history of the abbey of Ely, written in the twelfth century and dedicated to its founder, Æthelthryth, an East Anglian who had been married to a Mercian nobleman and then a king of Northumbria.

Roger of Wendover: a thirteenth-century chronicler who wrote the *Flowers of History* and died in 1236. He is noted more for his contemporary references than for those of earlier events, which he gleaned from other writers.

Ingulph's Chronicle of Croyland [Crowland]: Ingulph was an abbot at Crowland in the late eleventh century, but the chronicle is a forgery from either the thirteenth or fourteenth century.

Throughout the book there are also references to charters, most of which have a Sawyer, or S, number. Others have CS (Birch's *Cartularium Saxonicum*) and occasionally a K (Kemble) number.

PASE refers to the online database, *Prosopography of Anglo-Saxon England*.

CHAPTER 1

Penda the Pagan King

The first Mercian king about whom we have any definite information is Penda. The assumption is perhaps that we know rather a lot about him, and that the facts of his life are straightforward and easy to present: a relentlessly energetic king who rode north on many occasions, fighting his enemies and commanding huge numbers of troops. In fact, very little was written about this pagan warrior king. We cannot even precisely date his reign, but we know that he died in 655, and that he was a thorn in the side of the Northumbrians, West Saxons, and East Angles for most of the first half of the seventh century.

If it can be said that the history of Mercia is a history written by its enemies, then Penda's case can be held up as the prime example. We have no written sources from Mercia, in this case not because they are lost to us, but because Penda's was a pagan kingdom. With Christianity comes literacy.

It may be assumed, taking what we know from Bede and other sources, that Penda was no more than a savage heathen who attacked the kings of Northumbria for no other reason than rapacity. He is also remembered in the *Liber Eliensis* for having destroyed the church at Ely,[1] but it is possible to assign specific reasons to his actions by taking a view of the pervading political situation during his lifetime.

From the sources, we can gather some basic information, starting with his genealogy, although this in itself raises as many questions as it answers. Nennius, in his *Historia Brittonum*, lists the Mercian kings' genealogy, having them descend from Woden. 'Woden begat Guedolgeat, who begat Gueagon, who begat Guithleg, who begat Guerdmund, who begat Ossa, who begat Ongen, who begat Eamer, who begat Pybba. This Pybba had twelve sons, of whom two are better known to me than the others, that is Penda and Eowa.'[2] Simeon of Durham also believed that Penda was the son of Pybba.[3]

The *ASC* gives the genealogy back from Penda, the son of Pybba, to Woden, but the other names differ from those listed by Nennius: 'Penda was the son of Pybba, the son of Crida, the son of Cynewold, the son of Cnebba, the son of Icel, the son of Eomær, the son of Angeltheow, the son of Offa, the son of Wærmund, the son of Wihtlæg, the son of Woden.'[4]

Henry of Huntingdon calls him 'Penda the Strong' and gives his genealogy, but it is a different genealogy from that given in the *HB*. Henry says that Penda was the son of Pybba, who was the son of Crida. He also says that Pybba was succeeded by Cearl, who was 'not his son but his kinsman'.[5]

The problem is we have no proof that Pybba was ever himself a king, and little evidence about Cearl. Bede alone mentions Cearl, and only then because he is referring to Cearl's daughter, Cwenburh, as wife of Edwin, a Northumbrian. It has been suggested that Cearl had lowly origins and that his name was a nickname for a man of 'churlish stock'.[6]

It has also been suggested that for much of his young adult life, Penda was no more than a landless warrior nobleman, but Bede clearly sees him as royalty, calling him a 'most energetic member of the royal house of Mercia, who from that date ruled over [Mercia] for twenty-two years with varying success.'[7] There is even debate about Penda's name, with questions still hanging over whether it has its origins in British or Germanic tradition. Perhaps the *Pen* element derives from British. It is possible that the Penwalh mentioned in Felix's *Life* of St Guthlac and named as being from 'distinguished Mercian stock', was related to Penda.[8]

Much has been made of the alliterative nature of Anglo-Saxon names, so the suggestion that Penda was the son of Pybba and perhaps an antecedent of Penwalh fits with this notion. Much has also been made of the nature of the relationship of Penda with one of his sons, Merewalh, because the name is not alliterative, and the last element might suggest some connection with Wales, but this is to overlook the other men of this period whose names contained the same element, Penwalh being one of them, and Penda's West Saxon brother-in-law, Cenwalh of the West Saxons, being another.

Merewalh is cited in the *ASC* as being the brother of Wulfhere, who was indeed a son of Penda's, but the 'Welsh' element of his name leads to doubt that he was Penda's son. Merewalh later became a king in his own right, (*see* next chapter) and it may be that in fact he was a Welshman given his kingdom as a reward after one of Penda's campaigns. It is also possible that he was Penda's foster son. We only know the name of Penda's wife, Cynewise, through Bede, and the inference is that she was West Saxon, because of the alliterative name.[9] She may well have had a first husband, and perhaps he was Welsh. If Penda adopted her son this would not have been unprecedented – Sigeberht of East Anglia, for example, may have been King Rædwald's adopted or foster son.[10] It may also be the case that Merewalh was the son of a sister of Penda's. It is known that Penda gave another sister in marriage to Cenwalh of the West Saxons.[11] Suffice to say that he was considered by Penda to be close kin.

We do not know when Penda was born, but using such dates as we have, it is possible to say that he was born around 605, that he married a woman who was possibly a West Saxon and whose name might have been Cynewise. It is clear that he had several children, whose paternity is less in dispute than Merewalh's. Of the ones we can positively identify besides Merewalh were his sons Peada, Wulfhere and Æthelred, and daughters Cyneburh,[12] Cyneswith and possibly Cynethryth.[13]

Two more daughters may have been Edith, later St Edith of Bicester, and St Eadburh. Another possible daughter – Wilburg – was married to a man named Frithuwald. He was probably the sub-king of Surrey who endowed Chertsey Abbey in the 670s.[14]

There is one other reference to a son of Penda's, a man whose name was Osweard. He is mentioned in two charters of 714 (S1250, 1251) in relation to land granted to Bishop Ecgwine, or rather, how the bishop came by these lands. Both these charters are deemed to be spurious, however, and apart from a mention in the *Life* of St Ecgwine, which essentially repeats the information – 'A short time later, I acquired another estate with this one from Osweard, the brother of the aforementioned king [Æthelred], that is, twenty hides in the place called Twyford' –[15] Osweard makes no other appearances. It may be that he did nothing worth mentioning, for the reason we know what we do about Penda's other progeny is that they went on to become kings, or married kings, or became abbesses and saints. It is through mention of them in the annals and elsewhere that we find him listed as their father. All the recorded facts about Penda himself relate primarily to his warmongering. Even then, Penda is only really mentioned in passing, so what can we glean from reading between the lines? He must have been a worthy foe – and Mercia generally must have been powerful – but neither Bede nor the *ASC* were in the business of promoting him as a champion.

We must of necessity take most of our information about Penda from Bede[16] where he is presented as an enemy, and worse, a pagan. However, there is still much to be garnered from what Bede does and doesn't say. Bede championed the Northumbrian kings, understandably so, given that he himself was a Northumbrian. Indeed, it is impossible to piece together the few known facts about Penda's reign without examining the rivalry and feuding which went on between the kings who ruled north of the Humber. A brief outline of events is necessary before it is possible to discover the details of Penda's kingship.

The basic narrative is as follows: Penda fought the West Saxons in 626, he killed Edwin of Northumbria in 633, Oswald of Northumbria in 642, Anna of East Anglia in *c.* 654 and was himself killed by Oswiu of Northumbria in 655. (From the date of his death and the arguments about the length of his reign we can hazard a guess as to the date of his birth.) Most of the chroniclers barely expand on these basic facts, as if he is of little importance. Only the *HE* elaborates, and this is where we realise Penda's significance to Bede: as an enemy of Northumbria. There is no mention of Penda until Bede has cause to mention the birth of Edwin's sons by Cearl's daughter.

It is hard even to establish the date he became king of the Mercians, but the precise dates perhaps matter less than the sequence of events, if we are to gain any understanding of the man and his reign. To do this, we need to begin not in Mercia, but in Northumbria.

The story begins with Æthelfrith, a warlord and king of Bernicia, the north-eastern kingdom of Northumbria. Æthelfrith was an aggressor, who had in 603 defeated the king of the Irish, whose army was annihilated at a place called Degsa's Stone[17] and in about 604 he turned his attention to Deira. Bede called him a 'very brave king and most eager for glory... He ravaged the Britons more extensively than any other English ruler,'[18] and he was remembered in the *Life* of St Gregory[19] as a 'tyrant who drove [Edwin] from his country, so persecuted him everywhere that he even sought to purchase his death with his money.' He did not simply attack the rival Northumbrian kingdom and take it over, however; he also married Acha, a princess of the Deiran royal house. Whether this was consensual we cannot know, but the liaison produced a number of children. According to the *ASC* the sons of Æthelfrith were Eanfrith, Oswald, Oswiu, Oslac, Oswudu, Oslaf and Offa. Eanfrith was his son by a previous wife[20] and we only hear thereafter about Oswald and Oswiu. There was also a daughter, Æbbe, who is named in more than one source as the sister of Oswiu and the aunt of his son, but it is not clear whether she was Oswiu's full sister, or half-sister.

Meanwhile Edwin, who was probably the brother of the murdered Deiran king, and Osric who was in all likelihood his cousin, along with the murdered king's son, Hereric, were forced into exile. It is not clear whether this happened immediately, for we do not know the circumstances surrounding Æthelfrith's takeover of Deira.[21] For a time, it seems, they took shelter in the British kingdom of Elmet. Hereric, it must be assumed, stayed there, for it was reported that he was later slain by the king of Elmet.

Edwin travelled south. In around 605/6[22] he arrived at the Mercian court, presumably seeking the assistance of King Cearl. Penda was probably no more than an infant when Edwin arrived, but since he was a member of the Mercian royal house, and Edwin later married Cearl's daughter, they must have got to know each other reasonably well.

Nennius does not mention Cearl, but Bede is clear that Edwin had married a Mercian princess. When Edwin's sons by her received baptism, Bede explains that they were 'sons of King Edwin, their mother being Cwenburh, daughter of Cearl, king of the Mercians.'[23]

If, as is usually supposed, Pybba and Cearl were brothers, then Penda and Cwenburh were cousins. If Edwin stayed at the Mercian court long enough to father two sons, then the relationship between Edwin and the young Penda could well have been a close one. It is possible that Edwin was in Mercia for a decade, which is a long time for a child to have an adult in his life.

Edwin's marriage to Cearl's daughter produced two sons, who in theory might have been athelings to both the Mercian and Northumbrian thrones. But, presumably, Cearl did not provide the military assistance Edwin required and sometime before 616 Edwin moved to the court of East Anglia, where he sought the help of King Rædwald. Roger of Wendover says Edwin stayed in East Anglia for seventeen years,[24] omitting any mention of the sojourn in Mercia, but this seems unlikely, and that after the battle of the Idle, Edwin 'had all the kings, as well of the Angles as of the Welsh, subject to him.' Bede gives us much detail about what happened while Edwin was a guest here. 'When Æthelfrith learned that he [Edwin] had been seen in that kingdom … he sent Rædwald large sums of money to put Edwin to death. But it had no effect. He sent a second and third time, offering even larger gifts of silver and further threatening to make war on him if Rædwald despised his offer.' Bede goes on to relate that Rædwald finally agreed to the demands but was dissuaded by his wife, and 'as soon as the messengers returned home, he raised a large army to overthrow Æthelfrith.'

In 616, at the River Idle, the combined forces of Rædwald and Edwin (although whether Edwin had many men at his disposal, we cannot know) defeated Æthelfrith, and Edwin regained control of Deira and assumed the kingship of Bernicia too. At this stage it is possible that Edwin remained a client king of Rædwald, a situation which, if it existed, altered with the death of the East Anglian king and the succession of his son, Eorpwald. Bede lists Edwin as succeeding Rædwald as ruler of 'all the southern kingdoms' and goes on to say that Edwin 'had still greater power and ruled over the inhabitants of Britain, English and Britons alike, except for Kent only.' In 616, Æthelberht of Kent also died, and was succeeded by a son who in Bede's opinion was no replacement for his illustrious father.[25]

But if Edwin, having been restored to the throne of Deira in 616, had been hoping to gather his kin around him, or even to dispose of any potential rivals, it was not to be. We are not told what happened to his sister, Acha, but her children went into exile in the British kingdoms. Edwin began the expansion of his kingdom, conquering British territory, much as Æthelfrith had done before him. The subjugation of Elmet might have been as a direct result of Hereric's murder. Bede tells us that Hereric was poisoned while living in exile at King Ceredig of Elmet's court. He gives us this detail only in passing, as he explains that Hereric's wife had a vision during her child's infancy. Bede's interest here is that the child referred to is Hild, also known as St Hilda of Whitby. He does not tell us who poisoned Hereric, but it is possible that Edwin's motive for attacking Elmet was revenge.[26]

It must be assumed, for they later fought in battle with him, that Edwin's sons by his Mercian wife went with him to the north. But his wife probably did not, for in 625 Edwin married Æthelburh, daughter of Æthelberht of Kent, and received baptism from Paulinus, a Roman missionary who arrived in England at the beginning of the seventh century and became the first bishop of York. Bede tells us that the baptism occurred in the eleventh year of Edwin's reign, 'that is in the year of our Lord 627' and that he was baptised at York on Easter day, 12 April. The Welsh annals, on the other hand, recorded that Edwin was baptised not by Paulinus in the Roman tradition, but in the British tradition by Rhun, son of Urien.

Edwin survived an assassination attempt; Bede relates how an assassin by the name of Eomer was sent by Cwichelm, king of the West Saxons, and went to Edwin's court with a poisoned blade hidden under his cloak. Lunging forward he made a rush for the king and was only prevented from killing Edwin by the bravery of Edwin's thegn, Lilla, who put himself between the assailant and the king, although Edwin nevertheless sustained an injury.[27] All-powerful he may have been, but Edwin was not universally popular. And waiting in the wings were the sons of his sister, the progeny of his nemesis, Æthelfrith.

This then, is the background to relations between the kingdoms in the years immediately preceding Penda's ascendancy.

When Edwin left Mercia for East Anglia, Penda was probably still only a youth. In 633, Cadwallon of Wales, king of Gwynedd, a Briton and therefore a natural enemy, it would seem, of the Northumbrian

Angles,[28] rode against Edwin and defeated him at the battle of Hatfield Chase, near modern-day Doncaster. Bede tells us that 'Cadwallon, king of the Britons ... was supported by Penda, a most energetic member of the royal house of Mercia, who from that date ruled over that nation for twenty-two years with varying success.'[29]

Why was Penda riding alongside Cadwallon? Bede would have us assume that Penda was driven to acts of violence purely because he was a pagan. 'The paganism of Penda was important to the Church ... His role in Church Historiography was negative but vital.'[30] But Penda was not against Christianity per se; Bede tells us that he allowed Christian missionaries to preach in his lands, and that his only objection was when Christians 'scorned to obey the God in whom they believed.'[31] Evidently, then, he was no admirer of hypocrisy, so perhaps Edwin's personal morals had something to do with the antagonism.

At some point before 625, when he married his second wife, Edwin must have repudiated his first wife, if indeed, she was still alive. Bede makes it clear that at the time of the battle at Hatfield Chase Penda was not yet a king, so this was not a power struggle. We know that Penda later chased a West Saxon king into exile after that king repudiated Penda's sister, so it is possible that there was a revenge motive here. It may also have been an attempt to remove the onerous burden of tribute owed by the Mercians to Edwin, and of trying to shake off Northumbrian overlordship.

Cadwallon, although denounced by the chroniclers as acting like a heathen, was a Christian. Geoffrey of Monmouth wrote in the twelfth century of Æthelfrith of Bernicia banishing his pregnant wife to British territory where she gave birth to Edwin, while the Welsh king's wife bore Cadwallon, so the two princes grew up together.[32] This is clearly nonsense, and Geoffrey's 'history' has long been denounced as myth. He does, however, speak of Edwin's later aggression towards Cadwallon, claiming that Cadwallon took flight to Ireland. Initially, according to Geoffrey, Cadwallon's dealings with Penda were also hostile, and Roger of Wendover agrees with Geoffrey's story about Cadwallon routing Penda in a battle near Exeter, demanding hostages and an oath of fidelity.[33] There is no reason to doubt that Penda and Cadwallon were allies against Edwin, but it seems unlikely that Penda would have done so under duress. Cadwallon would have had reason enough to take on the might of Edwin. Even had Edwin not campaigned into the heart of Gwynedd, his subjugation of Elmet, perhaps as part of a general programme of expansion, perhaps as revenge for the death of his kinsman, Hereric, would have left no buffer between Northumbria and the lands of the Welsh.

Bede is specific when assigning roles, saying that Cadwallon was 'supported' by Penda.[34] It is clear then that Penda was a junior client of Cadwallon's at this point. It may be, though, that it was his 'pagans' who then burned and pillaged after Hatfield.[35]

So, Cadwallon had good reason to go after Edwin, but what was Penda's motive? The Mercians may well have had more in common with the British kingdoms even though ethnically they were closer to the Northumbrians.[36] Elmet was not just a buffer between Northumbria and the Welsh territory; it also bordered northern Mercia. If the Mercians were well-disposed towards the British kingdoms, then Edwin's treatment of Elmet may not have sat too well with them, especially given the proximity of Elmet to their own lands.

Henry of Huntingdon's entry for the year 633 reads: 'After Edwin had reigned seventeen years, he was slain in a desperate battle in the plain which is called *Hethfeld*, by Cadwallon, king of the Britons, supported by Penda the Strong, at the time king of the Mercians.'

But was Penda king in his own lands at this point? The *ASC* says that from 626, 'Penda held his kingdom for thirty years, and he was fifty years old when he succeeded to the kingdom.' This seems unlikely, given that we know Penda's death to have occurred in 655, on the battlefield, and he would hardly have been battle-fit at the age of nearly eighty. It might be better to assume that he succeeded in 626, reigned for thirty years and was fifty when he died. For as Dorothy Whitelock pointed out, the *ASC*'s reckoning 'would make him eighty when he was killed, but this must have arisen from some understanding, for he left two sons who were minors, nor would he, if so old, have been likely to have a sister young enough to marry Cenwalh of Wessex who reigned from about 642 to 673.' She also doubted the date of 626 for his accession, given that Bede implied that he was not king until 632.[37]

Patrick Sims-Williams said that in fact, 'Bede may not have known how long before 633 Penda began to reign. As a result of these uncertainties we cannot be sure, though it is the most natural and probable interpretation, that Penda was already king of the Mercians on his second appearance in the *ASC* in 628,' and Nicholas Brooks pointed out that the different years given for Penda's reign, of ten, twenty-two or thirty, may be the result of the fact that the sources are not Mercian, and Penda's power may have been perceived very differently by the Northumbrians, the Welsh, and the West Saxons.[38]

So perhaps we should examine Penda's dealings with the West Saxons. Roger of Wendover thought that Penda was king in 610 when Cynegils acceded to the throne of the West Saxons and he gave Cynegils' son Cwichelm's date of death as 626. His is a unique version of the death of Cwichelm, at the hands of Edwin who slew him 'at a place which is to this day called, in the English tongue "*Quicheleshlaune*"'. The dates, therefore, are somewhat garbled. But Roger of Wendover dated Penda's battle with Cynegils to 629, as did Æthelweard the Chronicler. Again, the precise dates are perhaps less important than establishing a sequence of events.

The *ASC* says the fight with the West Saxons took place in 628 and that they came to an agreement. 'In this year Cynegils and Cwichelm fought against Penda at Cirencester, and afterwards came to terms.' Henry of Huntingdon adds a little more detail and says that both sides had raised a powerful army: 'Both having vowed not to turn their backs on their enemies, each firmly maintained its ground until they were happily separated by the setting of the sun. In the morning, as they were sensible that, if they renewed the conflict, the destruction of both armies must ensue, they listened to moderate counsels, and concluded a treaty of peace.'

If the *ASC* is to be believed, then Penda was indeed king of the Mercians when he launched an attack on the West Saxons and fought against King Cynegils and his son Cwichelm at Cirencester, although Sir Frank Stenton described him at this point as being a landless noble. The *ASC* notes that they 'afterwards came to terms'; was this when Penda's unnamed sister was married to the younger son of Cynegils, whose name was Cenwalh? We know the marriage took place at some point, because Cenwalh's subsequent repudiation of her is recorded. King or not, it is likely that at this point Penda established his overlordship of the *Hwicce*, whose territory included Cirencester, although not necessarily establishing the kingdom (*see* Chapter Two).[39]

It has been suggested[40] that Penda might even have been acting on Edwin's behalf when he attacked the West Saxons, but it seems unlikely he would have come to terms with them, and indeed allow his sister to marry into the family if he was doing it all for Edwin. On the other hand, perhaps he didn't allow it so much as force it, if Cenwalh then later repudiated her. It should also be remembered that there was no love lost between the West Saxons and Edwin of Northumbria, given that the former sent a would-be assassin to the latter's court.

As to whether Penda was king in his own lands at this point, we might accept that he came to power in 626, or that he was king by 633 when he was joint victor over Edwin at Hatfield Chase, but this is to overlook his brother, Eowa. To assess this relationship and the bearing it might have had on Penda's power, we must turn back to Northumbria.

Edwin was succeeded by his nephew, Oswald, but not immediately. After the defeat of Edwin, a few exiled Bernician and Deiran hopefuls emerged from their hiding places: Eanfrith, the son of Æthelfrith by his first wife, came forward to claim Bernicia, while Osric, the exiled cousin of Edwin, made a bid for Deira. Cadwallon saw them both off, in short order.

Into the vacuum came Oswald, Æthelfrith's son by the Deiran princess, Acha. At Heavenfield near Hadrian's Wall, Oswald set up camp and ordered a wooden cross to be erected. In the ensuing battle, Oswald was triumphant, pursuing Cadwallon and killing him. It was all over very quickly. It is understandable why Cadwallon came so far north, but the short-lived claimants to the thrones of Bernicia and Deira also managed to appear on the scene without delay. Is it possible that for a short while they were in alliance with Cadwallon against Edwin?[41]

Oswald's reign is notable for his invitation to Bishop Aidan to establish the monastery at Lindisfarne, and to convert the Northumbrian people. The site of Oswald's death was associated with miracles. That site was Maserfeld, where Penda fought and killed him. Why? Do we now have the truth of the matter; that Penda killed Oswald simply because the latter was a good Christian king? Roger of Wendover said that Cadwallon was the one who sent Penda to slay Oswald, but this is clearly wrong, because Cadwallon was dead by this point.

It took some years for Penda to march against Oswald and we have to consider what took him so long. If he was avenging his Welsh friend's death, why the delay – was he building up an army? As Sir Frank Stenton wrote, 'the stages by which he came to power are unknown,'[42] so we do not know how large his powerbase was at this point.

The location of Maserfeld, associated with Oswestry in Shropshire, may be telling, for it might indicate that Oswald was coming south as an aggressor. Indeed, far from being a Christian king concerned only with good works, it seems likely that he, like his uncle and predecessor, Edwin, was not universally loved. If Oswald was exacting tribute, and forcing himself on the smaller kingdoms, it is possible that Penda was protecting Mercian rights against Northumbrian expansion.[43] Given that tribute was likely to have been in the form of easily moveable supplies of cattle, it might leave the tributary kingdoms hungry. Also, Geoffrey of Monmouth claimed that Cadwallon was married to a half-sister of Penda. It is probably not true, but perhaps hints at the depth of a personal friendship between the two men. Bede saw Penda as the aggressor and said that during the time of Bishop Aidan's episcopate, a hostile army, under Penda, ravaged as far as Bamburgh and attempted to set it on fire. The power of Aidan's prayer swerved the flames away from the target and towards the perpetrators.[44]

Eowa, Penda's brother, was reported as one of the casualties at Maserfeld in the Welsh annals. Therefore it seems that Penda may not, in fact, have been king of the Mercians from 626 onwards, or even after the killing of Edwin in 633. There are two things to consider: the first is Bede's suggestion that he ruled with 'varying degrees of success', possibly hinting that for some of those twenty-two years Penda lost overall control of Mercia. The second is the possibility that Eowa was not fighting against Oswald, but was part of his team, Oswald being his overlord.

Nennius clearly believed that the Mercians were under Oswald's yoke, suggesting that it was Penda who first freed them from the Northerners,[45] which adds strength to the notion that Eowa was fighting alongside Oswald.

If it can be accepted that Oswald was overlord of Mercia, it may help to explain a curious incident, recorded in a passage in *Marwynad Cynddylan* (the 'Death Song' of Cynddylan, a seventh-century Welsh prince) in which a certain Morfael carries off 1,500 cattle and five herds of swine, and gives no protection to the bishop and monks there. It has been argued that this occurred at what is now Wall, in Staffordshire, and that if Morfael was a contemporary of Cynddylan, and thus of Penda, it is strange that there were monks and a bishop in pagan Mercia. The suggestion is that Morfael's target was likely to have been Mercia under Eowa's kingship, and that the holy men were probably Northumbrians, or possibly Scots, installed by Oswald.[46] We know Penda was tolerant of missionaries, but this story suggests a rather more permanent establishment, and there is no mention in Bede of Eowa's conversion. A counter argument is that this attack was actually on Lichfield and is likely to have taken place after Penda's death, and that in fact it is unlikely that a bishopric was meant.[47]

It is not clear whether Oswald was indeed overlord of the Mercians, but with dates for the beginning of Penda's reign being given variously as 626, 633, or even, according to the *HB*, after the battle of Maserfeld and the defeat of Oswald, along with Bede's idea that his kingship was not unbroken, perhaps we can assume that somewhere along the line between 633 and 642 Penda was about the business of regaining, rather than acquiring, his throne. It is possible that after Cadwallon was killed, the Northumbrians placed Eowa as a sub-king of Mercia, under Oswald's overlordship, and that Penda regained this position in 642 at Maserfeld. This may cast light on Penda's motives for the attack on Edwin, for if his brother stood between him and the Mercian throne, and Penda was merely out for power, surely he would have taken care of his brother first, before riding with Cadwallon?

The death of Edwin's son, Eadfrith, while a guest at the Mercian court,[48] might also shed light on the relationship between the two kingdoms, if indeed Oswald put pressure on Penda to snuff out a member of the Deiran royal house. This young man was also a potential heir to the kingdom of Mercia, being the son of Edwin's Mercian wife, so it might have been in both their interests to remove him. However, if at this point Eowa was king, it might have been he who ordered the killing, at Oswald's bidding. It would also have been against Penda's interests to strengthen Bernicia by removing a Deiran claimant, unless pressured to do so.[49] Oswald's presence at Dorchester, where he married the West Saxon king's daughter, stood as godfather to the newly baptised West Saxon king, and appointed a bishop there, suggests that he was either fearful of Penda's increasing control, or at the very least looking to reassert authority south of the Humber. If we can agree that the battle was fought at Oswestry, then D.J.V. Fisher was of the opinion that this shows it was Oswald who was the aggressor.[50]

After Oswald's death, his younger brother Oswiu took over. He was altogether a different character. Bede's history is not quite so effusive about him. He followed his father's lead by finding a Deiran princess to marry, in this case Edwin's daughter, Eanflaed. She had grown up in Kent, having fled the wrath of Oswald's approaching army, a detail that rubs some of the sheen off Bede's whitewashing of Oswald's character. Oswald had left a son, Œthelwald, who was presumably too young to rule. Also still alive, and a claimant to the Deiran portion of the kingdom, was Oswine, son of Edwin's cousin Osric, whom Bede described in glowing terms, and who was murdered on Oswiu's instruction.

Little is heard of Penda between the battles of Maserfeld and Winwæd, where he was to meet his match and his death in 655. All we hear from the *ASC* is that in 645 he drove Cenwalh of the West Saxons out of his kingdom and in 654 King Anna of the East Anglians was slain, although the *ASC* does not say by whom.

Bede gives us a little more detail and says that Cenwalh 'repudiated his wife who was sister of Penda, king of the Mercians, and had married another woman; for this he was attacked by Penda and deprived of his kingdom.' Bede tells us that he then went to the court of 'the East Anglian king, whose name was Anna' and that he remained in exile there for three years.[51]

According to Henry of Huntingdon, Cenwalh, 'not being able to resist [Penda] as his father had done, was routed before him in battle and driven out of his kingdom.' The suggestion here is that Cynegils had not been defeated by Penda, which would tally with the idea of coming to terms and the subsequent marriage of Penda's sister to Cenwalh, but makes the claims that Penda gained enough control to establish a new kingdom of the *Hwicce* less convincing.

It is possible that Anna's sheltering of the exiled Cenwalh and his own death were linked. It is interesting that the year after Anna's death saw his brother, Æthelhere, joining the ranks of the Mercians when they rode to battle against Oswiu of Northumbria.

Bede records that Penda attacked the East Anglian kingdom, but he does not give a date. After the death of Rædwald's successor, Eorpwald, the kingdom was inherited by Sigeberht, (possibly the step- or foster son of Rædwald) who retired to a monastery and gave the kingdom over to a kinsman, Ecgric. Penda attacked, the East Anglians begged Sigeberht to come out from the monastery and lead them, but he refused to carry anything but a staff as a weapon. He and Ecgric were killed and 'the whole army was either slain or scattered by the heathen attacks.' His successor was Anna; he also was slain later on, like his predecessors, 'by the heathen Mercian leader'.[52]

Now, we know that by 645, the king of East Anglia was Anna, so Penda's attack must have occurred before then. In 645, Cenwalh of the West Saxons repudiated Penda's sister and was forced into exile for three years, finding shelter at the East Anglian court. Had Penda attacked the East Angles then, it would have made sense. But why did he attack earlier? Was this again on someone's orders, or was he flexing his muscles?

'The source of conflict between Mercia and East Anglia was presumably control of the East Midland peoples known ... as the Middle Angles.' It seems as if there may have been rising tension between the East Anglians and the Mercians. The *Life* of St Foillan records an attack on East Anglia around the year 650 during which a monastery was destroyed. A second attack 'brought about Anna's death' and was the turning point of Penda's career, 'one of the few East Anglian events to make it into the *ASC*.'[53]

The establishment of the kingdom of the Middle Angles occurred when Penda's son, Peada, married Alhflæd, Oswiu's daughter. According to Bede this was when Penda placed him upon the throne of the Middle Angles. This marriage, one of many between the two families, raises many questions. Who was wielding the power at this point: Penda, or Oswiu? Perhaps Anna of East Anglia had protested when Peada was made king of the Middle Angles. Was Anna appealing for help from Oswiu in the face of aggression from Mercia? Anna was succeeded by his brother Æthelhere who was, according to Bede, the cause of the war against Oswiu, so what was going on here?

The *ASC* entry for 655 says 'in this year Penda perished and the Mercians became Christians.' The *E chronicle* adds that 'in this year Oswiu killed Penda at *Winwædfeld*, and thirty princes with him, and some of them were kings. One of them was Æthelhere, brother of Anna, king of the East Angles.'

Why did Penda feel the need to go against Oswiu? Perhaps the East Anglians were negotiating with him; it may be that Anna was in league with him while Æthelhere wanted the throne and was prepared to treat with Penda. Oswiu was already wooing the East Saxons, with King Sigeberht of that kingdom making regular visits to his friend and sponsor in baptism, Oswiu.[54] Was this because the East Saxons feared Mercian expansion, or was it a sign of the encroachment of Oswiu's powers into the southern reaches? Penda may well have felt threatened. However, there is a clue which suggests that at this point, Penda was politically the stronger of the two, for he had as a hostage at his court Oswiu's young son, Ecgfrith.

We don't know how, when or why this had come about, but it may have had something to do with the 'savage and insupportable attacks of Penda' to which Bede says King Oswiu was exposed.

Whilst we have very few details of the battle at *Winwæd* (unidentified, but probably somewhere near Leeds), it is clear that a complicated political situation existed at the time, which saw some – at first glance – unexpected alliances.

Henry of Huntingdon echoes Bede by reporting that Œthelwald, King Oswald's son, 'who ought to have come to their aid, was on the side of their enemies.' Penda appears, then, to have had the upper hand. Men who ought to have been on Oswiu's side had rallied to Penda's instead, and he had the Welsh, as always, as his allies.

Yet, the *HB* says in Chapter 65 that 'Cadafael alone, king of Gwynedd, rising up in the night, escaped together with his army, wherefore he was called Cadafael the Battle Shirker.' The rest of the British kings who had accompanied Penda were killed in the ensuing battle, which the *HB* calls 'the slaughter of *Gai Campi* [the Field of Gai]'.

Penda's defeat can partly be explained by the appalling weather conditions, which saw as many men killed by drowning as by fighting. It was November, presumably the rivers were swollen, but it may be that Penda's forces were already in retreat. In which case it is possible that Cadafael's army merely left them to go home.[55]

It is not clear why Œthelwald, son of Oswald, was on Penda's side, but it seems that at the crucial moment he either deserted, or at any rate sat the battle out. Oswiu was obviously willing to risk his son's life, who was a Mercian hostage, but this is to assume that he was the aggressor. After the savage attacks by Penda he was 'forced to promise him an incalculable and incredible store of royal treasures.' According to Bede, this offer was refused.[56] However the *HB* says that Oswiu handed the treasure over and that Penda then 'distributed [the riches] to the kings of the Britons' and seems to imply that when Cadafael took off in the night, it was with pockets full of coin. Perhaps the payment went straight from Oswiu to Cadafael, a bribe to ensure he took no part in the fighting. This, of course, is conjecture.

Penda is not listed by Bede as a *Bretwalda* (over-king), but if he and Oswiu were on an equal footing, Bede would hardly have said so. Either way, it seems that Penda was the head of a huge network of peoples. He was happy to leave the kingdom for long periods, so he was clearly content to let his wife rule in his stead; or was he in fact leaving deputies in charge, from one of these other territories? We only know the name of Penda's wife because she was holding the young son of Oswiu hostage.[57] She is almost alone, in this period, as a Mercian noblewoman who is mentioned neither as a saint, nor in connection with a foul murder. Perhaps it is stretching credulity to read too much into this one sentence, but clearly Bede thought it important enough to mention that it was she, not her husband, or a nobleman, who was given the task of looking after the hostage. A flight of fancy, perhaps, but it is not wholly inconceivable that she looked after the boy in her own household where he had as playmates and companions various members of her own large brood, some of whom we know were still young when Penda died, and thus, presumably, of a similar age to Ecgfrith the hostage.

We should perhaps pause now to consider exactly what we know about the various Mercian tribes and kingdoms, and whether that knowledge informs our understanding of the power play between the Northumbrians and the Southumbrians.

Much of our interpretation of the situation relies on a document known as the *Tribal Hidage*. This document is a list of the tribes of the lands south of the Humber, and their representative hides, a hide being an area of land, traditionally one which could support one family. Debate continues regarding its origins and its purpose, and this will be discussed in more detail in Chapter Two. It has been described variously as having been drawn up under Penda (unlikely, given that there was no literacy in Mercia at this time) when his son took sovereignty of the Middle Angles and converted to Christianity, or that it was drawn up by later kings of Mercia. Dorothy Whitelock dated it to the 'late seventh or the eighth century' while Cyril Hart thought it was drawn up for King Offa (757–796).[58]

What the document is, and what it was used for, largely depends on where it was drawn up. If it was drawn up by any of the Mercian kings, then it can be seen as a list of the territories and peoples falling under Mercian control. If, however, the opposing – and probably minority – view is taken, that it was drawn up by the Northumbrians, then it becomes a list of tribute owed to Northumbria.

A Northumbrian origin would account for the inclusion of Elmet and the absence of the two Northumbrian kingdoms of Deira and Bernicia. It has been suggested that a Mercian tribute list would not have been headed by Mercia, as 'an early mediaeval king did not impose tribute upon his own kingdom' but must have been a list produced by another kingdom, perhaps with an altogether different purpose.[59] Nicholas Brooks suggested that the *Tribal Hidage* represents a reduction of Mercia back to its original area, giving the likes of the *Hwicce* and the Wrekin-dwellers their own assessment and showing that they were no longer part of Mercia.[60]

If we return for a moment to the beginning of the story and recall Æthelfrith of Bernicia's aggression, not just towards the neighbouring kingdom of Deira when Edwin was forced into exile, but examine his activities generally, we discover that he 'collected a great army against the city of the legions ... which is called Chester by the Britons and made a great slaughter of that nation of heretics.'[61]

So let us suppose for a moment that the document known as the *Tribal Hidage* does indeed represent the overlordship of the Northumbrians and the tribute owed by the peoples listed. This might throw some light on Penda's rise to power.

Sir Frank Stenton said that 'it was not until the reign of Penda that the Mercian kingdom became a great power.'[62] But when Edwin fled from Æthelfrith, he would have had to find refuge in a kingdom not subject to his persecutor. If Cearl of Mercia had been subject to Æthelfrith he would hardly have offered sanctuary to Edwin, much less allowed him to marry his daughter. So it seems that in fact Mercia might have been a great power before Penda's time. Indeed, if Edwin stayed in Mercia for most of a decade then Cearl was of similar standing in terms of power, and therefore status, to Æthelfrith, and may himself have been an over-king of other territories.

Cearl is not listed by Bede as a *Bretwalda*, unlike the kings of Kent and East Anglia, and Bede makes no mention of any effort to convert Cearl to Christianity, as he does with those other kings, although he suggests his high status when he records that his daughter married Edwin. Cearl must have been in some kind of alliance with Edwin and yet we hear no more about him, and Edwin subsequently moved to East Anglia. Why?

This line of enquiry goes to that battle of Chester, recorded by Bede, and suggests that Edwin was forced to flee Mercia after the battle in which, it is argued, Cearl perished. This scenario would see Æthelfrith of Northumbria temporarily supreme, and Edwin, without his protector, Cearl, once again in danger and on the run. Having found sanctuary with

Rædwald of East Anglia, and marched with him against Æthelfrith, he might then have been gifted the Northumbrian kingship by Rædwald. This, presumably, would have included any lands which Æthelfrith gained when he defeated Cearl at Chester.

If Æthelfrith had replaced Cearl with a puppet king from an alternative line – perhaps Pybba or even Eowa – then an oft-quoted line in the *Historia Brittonum* makes a bit more sense: that Penda first 'separated the kingdom of the Mercians from the kingdom of the northerners'. This would weaken the case for Penda being king from 626, unless we see the *Tribal Hidage* as being drawn up in two stages, with Edwin adding several southern kings to his tributaries around the time his representatives were in Kent sorting out the terms of his second marriage in 625.[63]

If, however, Eowa was indeed a puppet king, but installed by Oswald, from the death of Cadwallon to his own death in 642, then perhaps it was during this time, under Oswald's direction, that the territory of the *Hwicce* was established. It has been argued that their leaders had names that indicated they were linked to the Bernician family. This argument is predicated on Penda's having been king before Cadwallon's death, and the suggestion that Eowa was not allowed the whole territory that Penda had been ruling hitherto, so that Eowa was given a reduced kingdom, restricted to the Mercian heartland, which the *Tribal Hidage* assessed at 30,000 hides. Therefore, the function of the *Tribal Hidage* was to assert that people in certain named tribes were no longer part of the Mercian kingdom.

But the counter arguments suggest that 'the greater Mercia which Penda created is set out in the tax list known as the *Tribal Hidage*' and that we 'should not assume that all the provinces in the *Tribal Hidage* had rulers of Germanic birth,' for example, Elmet.[64] Further, the *HB* dates the end of independent Elmet to the expulsion of Ceredig by Edwin in 616, yet it is shown as an independent unit in the *Tribal Hidage*, suggesting that it had detached itself from Northumbria by the second half of the seventh century and moved into the Mercian sphere.[65] One further argument for the *Tribal Hidage* being Northumbrian in origin is exactly that point, that the *Elmetsæte* – the people of Elmet – are included, whereas the Deirans and Bernicians are not.[66]

What may not be in dispute is that the *Tribal Hidage* 'provides the clearest evidence for the transformation of areas of primitive settlement into units of royal administration' even though it may not be possible to establish which particular royal administration.[67] Whatever the conclusions we come to about the *Tribal Hidage*, Bede suggests that Penda was nevertheless the overlord of a wide-ranging area. He had with him 'thirty *duces*' at Winwæd, and his army also included Æthelhere of

East Anglia, Œthelwald of Deira and probably several British princes, including Cadafael of Gwynedd.

Had there been someone in Mercia writing such a history as Bede's, we might know a little more about how Penda achieved this yet, although he was clearly as powerful as any of the other *Bretwaldas*, quite how he achieved this status is 'irrecoverable'.[68] It seems that, king or not, Penda was the junior partner in the alliance with Cadwallon and his motives for joining the fight may have been a mutual interest in restraining Edwin's aggrandisement, a personal quest for vengeance because Penda's kinswoman had been abandoned by Edwin, or naked ambition. This latter seems unlikely, given that his brother was the most immediate block to Penda's advancement, yet remained unharmed until he rode out with Oswald at Maserfeld.

It seems possible that Oswald's power and influence must have been limited by that of Penda. Was Oswald's visit to Dorchester, where he stood sponsor for the West Saxon king's baptism an assertion of power, or a strategy against Penda's authority? Oswald saw fit to take the fight to Penda, if Oswestry is indeed the location of the battle.[69] Oswiu copied his uncle Edwin, using marriage alliance to his advantage. But he must have made enemies along the way, because those who should have been on his side, were on Penda's at the *Winwæd*. Surely Penda can't have coerced them all? It may have been the case that for Oswiu's natural allies, with a friend like Oswiu they had no need of enemies. For a short period during his reign, Northumbria was once again divided into the two kingdoms of Bernicia and Deira, and a kinsman of Edwin was ruler of the latter.

This ruler, Oswine, who was, according to Bede, 'tall and handsome, pleasant of speech, courteous in manner and bountiful to nobles and commons alike' was cruelly made an end of, murdered by a thegn, whom he believed to be his friend but who was in the pay of Oswiu. If we may add bribery – in the form of the tribute carried away by Cadafael of Gwynedd – to the list of crimes committed by Oswiu, then we might have some idea as to why his own nephew decided not to fight for him, and why Æthelhere of East Anglia threw in his lot with Penda.[70]

There may be a case for stating that Penda was in fact overlord of Northumbria for a while. Bede lists the dates of the reigns of the various kings, but these are not consecutive, thus Osric (killed by Cadwallon) has his reign included in Oswald's timeline, while the seven-year reign of Oswine ends in the ninth of Oswiu's. It may be deduced from this that Oswiu reigned for some time without Oswine, but 'whether this means that he reigned also in Deira, or that there was a long interregnum there, or that Penda was king, is not clear.'[71]

Whatever his status, the length of his reign, and the extent of his power, Penda was a fearsome warrior and obviously a skilled general. Given that we know he was powerful enough to take royal hostages, it is safe to assume that he was at least equal in status to the Northumbrian; which, presumably, is why we find so many marriages between the offspring of these two warrior kings.

The first of these marriages was between Alhfrith, Oswiu's son by his British wife, and Cyneburh, daughter of Penda. We cannot know what brought about this marriage, or whether it was part of any agreement, but we know that this was the first of the intermarriages because of what Bede tells us about the second, which took place between Peada, Penda's son, and Alhflæd, Oswiu's daughter by his British wife. Bede says that as soon as Peada had been created king of the Middle Angles, he 'thereupon went to Oswiu and asked for the hand of his daughter. But his request was granted only on condition that he and his nation accepted the Christian faith and baptism.' Bede goes on to say that Peada was 'earnestly persuaded to accept the faith by Alhfrith, son of King Oswiu, who was his brother-in-law and friend, having married Penda's daughter, Cyneburh.'[72]

The interesting aspect of these marriages is that the feud did not end with Penda's death, and in fact, the marriages had not prevented the showdown at the *Winwæd* either. But on paper, it might look as if the antagonism between the kings of Northumbria and Mercia did not filter down to the next generation. It is hard to read Bede's words and conclude that these marriages were forced or formed part of any political agreement. Were they genuine love matches, with the younger generation ignoring the antipathy of the older? We have seen that Penda was not averse to others converting to the new faith, but this goes further and seems to suggest that Peada was acting with a fair amount of autonomy.

Nor were these the only marriages between the two families. There was to be yet another wedding, that of Penda's son Wulfhere to Oswiu's daughter Osthryth. However, a knowledge of what happened when this next generation came into their ascendancy demands a fair amount of caution when presuming long-standing personal friendships. It has been suggested that these intermarriages may have been an attempt to stop the ambitions of any claimants from other families, in other words limiting the royal gene pool,[73] but it certainly didn't bring peace. In truth, we can't know what these marriages were for.

If Peada had been installed king of the Middle Angles by Oswiu, one might imagine this would affect his relationship with his father, and yet Wulfhere and then his brother Æthelred had no compunction in attempting to take back supremacy. Florence of Worcester says that Oswiu reigned three years over the Mercians and made his 'cousin' Peada king of the southern Mercians. A better translation in John of Worcester calls him his 'kinsman'. But Bede was clear that Peada was made king of the Middle Angles by his father in 653, although it could be argued that it was only with Oswiu's leave. And Peada was not *in situ* for the whole of those three years but was poisoned by his wife, Oswiu's daughter. Whatever the nature of the relationships it is clear that we cannot liken them to any modern family dynamic, much less imagine them all sitting round the meal table together.

The first half of the seventh century saw an extraordinary amount of fighting, battles for supremacy, and marriages of alliance. It was the time of the conversion, a time when England was becoming literate, and its map was changing. Yet without Bede's narrative, we would know little. And even with it, we still know only a small amount about Penda.

However, albeit that most of that small amount relates to his violent heathenism, we find snippets of information that allow us to build a picture of the man. Bede is very clear that Penda attacked Cenwalh because he'd repudiated Penda's sister; perhaps he was similarly motivated when it came to attacking Edwin? If Merewalh was not his son, then he was generous in taking him in. It shows him as a family man and gives added credence to the idea that his battles had a personal element, too.

To Bede, he was the pagan enemy, important in demonstrating the wickedness of not embracing the true faith, and as a foil to highlight the attributes of those such as Oswald, who did. Bede was not interested in private, family matters, any more than the other chroniclers were. So his brief mention of the repudiation of Penda's sister carries weight, as does his assertion that Penda was tolerant of Christians and Christian preachers. 'Now King Penda did not forbid the preaching of the Word, even in his own Mercian kingdom, if any wished to hear it. But he hated and despised those who, after they had accepted the Christian faith, were clearly lacking in the works of faith.'[74] Given that he appears only to have had one wife, and maybe even adopted her child, could it be that Penda didn't like these Christian kings putting aside their wives?

He was capable of loyalty and friendship. The relationship between the Mercians and the Welsh is a long and at times complicated story, one often as much about war as about amity, but the alliances with the Welsh were pivotal in Penda's career. In Welsh tradition, Penda's nickname was *Panna ap Pyd* (Penda son of Danger).[75] It is doubtful that he could have defeated Edwin without Cadwallon, it is possible that Cynddylan of Powys was supporting him when he defeated Oswald[76] and it might have been a very different picture in 655 if Cadafael had not proved untrustworthy. The incident shows, and not for the last time, that these cross-border relationships were built not just on national interest, but on personal friendship.

Penda's refusal to convert might have been not just religious but political. By converting, he may have implied acknowledgement of Oswiu's supremacy.[77] Penda was happy to work alongside – and accept a role as junior partner of – Cadwallon, who was a Christian. J.M. Wallace-Hadrill suggested that Penda was not aiming to eradicate Christianity but that his paganism was important because the kings he killed were all martyred. Presumably he meant by this that he was important to his enemies and/or the chroniclers, for it is clear that whatever his motives, Penda was not killing these kings, particularly not Edwin and Anna, for their religious beliefs.[78] It is hard to put forward a convincing argument for Penda's wars being motivated by religion. He was not averse to allowing preachers and clearly his children were not intimidated by him, for they all converted, some of them in his lifetime. The *Winwæd* may have been seen as a victory for Christianity because of Oswiu's promise to give his daughter to the Church if the battle went his way,[78] but we must remember that all this was written with hindsight and the knowledge that the Christian king triumphed.

If we accept the idea that Cearl was more powerful than usually supposed, then it might be seen that Penda's aggression was simply an attempt to restore the status quo. It may be that we should not take the comment about separating the kingdom from the north too seriously, and that his achievements have in fact been exaggerated because of Cearl's strength.[79]

On the face of it, religion aside, it looks as though Penda's main aims were to maintain, or achieve, or regain, independence from Northumbria.[80] In fact, we know little else of his activities because we hear only of Northumbrian kings from a Northumbrian narrator. On his last campaign he was the head of an army drawn from across the southern kingdoms, but we cannot be sure whether they were there because he was their aggressive overlord, or whether this was an alliance against the overbearing Northumbrian, Oswiu. This mighty army, incorporating not only the southern English, but the Welsh too, might say as much about the unpopularity of Oswiu as it does about Penda's attitude towards his southern neighbours.

It was said of Edwin's dominion that if a woman with her new-born babe chose to wander throughout the island from sea to sea, presumably from the east to west coast, she could do so without molestation.[81] Edwin, seen as the saviour of Northumbria, could well have been seen an oppressor of the Welsh, the West Saxons, and of Elmet. The small kingdom of Lindsey was not kindly disposed towards Oswald. Penda, perhaps, rather than being an aggressive pagan warlord, was simply fighting back.

Despite the difficulties presented with the confused dates, and the paucity of written sources, it has been possible to present a sequence of events during Penda's lifetime. Now we must set this in context and consider who the Mercians were, and how they interacted with their neighbours. What about this confederation, which Penda seemingly led at the *Winwæd*? Did they have more in common than a shared hatred of Northumbria?

CHAPTER 2

The Origins of the Mercian Kingdom

7th Century
Britain

PICTS

DALRIADA

STRATHCLYDE

LOTHIAN

BERNICIA

RHEGED

MAN

DEIRA

ANGLESEY

ELMET

PECSÆTE

GWYNEDD WRECONSÆTE

LINDSEY

MERCIA

POWYS

MAGONSÆTE

AROSÆTE

MIDDLE ANGLES

EAST ANGLES

GWENT HWICCE

CHILTERNSÆTE

EAST SAXONS

WEST SAXONS

KENT

0 20 40   80KM

Map of Seventh-century
Tribes and Kingdoms.

Who were the Mercians? The nature and magnitude of the Germanic settlement of the British Isles is a topic for another book. Suffice to say here that it has generally been accepted that after the initial settlement the political landscape grew into what has been called the Heptarchy; seven kingdoms dominating what eventually became England. These were Wessex, Essex, Sussex, East Anglia, Kent, Mercia and Northumbria, which was originally split into the two kingdoms of Deira and Bernicia. Most of these kingdoms have recognisable names, but this list is perhaps simplistic; the boundaries were not fixed, and the borders moved frequently even after the main kingdoms emerged.[1]

Indeed, there were also smaller territories, many of them in the Mercian region, which survived until quite late. It is hard to know whether all these 'kingdoms' did indeed have dynastic leaders ruling over them, although we do know about two or three of them and we will look at their history in a moment.

Of the major kingdoms, many kept their ethnic origins intact; the West, East, and South Saxons, for example. It seems to be accepted that the Mercians were most likely Angles in origin,[2] but of the possibility that they came originally from East Anglia, the evidence, based on place names which incorporate the name *Icel* – one of the supposed founders of the Mercian royal dynasty – is 'slight and inconclusive'.[3] If there was an East Anglia, why no West Anglia? There was, briefly, a kingdom of the Middle Angles, one of many tribes eventually to be absorbed into Greater Mercia.

So if the East Angles kept their ethnic name, why didn't the Mercians? Where does this name come from? The Mercians were the *Myrcne,* (*Mierce*) or Marcher/Border people.

Given that there were British kingdoms between the north Mercians above the River Trent and the Anglian Northumbrian kingdoms, it is reasonable to suppose that the name refers to the border with the British kingdoms in what we know now as Wales, although a case has been made for the border in question being the one between the southern and northern English.[4]

Also, since most of the written sources come from their enemies, the name – the border people – might even suggest that the Mercians were named by other people, that it was their description of them. The point has already been made that the Mercians do not make an appearance in the *HE* until Bede has cause to mention Edwin's sons by Cearl's daughter. Similarly, the tribe known as the *Hwicce* first come to be mentioned because a Northumbrian, St Wilfrid, met a *Hwiccian* princess in Sussex. 'It is oddly symptomatic' of the way that we know of the Mercians only from the point of view of their neighbours that their name means 'frontier folk.'[5]

It is possible that the name, *Mierce*, like that of the *Hwicce* and *Gewisse* (the old name for the West Saxons, specifically for a tribe based in the area around Dorchester) might indicate kingdom names which incorporate a geographical location. The origin of the names may have been in the names of 'mobile *comitatus* groupings' rather than of settled peoples.[6]

Bede describes the Mercians as being the people who lived north and south of the River Trent, and this is a far-reduced area from the later Mercian kingdom. His statement doesn't tell us whether they were originally divided as North and South Mercians, either side of the Trent, but it is clear from what he says that the Trent ran through Mercian territory. It is hard to say for certain, but we can assume that the original Mercia was an area which roughly equated to modern-day Staffordshire, Leicestershire, Nottinghamshire, south Derbyshire and north Warwickshire.[7]

We are almost entirely dependent on Bede for this portion of Mercian history, but for the most part, the process by which the dwellers of the area around the Trent became a great midland people is 'hidden from our sight'. We know that they controlled the Middle Angles in 653, but not for how long before this date.[8]

'All the narrative sources which claim to go back before Penda are all post-conquest.' For example, Henry of Huntingdon said that Crida began to rule in 585, when the kingdom of Mercia began, but there is no evidence that he was using an independent source and may well have been copying Bede. Barbara Yorke also pointed out that none of the later kings claimed descent from Cearl: 'If we can trust the tradition that Crida ruled before Cearl ... men were probably calling themselves kings of Mercia by *c.* 600 but we don't know precisely what is meant by that title.'[9]

Who, at the time, would have called themselves 'Mercian'? Was it a name they applied to themselves, and did it define them as living in a particular geographical area, or that they had accepted the authority of the king of Mercia?

If we accept that Cearl harboured Edwin and even the argument about the battle of Chester explored in the previous chapter, then we might suppose that Mercia was strong, and well-established by very early on in the seventh century, but the case has also been argued for a later emergence of the kingdom. Certainly by the eighth century the Mercian kings were known as the Iclingas, but even if there were any stories about their origins, they have not survived.[10] The genealogy of the Iclingas is preserved in Felix's *Life* of St Guthlac, which traces the line back to Icel. Perhaps, after all, there was a 'foundation account of how the kingdom and its dynasty came into being'?[11] The previously mentioned Penwalh could, according to the *Life*, trace his lineage in 'set order through the most noble names of famous kings, back to Icel,' Icel appearing five generations above Penda in a genealogy contained in the Anglian Collection.[12]

The later dynastic centres of Mercia lay at Lichfield, Breedon-on-the-Hill, Repton and Tamworth, which all fell within the territory of a people called the *Tomsæte*, 'the dwellers by the River Tame' and the Iclingas perhaps began as the leaders of this people.[13] A charter of 849 mentions the boundary of a folk called *Tomsætan* and they appear in another document, showing that they were ruled by their own ealdormen in an area of north Leicestershire where the monastery of Breedon-on-the-Hill was situated.[14] The process of how, and when, they became part of Mercia proper is a subject of debate. The borders were seemingly not fixed, the old British kingdoms were subdued in some cases, but survived in others, and as we shall see, at any given time some or all of the smaller regions and larger kingdoms were subject to overlordship by kings who were in the ascendancy. Many of the smaller kingdoms found their kings reduced in status to that of ealdorman.

There is virtually no written evidence to help us. Although Bede gives us some information, and he makes a clear distinction between the Angles and the Saxons, unlike some of the other chroniclers,[15] the *ASC* is not very informative.

The smaller provinces and/or kingdoms were absorbed into larger ones. The Mercian expansion eventually saw the subjugation of the kingdoms of the *Hwicce*,[16] the *Magonsæte* and the Middle Angles. The South Saxons, threatened by Wessex, allied with the rulers of Mercia. The Mercian supremacy saw the South Saxon kings reduced in status to sub-kings and then to ealdormen. Independence was never regained, and in the ninth century they were absorbed into Wessex. Lindsey, as we will see, had a changeable history, belonging to Northumbria in Edwin's reign, and in part of Oswald's, who was not remembered fondly there, but often associated with Mercia.

Further difficulties arise because some depositories were destroyed by the Vikings and then the shiring of the Midlands later on.[17] The only other written source to give us any detailed information about these early midland tribes is a document known as the *Tribal Hidage*, which was briefly mentioned in Chapter One.[18] Its author, and purpose, are unknown, and possible contenders are many and varied, but for now it is useful to see what it can tell us about the formation of the heartland of England.

'During the years of expansion, many minor kingdoms and principalities were absorbed into the Mercian kingdom either through subjugation or voluntary alliance and the only record we now have of these "lost" peoples is in the assessment known as the *Tribal Hidage*.'[19]

The *Tribal Hidage* is a document which lists the names of thirty-five 'tribes', given in the genitive plural,[20] along with an assessment in hides, all of which are given in round figures. Some of the names do appear to refer to geographical areas or features: *Pecsætan* (dwellers in the Peak), *Gyrwe* (dwellers in the Fens, Old English *gyr* – mud, or marsh).

The *Gyrwe* are one of the very few peoples to be mentioned in other sources. In the preface to Book One, the *Liber Eliensis* defines the region of the *Gyrwe*: 'The *Gyrwe* are all the South Angles who live in the great fen in which the isle of Ely is situated.' Bede mentions the monastery at Medeshamstede (Peterborough) in the land of the *Gyrwe*. We know that King Ecgfrith of Northumbria married the daughter of Anna, king of East Anglia, and according to Bede she had previously been married to a nobleman, Tondberht, of the South *Gyrwe*.[21]

Some of the tribe names are not so easy to define, and it is difficult to establish whether they were 'actual tribes, without kings, who had retained their identity but been absorbed by Mercia, or ... what appeared to be tribal names [were] actually administrative areas'. In the example given by James Campbell,[22] the *East Wixna* might have been a tribe, perhaps dating back to the invasion period, with the round figure of 300 an indication of expected tribute, or an organised administrative unit.

The *Tribal Hidage* is often referred to as a tribute list, but nothing in the text confirms this, and its origins and purpose have continued to tax historians. It is possible that the text has been altered,[23] which suggests that it in fact meant different things to different people over the centuries and the manuscripts themselves throw up problems, with copying errors as well as the amendments and additions. It may be that it is a composite document, which cannot be ascribed to any particular reign.[24] According to Sir Frank Stenton, it was 'almost certainly compiled in Mercia'.[25]

As we saw in Chapter One there is an argument for suggesting that since it includes Elmet,[26] which as far as we know was never under Mercian but rather under Northumbrian control, and that it doesn't include lands north of the Humber, then the *Tribal Hidage* must be Northumbrian in origin.

The round figures suggest that whatever it is, and whoever compiled it, it is not an accurate assessment of the landholdings. If it is indeed a tribute list, the payment was unlikely to have been in coin. The likelihood is that it was paid in cattle, a moveable commodity that held its value.

Mercia proper tops the list, which then goes out clockwise from the Mercian heartlands, beginning with the *Wocen sætan* (*Wreoconsætan*) from an area between Wroxeter and the Mersey to the west of the Trent valley, then the *Westerna*, associated with the *Magonsætan* whose lands were around Leominster and Hereford. This area might once have been part of the kingdom of Powys, if Welsh legend lamenting its loss to Penda can be believed.[27]

Next on the list are those living to the north of the Mercian heartlands: the *Pecsætan* of the Peak District and the people of Elmet, near Leeds.[28] There is no information regarding how or when the area of *Pecsæte* in the Derbyshire Peak District passed into the hands of the Mercian kings. Many of the names on the *Tribal Hidage* hint that the tribes had no corporate identity before they reached the area where they settled, given that the element *sætan* means 'a resident inhabitant holding of land.' Their identity may also have been influenced by the identity of the local lord, and as pointed out by Barbara Yorke[29] a person living, for example, in the area of the *Pecsætan* (Peak District) may have paid tribute to Northumbrians and Mercians at different times.

To the east we have Lindsey, Lincolnshire, and the North and South *Gyrwe*, around modern-day Peterborough. This last were obviously reasonably prestigious if, as noted above, Tondberht of the South *Gyrwe* was allowed to marry a princess.

Of Lindsey, we have a little more information. It had its own ruling dynasty which, according to the Anglian genealogies, could trace its lineage back to Woden.[30] Given that one of the names has a first element Cæd (Cædbæd), which may be a British name-stem,[31] it is possible that their origin was part British. Lindsey's geography was important: Hatfield Chase, the site of Edwin's demise at the hands of Penda, is on its borders. As with the later questions about Oswald and the extent of his encroachment south, this raises questions about who was taking the fight to whom when Mercia and Northumbria fought at Hatfield Chase. Bede makes reference to the monastery at Bardney – we know that the later monks of Bardney in Lindsey were reluctant to take Oswald's remains when his niece had them translated there – and it is likely that it was a royal residence.[32]

Penda's son, Æthelred, married Osthryth of Northumbria, and she was the niece of Oswald. It was she who brought Oswald's remains from their resting place to Bardney, and she was herself buried there. In 704 her husband withdrew to Bardney and died there as abbot. This would add weight to the notion that Lindsey was, originally at least, more connected politically with Mercia than with Northumbria, although the lordship of the province passed back and forth from one to the other until Æthelred's victory at the battle of the Trent in 679 brought it back under Mercian control. Henry of Huntingdon believed that Lindsey belonged to the Mercians and there is much about the early ecclesiastical history of this region, generally, to connect it with Mercia. Guthlac, the founder of Crowland Abbey, belonged to the royal house of Mercia and was related to Penwalh, who could trace his lineage back to Icel. The monastery at Crowland was dedicated by Headda, the bishop of Lichfield.

It was thought that the last king of Lindsey, Aldfrith, attended Offa of Mercia's court between 787 and 796, but this suggestion has been discounted and it is now thought that the Lindsey royal dynasty did not survive as late as this.[33] Lindsey was a sizeable kingdom, assessed in the *Tribal Hidage* at 7,000 hides.

Some of the smaller groups can be pinpointed to the east midlands, including the *Spalda* – Spalding – and the *Sweodora*, which may be identified with Sword Point in Whittlesea Mere, Huntingdonshire.

Next comes the incongruous *Wihtgara* (Isle of Wight) before the list continues in its clockwise circle to south of the Mercian heartlands with the *Hwinca (Hwicce)* of Worcestershire/Gloucestershire, the *Ciltern sætan* of the Chilterns and the *Færpingas*, probably the *Feppingas* of north Oxfordshire.

Today there is still an area known as Phepson, in modern-day Worcestershire, which may well allude to the settlers known to Bede as *Feppingas*. To the south of Phepson there is a stream called Whitsun Brook, which takes its name from the *Wixan (Wixna)* who appear in the *Tribal Hidage* in close association with the *Gyrwe*.[34] At the bottom of the list all the other kingdoms of the 'Heptarchy' appear, with the exception of Northumbria. The West Saxons are listed with a figure of 100,000 hides.

The *Tribal Hidage* gives Mercia an area of 30,000 hides, as opposed to Bede's figure of 12,000. What are we to make of this discrepancy? If this is not a 'punitive figure', then we must assume that the hidage attributed to Mercia took in the neighbouring territories[35] and they may have gone from one figure to the other in a short space of time. The extent to which the kings held sway over the larger areas may have been changeable indeed.

Were it not for the survival of the *Tribal Hidage*, we might in fact be surer of the origins of the Mercians and the people who came under the umbrella of that name. The document creates as much confusion as it provides answers.

An interesting proposal over its use was put forward by Peter Featherstone, after he examined the details pertaining to the Mercian heartlands. Royal lineages exist for the larger of the units: Lindsey, and the *Grywe*, as we have seen, and the *Hwicce*, which we will come to in a moment. Featherstone concluded that the *Tribal Hidage* was a 'catalogue of kingdoms and principalities, some of whom boasted their own royal lines, assessed in figures that were symbolic of relative status.' He went on to say that whoever compiled the list was interested in 'the total hidation of Southumbria; however, it must be stressed that this information might be of use whether the compiler were levying taxes or merely taking a rough count of heads.'[36]

What was the the date of the document? One area is not listed, and it is one which we know existed, that of the kingdom of the Middle Angles. Its constituent parts must be listed separately, suggesting that at the time the *Tribal Hidage* was compiled, it had not yet been 'welded into a simple unit'.[37] Yet it seems hard to believe that the document dates from so early a period.

What is clear is that for a long time there was no love lost between the rulers of Bernicia and Deira and in 655 the Mercians under Penda may have hoped to separate them and bring Deira under Mercian control (Œthelwald of Deira was fighting on Mercia's side, despite being the nephew of the king of Bernicia.) In Penda's time, or certainly by the time of his death, he had thirty *duces regii* under his command and had the king of Bernicia's son as a hostage. Surely, though, we don't know enough about the administration of his reign to know whether there was even the wherewithal to draw up such a document, nor was anything stable enough at this time to warrant its being committed to 'paper'. This alone would point to a later date for the *Tribal Hidage*.

The reason we know of Middle Anglia is that it seems to have been created when Penda made his son Peada king of that territory in 653. It is not stated just which particular peoples this kingdom incorporated, and it ceased to exist after Peada's murder in 656. Was he simply an overlord of a number of tribes? It must all have been very fluid. Some areas were kingdoms, some were not. Changes were not always permanent. Peada was given a territory and it was turned into a kingdom, but there were no more kings of Middle Anglia after his death.

A date for the *Tribal Hidage* as early as Penda's reign seems unlikely, but let us suppose that its origins were, indeed, Mercian. The discrepancy between the 30,000 hides figure and the 12,000 given by Bede has led some to think that it must date to around the time of King Offa (757–796) when we know that Mercia had expanded considerably. On the other hand, it might have been earlier, perhaps during the reign of Wulfhere, son of Penda, who also expanded the kingdom, particularly in the south. But many of the kingdoms which recognised his overlordship retained their royal dynasties well beyond his reign. As we've already seen, others have argued that it must have been Northumbrian in origin, possibly as early as the reign of Oswiu, and on the grounds that if it is a tribute list, this explains why Northumbria is not on it.

This of course is to suppose that it is, indeed, a tribute list, and there is no certainty of that. That very large figure for Wessex, 100,000 hides, could be evidence of an earlier date, when Wessex owed tribute to Mercia, or to a much later date when the kingdom of the West Saxons was much enlarged. Not only does the survival of the *Tribal Hidage* cause difficulties in terms of interpretation, but the very fact of its survival is itself a mystery. How, if this was indeed a Mercian document, did it survive when so much else did not? This alone may point to its not being Mercian in origin, or that it was very deliberately preserved.

If we go back and consider the areas that were subject to Mercia but retained their own kings, it is clear it was a gradual process by which those kingdoms were absorbed into Mercia and the status of those kings reduced to that of ealdorman.

To return to Featherstone's supposition about the *Tribal Hidage*, he examined the charter evidence, particularly the witness lists, and concluded that these contained a graded hierarchy, one which was not dependent on royal favour, because it did not seem to change wholesale when there was a succession. What he saw was a system where men who served the king had power bases, which made it difficult to dislodge them, a nucleus of about ten or eleven men. In the *Tribal Hidage* he saw that, discounting the larger and most obvious – Wessex, Kent, East and South Saxons etc. – there were ten or eleven units with assessments of more than 1,000 hides. His contention was that an ealdorman of such an area would have a greater position at court than one of a unit based on, say, 300 hides.

However, whilst the leaders of these provinces came to court in a pecking order, it doesn't show why or when the *Tribal Hidage* was drawn up, just that the areas existed and had ealdormen leading them. What it does show is how gradual the process was. The kings of the *Hwicce* were not replaced, but demoted. This attestation of a pecking order proves the truth of the *Tribal Hidage's* assessments, maybe, but not its original purpose. The main problem is that we simply don't have a precise date for it, and without that, its original purpose cannot truly be discerned, for as Featherstone pointed out, it meant different things to different people throughout the centuries. It was more like a working document, amended as the times and needs changed. It is possible and even likely that the minor tribes remained as such under ealdormen. But we know that the *Hwicce* royal line continued into the 780s.

Historians have been troubled by the kingdom of the *Hwicce* and whether it existed before Penda's reign. It is often supposed that the kingdom was created when Penda fought the West Saxons at Cirencester.

It was Penda's son, Wulfhere, who drove the West Saxons out of the old *Gewissan* lands in the upper Thames Valley, so the *Hwicce* may originally have been dependents not of the Mercians but of the West Saxons, and we should perhaps not assume that it was Penda who either liberated or created the kingdom.[38]

Do we know where the name *Hwicce* came from? One theory is that it is an old folk name, possibly from the pre-migration age.[39] Alternatively it may be linked to the landscape, meaning ark, or chest, and referring to the flat-bottomed valley where they lived, between the Cotswold and Malvern Hills. A charter of 840 refers to a stretch of woodland in the west of the region, called Wychwood Forest (*Huiccedwudu*).[40]

We know from Bede that they were the northwest neighbours of the West Saxons in Warwickshire, Worcestershire and Gloucestershire, with their own royal dynasty and a bishopric.[41] The territory was formed into a diocese with its seat at Worcester, the bishops there describing themselves as *episcopi Hwicciorum*.[42] Florence of Worcester's entry for 731 describes the *Hwicce* as 'the people who live beyond the River Severn towards the west.'

There is a lot of extant material from Worcester, with the large collection known as *Hemming's Cartulary*, and many other charters which survived, helped by the monastic revival of the tenth century promoted by St Oswald, bishop of Worcester.[43]

Bede mentions the royal line and talks of Queen Eafe who was of the *Hwicce*, daughter of Eanfrith and he also wrote that Osric was king of the *Hwicce* and that 'At the present time ... Wilfrid is bishop of the kingdom of the *Hwicce*.'[44] They may themselves have been rulers of a number of smaller 'tribes'; an early charter (S1272) makes reference to the *Pencersætan* (southwest of Birmingham) and the people known as the *Weogoran*, who gave their name to Worcester itself.[45]

Sir Frank Stenton and H.P.R. Finberg both thought that it was Penda who created the territory of the *Hwicce*. Stenton was of the opinion that the area came into English possession as a result of a victory over the British in 577 and that it stayed in West Saxon hands until 628. He believed that, at that time, Penda was a 'landless noble' and it was he who brought the 'Angles and the Saxons of the lower Severn under a single lordship'.[46]

The *Hwiccian* kings ruled for over a century and it is hard to see how they could have done so without Mercian support. Their reducing status does not necessarily mean a loss of real power; is there any reason to believe that the *Hwiccian* dynasty itself was foisted on the kingdom by the Mercians? It may be that the *Hwiccian* kings gained, rather than lost, by being subordinate to Mercia, and that their overlords in turn helped them to establish dominance over these smaller peoples.[47] As in all the midland tribes, their origins are obscure. However, there is a possibility that the origins of the *Hwicce* are slightly different, and that they were not so linked to the Mercians as might be supposed. If it can be generally accepted that the *Hwicce* moved from West Saxon to Mercian control at Cirencester, we must remember that in all likelihood Penda was not yet a king.

Finberg suggested that Penda had fighting alongside him a war band who were Northumbrian in origin, and that Penda was not liberating the *Hwicce*, but rather he was appropriating land held by the West Saxons, which he then gave to his allies as a reward. This theory rests partly on the similarity of royal names, common to the *Hwiccian* and Northumbrian royal houses – Oswald, Osric, Oslaf and Osred, for example – and the possibility that some of the Bernicians who were driven into exile after Edwin regained control in the north might have had everything to gain by throwing in their lot with Penda.[48]

Another story, offered by Finberg to prove a link between the *Hwiccian* royal house and Bernicia, begins with Offa, king of Essex. The point is made not only that his name is unusual, but that it is especially unusual for a king of the East Saxons, where regnal names tended to begin with 'S', such as Sigehere or Sebbi. The only appearance of the name before the famous king of Mercia, was one of the otherwise unmentioned younger brothers of the Bernician kings Oswald and Oswiu. This Offa of Essex also owned property in the kingdom of the *Hwicce*. Finberg argued that Offa's father, as king of the East Saxons, was unlikely to have owned land in Mercia, and thus Offa must have inherited from his mother. She, Osgith, is a little-known figure, and really all that is known of her is that she founded a monastery at Chich. The *Evesham Chronicle*, though, recorded that Æthilheard of the *Hwicce*, son of King Oshere, was a kinsman of Offa. This suggests that Offa's mother was a *Hwiccian* princess. In view of her name, Finberg thought it plausible to picture Osgith among the Osrics, Osheres, Oswalds and Osreds of that family. If, for example, she was Oshere's sister, her son and Æthilheard of the *Hwicce* would have been first cousins. He also suggested that this scenario sat well with what Bede had to say about King Wulfhere of the Mercians and his dealings with the South Saxons, where, to consolidate conversion to Christianity, he had given to the newly converted King Æthelwalh a wife chosen from the *Hwiccian* royal family.

Conversely, Patrick Sims-Williams was of the opinion that the connection with the Northumbrian royal family was 'implausible.'[49] But the alliteration does make one thing almost certain: that the kings of the *Hwicce* were all related, and it is possible to construct a list of the *Hwiccian* kings, using charter and chronicle evidence.

Bede gives us the names of the brothers Eanfrith and Eanhere in his account of St Wilfrid's conversion of the South Saxons and his talk of Queen Eafe, who had been 'baptised in her own province, that is, that of the *Hwicce*. She was the daughter of Eanfrith, the brother of Eanhere, who were both Christians, together with their people.' It is not clear whether these two ruled jointly, or whether Eanhere was sole king. Bede then gives us another name, albeit in passing, in the same section of the *HE*, when he says that Oftfor, later bishop of the *Hwicce*, went to the province of the *Hwicce*, 'which King Osric then ruled'.

A possible date for King Osric is provided by two charters, one dated between 672 and 674 (S1165) where an Osric attests as a *subreguli*, and in a charter of 675, for the foundation of Bath Monastery, granted by Osric *rex* with the consent of King Æthelred of Mercia. Osric was succeeded by Oshere, who may have been the son of Eanhere. He probably died before 709 because in charters S1177 and S64, his four sons were attesting without him.[50]

Of these four sons, only Æthelric was given titles, and attested a charter of King Æthelbald of Mercia as *subregulus* (S89). Since he appears in a charter dated between 693 and 699 (S53) it is possible that he reigned directly after Oshere, but we cannot be sure that one or more of his brothers didn't rule before him.

King Æthelbald of Mercia called a certain Osred his 'most faithful servant who is of the not ignoble royal stock of the *Hwiccian* people' (S99), but there is no evidence that Osred was a ruler of the *Hwicce*.

After a gap in the documentary evidence, three brothers – Eanberht, Uhtred and Ealdred – appear, each of them as *regulus*, in charters of 757 and 759, but there is no mention of their having had any children, and by the time of a charter of King Offa in 778, Ealdred is styled *subregulus* and *dux* (S113).

An ealdorman, Æthelmund, was killed attacking the people of Wiltshire at Kempsford in 802. He was granted land by Uhtred, 'ruler of the *Hwicce*', in 770, who called him his 'faithful servant'[51] but made no mention of any blood tie, and King Offa granted him land at Westbury in a charter (S139) in the absence of any *Hwiccian reguli*. In S148 Æthelmund was described by King Ecgfrith merely as a faithful *princeps*. His son was embroiled in a legal wrangle to stake his claim to Westbury[52] but the relevance of this story here is the proof that the *Hwiccian* kings were relegated to the status of noblemen.

Even if the theory about the Bernicians is correct, it doesn't seem plausible that Penda would have been strong enough, in the days when he was not yet king of Mercia and still a junior partner to Cadwallon, to reward his allies with a kingdom and, whilst it is clear that the *Hwicce* were under the domination of the Mercians from an early stage, this theory, not universally accepted, is not proof that Penda created the kingdom. It is more likely that amongst others of the lesser kingdoms, the *Hwicce* were part of a narrative that saw Mercia expanding to incorporate surrounding territories;[53] they survived, as a kingdom, for far longer than others which were more likely to have been artificially created by the Mercians: the kingdom of the Middle Angles, and the *Magonsæte*, which both had sons of Penda as kings.

'Now there was in the days of Æthelred the illustrious king of the English a certain man of distinguished Mercian stock named Penwalh, whose dwelling, furnished with an abundance of goods of various kinds, was in the district of the Middle Angles.' So begins the *Life* of St Guthlac, with a reminder of both the Middle Angles and the *-walh* name ending.

The name Penwalh would seem to provide a possible link of nomenclature between Penda and Merewalh, but Merewalh's story is linked more to that of the *Magonsæte* than of Mercian politics generally.

The name *Magonsæte* first appears in a document of 811 in a charter in which Archbishop Wulfred of Canterbury gave land to King Cenwulf of Mercia.[54] We know less about the *Magonsæte* because so many of the records from Hereford were lost, but just as the *Hwicce* kingdom appears to have been coterminous with the diocese of Worcester, so the province of the *Magonsæte* corresponds to the diocese of Hereford.[55]

The *Magonsæte* are not explicitly mentioned in the *Tribal Hidage*, and neither does Bede mention them by name. In his summation of the 'present time' i.e. 731, he tells us that 'Ealdwine is bishop of the province of the Mercians and Walhstod is bishop of the peoples who dwell over the River Severn to the west.'[56]

It may be that this area was more ethnically diverse than the others named by Bede – Wilfrid as bishop of the province of the *Hwicce*, Cyneberht as bishop of the province of Lindsey – a fact reflected in the name of Bishop Walhstod, whose name means 'interpreter'. Later sources give us details of their dynasty, beginning with Merewalh, possible son of Penda, but if we consider the name of Bishop Walhstod we might glean a little of the history before Merewalh's rule. It may be that in fact Merewalh was indeed a Welshman, who was rewarded after the success at Maserfeld. This being so, it might be that the lands had been in his family long before Penda's time. Bishop Walhstod's name might then reflect the fact that there were still many Welsh speakers living in the area.[57]

Still, the appearance of the name *Magonsæte* is relatively late. 'The inhabitants of the country between the Wrekin and the Wye appear to have been known in the seventh century as the Western *Hecani*.'[58] From the ninth century until the eve of the Conquest the people living in south Shropshire and north Herefordshire were called the *Magonsæte*, with a name which seems to derive from the district of *Magana* (Maund) near Leominster.[59]

The first known king of the *Magonsæte* was Merewalh, who may or may not have been Penda's son. Given that we know that Penda made his son Peada king of the Middle Angles it is believable that some similar arrangement, familial or not, came to pass, whereby he set Merewalh over the people who came to be known as the *Magonsæte*.

Merewalh was married to Eormenburg, a lady from the Kentish royal house.[60] Their children were Mildburg, who was the foundress of Much Wenlock Abbey; Mildthryth, or Mildryth, the abbess of Minster-in-Thanet; Mildgyth, a nun at Eastry; and a son, Merefin, of whom nothing more is known.

Florence of Worcester describes Merewalh as king of the Western *Hecani* and adds that a brother, Merchelm, reigned after him. The strong alliteration probably confirms that these people all belonged to the same family but has also been used to argue that they could not have been related to Penda.[61] This regnal list is supported by the chronicler William of Malmesbury, who claimed to have seen a cross in Hereford inscribed with the name of a *regulus*, Milfrith, and his wife Cwenburh. Milfrith is otherwise not accounted for in this list, but the alliteration, and the association with Hereford, suggests some connection.

The family disappeared from the records, and it may be that the dynastic status was lost when King Offa began the process of absorption of the smaller kingdoms into greater Mercia in the eighth century. The beheaded Æthelberht of East Anglia's body was taken to Hereford, and this, as well as the building of Offa's Dyke, points to Offa's having been in direct control of the area.[62]

Goscelin of St Bertin's *Life* of St Mildburg says that Merewalh was the third son of Penda and that he was a pagan until 660 when a Northumbrian missionary named Eadfrith converted him. It was after this that Merewalh founded a church at Leominster, but the people of this area were probably already Christian at the time of Bede.[63] It should be noted that if Merewalh was indeed a son of Penda, it is unlikely that he would have been the third son. He was old enough to be given a kingdom in his father's lifetime, whereas Penda left young, possibly not even teenage, sons when he died.

A document called *The Testament of St Mildburg* survives and, in it, St Mildburg calls her brother, Merchelm, son of Merewalh, '*rex*'. She names Æthelred, another son of Penda's, as her uncle.[64] It has been argued that

Merewalh was not Penda's son, because of the non-alliteration,[65] but then only one of Penda's known sons had an alliterative name. Stenton noted that Merewalh alliterates with *Magonsætan*, but it has been pointed out that alliteration between place names and personal names is uncommon and, in this case, probably coincidental.[66]

Much has been made already of Merewalh's name. The Welsh connection may be unsecure, given that it might derive from the same source as the Old English term for 'slave' and seems therefore to be an odd name for English nobility[67] and, as we know, there were also men of royal blood called Cenwalh, Æthelwalh (of Sussex, d. before 685), and Penwalh. It seems likely that Penwalh was closely related to Penda, and with Merewalh we see British elements in the names, possibly implying some degree of intermarriage.[68]

Certainly, Merewalh's family was alliterative. As well as sons Merchelm and Mildfrith, he had daughters Mildburg, Mildthryth and Mildgyth, along with the son Merefin who did not survive infancy.

We wouldn't know much about them at all were it not for St Mildburg. Mildburg became the second abbess of Wenlock, and many miracles were associated with her. William of Malmesbury's *Gesta Pontificum* gives details of her, telling us that 'the blessed Mildburg, sister of the holy Mildryth and a daughter of the son of Penda, king of Mercia, lived and was buried there [Wenlock].' The crypt was broken into, her body revealed, and many miracles began, including the 'king's disease' vanishing 'before the powers of the virgin'.[69] In Chapter 172 William relates the story of some geese and a bailiff, who was told by St Mildburg to shut the geese up in his house to stop them pecking at the crops but he ate one of the geese for his supper; the remaining geese crowded round St Mildburg and revealed what had happened, whereupon, with the divine hand of God, she was able to bring the deceased bird back to life.

Goscelin chose not to edit but to copy verbatim her *Testament* – contained in his twelfth-century *Life* and preserved in a thirteenth-century manuscript – which was allegedly written or dictated by the lady herself. In it, she explains that she gained possession of 'several landed properties in sundry places by sundry gifts of my brothers King Merchelm and Mildfrith'.[70] The charter referred to cannot be dated with any precision. In the document they refer to her as their sister (*Germana ac soror*) and as we have seen, she referred to them as her brothers. '*Germana*' sometimes means half-sister, so perhaps Merchelm and Mildfrith were Merewalh's sons by a previous wife, or mistress.

Mildfrith was named *regulus* in a monumental inscription set up by Cuthbert, bishop of Hereford, in the eighth century. Here his wife's name is recorded as Quenburga [Cwenburg]. The last lines of the inscription read:

> The fourth, a chieftain, Mildfrith called, and fifth
> His fair wife Cwenburg. Sixth and last
> Is buried Osfrith, son of Oshelm here.[71]

It is possible that Mildfrith shared authority with Merchelm, the brother who was styled in Mildburg's *Testament* as *rex*.

The only other mention of the family is the apocryphal story of Mildfrith. The story concerns the murder of Æthelberht of East Anglia. Upon hearing reports of miracles associated with the victim, Mildfrith founded a minster at Hereford. Mildfrith must have been long dead by the time of this murder, which occurred in the reign of Offa, and the inscription which bears the name of Mildfrith and his wife was set up by a bishop, Cuthbert, who was incumbent from 736–740, which means that Hereford was well-established before the date of the king of East Anglia's murder.[72]

Nothing more is heard of the dynasty after Mildfrith. A grant of land to Gloucester Monastery (S1782) by the permission of Beornwulf, who was king of Mercia in the mid-ninth century, was given by Nothheard, who appears in the charter as *praefectus et comes regis in Magansetum* and Nothheard was thus presumably a nobleman of only local importance.[73] The name *Magonsætan* was mentioned as late at 1041, but only in terms of ealdormen or *comes*.[74]

The kingdom of the *Hwicce*, centred as it was around the Avon and Lower Severn valleys, was surrounded by other Angle and Saxon kingdoms. The *Magonsætan*, on the other hand, occupied a border position, and its western border may have been established by force against an indigenous Welsh population.[75]

The *Magonsætan* kingdom, whilst being subordinate to the wider Mercian kingdom, may yet have benefited from the connection. Merewalh could have been Penda's son, put into power like his brother, Peada, and the *Magonsæte* must have been reliant on Mercian support in their dealings with the Welsh along their border. The *Life* of St Guthlac speaks of attacks by the Welsh in the reign of King Coenred at the beginning of the eighth century and the Welsh annals reported British victories in 722. The *ASC* informs us that in 743 Æthelbald of Mercia and Cuthred of Wessex fought against the Britons (*Walas*).

If only we could be surer about the ethnic identity of the area. 'A degree of intermarriage is suggested by the discovery both of studded boots and of material woven by traditional Romano-British methods.'[76]

Certainly, it has been pointed out that in these early days, in any conflict, the Mercians tended to side with the Britons rather than other Angles or Saxons, although the animosity with the West Saxons could simply have been due to the Mercians' tendency to support others of their ilk (the *Hwicce*). As previously noted, Bede made the distinction between Angles and Saxons and it could be that this was a difference still clearly felt, certainly closer to 'home'. Or it may simply have been a case of 'the enemy of my enemy is my friend'; Edwin of Northumbria had been aggressive towards the British kingdoms just as much as he had Mercian territories. That Penda was the junior partner in the alliance with Cadwallon of Gwynedd may be significant, but may also simply prove that at that stage, whatever his royal lineage, Penda was not a king.

What of the Mercians, i.e. Penda's 'tribe' themselves? The possibility has been discussed of the Iclingas absorbing the *Tomsæte*. Although Bede clearly calls Cearl a king, he does not appear on any of the genealogies.[77] If, indeed, his name was a nickname for an upstart of less than noble stock, could it be that there was something in what Stenton said; could Penda have been a landless noble and the first to rise up and grab himself a kingdom? If so, then we might think of him not only as energetic, but also ambitious, and possessed of a phenomenal amount of daring and self-belief.

Bede is the only source to mention Cearl, and he only mentions him when explaining Edwin's marriage to Cwenburh. Whilst not all the sources mention Edwin's period of exile in Mercia, it seems clear that it happened, and that the marriage produced two children. Whether or not these children were born while Edwin was still in exile, they must have been the product of his first marriage to have been old enough to fight with him at Hatfield Chase. Presumably Edwin fled to a country that could offer him some form of protection, although it seems likely that his nephew Hereric found sanctuary in the British kingdom of Elmet, which can be deduced from Bede's comment that he was later killed there. If Rædwald of East Anglia only felt able to move against Northumbria once Æthelberht of Kent had died and he, Rædwald, was the new *Bretwalda*, then it is possible that Edwin fled initially to a province where the king was more powerful, that being Mercia, and only left when Rædwald gained ascendancy.

Stenton pointed out that the marriage between Edwin and Cwenburh proves that the Mercians were independent of Northumbria at that point, and that 'there is no reason to doubt that they formed part of the southern confederacy led by Æthelberht of Kent.'[78]

As seen in the previous chapter, it has been suggested that Cearl was not only a powerful king, but that he led Mercian forces alongside the

Welsh/British at the battle of Chester in 613. Cearl was certainly powerful enough, then, to protect the exiled Prince Edwin, but what happened; why did Edwin leave? Perhaps it was more than a simple case of a new *Bretwalda* coming to prominence in the east. It may be that Cearl fell at the battle of Chester, and with him, the power of Mercia to promise help to Edwin. If so, then it might shed different light upon the *Tribal Hidage* and prove that it was indeed drawn up in Northumbria.

Nicholas Higham argued that the two lists of the *Tribal Hidage* were drawn up at Edwin's court, the primary list in the latter part of 625, and the secondary twelve months later, and that the list is, in fact, a tally of all the lands recently lost to Northumbria.[79] The two-phase construction of the list might be argued to show that the first list was borrowed from an existing, not necessarily written, list, and that perhaps Edwin inherited these territories from Æthelfrith of Bernicia. It may even be that Æthelfrith, having defeated Cearl at Chester, then placed a king from an alternative line, in this case Pybba's, on the Mercian throne as puppet. It very much depends how we interpret that line in *HB*, 'He first separated the kingdom of the Mercians from the kingdom of the Northerners.' If Cearl was an important and powerful king, then it means that the Mercians were a dominant force before Penda's rise to power.

But Stenton, whilst arguing for Mercian independence at this point, also stated that the Mercian kingdom was not so much a state as a group of peoples, the boundaries of whose lands were 'ill-defined', and that it was not until the reign of Penda that the Mercian kingdom became a great power, although he acknowledged that 'the stages by which he came to power are unknown.'[80]

With the *Tribal Hidage* casting as much shadow as it sheds light, we will probably never know. Clearly, however, nothing had been definitively settled at the battle of the *Winwæd*, and both Oswiu and Penda had sons. Sons who would grow up, and one day be kings.

CHAPTER 3

The Sons of Penda

In the aftermath of the *Winwæd*, Oswiu was supreme – for the time being. Of Penda's widow, we hear nothing. As, presumably, she was a pagan, it seems unlikely that she would have voluntarily gone to a nunnery. Her younger sons went into hiding; perhaps she went with them. Peada, king of the Middle Angles, kept his position there, no doubt benefiting from his Christianity and the fact that he was married to Oswiu's daughter, Alhflæd, at least in the short term. After 656, when Peada died, Oswiu did not appoint another puppet in his place, and all of the Mercian lands were under Northumbrian control.

Little is said of Penda's sons in the chronicles, and most of what there is focuses on the religious foundations, but there is also surviving, albeit scant, charter evidence for this period. All of Penda's offspring were Christians, and according to the *ASC*, Peada and two of his brothers were instrumental in founding the monastery at Medeshamstede (Peterborough).

Stenton pointed out that there is no surviving genuine foundation charter for the abbey, and many documents which appear to date from this period have been declared spurious. The earliest land-book relating to the abbey can be dated to 679. Such an important institution must have received earlier endowments, perhaps without written record.[1]

Henry of Huntingdon says Peada governed the Middle Angles 'for his father Penda' but there seems little doubt that he was more of a puppet of Oswiu's. He and Oswiu founded Medeshamstede jointly, though, so they must have been working in at least nominal harmony. Hugh Candidus, a Peterborough monk writing in the early twelfth century, recorded that 'in the region of the men of *Gyrwas* stands a famous monastery that was once called Medeshamstede. Those men are called *Gyrwas* who dwell in the fen, or hard by the fen, since a deep bog is called in the Saxon tongue,

"*Gyr*".' He then provides the names of those who built the monastery and says that there were 'three brothers, Peada, Wulfhere and Æthelred, each a most Christian prince, albeit a son of the heathen king Penda, who slew the right holy Oswald. For these men with their holy sisters Cyneburh and Cyneswith, who now rest there, and with King Oswiu, built this monastery from its foundations.'[2]

The *ASC* entry for 654 says Peada succeeded to the 'kingdom of Mercia', which is not quite right, and the *Liber Eliensis* says he held the kingdom of the Southern Angles.[3]

The name *Middle Anglia*, which does not appear on the *Tribal Hidage*, was a loose term, incorporating a number of peoples within an area, but its location is not in dispute, for the sources agree about the site of Medeshamstede.

Bede described how the Isle of Ely was given to Æthelthryth – indeed, the *Liber Eliensis* was written in her honour – as a dowry by her husband Tondberht of the South *Gyrwe*. Medeshamstede was perhaps 'central to the two regions of the *Gyrwe* and the *Widderingas*'.[4] Not all the versions of the *ASC* mention the founding of Medeshamstede. Likewise, they vary in their account of the other main event of this short-lived kingdom, that of the death of its first and only king.

One version of the *ASC* says that Peada died, while the E version of the *Chronicle* says specifically that he was 'slain'.[5] Hugh Candidus tells us that 'the Middle Angles adopted the faith of the Lord under Peada their ruler and king, two years before the death of Penda' and that his wife was 'enticed by the devil to kill him'. Bede says that Peada was 'most foully murdered in the following spring by the treachery, or so it is said, of his wife during the very time of the Easter festival.'[6] The *LE* has the same statement, almost verbatim, although it removes any doubt by omitting the qualifier 'or so it is said'.

We cannot ignore the fact that his wife was the daughter of Oswiu. Was she pressured to kill her husband? Or was she just the victim of a tradition which blames women for the murder of kings? On the face of it, it seems hard to understand why, following his resounding victory at the *Winwæd*, Oswiu would have not only spared Peada but allowed him to reign, only to order his dispatch less than a year later. Especially, if, as many of the sources state, they co-founded the monastery at Medeshamstede.

An interesting point from Sharon M. Rowley is that Bede never says that the marriage took place, but rather he concentrates on the baptism of Peada. Peada returns home with four priests, rather than a bride, although Alhflæd did go home with him. Rowley's contention is that Bede mentions little else about the marriage because of the subsequent murder.

The suggestion of Alhflæd's involvement in the killing raises questions about Oswiu's motives when allowing his daughter to marry the son of his enemy. For, despite two marriage alliances, he was still beset by Penda. With his daughter's connivance he managed to rid himself of Peada not long after the pretence of a settlement. Rowley points out the contrast between the Old English version of the *HE*, which misses out much of the religious aspects of this story and leaves only a tale of a violent end to a marriage for political purposes.[7]

Alhflæd, coming to us through history only as a means to tell a political or religious story, promptly disappears. Nothing is mentioned of what happened to her afterwards. Did she simply walk away having murdered her husband the king? It seems unlikely, and this was certainly not the fate of her sister, and indeed sister-in-law, Osthryth, who appears to have died for much less of a crime, as we shall shortly discover.

Clearly Oswiu didn't feel the need to install a puppet king in Middle Anglia after Peada's demise, and it seems that no sub-king was appointed in Mercia proper either, after Penda's death. The next we hear of Mercia is the emergence from hiding of Wulfhere, who was 'probably in his mid-teens when he became king'.[8] Wulfhere came to the throne three years after the death of his father, Penda, and it seems as if he succeeded to the whole of the Mercian kingdom. Bede talks of a rebellion: 'Three years after Penda's death the ealdormen of the Mercian race, Immin, Eafa, and Eadberht, rebelled against King Oswiu and set up as their king Wulfhere, Penda's young son, whom they had kept concealed; and having driven out the ealdormen of the foreign king, they boldly recovered their lands and their liberty at the same time.'[9] One wonders why this was such a simple enterprise, and that there was no reprisal. There are no details given regarding the level of Northumbrian occupation in Mercia, but it is clear that Oswiu left ealdormen in charge, rather than installing a sub-king, so presumably these were ealdormen appointed by Oswiu who had only small numbers of men loyal to them. That said, Wulfhere subsequently and almost exclusively restricted his activities to the south and kept out of Oswiu's way. Was Oswiu kept occupied elsewhere? A record in the Welsh annals for 658 that 'Oswiu came and took plunder' suggests so. There may have been some sort of agreement, whereby Wulfhere promised to recognise Oswiu's supremacy, for Bede tells us that the first bishop of Mercia was Trumhere, was a kinsman of the murdered king of Deira, Oswine, and therefore a Northumbrian.

We can only speculate as to where Wulfhere was hiding during his exile. Were the Welsh alliances useful at this point? How long had the uprising been planned? As with so much of Mercian history, the details, if ever recorded, are now lost.

Wulfhere's reign mirrored his father's in that by the end of it he was leading a combined force, having 'stirred up all the southern nations against Northumbria'. Very little was written about this or the succeeding reigns and yet, between them, Wulfhere and his brother Æthelred ruled Mercia for a total of forty-six years.

Bede mentions them only in terms of religion (naturally enough) and because they hardly troubled the Northumbrians. It is likely that the *Vita Ecgwini – Life* of St Ecgwine – was written in the early eleventh century, and whilst we don't know when Ecgwine was born and died, we do know that he had dealings with Æthelred of Mercia, and yet Bede doesn't mention him at all. Bede was interested mainly in ecclesiastical matters, and Northumbria, but more specifically, Northumbrian ecclesiastical matters. However, we can glean a fair amount of information about the activities of Penda's sons in the south. Indeed, by the end of his reign, we know that Wulfhere was in possession of West Saxon territory, and had a residence at Thame. He had the king of Surrey, which may have been under West Saxon control, as his sub-king,[10] nor was this the only region subject to his rule.

There is also an interesting crossover here as we move into a period when the written records increase and at the same time the chroniclers are contemporary with their subjects. Thus we have the *Lives* of Wilfrid, friend of both Wulfhere and his brother Æthelred, and Guthlac, the man who was of noble, possibly royal stock, born during the reign of Æthelred, who began his career as a warrior, perhaps fighting in Æthelred's army. Both *Lives* were written by men who probably knew their subjects. Also, insofar as there is any detail therein, we get close to Bede's own lifetime, so that he is recording far more recent events.

With the available sources it is possible to build a picture of Wulfhere's reign, showing how he eventually became strong enough to stir up the south against the north.

The *ASC* tells us that in 661 Wulfhere 'harried in the Isle of Wight and gave the people of the Isle of Wight to Æthelwalh, king of the South Saxons, because Wulfhere had stood sponsor to him at baptism.' There is a little more to this story than is suggested by the *Chronicle*, however. Bede furnishes us with the details of the baptism and says that Æthelwalh was baptised 'at the suggestion and in the presence of Wulfhere, who, when Æthelwalh came forth from the font, received him as a son. As a token of his adoption Wulfhere gave him two provinces, namely the Isle of Wight and the province of the *Meonware*, in the land of the West Saxons.'[11] This is an interesting passage, because it indicates, firstly, that these territories were subordinate to Wulfhere. Æthelwalh, by agreeing to baptism in this way must surely have been signalling his recognition of Wulfhere as his overlord. Equally of note is the *ASC*'s omission of the gift of the province of the *Meonware*, the Meon Valley being an area in modern-day southern Hampshire, an act which represented an encroachment into the lands of the West Saxons.[12] Wulfhere was demonstrating his strength to the West Saxons by giving lands in that area to a weaker state. The *ASC* makes little comment on this development, in one of the earlier examples, perhaps, of West Saxon bias in its record-keeping.

Another part of the entry for 661 includes the detail that Wulfhere 'harried on Ashdown'. Clearly Wulfhere was on the offensive, and Bede mentions that Cenwalh of the West Saxons continually suffered 'heavy losses in his kingdom at the hands of his enemies.'[13] We might reasonably put two and two together and conclude that Wulfhere was responsible. At around this time, the see at Dorchester became a Mercian bishopric. Bede was of the opinion that it was abandoned because the then bishop, Agilberht, could not speak the West Saxon language. But the *ASC* records that he had arrived from Gaul in 650; plenty of time, surely, to have grasped the basics. It has been pointed out that if Wulfhere raided Ashdown then he would have passed Dorchester on his way, so it is likely that the bishopric changed hands as a result of Wulfhere's campaigning.[14] It is tempting to wonder whether personal enmity played a part in the animosity between these two kings; Wulfhere had been in exile, but it is possible he remembered, or knew about, Cenwalh's repudiation of his aunt, and Penda's subsequent retaliation.

The only other detail in the *ASC* entry for this year states that Cenwalh fought at Easter at *Posentesbyrig*. It doesn't say whom he fought, nor does it give the outcome. Curiously, Æthelweard the Chronicler says that Cenwalh fought Wulfhere at Pontesbury, near Ashdown, and took Wulfhere prisoner 'when he had defeated his army.' William of Malmesbury said that Cenwalh 'deprived Wulfhere of the greatest part of his kingdom.' This would suggest a West Saxon victory, in which case it is surprising not to see more detail in the *ASC*, so it must be presumed that Æthelweard, and later William, had their facts muddled.

Bede records that not long after Agilberht returned to Gaul, his replacement, Wine, had cause to seek refuge with Wulfhere, and then bought the see of London from him. The inference here is that London, in the kingdom of the East Saxons, was also under the control of Mercia. Bede confirms this by recording that when the East Saxon kings, Sigehere and Sebbi, succeeded they were subject to Wulfhere.[15] Thereafter, the Mercian kings did not lose control of London until the Viking age.

As seen in Chapter Two, Æthelwalh of the South Saxons was married to Eafe, a princess of the *Hwicce,* and the kings of the *Hwicce* witnessed charters as sub-kings of Wulfhere in the 670s. Lindsey, too, must have been under his control, for he lost it to Ecgfrith of Northumbria in the last years of his reign. When Chad was appointed bishop of Lichfield by Wulfhere in 669, he was given land at Barrow in Lindsey, where he founded a monastery.[16]

A charter, (S1165), probably a forgery but based on an original grant, shows Wulfhere to be overlord of Surrey in the 670s. It concerns 'Frithuwald ... sub-king of Wulfhere, king of the Mercians ... of the province of the men of Surrey', but his kingdom seems to have extended north of the Thames into south Buckinghamshire. It has been suggested that he was a Mercian; Frithuric, who is the first on the witness list, was 'probably a kinsman and the donor of Breedon-on-the-Hill, Leicestershire, and Repton, Derby, to the monastery of Medeshamstede'.[17]

Whether or not the East Saxons fought under Penda at the *Winwæd*, and it seems unlikely given that Oswiu was making overtures to them with offers to sponsor baptism, the East Saxons had fallen under Mercian lordship by the last part of Wulfhere's reign.[18] *The Tribal Hidage* may have been compiled during the reign of Wulfhere. The reason for this argument would be that he was seemingly overlord of most of southern England and he remains a possible, although unlikely, candidate.

Concerning the north, it is possible that Wulfhere attempted to take advantage of regime changes. In 670, Oswiu, the mighty king who had killed Wulfhere's father, died. He was succeeded by his son Ecgfrith, who had been a hostage at Penda's court in the 650s. Wulfhere and Ecgfrith would have known each other as small boys and could well have been of similar age. Presumably the hostage's lot was a comfortable one, and they might even have played together? It is at once interesting and frustrating that these two families were so closely connected, by marriage and by circumstance, and yet little of these personal relationships is revealed to us by the documentary evidence.

Cenwalh of Wessex died in 672, and perhaps it was after this that Wulfhere made his move against the north. The death of the West Saxon king just two years after the demise of the Northumbrian overlord may have presented the perfect opportunity for Wulfhere to turn north. It was Eddius Stephanus (also known as Stephen of Ripon), writing the *Life* of St Wilfrid, who declared that Wulfhere 'stirred up all the southern nations' against Northumbria.[19] Bede gives no information about this, and it is not mentioned in the *ASC*, but a likely date would be 674, and it may be that in fact Wulfhere had no choice in the timing, and that his gaze was drawn north by Ecgfrith, challenging the Mercian hold on Lindsey. We know from Bede that at the time of Wulfhere's death, Lindsey had 'recently' been lost to Northumbria, but not who was the initial aggressor.[20] For, despite the large numbers at his disposal, Wulfhere was not victorious.

Simeon of Durham records the battle: 'In that time King Ecgfrith fought against the king of the Mercians, Wulfhere son of Penda, and having cut down [his] army he vanquished him and put him to flight with only one small boy accompanying [him].'[21] It would be interesting to find out more about this small boy, but there is no other mention of him. The *Life* of Wilfrid tells us only that the kingdom of Mercia was put under tribute and Ecgfrith 'ruled a wider realm in peace.'[22] William of Malmesbury added that Wulfhere 'led an army against the Northumbrians, recalling with resentment how they had killed his father. On he came, confident that he would make good the loss, or win a kingdom. But fortune did not favour him – hardly more than it favoured his father; but he did live to turn tail in shameful retreat.'[23] It was a blow for the overlord of southern England; 'Only an unsuccessful battle prevented Wulfhere of Mercia from bringing Northumbria under an overlordship which was already effective throughout the south.'[24]

Wulfhere was down, but not quite out. The *ASC* entry for 675 finds him in one last battle, against Æscwine of the West Saxons at a place called *Biedanheafde* – though the outcome is not recorded – and Wulfhere died 'later that year'. It might be that he sustained fatal wounds in the battle, but Henry of Huntingdon said that he died of disease, while Stephen in the *Life* of Wilfrid confessed that he did not know the cause of Wulfhere's death. William of Malmesbury thought he died a few days after his battle with Ecgfrith, so his evidence here can be discounted.

Wulfhere was evidently keen, and more than capable, to take the baton, as it were, and continue his father's efforts to keep Northumbria out of Mercia, and 'at the height of his power, he must have been a *Bretwalda*.'[25] His vigorous campaigning in the south reaped dividends but, ultimately, he was unable to arrest Northumbrian aggrandisement. His reign was not simply a tale of aggression and warfare, however.

John of Worcester wrote that Wulfhere 'ordered the name of Christ to be preached everywhere in his kingdom and built churches in many places.' He stated that Wulfhere's queen, 'St Eormenhild ... bore him a virgin of great virtue, St Werburg, who on the death of her father renounced the world to take the habit of the holy monastic life and entered the convent of her mother's aunt, named of St Æthelthryth, where with God's help she performed many miracles.'

Wulfhere's wife Eormenhild was the daughter of Eorcenberht of Kent and his wife, Seaxburh (whose sister was St Æthelthryth, married to Tonberht of the *Gyrwe*, then Ecgfrith of Northumbria, and finally founder and abbess of Ely). The stories concerning Wulfhere's wife and offspring are varied and, at times, puzzling. Their two identified children were Coenred and Werberg, but there may have been others.

A curious seventeenth-century anecdote about Wulfhere comes under an entry for Stone, in Staffordshire.[26] It states that Wulfhere and Eormenhild had two sons, Wulfad and Ruffin, as well as their daughter, Werburg, who was born at Stone. The sons were baptised by St Cedd (who had accompanied Peada back to Middle Anglia) which, according to this story, offended their father, who then 'killed them both with his own hands.' Wulfhere was horribly tormented by what he had done, and 'could find no ease' until he went to St Cedd, who absolved him if he would suppress idolatry and establish Christianity throughout Mercia. It also says that the king built many churches and monasteries, among them Peterborough, although as we have seen it is likely that the monastery there (Medeshamstede) was perhaps founded earlier, and by Wulfhere's brother, Peada. We also learn from Hugh Candidus that Wulfhere 'continued [Peada's] good work at Medeshamstede and had his sisters helping him', and that 'he endowed the monastery.'[27]

It has been pointed out that Ruffin, or Rufinus, is an odd name for a Mercian prince, although Wulfad, or Wulflad, is alliterative.[28] Given that St Werburg was the daughter of Wulfhere, and thus would have been the sister of these two boys, the scenario in which her father kills them for having been baptised seems unlikely to say the least. Werburg's *Life*, which probably preserves earlier material, tells how she was a nun at Ely before living on her father's estates.[29] It is hard to see how a murderous king would allow her so to do.

There is no other source which corroborates this story. Bede even tells us that when Wulfhere discovered that part of the East Saxon kingdom had apostatised, he sent Bishop Jaruman to 'correct their error.' Although Bede does have a story about two young princes being killed immediately after baptism, the story is later than Wulfhere's death, and takes place on the Isle of Wight.[30]

What is true is that Wulfhere married a Kentish princess, whose name was Eormenhild. She was the daughter of Eorcenberht and a brief overview of the Kentish kings at this time shows that King Eorcenberht seized Kent from his brother, Eormenred.

Eormenred was married to Oslafa and their children were (Domne) Eafe, Eormenburg, Æthelberht and Æthelred. Domne Eafe, sometimes called Domneva, was the wife of Merewalh, king of the *Magonsæte*.

Eorcenberht was married to Seaxburh. She had a son, Ecgberht, who murdered Æthelberht and Æthelred, the brothers of (Domne) Eafe.

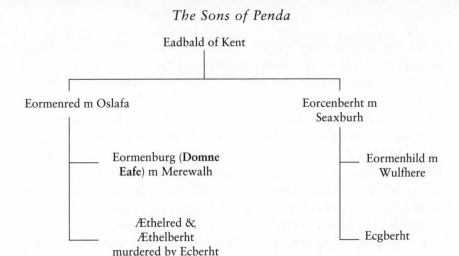

Domne Eafe's Family Connections.

Thus, in this very tangled family web, it appears, firstly, the wives of Merewalh and Wulfhere were cousins, and that the brothers of Wulfhere's wife were killed by the brother, or half-brother, of Merewalh's wife.

Of the murder, William of Malmesbury reported that Ecgberht's servant, Thunor, deceived them with daily kisses, then, while hugging them, stabbed them, and buried them deep in a pit right under the king's throne, where no one would think to look. But the king was scorched by divine fire, which caused him to dig away the stones, and the earth opened up and swallowed Thunor alive.[31] Stories about this and other family connections come to us via the *Life* of St Wilfrid.

St Wilfrid (634–709) was a monk and then bishop of York. Bede had met him and was 'probably familiar with Eddius [Stephen]'s *Life* of Wilfrid'.[32] His monastic life began under the patronage of King Oswiu's third wife Eanflaed, daughter of Edwin, and he went to Lindisfarne during the tenure of Aidan. In about 652 he went on pilgrimage to Rome, first spending a year at the Kentish royal court. Eanflaed, his sponsor, was the daughter of a Kentish princess and had grown up there during the reign of Oswald. The fact that it was seen sensible for Edwin's widow and children to flee to Kent when Oswald became king is, as mentioned in Chapter One, another indicator that he was seen by some as an aggressor.

Returning from his pilgrimage, Wilfrid struck up a friendship with Alhfrith, son of Oswiu by a previous wife, who was ruling Deira for his father as a sub-king. Alhfrith gave Wilfrid the bishopric of Ripon, and Wilfrid was ordained there, probably by Agilberht, the bishop who had abandoned his see at Dorchester. In 664 Wilfrid attended the famous Synod of Whitby, where the question of the observance of Easter was decided. Not long afterwards, Wilfrid became archbishop of York, but could not be consecrated because the see of Canterbury was vacant. Instead, Agilberht consecrated him at Compiègne.

While he was away, a row broke out between Alhfrith and his father Oswiu, which may be connected to the fact that Oswiu had installed Chad as archbishop of York. Surviving shipwreck, Wilfrid returned to Northumbria and retired to his monastery at Ripon. While he was there, he conducted duties for Mercia and founded monasteries there, with the benefit of endowments from Wulfhere. William of Malmesbury: 'For three years Wilfrid lived a humble life at Ripon ... he was often called in by Wulfhere king of the Mercians, who gave him a site called Lichfield, on which to build a cathedral or a monastery, as he chose.'[33]

When Archbishop Theodore visited England in 669, he restored Wilfrid to York, giving Chad the see of Lichfield instead. It is interesting to note that the *Life* of Wilfrid says this happened 'during Wulfhere's reign' rather than naming the Northumbrian king. The chapter in question is dated 669–671, and Oswiu died in 670. Perhaps Stephen was not sure just in whose reign this occurred.[34]

Oswiu of Northumbria was succeeded by his son Ecgfrith who, in 678, quarrelled with Wilfrid. The opportunist Theodore took advantage of the standoff and consecrated three new Northumbrian bishops. Wilfrid went back to Rome to petition the pope. The pope supported him but when Wilfrid returned, Ecgfrith ignored the ruling, imprisoned Wilfrid for a short time and then banished him.

Wilfrid's fortunes turned when Ecgfrith died and was succeeded by Aldfrith – yet another of Oswiu's sons – although the see of York had been much reduced in size and status. But he quarrelled with Aldfrith and was banished again, for a longer and less well-recorded period. He was, occasionally, to be found in Mercia and was there, at his foundation at Oundle, when he died.

There are two aspects of Wilfrid's story especially pertinent in identifying members of Penda's dynasty. The first indicates that Wulfhere had an otherwise unknown son, called Berhtwald.

In a later chapter of the *Vita Wilfridi* – *Life* of Wilfrid – we find Wilfrid setting off 'in exile for the kingdoms of the south. God ... sent a kind-hearted man to meet them on their way, a sheriff of noble birth called Berhtwald, nephew to Æthelred, king of Mercia. But King Æthelred and his queen, Ecgfrith's sister, hearing that Wilfrid had been staying there awhile in peace, forbade Berhtwald, as he valued his safety, to harbour him another day. They did this to flatter Ecgfrith. The monks remained, but Wilfrid was spitefully driven out and made his way to Centwini, king of the West Saxons.' He wasn't there for long though because Centwini's queen, who was sister to Ecgfrith's second wife, 'detested him'.[35]

William of Malmesbury, when writing about Æthelred of Mercia, said that, 'The same king has by his brother Wulfhere a nephew called Berhtwald of whom I spoke in my account of Bishop Wilfrid. He did not have a king's powers but was a chieftain in one part of the kingdom.' Berhtwald appears to have been a *subregulus* on the borders of the kingdoms of the *Hwicce* and the West Saxons and able to grant an estate in Wiltshire to Aldhelm, abbot of Malmesbury.[36]

The other aspect of Wilfrid's tale at first muddies the waters and makes it difficult to identify the women of the story. It cannot have brought the Northumbrian kings any comfort that Wilfrid was on such friendly terms with Wulfhere of Mercia and, later on, his brother and successor, Æthelred, but it is likely that the quarrel between Wilfrid and Ecgfrith had a fair bit to do with the fact that Wilfrid had encouraged Ecgfrith's queen, the aforementioned Æthelthryth, in a vow of virginity.

According to Bede, he asked Wilfrid if this was true and Wilfrid had confirmed it, saying that Ecgfrith had promised Wilfrid estates and money if he would persuade her to consummate the marriage.[37] The truth of this cannot be proven of course, but if it is, she must have been a determined woman, for this was her second marriage, the first having been to Tonberht of the *Gyrwe*. Having, it seems, left a nunnery to be married for a second time, she returned to the religious life, and Ecgfrith married again. His new queen, variously Iurminburg, Ermengburga, or Eormenburg, was openly hostile to Wilfrid. We know that she came from Kent, for it was her sister, the 'Centwini queen,' who detested Wilfrid.

This Eormenburg is often cited as being the mother of St Mildburg, and thus of St Mildthryth. But these women were the daughters of Merewalh, king of the *Magonsæte* and possibly the son of Penda. Is it possible that Eormenburg was married to a son of Penda and a son of Oswiu? The entry in *PASE* would suggest so, but it seems not.

The earliest written legend of St Mildthryth in the eleventh century, and some versions of her genealogy, say that Domne Eafe (Domneva), Mildthryth's mother, was also called Eormenburg. However, in a charter of 699, in which King Wihtred of Kent grants privileges to the churches and monasteries of Kent, both Eafe [Aebbe] and Eormenburg [Irmingburga] were among those present, along with a third abbess, Eormenhild (Hirminhilda) These women have been identified as Eormenhild, wife of Wulfhere, mother of St Werburg, and her cousins (Domne) Eafe, wife of Merewalh and mother of Mildburg and Mildthryth, and her sister, Eormenburg. There is nothing to connect this Eormenburg with the second wife of King Ecgfrith, who, after Ecgfrith was defeated and killed at *Nechtanesmere* in 685 retired to a monastery in Carlisle which had been founded by her sister.[38]

Thus Ecgfrith of Northumbria's second wife was not connected to Mercia, nor was she the woman who married Merewalh, but this story serves to show how difficult the task can be of piecing these family connections together.

We have already met Merewalh, who may or may not have been Penda's son. The *Liber Eliensis*[39] says that Merewalh was a son of Penda who 'held a kingdom in the western part of Mercia.'

Did he survive untroubled by Oswiu? His brother, or half-brother, Peada, seems to have held the kingdom of the Middle Angles with Oswiu's 'permission', but no more is heard of the kingdom of the Middle Angles after Peada's death. Presumably, since his dynasty survived, Merewalh was left unmolested. Does this add weight to the possibility that he was not, in fact, Penda's son?

Goscelin of St Bertin wrote the *Life* of St Mildburg, daughter of Merewalh and his Kentish wife, (Domne) Eafe, whom he calls Domneva. As mentioned in Chapter Two, Goscelin said that Merewalh was the third of Penda's sons, which seems unlikely. According to Goscelin Merewalh converted to Christianity in 660 and founded the church at Leominster soon afterwards. The suggestion is that he already had his two sons, Merchelm and Mildfrith, when he married his Kentish bride. Domneva then bore their three daughters Mildburg, Mildthryth and Mildgyth, and a son Merefin, who died in infancy. At some point, probably before 673, the royal couple separated. When her brothers, Æthelberht and Æthelred were murdered, she was given land on the Isle of Thanet as their *wergild* (man-price) and she founded a convent there. It has been pointed out that her daughters must have been quite young when their mother left Mercia for the 'bracing air of Thanet'.[40] Goscelin's account of Merewalh's relationship with Penda is borne out by St Mildburg's *Testament* where she refers to Æthelred, another son of Penda, as her uncle on the father's side.[41]

Æthelred succeeded his brother to the throne of Mercia; presumably Wulfhere's son was not old enough at this point to do so. If Wulfhere had been only a teenager at the time of Penda's death, then Æthelred must have been a young child in 655. Whether he was in exile with his brother, we do not know. Presumably he came back to Mercia once the overthrow of the Northumbrian ealdormen had allowed Wulfhere to take back the kingdom. Perhaps his memories of his father flickered more dimly than they did for Wulfhere, for his reign, though reasonable in length, is relatively incident-free. He seems to have been more concerned with religious matters than with politics, eventually retiring to a monastery, so much so that it seems almost out of character that he took on the might of Northumbria and destroyed the supremacy of the north.

The only significant dates we have for his reign are that in 676 he devastated Kent at the head of a 'cruel army ... profaning churches and monasteries without respect for religion or fear of God,' and that in 679 he regained Lindsey at the battle of the Trent, after which, according to Bede, there was a long peace between Mercia and Northumbria.[42] The *ASC* mentions the attack on Kent, without supplying any further information. It is possible that Æthelred's action was an attempt to secure border territories and prevent the king of Kent from repossessing Surrey.[43]

In 690 it appears that Æthelred involved himself once again in the affairs of the Kentish kingdom, supporting the – ultimately unsuccessful – claims of Oswine, who was probably the nephew of (Domne) Eafe and therefore a nephew by marriage of Æthelred[44] but there is very little other recorded activity of this nature for his reign. It is possible that he had problems with the Welsh, for we are told that the young Guthlac spent his time fighting in Wales and perhaps this was part of an ongoing campaign.[45]

He seems to have been consolidating the principal lands of Mercia. Charter evidence shows the kings of the *Hwicce* were granting land, but only with Æthelred's consent,[46] however, it seems his attempt to hold onto Surrey was unsuccessful and he lost it – and Sussex – to Cædwalla of the West Saxons. A charter of 688 (S235) shows Cædwalla granting land in Surrey, from which the inference can be drawn that he had captured it from Æthelred.

In the late 680s members of the East Saxon royal family were ruling in Kent with Æthelred's support. He granted land at Ealing to the bishop of London (S1783) and a grant of King Swæfred in Middlesex was made with his consent and confirmed by Æthelred's successors Coenred and Ceolred (S65). From 704, the last year of the reign of Æthelred, a brief series of five documents 'attests to the overlordship of Æthelred and his successor Coenred in Essex.'[47]

But by the 690s, the strong kingship of both Wihtred of Kent and Ine of Wessex halted any further expansion of Mercia. In 704 Æthelred abdicated and became a monk.

Hugh Candidus remembered him for honouring Medeshamstede and extolling it 'beyond all others in the granting of lands and privileges'[48] but it was to Bardney that the king retired, to become first monk, and then abbot, there.

The *Life* of Wilfrid gives many examples of the loyalty and piety of Æthelred. It recounts that 'Æthelred treated [Wilfrid] with the deepest respect and remained his faithful friend for ever' and that when Wilfrid and Aldfrith had their altercation, 'Wilfrid refused to submit and betook himself to his friend the king of Mercia. Æthelred welcomed him with great honour.' In a later chapter, the contents of a letter from Pope John are recorded, and the letter opens with the words, 'Pope John to their most noble majesties, Æthelred, king of Mercia and Aldfrith, king of Deira. We fully recognise your zeal for the faith which you received when God illuminated your hearts.' It is interesting to note that he addresses Mercia first and puts the two kings on equal footing. After the king's abdication, Wilfrid went to visit 'that faithful friend whose loyalty had never wavered, Æthelred, the former king of Mercia.'[49]

Æthelred was not just associated with St Wilfrid, but with St Ecgwine, too, a monk of Evesham who became bishop of Worcester. From Byrhtferth's *Life* of St Ecgwine we learn that 'He [Ecgwine] was chosen by all the noblemen and ealdormen in the days of Æthelred, king of the Mercians who entrusted to him the episcopal see located in the town of Worcester. Æthelred always loved discussions with him, because Ecgwine was a revered counsellor and spokesman.' On the subject of God-fearing kings, it is noted: 'Of these, King Æthelred shone particularly with his diadem; he entrusted his illustrious children to the aforementioned bishop to be instructed in the ways of justice, so that they would discern the pre-eminence of wisdom and the discipline of moderation and the garland of courage.'[50]

Æthelred granted Ecgwine Evesham and Fladbury, which Ecgwine says he had acquired from the dowry of his wife.[51] He goes on to say that, 'after a short space of time I willingly gave it to the sub-king Æthelheard (who was king of that region which is called the "*Hwicce*"). A short time later, I acquired another estate with the one from Osweard, the brother of the aforementioned king, that is, twenty hides in the place called Twyford.'[52]

Æthelred, having taken on the might of Northumbria and won, died peacefully in his bed. His wife did not fare so well, for she was murdered in 697 by the Mercian nobles.

Yet another marriage had taken place between the two families of Penda and Oswiu, this time between the last of Penda's sons to become a king in Mercia, Æthelred, and the daughter of Oswiu and his second wife. This daughter was called Osthryth. According to the *ASC*, 'the Southumbrians slew Osthryth, Æthelred's queen and Ecgfrith's [king of Northumbria] sister.'

No explanation is given for the murder. It is known that Osthryth oversaw the removal of the bones of St Oswald, her uncle, to the abbey at Bardney, in an area where he might not have been fondly remembered. Oswald had been an enemy of Mercia, so perhaps they didn't like her highlighting his memory, but this seems a poor excuse for killing her. Was it retribution for her half-sister's murderous act, when Peada of the

Middle Angles was allegedly poisoned in 656? Again, it seems an over-reaction, especially given the amount of time which had elapsed.

It must, however, have been a tense situation, given that her husband had waged war on her brother, and in that ensuing battle of the Trent, in 679, another brother of hers had been killed. Bede noted that this young man was about eighteen years of age, and beloved in both kingdoms.

The battle of the Trent must have been an intensely personal battle. It was waged between members of the original feuding families, only one generation on. This went deeper still with the death of Ecgfrith's brother Ælfwine, who was, as the tangled interconnection continued, also the brother-in-law of Æthelred. All-out vengeance was prevented by the brokering of a deal by Archbishop Theodore, through which the Northumbrians were persuaded to accept *wergild* for the death. There might have been some satisfaction for the Mercians when Ecgfrith was killed in 685, fighting the Picts at the battle of *Nechtanesmere*, but it seems that although they were successful as kings, none of Penda's sons was able fully to avenge his death.

William of Malmesbury mentions only that Ælfwine was routed, not killed, but contradicts this by saying that the marriage between Osthryth and Æthelred took place after the death of her brother and was specifically designed to heal the rift after the killing. It was during the course of Wilfrid's journey to Wessex and the encounter with the previously mentioned Berhtwald. Wilfrid was 'only safe for a few days, for Berhtwald was the vassal of Æthelred, king of the Mercians, seeing that he was the son of Æthelred's brother, and Æthelred sent him fierce messages, warning him not to keep Wilfrid for even one day. He was doing this as a favour to Ecgfrith, for Osthryth, Ecgfrith's sister, had recently married Æthelred to comfort herself for the death of her brother Ælfwine and had established a peace between her husband and her brother Ecgfrith.'[53] Bede is clear, however, that the marriage had taken place before the battle. Whatever the sequence of events, it is evident that even while these marriages were occurring, the two royal houses were still bitterly opposed to one another and that there were conflicting loyalties. It is perhaps in this context that the murder of Osthryth should be viewed, but whatever she had done, or been accused of, we shall never know.

However, if the link between the royal dynasty of the *Hwicce* and the Bernicians, discussed in Chapter Two, stands up at all to scrutiny, then a charter suggests a link between Æthilheard, under-king of the *Hwicce*, and Osthryth, daughter of King Oswiu and niece of King Oswald. Finberg tentatively suggested that her murder may have been connected to the 'tragic' death of Oshere king of the *Hwicce*, father of the previously mentioned Æthilheard and that it is possible that they were suspected of attempting to detach the kingdom of the *Hwicce* from the overlordship of the Mercians. D.P. Kirby went further and suggested that it might have been Æthelred of Mercia who was responsible for the death of Oshere.[54]

Another feature of the battle of the Trent is the story related by Bede of a man named Imma, who was struck down during the fighting and rendered unconscious. When he awoke, he set off to find his companions, but he was captured and taken to the enemy king, Æthelred. When questioned, he was fearful of admitting his identity as a thegn and claimed to be of peasant stock. He was taken prisoner and as he grew stronger, he was bound every night to prevent his escape, but every time he was bound, the fetters loosened themselves. When asked about this he explained that his brother, a priest, would be out looking for him and offering prayers for his release, and thus the loosening of the bonds was a result of masses being said for him. The story concludes with the reuniting of Imma with his brother and their experience inspiring others to prayer, hence Bede's interest in the tale. But it also offers a glimpse into the expectations of the warrior class at this time, because when Imma's guard, who has been watching him closely, concludes that he is of noble status, he asks him to be truthful about his origins, promising that no harm shall befall him as long as he is honest. Imma reveals that he is in fact a king's thegn, and the guard responds that 'now you ought to die, because all my brothers and kinsmen were killed in the battle, but I will not kill you for I do not intend to break my promise.'[55] Clearly the guard is honour-bound to avenge his kin, but equally, his word is his bond.

Ecgfrith of Northumbria, though defeated, was not killed at the battle of the Trent. The northern expansion of his borders came to a halt, though, when he was killed in 685 by the Pictish king Bruide (his cousin) at the battle of *Nechtanesmere*. His successor was his half-Irish half-brother Aldfrith. Though Northumbria flourished as a centre of cultural and artistic richness, its supremacy was over, and the kingdoms south of the Humber were being drawn into the Mercian orbit, by varying degrees.

'Accordingly, as Æthelred, king of the Mercians, withdrew from the kingdom of this life, Coenred succeeded to the throne. He took over the kingdom honourably and duly held it, surrounded with royal splendour, ruling his people with unconquerable strength; barbarian peoples on all sides feared him.'[56]

Æthelred was succeeded by his nephew, Coenred, son of Wulfhere, about whom we know virtually nothing. It is interesting to note that within a generation of kings where alliterative names or lack thereof are used to weigh up the likelihood of familial connection, there is little alliteration. Cousins Coenred and Ceolred had alliterative names, but their fathers and the rest of their aunts and uncles did not, with the exception of Merewalh and his family.

There is very little information about Coenred's reign. Bede mentions him only briefly, but seems to have approved of him, relating a story in which an unrepentant layman, holding military rank, who despite being warned frequently by the king, would not mend his ways and give up his sins. Bede also summed up Coenred's reign by saying that he had ruled the kingdom of Mercia 'for some time and very nobly'.[57]

Felix's *Life* of Guthlac mentions unrest: 'It happened in the days of Coenred king of the Mercians, while the Britons the implacable enemies of the Saxon race, were troubling the English with their attacks, their pillaging and their devastation of the people,' but that is all the information we are given and the chapter then goes on to relate the story of Guthlac recognising the British and their 'sibilant' speech, and causing them to disappear by reciting the sixty-seventh psalm.[58] The Welsh annals do not give any details relating to the Mercians for this period.

We have a little more from the *Vita Ecgwine* which, apart from giving the abovementioned clue about the barbarians fearing him on all sides, tells us that Coenred was generous and pious. 'As he took over the kingdom, therefore, he granted to me by royal bequest – not only out of the warmth of his human friendship, but for his love of God – eighty-four hides … [58] He did these things because he was a devout king and wise in his actions, just as in his dealings and the friend of his own should, as his father [– to wit – Æthelred?] had been. To this bequest, one Æthelric, the son of King Oshere, an outstanding youth devoutly following his father's achievements in his own holy undertakings … spontaneously granted to me eight hides …'[59]

Three surviving charters for this period show Coenred granting land to Ecgwine for the monastery at Evesham (S78, 79) and, with Offa king of the East Angles [sic], land to Evesham (S80), but this last, purporting to indicate Coenred's overlordship of the East Angles, has been shown to be spurious.[60]

Æthelred, although retired, retained some influence. Wilfrid went to see him, and Æthelred summoned Coenred 'whom he had appointed his heir.'[61] Æthelred had a son of his own, who might have been too young to succeed, or, it may be that the king knew his son was not up to the task of ruling.

In 709, a mere five years after he succeeded, Coenred went to Rome to become a monk, taking with him King Offa of the East Saxons. How devout they were in their expedition is unclear, for Bede seems to imply that they were political exiles.[62]

From the *Vita Ecgwine*: 'At that time Coenred, the renowned king of the Mercians and my beloved friend, and Offa, king of the East Angles [sic],[63] decided to go to Rome together with their retinue.' Byrhtferth says nothing, unlike Bede, about them taking the habit and ending eir days there. Thus, when he continues that 'when the valiant King Coenred, after he arrived safely back in his kingdom, ordered a synod to be convened in the well-known place which is called Alcester,' and that Wilfrid was there, he is inaccurate, for Wilfrid was dead by then, and Coenred did not return from Rome.[64] He was succeeded by Ceolred, the son of Æthelred, about whom little is said, and almost none of it good.

The *ASC* mentions a battle between Ine of Wessex and Ceolred at Woden's Barrow in 715 but gives no detail. Most of the other information we have about this king comes from Felix's *Life* of Guthlac, where we hear that Boniface (a West Saxon missionary living and working on the Continent) wrote to his successor, reminding him that he had lived a sinful life. Ceolred was one of two kings (the other being Osred of Deira), who showed by 'wicked example an open display of these two greatest sins in the provinces of the English ... that is, debauchery and adultery with nuns and violation of monasteries.'[65] In the same letter, Boniface describes the death of Ceolred who, 'feasting in splendour amid his companions' was suddenly send mad 'by a malign spirit ... so that without repentance and confession, he departed from this light without a doubt to the torments of hell.' It may be that there were sound reasons behind Æthelred's decision to nominate his nephew, rather than his own son, as his heir.

One version of the Worcester regnal list has Ceolred succeeded by an otherwise unknown Ceolwald, who, if he existed, was perhaps the brother of Ceolred.[66]

It is true that the reigns of Coenred and Ceolred contained little of note. But whilst they may not have expanded the kingdom of Mercia, both granted land beyond the Mercian heartlands and confirmed charters of the rulers of the *Hwicce* – S54 shows Æthelweard, *subregulus*, with the consent of Coenred, king of Mercia, granting land to Ecgwine, bishop, for St Mary's Church at Evesham, with later confirmations by Ceolred, Æthelbald and Offa, kings of Mercia – the *Magonsæte*, and the East Saxons: S65 is a grant by Swæfred, king of Essex, with the consent of Æthelred, king of Mercia, to Waldhere, bishop ... with confirmation by Coenred and Ceolred, kings of Mercia. The Fenland, however, once under the auspices of Middle Anglia, seems to have come under the control of the East Anglians.[67]

We know that Coenred was faced with hostility from the Welsh and that Ceolred fought Ine of Wessex, but we don't know whether his role was as aggressor. We first hear of his successor as an exile who visited Guthlac at Crowland. This successor was the first since Penda not to be directly related to that king. He was Æthelbald, and Ceolred apparently 'chased him hither and thither.' Exile was not something to be borne lightly[68] and the inference here is that members of other branches of the royal family were becoming discontented, a danger, or both.

The succession was about to pass out of the hands of the direct descendants of the warlord Penda, but there is a curious story concerning a supposed grandson of Penda's, a certain St Rumwold. According to tradition, he was a baby who died at just three days old, and one scholar who tried to discover more about him pleaded, 'Reader, I request thee to take this ... on my credit for thy own ease, and not to buy the truth of so difficult a trifle with the trouble I paid for it.'[69]

According to the *Vita Sancti Rumwoldi*, the eleventh-century account of his life, he was able to speak at birth, preached on wisdom and the Trinity, and predicted his own death, giving precise instructions regarding where his body was to be laid to rest, namely Buckingham. A cult of St Rumwold grew up centred around Buckingham, and his bones rested there until the sixteenth century, but it seems the cult was comparatively short-lived.[70]

It is said that he was the grandson of Penda and the son of an unnamed king of Northumbria. In which case, he can only have been the son of one of Penda's daughters married to the Northumbrian line – except that none of those husbands was king of Northumbria. We know that Cyneburh married Alhfrith, son of Oswiu, but he was never king of Northumbria. He was, however, given authority over Deira and was king there from 655 until 664. While there were a number of marriages between the children of Penda and those of Oswiu, this is the only one which could be linked to the parentage of Rumwold. The other marriages involved Penda's sons marrying Oswiu's daughters and we know that none of Penda's sons was ever king of Northumbria. Was the fact that Alhfrith was king only of Deira a point of confusion for Rumwold's hagiographer? It is likely we will never know, and it matters little, except that it is interesting to note that here, along with Merewalh's daughters, Mildburg and Mildthryth, and Wulfad and Ruffin, the reputed sons of Wulfhere, and his daughter, Werburg, is yet another saint associated with Penda the pagan's extended family.

John of Worcester said of St Werburg: 'When her uncle King Æthelred learnt of her reputation for holiness, he set her as abbess over several monasteries of virgins devoted to God; living with them and among them according to the rule, and piously advising them in everything, she strove for Christ, the true king, until the end of her life. She departed this life in one of her monasteries called Threckingham.'

Her *Life* gives an account of her time at Ely and how she later lived on her father's estates, having been given authority over the Mercian monasteries. She was buried at Hanbury in Staffordshire but her remains were elevated in the reign of her cousin, Ceolred.[71] Of her father, John of Worcester sums up, 'These were the brothers of King Wulfhere: Æthelred, who ruled the kingdom with royal sway after him; Peada, who had the kingdom of the South [sic] Mercians, as we have indicated briefly; Merewalh, who held the kingdom in the western part of Mercia, whose queen, St Eormenburg, (note the confusion of names again. This should read Eafe, or Domne Eafe) daughter of King Eormenred, bore him three daughters, namely St Mildburg, St Mildthryth, and St Mildgyth, and one son, Merefin, a boy of exceptional sanctity.'

The list of saints does not end there, for Penda's own son, Æthelred, (both he and his wife Osthryth may have been revered as saints at Bardney) and his daughters Cyneburh and Cyneswith, should also be added. 'Those famous virgins, Cynethryth and Cyneswith, daughters of king Penda, keep the relics of their bodies cherished [at Peterborough.] Both were dedicated to God from infancy.'[72]

Also meriting possible inclusion on this list would be Penda's daughters Edith and Eadburh. Eadburh may have been the saint associated with Bicester, although another focus of the cult was Adderbury (in modern Oxfordshire) which means Eadburg's *byrig,* indicating that the place was named after her.[73] Traditions were preserved at Aylesbury of these two, along with a supposed granddaughter, St Osyth. Osyth was said to be the child of Frithuwald of Surrey and Wilburg, daughter of Penda, and that she was brought up by her maternal aunt Edith.[74] Osyth's story may have been confused with that of another lady of the same name, for it seems that both Aylesbury and Chich claimed to hold her relics. Apparently, she was married – unhappily – to Sigehere of the East Saxons and she put herself under the protection of a bishop by the name of Beaduwine. She was described as 'a virgin, famous for her miracles'.[75]

It is an illustrious list, made all the more remarkable for the short amount of time which had elapsed between the death of Penda and the good works of these saints. From what Boniface had to say, though, it is clear that Ceolred did not follow the same righteous path. His reign marked more than one change, too. After Ceolred, the kingship moved to a different branch of the Mercian royal tree.

Æthelweard the Chronicler, with what seems to be a strong Wessex bias, has virtually nothing to say of this period. In his chapter on Wulfhere he mentions one battle of 674 and records that 'after three years a comet was seen.' The next mention of the Mercians is entitled *Of the Acts of King Æthelred of the Mercians* and all we have is that in 704 'after ten years Æthelred king of the Mercians assumed the monastic habit. He had completed twenty-nine years of his reign.'

The Mercian kingship would, in time, pass back to this branch of the family, but the next nearly 100 years saw the kingdom ruled by perhaps the strongest, and most ruthless kings of Mercian history.

CHAPTER 4

Æthelbald the Elusive King

Æthelbald reigned from 716 to 757, a period of forty-one years, most of which was a story of overlordship, power, and strength. He is perhaps the most successful king of whom few people have heard. Spanning the second quarter of the eighth century, his rule coincided with the burgeoning of literate England, but we still know very little about him and his fame is eclipsed by that of his successor, Offa.

It is hard to get the measure of him because we do not have his family background, so there are no relationships to give any clue to familial dynamics, good or bad. With Penda and his sons, daughters and grandchildren, we can see the extended family, the interaction between them and their wider family, and the intermarriages with Northumbria and with Kent, but Æthelbald as a man is more elusive. He didn't marry, as far as we know, or have children. But he was more than just a philandering irreligious warlord.

He is mentioned in the regnal lists[1] and Roger of Wendover called him a 'brave and powerful man'. Much was said by Boniface about his morals, but perhaps his lasciviousness was overstated, much as it would be with later kings. He obviously didn't feel the need to get married to secure the prestige of a wife's royal connections.

Previous queens of Mercia did not leave joyous legacies – Alhflæd accused of murder, Osthryth a victim of it – and it might be that Æthelbald made it a deliberate policy not to be ensnared, either by political alliance or by intrigue.[2] He was accused of failing to take a wife and instead fornicating with nuns but perhaps his behaviour was brought into sharper focus because of his attempts to control monastic lands. It is frustrating that we know no more. If Boniface accused him of failing to take a legitimate wife, perhaps he had a long-standing companion?

73

No children are recorded, and in the battles which followed over the next century or so for control of the kingship of Mercia, none of the contenders appears to have claimed descent from him.

The *ASC* entry for 716 says that he was the son of Alweo, the son of Eowa, the son of Pybba, so he came from a different line of the Mercian Royal family and was not directly descended from Penda but from his brother. He was in exile during Ceolred's reign, and we may wonder why. If we have summed up the events leading to Penda's kingship correctly, then it might be that there was a long-standing family feud. Eowa would seem to have been king first, possibly, and thus might his children have had some claim to the throne which was denied them? Whatever the reason, we know that Æthelbald was in hiding, certainly during the reign of Ceolred, for we have details from the near-contemporary *Life* of Guthlac.

Guthlac had begun his career as a warrior, fighting the Welsh, presumably in Æthelred's army. In around 699 Guthlac took up his solitary life at Crowland in the fenlands of Cambridgeshire, which at that time could be reached only by boat. The story of his life, recorded by the monk Felix, was written when Æthelbald was in power, and so it naturally paints him in a good light, but the work was commissioned by King Ælfwald of East Anglia (713–749) and it seems that Felix himself may have been an East Angle.[3] It might be interesting to ponder why an East Anglian king would wish for a *Life* of a Mercian, but more intriguing is the possibility that Æthelbald spent his years of exile in East Anglia, for Crowland was on the border between the kingdoms, and he was a frequent and welcome visitor there.

Felix tells us that Æthelbald was in exile because, as the grandson of Penda's brother, he was a rival to Ceolred. One chapter tells of a visit by the exiled king-in-waiting, who was accompanied by Wilfrid, later St Wilfrid. Guthlac asked the pair if they had left anything in the boat, to which Wilfrid replied that he had left his gloves. Jackdaws had stolen the gloves and Guthlac restrained one of the birds with 'gentle words,' whereupon it left the glove on the top of the cottage and fled.

On another occasion, a retainer of this 'same exile', a man named Ofa, went to speak to Guthlac. Walking through the fields, he trod on a thorn which, perhaps incredibly, went through the middle of his sole, tore it as far as the heel and 'pierced right through the framework of the foot.' More believably, it seemingly caused an infection and Guthlac, when informed how ill the man was, wrapped him in the sheepskin rug 'in which he was accustomed to pray' and once Ofa was wrapped in the garment, the thorn fell from his foot and he immediately rose and was able to walk. 'Then all who were present to witness the miracle returned glory to the Lord.'[4] We might assume that Æthelbald was among their number.

In Chapter xlix of the *Life,* Æthelbald comes to Guthlac full of despair, having been 'driven hither and thither by King Ceolred and tossed about among divers peoples'. Guthlac demonstrates his powers of prophesy by predicting that God will make Æthelbald ruler over his race and chief over the peoples.

In 716 Æthelbald did indeed peacefully accede to the throne. Presumably there was something in what was said about Coelred's character, if this change of 'dynasty' was acceptable. Later tradition had it that Æthelbald visited Guthlac after he became king, but it seems that this was an invention designed to support a forged charter, which Æthelbald was said to have given to the abbey shortly afterwards.[5] One has to wonder why, and indeed how, if Æthelbald feared for his life so much as to remain in exile during the reign of Ceolred (and, perhaps, during the reign of his predecessor, Coenred) he was able to take over the throne without a fight. Hindsight presents him as a capable warrior, but we cannot know of his reputation in 716. Perhaps Ceolred's death was a welcome relief to his subjects? As we have already seen, Boniface was disapproving of him. He wrote of a monk at Wenlock who had a vision of Ceolred being carried into hell by devils.[6]

It is difficult to piece together the circumstances of Æthelbald's exile. It doesn't appear that Ceolred was a strong enough king to stave off contenders, particularly not ones of the calibre Æthelbald would prove to be. Perhaps, then, he had been in exile since the time of Æthelred, yet he did not emerge until after Ceolred's death. Were there other contenders to the throne? Had he been chased out of Mercia because the kings there were strong, or because he was, and thus he was a threat? Dynastic disputes would become a feature of Mercian politics, particularly in the next century.

There is, in fact, a hint that the takeover was not so peaceful, provided by a reference in one source[7] to a Ceolwald reigning between Ceolred and Æthelbald. This man, briefly mentioned in Chapter Three, could, if he existed at all, have been the brother of Ceolred. If so, and if he became king, he did not reign for long, for Æthelbald became king in the same year in which Ceolred died. Perhaps there was a coup? If only we knew; but as we have seen, particularly when it comes to Mercian history, absence of evidence is most assuredly not evidence of absence, and we can only speculate when we come across these tantalising nuggets of information.

Æthelbald honoured Guthlac after his death by enriching his shrine: 'We behold wonderful structures and ornamentations put up by King

Æthelbald' and Felix's *Life* writes highly of the king at all times, speaking of the king's grief upon hearing of the Saint's death 'who alone had been his refuge and consolation in his affliction.'[8] The bias is to be expected though, because at the time of writing the king was at the height of his powers.

By 731, according to Bede, though he never classes Æthelbald as a *Bretwalda*, all the southern kingdoms were subject to him, i.e. Kent, Essex, East Anglia, the kingdom of the West Saxons, the Mercians, the *Magonsæte*, the *Hwicce* and Lindsey. Bede says that in 731 the archbishop of Canterbury was Tatwine, who was a Mercian. His successor, Nothelm, was also a Mercian.[9]

If Mercians were being appointed to the see of Canterbury, this suggests dominance over Kent, although this may not have lasted beyond Æthelbald's death. The rulers of the *Hwicce* signed as his sub-kings, and a charter of 726 (S93) seems to show Æthelheard, king of Wessex, in Æthelbald's entourage.[10]

So it would seem that Bede's assessment was not wide of the mark; further, it appears that Æthelbald claimed an overlordship of not just southern England, but of southern Britain, too. The Pillar of Eliseg, erected in 855 by the king of Powys, bears an inscription which commemorates the liberation of Powys from English rule, attributed to Elisedd ap Gwylog, who died around 755, and suggests that during Æthelbald's reign, Powys was under Mercian domination.[11]

Therefore, we have documentary and physical evidence of his power and status in the south. His early charters invariably style him king of Mercia, but of special note is a charter of 736[12] in which he is styled r*ex Britanniae*. The Ismere charter, as it is known, demonstrates that Mercia had direct authority in the territory of the *Hwicce*, and is attested by Æthelric, *subregulus*, who was one of the sons of Oshere of the *Hwicce*. The reduction of status of the kings of the *Hwicce* has been shown to be a gradual process and the Ismere charter is just another such example. The point of real interest here is the wording used to describe Æthelbald.

He is styled 'Ruler not only of the Mercians but of all the provinces that go by the general name of 'South English' (*domino donante rex non solum Marcersium sed et omnium provinciarum quae generali nomine Sutangli dicuntu*) and he heads the witness list as 'Ruler of Britain' (*rex Britanniae*).

Stenton argued that this last title was of particular importance, opining that the bearing of the style *rex Britanniae* upon the significance of the term *Bretwalda* had been overlooked[13] and that in the past the scribes had used succinct and precise terms, such as *rex Cantuariorum*, or *dux*

Suthsaxorum. He believed the phrase *rex Britanniae* was something altogether different.

Perhaps equally important though was the *rex Suthanglorum* and *rex non solum Mercensium sed Anglorum*, suggesting that Æthelbald was extending the borders and establishing a kingdom more akin with what we now tend to think of as Mercia.[14]

The word *Sutangli*, Stenton said, had been used in earlier documents, and he gave the example of the – admittedly corrupt – Whitby *Life* of Gregory the Great, where the context suggested that the South English represented the Mercians, Middle Angles and the people of Lindsey.

The information of Bede's summation of the situation in 731 when added to the details of the Ismere charter, dated only five years later, prompts the conclusion that the *Sutangli* were not only the Mercians, but those who lived in all the provinces south of the Humber, of whom Æthelbald was overlord.

For Stenton, the combination of the title *rex Brittaniae* and the definition of the authority over the Southern English was what gave the 'unique interest' to the Ismere charter. It was his conclusion that the power so defined exactly equated to that assigned to those on the list of *Bretwaldas*, and that the information in the Ismere charter should be treated in the same way as that which led to the name of Ecgberht of the West Saxons (802–839) being added to the original list of seven *Bretwaldas*.

D.P. Kirby was of the opinion that there is no reason to suppose that something significant happened in 736 to herald this change in title and that it might, in fact, have been a style peculiar to Worcester, pointing out that this is the oldest surviving original Mercian text, but the new title does seem to coincide with the takeover of the archbishopric. The charters of the kings of Kent make no reference to Æthelbald's overlordship, but it can be inferred by the abovementioned elections of Mercians to the archbishopric of Canterbury.[15]

We have no information about how Æthelbald achieved this dominance over the southern kingdoms, with the first reference being to his dealings with the West Saxons in 733, but there must have been some hostile activity beforehand, or a process by which the subdued states rose up later in his reign.

We know that the *Life* of Guthlac was commissioned by King Ælfwald of East Anglia, and given that Felix wrote so favourably of Æthelbald in a work commissioned by another king, it might be reasonable to suppose that the two kings were on good terms. Whilst the story of Æthelbald's reign seems to be one of aggression, none is directed towards East Anglia. If the East Anglians were subordinate to him, it seems to have been an acceptable arrangement. If we remember that Æthelthryth, a princess of East Anglia who had married Tondberht of the South *Gyrwe,* later founded a monastery at Ely, it shows a connection with Middle Anglia which may well have continued and allowed the shelter of Æthelbald and the interest taken by Ælfwald in the life of the Mercian Guthlac.[16]

At the beginning of the eighth century there were powerful kings in the south: Wihtred of Kent and Ine of Wessex. Wihtred's death in 725 and Ine's abdication in 726 would potentially have made it easier for Æthelbald to establish Mercian dominance over the southern kingdoms. Bede mentions the abdication, but not that there was then a succession dispute. According to the *ASC,* Æthelheard, Ine's successor, and 'the atheling Oswald' fought. Given that we know of Æthelheard's later association with the Mercian king, it is possible that Æthelbald took advantage of, and possibly intervened in, the succession dispute. The outcome certainly seems to have been to Mercian benefit.

Æthelbald made grants concerning London and elsewhere in Middlesex and there is no reference to kings of Essex. It seems likely that it was during his reign that Middlesex was brought under direct Mercian control.[17]

In 740 he devastated Northumbria. The eighth-century annals appended to Bede[18] say Æthelbald 'treacherously devastated Northumbria, while Eadberht was occupied with his army fighting against the Picts.' The *ASC* mentions the burning of York, as does Simeon of Durham. His entry for 741 says that 'the minster in the city of York was burnt on Sunday, 23 April'. Perhaps the burning was part of the 'devastation'. The Bede continuations say that Æthelbald's raid was treacherous, but there is no explanation given. It might be that the Northumbrian, Eadberht, had negotiated a peace before he went north, or it might be that the Picts were in alliance with the Mercians.[19] However, while he clearly posed a threat to Northumbria, Æthelbald never seems to have focused his attention on the north in the way his predecessors did.

In fact, the following year, in 741, according to Roger of Wendover, 'Æthelbald, the proud king of the Mercians, harassed Cuthred, king of the West Saxons, at one time by making war on him, at another by stirring up seditions: they frequently made peace between them, which was kept but for a short time.'

This seems to have been a long-running saga. In 733 Æthelbald had occupied Somerton in the kingdom of the West Saxons. Æthelweard the Chronicler put it that 'King Æthelbald received under his dominion the royal vill which is called Somerton', and Roger of Wendover's entry describes how 'Æthelbald, king of the Mercians, assembled an army and laid siege to the castle of Somerton, which he reduced under his own dominion, there being none to afford assistance to the besieged. The aforesaid king afterwards subdued all the kings of England south of the Humber, and reigned over all those provinces.'

But although Æthelbald had harassed Cuthred of Wessex in 741, in 743 he and Cuthred fought the Britons, perhaps with Cuthred acting under Æthelbald's orders. Roger of Wendover said that, 'having made peace with each other, [they] united their forces and fought against the Britons' but bearing in mind the relationship between Æthelbald and Cuthred's predecessor, Æthelheard, it is likely that it was a joint campaign under Mercian control. This is not to say that Cuthred was a willing subordinate, however. In 752 he fought Æthelbald and 'put him to flight'.

The date of 752 is given in the *ASC*, but both Simeon of Durham and the Bede continuations date the uprising of Cuthred to 750, with the Bede continuations saying that Cuthred was fighting both Æthelbald and Angus, king of the Picts. Either the date of 752 is incorrect, or there may have been more than one battle, which, given what the Bede continuations have to say about this chequered relationship, is not impossible to believe.[20] The *ASC* gives the location of the battle as *Beorhford* (Burford).

The *ASC* does mention a battle in 750, but it records that Cuthred of Wessex fought an 'arrogant' Ealdorman Æthelhun. If this arrogant ealdorman was a Mercian then this may be the same incident referred to in the Bede continuations for that year. Alternatively, perhaps this Æthelhun was merely taking advantage of Cuthred's being distracted by his fight with Æthelbald. Certainly, if Æthelbald was indeed allied with the Picts, then it was not unprecedented for him to use decoys to divert the attention of his enemies. But if this is the case, it seems not to have paid off on this occasion.

Other chroniclers appear to conflate the two incidents. Æthelweard the Chronicler paints Cuthred in less than a good light: 'After twelve years, King Cuthred began to make war on Duke Æthelhun, for some state-jealousy,' while Roger of Wendover also says it was in 752 that Cuthred, 'unable to endure the overbearing exactions and insolence' of Æthelbald, met him in the field at *Beorhford*, where 'these kings had a most severe engagement. King Æthelbald, preceded by Æthelhun who bore his standard, on which was painted a golden dragon, made a fierce attack on the enemy.' But, 'terrible was the thunder of the battle ... each side was confident of victory; but at last God ... turned Æthelbald to flight and rejoiced Cuthred with the victory.'

Henry of Huntingdon, conversely, says that Æthelhun was leading the West Saxons and was the 'aforesaid chief with whom [Cuthred] was now reconciled.' He gives yet more florid detail about the battle, even talking of Amazonian battle-axes, and adds that 'the arrogance of their pride sustained the Mercians, the fear of slavery kindled the courage of the men of Wessex.' He goes on to report that 'wherever the brave King Æthelbald turned, the enemy were slaughtered, for his invincible sword rent armour as if it were a vestment, and bones as if they were flesh.'

There are hints of trouble elsewhere. In 749, Ælfwald of East Anglia, friend of Æthelbald, was succeeded by joint rulers Hun, Beonna and Æthelberht and there was an attempt at a reformed southern coinage. Beonna's coinage probably dates to the later 750s and might represent a bid for independence after the death of Æthelbald.

However, by 757 it looks as if Æthelbald's fortunes might have been reversed once again, for a charter of that year (S96) styles him 'king not only of the Mercians but of the surrounding peoples', attested by Cynewulf of Wessex and, in it, he is granting land in Wiltshire, a West Saxon shire.

Cynewulf of Wessex, the witness to that charter, acceded to the West Saxon throne in 757. The earliest known charter of Cynewulf's (S265) is confirmed by Offa, Æthelbald's successor in Mercia, so this might denote West Saxon dependence, but on the other hand, it is the only one of Cynewulf's charters to hint at Mercian overlordship.

After what seems to have been a hectic reign filled with violence, Æthelbald was killed in 757. The *ASC* says that he was killed at Seckington (North Warwickshire) and that he was buried at Repton. Simeon writes: 'Æthelbald, king of the Mercians, was treacherously killed by his bodyguard, and in the same year the Mercians commenced a civil war among themselves. Beornred being put to flight, King Offa remained victor.' According to the *ASC*, Beornred held the kingdom 'for but a little space and unhappily'.

Roger of Wendover said that Æthelbald had a 'severe engagement at Seckington ... and would not flee to save himself,' while William of Malmesbury wrote that 'this king, enjoying the sovereignty in profound and long-continued peace, that is, for the space of forty-one years, was ultimately killed by his subjects. Beornred, the author of his death, left nothing worthy of record, except that afterwards, being himself put to death by Offa, he received the just reward of his treachery.'[21]

Æthelbald was buried at Repton, a place with strong and what would be continuing links with the Mercian royal house, and where his friend Guthlac was said to have been tonsured. As we have seen, the history of Mercia is one of lacking or lost written evidence, or it is the story written by the enemies of Mercia yet in the *Life* of Guthlac there is a different portrayal of the kings of Mercia, and in particular, of Æthelbald. What a different perspective there might have been, had more works like this been written and/or survived. Henry of Huntingdon was certainly no fan of Æthelbald's, calling him the 'haughty king of the Mercians' who despised holiness.[22] So the reign would seem to be one of brutal fighting, dominance over the other southern kingdoms, and a king of Mercia who, even as the kingdoms of England moved even further into the Christian, literate age, behaved more like a pagan warlord. But this was not the only aspect of his rule.

In about 747, Boniface wrote to Æthelbald castigating him for not taking a wife and instead fornicating with nuns, and violating the privileges of the Church, but also complimenting his alms-giving and peace-keeping.[23] In 747, too, the Council of Clofesho[24] took place, attended by Æthelbald, resulting in the issuing of thirty canons and a set of reforms. William of Malmesbury's *Gesta Pontificum* lists them all. He describes the proceedings, which began with two documents of Pope Zachary being read out, 'in which he warned the English to live more soberly and threatened to excommunicate those who ignored this.'[25] In 749 Æthelbald responded by issuing a charter at Gumley, in modern-day Leicestershire (S92), which set out clearly that churches were free from all tax, works and burdens.

A charter issued at Clofesho in 798, which ended a long-running dispute concerning the monastery of Cookham, Berkshire, mentions that it was 'Æthelbald, the famous king of the Mercians' who had given the 'monastery and all the lands belonging to it' to Christ Church, Canterbury[26] and the monks of Abingdon appear to have regarded Æthelbald as their protector.[27]

A womaniser, a bloodthirsty warrior, but also a religious benefactor: is it possible to get a measure of the man? Was he full of bluster and totally unafraid, refusing to flee to save himself? Was he paying lip service to the Church, or was he genuinely repentant?

The charter issued at the Council of Gumley in 749 outlined the freedom from dues, but it also outlined the services which the churchmen of Mercia owed to King Æthelbald.[28] Furthermore, it was witnessed only by Mercian bishops and therefore might have been confined to Mercia. Perhaps he was more shrewd than sorry. As to the nuns, they may have been hard to distinguish from noble ladies, a problem which would similarly trouble King Edgar in the tenth century. It might also have been that Æthelbald saw little difference between the powerful monasteries and the secular halls, in that they took land and resources from royal hands.[29]

But Boniface also had good things to say about Æthelbald: 'We have heard that thou givest many alms and upon this we congratulate thee ... We have heard too that thou dost strongly check theft and iniquity, perjury and rapine, and art known to be a defender of widows and the poor and hast peace established in thy kingdom.'[30]

So although he seems to be somewhat of a throwback character, we know that Æthelbald wasn't quite so two-dimensional. Had Bede lived even just a little longer, we might have found out more about the king who to all intents and purposes seems to have been a *Bretwalda* just as much as Rædwald, another Southumbrian king. There is more charter evidence relating to him and yet we just don't know as much about his nature as we might feel we do about other, earlier, Mercian kings. Perhaps if he had attacked Northumbria more often, or if there had been a Mercian Bede, or if Æthelbald had had more dealings with the Continent, then we might have learned a little more. Æthelbald didn't marry, so had no children – that we know of – and thus was not able to negotiate any diplomatic marriages, and perhaps in these last two points he was overshadowed by his successor, Offa, who famously had dealings with the court of Charlemagne and married off his daughters to useful effect.

A ninth-century list of benefactions to Gloucester Abbey includes details of a grant of Æthelbald's 'in recompense for having struck Æthelmund, son of his kinsman Orwald.'[31] Could this provide a clue to his demise at the hands of men who had sworn oaths of loyalty to him? If Æthelbald was killed by his own men this was a serious breach of the code of fidelity and suggests that his popularity, or his strength, or both, was on the wane. But his reign of forty-one years was not only characterised by aggressive warfare. There are hints of the increasing wealth of Mercia during his reign. There are charters, for example, S103a and S103b, which mention tolls and toll collection as well as demonstrating the king's control over London. S103a states:

> I, Æthelbald, king of the Mercians, for the eternal salvation of my soul and also out of pious love for the Saviour of the world, have decided to give a portion of my property to the Almighty Giver of all good things. For that reason I am giving to Ingwald, bishop of the city of London, into his own possession eternally by perpetual right the toll on one ship that he might have it without any fear of change, nor, concerning that, that any kings and my successors or person of rank of any kind should presume to take possession of anything for themselves against your will, but may it be favourably preserved as a lasting gift for me in blessed repose.

S103b is also a grant to Ingwald, along similar lines, with the added 'augmenting of this gift that when that ship either gets old or is damaged through being wrecked, that another and another be built and held in accordance with the place and terms of this gift.'

A charter from the very earliest part of his reign, dated either 716 or 717, shows the king granting land to the Church of Worcester 'for the construction of salt works, in exchange for salt works north of the same river' and offers proof of the burgeoning salt production industry.[32]

The charters, and the references to salt workings, point towards a strong economy and administration. It is just possible, although not widely postulated, that the *Tribal Hidage* might even date to his reign.[33]

There is only one other place to turn for information about this obviously successful and yet elusive character, and that is through the study of the coinage of the times. As mentioned above, in the decade of Æthelbald's death, Beonna of East Anglia was minting his own coins, which included both his name and his title. Perhaps this was a sign that the kingdom was detaching itself from Mercian domination and thus there is a hint that Æthelbald's power was waning.[34] It is perhaps not surprising, though, given that he must have been of fairly advanced years by the mid-750s.[35]

The sceatta was a small silver coin, pre-dating the penny, and silver sceattas were in circulation in Mercia during Æthelbald's reign. We know he had control of London in the early 730s, and it seems that he had a mint operating there, as well as one in the Oxford area. Both these mints struck sceattas showing figures holding two long crosses, often thought to depict a bishop, although it has been argued that the figure is wearing a *cynehelm* (kinghelm, or crown).[36] But whilst Æthelbald may have been the first king to mint coins, it was his successor and kinsman Offa who first had his name on the Mercian coinage.

It was also likely to have been Offa who commissioned a lasting memorial to his predecessor, in the form of what is now known as the Repton Stone. This was found in the churchyard at Repton, and was originally part of a cross, erected, it is thought, by King Offa in honour of Æthelbald. Its position, just outside the Anglo-Saxon crypt, is thought to add weight to the suggestion that Æthelbald was laid to rest at Repton. If it were, indeed, commissioned by Offa, who was not especially directly related to Æthelbald, it is a telling memorial to one who was obviously considered to be worthy of such commemoration.

CHAPTER 5
Offa the Great

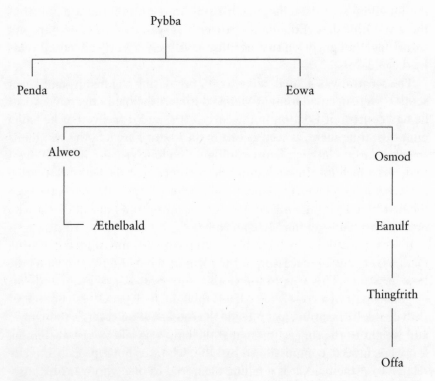

Æthelbald's relationship to Offa.

In the year of our Lord 757 the people of the kingdom of the Mercians rose against Beornred their king, because he did not govern his people by just laws, but tyrannically; and assembling together, high and low, they, under the direction of a most courageous youth named Offa, expelled him ... King Offa was a terror and a fear to all the kings of England, for he overcame in battle the king of Kent, the king of the South Saxons, the king of the East Angles.

This summary comes to us via Roger of Wendover, while Æthelweard the Chronicler says, more succinctly, that in 756 Offa – 'a remarkable man' – succeeded.

There is no more information about Beornred. His name is interesting, not least because of later dynastic disputes between the so-called 'B' and 'C' dynasties of Mercia, of which more in Chapter Six, but also because of a theory connected with the minting of coins by Beonna in the later stages of Æthelbald's reign, briefly mentioned in Chapter Four.

It is just possible that Beonna, who seems to have been making some move towards independence from Mercia, was a kinsman of Beornred. His name sits better with the 'B' family of Mercia than it does with the list of kings of East Anglia, of which no other member had a name beginning with B. It has been further suggested that Beornred and Beonna were the same person, striking coins to meet military needs prior to a campaign against Mercia.[1] If this is the case, it was a short-lived coup. Offa established himself in Mercia and in the early 760s also asserted his authority over East Anglia.

Æthelbald was descended from Eowa, brother of Penda who may have been king before and even during Penda's reign. His successor, Offa, was also descended from Eowa and according to the genealogies of the Anglian collection, the two kings were first cousins twice removed.[2]

Offa was a son of Thingfrith, whose father, Eanwulf, was a first cousin of Æthelbald's. He was the recipient of land at Westbury and Henbury in *Hwicce* territory, and was granted land by Æthelbald, which, traditionally, he used to establish the monastery at Bredon, in modern-day Worcestershire, but this tradition may be incorrect. A foundation charter, now lost, was seen by Dugdale, but can now be considered faulty with 'anachronistic references'.[3] There is no certain proof that Offa was related to the princes of the *Hwicce,* although some connection has been suggested between an Æthelburh mentioned in a charter as a kinswoman of Ealdred, *subregulus* of the *Hwicce*, and Æthelburh, daughter of Offa who became an abbess and witnessed a grant of Offa's.[4]

Whatever his connections, none of Offa's immediate family had been kings before him, and in this respect his circumstances were the same as Æthelbald's. It is likely that mindfulness of this fact informed some of his decisions throughout his reign.

Unlike his predecessor, Offa was aware of the need for legitimate marriage, and pushed for his son to be recognised, not only as his heir, but as his anointed heir. He married Cynethryth, and they had at least three daughters: Eadburh, who married the king of Wessex; Ælfflæd, who married the king of Northumbria; and Æthelburh, who became an abbess. Later legends suggest that the king of East Anglia was harbouring hopes of marrying a fourth daughter when he was murdered. Offa and Cynethryth also had at least one son, Ecgfrith. A charter of 787 (S127) names three more daughters, Cynedritha, Æthelflæd and Æthelswith, but it may be spurious, although perhaps based on an original charter of Offa's.

Despite Offa's being a well-known name, his reign has not had as much attention as might be supposed.[5] It seems that learning about Offa is a matter of deduction; it is necessary to research the lives of people who came into contact with him, to form a notion of the man and his character. A brief look at the *PASE* page tells us that most of the references to him relate to coins and charters. This is solid evidence. Yet he is barely mentioned in the writings, and we have no account from the equivalent of Bede, no association with a saint that might include him in a *Life*. Asser mentions him, briefly, as does Æthelweard, so too Alcuin, but this is largely with reference to Charlemagne. Offa was king from 757–796, nearly 40 years, and as Sir Frank Stenton said, 'The re-establishment of Mercian supremacy by Offa is the central fact in English history in the second half of the eighth century. But the stages by which it was brought about cannot now be reconstructed.'[6]

Researching Offa, it is hard to get a sense of the man. It is as if reading a novel where the main character is only talked about by other characters and we don't really see him in action. There is a detachment, even more so perhaps than with Æthelbald. The main evidence is the charters and, fortunately, those which survive show us enough to piece together Offa's relationships with the other kings. It is possible that the *Tribal Hidage* dates from this time. His policies were those of a king of the English, perhaps, rather than a king of Mercia, but he was ultimately unsuccessful in any ambition to become king of the English.[7] Perhaps a good place to begin a survey of his reign is to explore what was happening in Northumbria at the time.

In 758, King Eadberht of Northumbria retired to a monastery, resigning the throne to his son Oswulf, who was then, according to the Bede continuations, killed by his thegns. Æthelwold 'Moll' was elected. He was a man who appeared to have no connection to the royal house, and after a battle of 761 in which he killed a man named Oswine (possibly a relative of the murdered Oswulf), he was exiled in

765. Alhred, who seems to have claimed royal descent, ruled from 765 but was ousted by Æthelwold Moll's son, Æthelred, in 774, who was then, in turn, expelled in 778. In 769 Catterick, according to Simeon of Durham, was burned down by Eanred 'and by the judgment of God he himself perished miserably by fire in the same year.' Eanred is described as a 'tyrant' but is unlikely to be the later King Eanred, who ruled from 808 to 840/1. Nevertheless, the entry shows the northern kingdom in turmoil. The troubles in Northumbria indicate the same kind of strife between rival families that would come to afflict Mercia in the ninth and early tenth centuries.

One would expect Northumbria's traditional enemy, Mercia, to take advantage of such infighting, yet it appears that Offa did not. Æthelred of Northumbria, son of Æthelwold Moll, regained the throne in 790 and drove out his rival, Osred. In 792 he married Offa's daughter, whose name was Ælfflæd. Simeon of Durham gives us both the date and location for the wedding, which was held at Catterick in modern North Yorkshire, on 29 September. So a new situation appears to have emerged, in which the king of Northumbria was looking for support from, and alliance with, a far more powerful Mercian king. The alliance did not save Æthelred, however, and he was killed in 796. Presumably the motive for the marriage was to boost Æthelred's strength by allying to a stronger partner, so we can probably safely assume that Offa was fairly powerful by the 790s, but what was keeping his attention in the south before this? The charter evidence suggests that his hands were rather full.

He seems fairly quickly to have established dominance over the *Hwicce*, with the rulers there, 'brothers and under-kings of the *Hwicce*', Eanberht, Uhtred and Ealdred, acknowledging their position as his sub-kings in charters of 757 and 759 (S55, 56.) There is no reason to assume any hostility to, or resentment of, this arrangement. By the 790s the ruling family had disappeared, the role of leader there reduced to ealdorman.

Elsewhere we find suggestions of Offa's activities in the south. In 760 a battle at Hereford between Britons and Saxons was recorded in the *Annales Cambriae*. Offa is not specifically mentioned but was more than likely involved. Simeon of Durham mentions that Offa conquered the people of Hastings and that they were 'subdued by the force of arms.' Hastings here means not only the town, but the district of East Sussex. S49 is a charter of 770, issued in his own name by Osmund, king of the South Saxons. By 772, after the attack, his status had been reduced to that of ealdorman.[8]

Offa's dealings with Kent were long and complicated. A charter of 764 appears to show that by this point Offa had taken control of Kent. S105 records him granting land to the bishop of Rochester, and it has been pointed out that this was the first occasion on which a Mercian king is known to have done so, and that Heahberht, king of Kent at the time, was secured in power by Offa's intervention.[9]

There are instances of kings of Kent issuing charters free from Mercian permission, for example S25 and S32, both dated 762[10] but a charter of the early ninth century mentions Offa's revocation of land granted by Ecgberht I of Kent (reigned 664–73 or possibly later), on the grounds that 'it was not right for a man to grant away land which his lord had given him, without his lord's assent.'[11] But Offa did not hold sway over Kent for the whole period. Two charters of 774 (S110, 111) show Offa granting land in Kent to Jænberht, archbishop of Canterbury, so he still had control of Kent then, seemingly, but in 776 at the battle of Otford it seems that Offa lost control of Kent, not regaining it until about 784/5. It is possible there may have been an uprising following the death of Heahberht. In 765 Offa had confirmed a grant by King Ecgberht II of Kent, which was also witnessed by Heahberht, so perhaps it was Ecgberht's emergence that was the catalyst for this battle.[12]

The *ASC* entry for the year 776 is somewhat less than enlightening, reporting only: 'In this year a red cross appeared in the sky after sunset. And that year the Mercians and the people of Kent fought at Otford. And marvellous adders were seen in Sussex.' It would be helpful to have been told who won this fight. Roger of Wendover mentions a battle at Ottanford and says that 'after a fearful slaughter on each side, Offa gained a signal victory.' Henry of Huntingdon has Offa in 773 fighting 'a battle with the Kentish men at Ottanford, in which, after a dreadful slaughter on both sides, Offa gained the honour of victory.'[13] Æthelweard the Chronicler recorded a civil war – by which he means within the 'English' – between Kent and Mercia at a place called Cittanford, which should be Ottanford/Otford.

Sir Frank Stenton thought the battle probably resulted in a Mercian victory,[14] but charters issued by kings of Kent in the years following the battle might give some clues. S35, dated 778 and S36, dated 779, record grants to the bishop of Rochester; S38, from 784, is a grant of land at Reculver to an Abbot Wihtred. These documents all show King Ecgberht II and his successor King Ealhmund issuing charters independently of Mercia, so it looks as if Otford was indeed a Mercian defeat, resulting in the loss of control over Sussex and Kent.[15]

But it seems that Offa was not too defeated, for the 778 entry of the *Annales Cambriae* records the 'devastation of the Southern Britons by Offa' and the following year, at the battle of Bensington, Offa defeated Cynewulf of Wessex. The *ASC* recorded: 'In this year Cynewulf and Offa fought around Bensington [in present-day Oxfordshire] and Offa captured the town.' Stenton pointed out that apart from his appearance at Offa's court in 772 (S108) there is no evidence of Cynewulf's being under Offa's direct and recognised control,[16] and, in his study of the early history of Abingdon Abbey, he wrote that it was probably between the death of Æthelbald and Offa's establishing his kingship, that the Thames valley passed back under the control of the West Saxons. He believed it was 'certain that the royal estate of Bensington was in Cynewulf's hands when the war broke out' and that the capture of it decided finally the ownership of what he famously called 'the debateable land east of the Thames along the Chilterns.' He went further, saying that the battle not only gave Mercia the whole line of the middle Thames as a boundary, but that Mercian dominion crossed the river to include Berkshire, as it may have done in Æthelbald's time. This contention, he said, was 'immensely reinforced by an incidental statement in [a] Canterbury document which proves the Berkshire dominion of Æthelbald.' Offa of Mercia, according to this record, 'took away the monastery of Cookham and very many other towns from King Cynewulf and added them to the Mercian imperium.'[17]

In 784 Offa seems to have turned his attention to Wales again, and caused the *Annales Cambriae* to report 'the devastation of Britain by Offa in the summer'. But he did not look westwards for long.

Just as Æthelbald had benefitted from the death of Wihtred and the abdication of Ine, so it would appear that Offa gained power in the aftermath of the deaths of Ecgberht of Kent in 784 and Cynewulf of Wessex in 786.

It appears that in 784/5 Offa managed to regain control of Kent. The chroniclers don't furnish us with any information about this, but charters S123 of 785, S125 of 786, S128 from 788, and S134 of 792 all show that throughout the later 780s and early 790s he was granting land in Kent with no reference to local kings.[18] According to the *ASC*, Ealhmund succeeded to the Kentish throne in 784, so it appears that Offa's loss of control over Kent did indeed coincide with Ecgberht II's dominance, with the previously mentioned charter of Ealhmund's, S38, dating to the same year as Ecgberht's death and thus very early in Ealhmund's reign.

Meanwhile in Wessex there was a succession struggle, recorded in detail in the *ASC*. It is under the entry for the year 757 but it implies that the story it relates pertains to the end of Cynewulf's reign, for it begins by saying 'and when he had held the kingdom for thirty-one years...' It tells how Cynewulf, visiting a woman, and with only a small fighting band accompanying him, was overtaken by Cyneheard, 'the atheling'. The king fought back, and severely wounded Cyneheard before he himself was killed. His retainers fought on until they were all killed, with the exception of one British hostage. When, the next morning, the rest of the king's men arrived, they found Cyneheard barricaded in, and he offered them money and land if they would accept his claim to the throne. But these loyal retainers would no more accept this offer than had their dead comrades, and in the ensuing fighting, Cyneheard was killed.[19] Whether these men were seeking heroic death in the manner of their own beloved lord, or whether they were merely impelled to have vengeance, is debatable.[20] Either way, their loyalty is laudable.

The story is followed in the *ASC* by the reporting of the death of Æthelbald, killed by his own men at Seckington. The contrast is no doubt deliberate. If Anglo-Saxon men would demonstrate loyalty unto death, then Æthelbald must have been somehow undeserving of such steadfastness. Perhaps the two stories are designed to show the difference between the standards of devotion between the West Saxons and the Mercians?

In 786, Cynewulf of Wessex died and was succeeded by Beorhtric, who was later to become son-in-law to Offa of Mercia. 786 was also the year of the visit of the papal legates. Pope Hadrian sent George, Bishop of Ostia (an area of Rome), and Theophylact, Bishop of Todi (in Perugia), to investigate the English Church and suppress heresy.

Their report survives[21] and they explain that they were 'first received by Jænberht, archbishop of the holy church of Dorovenia (Canterbury)... Journeying from there we arrived at the court of Offa, king of the Mercians.' They go on to explain that Offa and Cynewulf of Wessex met in council, where they received the pope's 'holy writings' and agreed to reform their vices. We are told that while George went north to Northumbria and met Alcuin of York at the court of King Ælfwold, Theophylact stayed, visiting other parts of Mercia and then moving to Wales.

Was Offa being especially pious because he had ulterior motives? His actions of the following year might suggest so; in fact, it appears that Offa had ambitions for his son, unprecedented in Mercia. As Stenton pointed out,[22] Offa must have been aware that Charlemagne's sons had been anointed by Pope Hadrian so there would have been an element of 'status-chasing' and perhaps it is with this in mind that the events should be viewed.

In 787, a year after the visit of the papal legates, at a synod in Chelsea, Offa established a new bishopric at Lichfield. This newly-established see only lasted for six years and the only archbishop was a man named Hygeberht. Alcuin of York wrote a letter to the archbishop of Canterbury supporting the idea, for the sake of unity, but it looks as if discussions for abolishing the see had already occurred, for Alcuin said that Hygeberht should not be deprived of the pallium in his lifetime.[23] Was Offa acting sincerely, claiming that the archbishopric was simply too large to cater for the house of Southumbria? The entry in the *ASC* reads: 'In this year there was a contentious synod at Chelsea, and Archbishop Jænberht lost a certain part of his province and Hygeberht was chosen by King Offa. And Ecgfrith was consecrated king.' This last sentence, short though it is, is hugely significant. It is the first mention of the consecration of a king, and it refers to Offa's son.

Could it be that Jænberht had refused to anoint the atheling? Perhaps there were fears that if this was done from Canterbury then in some way it would endorse not just Offa's control of the whole of southern England but that some hereditary right would be conferred on his son to rule Kent. Cenwulf, Offa's eventual successor, admitted to Pope Leo III that he had desired the new archbishopric of Lichfield because of his hatred of Jænberht.[24] A year or so before the papal legates had visited, the pope had written to Charlemagne; he mentioned a rumour about Offa plotting to dethrone him, that is, the pope. That the pope did not believe the rumour – had it been started, or spread, by Jænberht? – and the fact that it had reached his ears at all, attests perhaps to the high esteem in which Offa was held, and the status he had attained. Pope Hadrian, after all, agreed, however reluctantly, to the establishment of the Lichfield see.

Why would Offa have wanted his son consecrated? Perhaps he simply felt the need to confirm Ecgfrith's status as heir. After all, it had been a long time since the kingship of Mercia had passed from father to son. There may have been more to the ambition than mere 'status chasing'.

In a letter to an ealdorman by the name of Osbert, Alcuin wrote that 'you know very well how much blood [Offa] shed to secure the kingdom on his son.'[25] So there were rival claimants and the inference must be that Offa was doing all he could to ensure his son's succession. Given the circumstances surrounding his own accession and that of his predecessor, who was in exile before he succeeded and may have had to mount a palace coup if the odd mention of the king Ceolwald can be considered significant, then surely Offa was right not to assume that Ecgfrith would succeed uncontested.

S129 is a charter dated 788 confirming a grant of Offa, king of Mercia, to the bishopric of Rochester and is attested by Ecgfrith as king: *Ego Ecgfrid rex Merciorum testis consentiens subscripsi.* Offa was successful in emulating Charlemagne; but this was not the only connection between the two kings.

The *ASC*, recording the death of Ecgberht of Wessex in 839, says that before he became king he had been driven from England to exile in France by Offa and that 'Beorhtric had helped Offa because he had married his daughter.' A show of strength then, and a wise marriage alliance which saw Offa driving off a contender to the West Saxon throne using his West Saxon son-in-law. (Ecgberht did become king though, upon the death of Beorhtric in 802, an event which would have immense consequences, ultimately, for Mercia.)[26] In the last decade of his reign, Offa became embroiled in a standoff with the powerful Charlemagne, ruler of the Franks, and the exile of Ecgberht may have been a factor.

Alcuin wrote a letter in 790 speaking of a dissension, lately arisen, 'between King Charles and King Offa, so that on both sides the passage of ships has been forbidden to merchants.' Alcuin went on to say that he thought he might be about to be sent as a peace envoy.[27] Light is thrown on this episode by a work composed towards the mid-ninth century; a passage from the *Acts of the Abbots of Fontenelle* explains that a number of diplomatic missions were discharged by Charlemagne: 'Finally one on account of the daughter of the same king, who was sought in marriage by the younger Charles (Charlemagne's son).' It goes on to report that 'Offa would not agree to this unless Berta, daughter of Charles the Great, should be given in marriage to his son,' and that 'the most mighty king being somewhat enraged gave orders that no one from the island of Britain and the English race was to land on the coast of Gaul for the sake of commerce.'[28] Clearly Offa's presumption that his status was equal to that of the leader of the Franks did not go down well with Charlemagne.

There might have been more to the disagreement than that, however. Ecgberht had been driven across the sea, as we've already seen. Is it possible that he sought, and was given, refuge at Charlemagne's court?

In a letter dated between 793 and 796, Charlemagne wrote to Æthelheard, archbishop of Canterbury, and Ceolwulf, bishop of Lindsey, in which he asked them to intercede with Offa on behalf of 'miserable exiles ... that they may be allowed to return to their native land.' They had, as loyalty oaths dictated, followed their lord, Hringstan, recently deceased, who, Charlemagne felt, would have been faithful to his own lord had he been allowed to stay in his own country. If Offa could not be persuaded to allow Hringstan's retainers to return home, he enjoined the bishops to 'send them back to us uninjured. It is better to live in exile than to perish.'[29] So here is evidence that Charlemagne had no compunction in offering shelter to those fleeing Offa. We might also wonder why Hringstan and his men were compelled to flee, but history provides no answers, although the episode might offer an insight into the tone of Offa's reign.

It is supposition, but Charlemagne might also have offered sanctuary to the exiled Ecgberht of Wessex. We know that it had been Offa and Beorhtric who had driven him away in 789. We also know that

Ecgberht's eventual succession to the throne of Wessex was to have wide-ranging consequences for Mercia. Offa evidently had reason to view Ecgberht as a potential threat even as early as forty years before his own death; he would not have been pleased had Charlemagne harboured the exile.

If Ecgberht was indeed being given shelter at Charlemagne's court, it might add another dimension to the consecration of Offa's son Ecgfrith, that of seeking to secure the hereditary nature of kingship, knowing that Ecgberht was in fact still alive and posed a potential threat.

Further, we know that Ecgberht and Jænberht had a good relationship, with Ecgberht referring to him in a charter of 765 (S34) as dear to him in all things: '*archiepiscopi Genberhti qui michi in omnibus carus est.*'

It was during Beorhtric's reign that the first Viking raid occurred. Three ships arrived, and the local reeve assumed they were traders 'for he did not know what they were; and they slew him.'

The significance for England cannot have been contemplated. It might have been considered a one-off incident of little import. It was to signal a devastating period for the Anglo-Saxons, but it was also a pivotal event in Mercian history. During Offa's reign, at the height of the Mercian supremacy, two things heralded the beginning of the decline: the Vikings, and Ecgberht of Wessex.

While all this is clear in hindsight, it would not have been obvious at the time. Offa saw Ecgberht as a threat, but he cannot have known that his West Saxon rival would found a dynasty whose members would include Alfred the Great and Athelstan. In the mid-790s, Offa had his mind on other matters.

In 794, the *ASC* informs us that the king of East Anglia was killed. The entry simply reads: 'In this year Offa, king of the Mercians, had Æthelberht beheaded.' No further detail is given.

The earliest version of Æthelberht's *passio* tells how he succeeded to the kingdom of East Anglia aged only fourteen and was required by his nobles to marry. He rejected their first choice and followed the second recommendation, to marry Ælfthryth, daughter of Offa of Mercia. He travelled to meet her at the Mercian royal vill of Sutton (probably Sutton by Hereford) but Offa suspected him of planning an invasion. Having consulted his queen, Cynethryth, Offa decided upon murder and an East Anglian exile, Winberht, committed the act and threw Æthelberht's beheaded body into the River Lugg. Soon after, a column of light shone down on the burial place, visions appeared, and Offa ordered the body retrieved and carried to Hereford, where later a king named Mildfrith founded a monastery. Offa's grieving daughter Ælfthryth retired to a hermitage on the island of Crowland.[30]

One problematic aspect of this story has already been discussed in Chapter Two, that of the anachronism which suggests that Mildfrith reigned so much later than he in fact could have done. However, there are other details, particularly the use of correct names, such as Cynethryth rather than Quendrida, and a good working knowledge of Hereford, which suggests that much of the *passio* can be assumed to be reliable.[31]

Hereford Cathedral was dedicated to Æthelberht, 'certainly by the time of its destruction in 1055, but possibly earlier.'[32] The details only come to us from later sources, such as Roger of Wendover, the twelfth-century *passio* and later versions such as those by Osbert of Clare (who wrote a *Life* of St Æthelberht around 1138) and Gerald of Wales (*c.*1146 – *c.*1223).

David Rollason made a connection between the proliferation of stories about murdered royal saints, the greatest concentration of which arose not long after the visit of the papal legates in 786.[33] The twelfth of the thirty canons promulgated denounced the killing of kings: 'Let no one dare to conspire to kill a king, for he is the Lord's anointed, and if anyone take part in such a crime ... let him be expelled, everyone who has consented to such sacrilege shall perish in the eternal fetters of anathema,' and this may have an especial connection with the veneration of those murdered kings.

What of the king, rather than the saint he was to become? William of Malmesbury stated bluntly that 'Offa, king of Mercia, murdered him'[34] but Roger of Wendover blamed Offa's wife, saying that it was she who had counselled the murders.

Roger's story gives great detail: Æthelberht left his territories, 'much against his mother's remonstrances, and came to Offa, the most potent king of the Mercians, beseeching him to give him his daughter in marriage.' On learning the reason for his visit, Offa apparently entertained him with 'all possible courtesy'. But when he consulted his queen, she said 'God has this day delivered into your hands your enemy, whose kingdom you have so long desired; if, therefore, you secretly put him to death, his kingdom will pass to you and your successors forever.'

The king was 'exceedingly disturbed in mind at this counsel of the queen' and rebuked her as a 'foolish woman'. But she nevertheless hatched a complicated plan, which involved the digging of a pit underneath the visitor's chair, into which he fell and was there 'stifled by the executioners placed there by the queen.' The noble King Offa, when he heard the news, 'shut himself up in grief ... and tasted no food for three days.' Still, it seems he was not one to miss an opportunity and set out on a great expedition and 'united the kingdom of the East Angles to his dominions.' Roger records that Æthelberht was initially buried 'ignominiously in a place unknown to all'.[35]

John of Worcester was unequivocal in his condemnation: 'The most glory and most holy Æthelberht, king of the Angles, pleasing to Christ by reason of his virtues, gracious to all with his agreeable speech, was robbed of his kingdom and his life by decapitation at the loathsome command of Offa, the very powerful king of the Mercians, and at the wicked urging of his [Offa's] wife, Queen Cynethryth.'[36]

Queen Cynethryth joins the list, then, of 'wicked queens' but we have a great deal more information about her beyond her supposed involvement in the murder of Æthelberht. Her name might suggest a connection with Penda's family, given that his wife was Cynewise, and their daughters were Cyneburh and Cyneswith, but assuming familial connections purely on alliterative names can never be more than speculation. However, had Offa married into this branch of the family, it would have added weight to his claim to the throne.

We don't know when she married Offa, but the first charter she witnessed, and the first of a Mercian queen since Osthryth, given that Æthelbald remained resolutely single, was as the mother of Ecgfrith.[37] She often appears in charters without him, but after he gained his majority, his own regular appearances on the witness lists seem to have replaced hers.[38] She did not witness after the late 780s but made a brief appearance during the short-lived reign of her son, which could either be interpreted as a takeover, or simply the strong presence of a mother whose young son was now king.[39] However, it seems her authority was acknowledged and legitimate; Alcuin wrote to Ecgfrith, telling him to learn compassion from his mother, and to send greeting to her, for he would have written to her himself but knew that the king's business kept her too busy to read letters. Cynethryth was referred to as 'queen', 'queen of the Mercians' and 'queen of the Mercians by the grace of God'.[40]

Another sign of her authority is that coins were struck in her name. It might be only, as Pauline Stafford suggested, an accident of survival, but at a time when coinage generally in southern England was, after the 770s, becoming specifically more royal in nature, it was still 'exceptional' to find the name of a queen on the coins.[41] Like future royal women, she had disputes with the Church and clashed with the archbishop of Canterbury over Cookham, which was resolved with a charter of 798 in which she was given another monastery, *Pectanege* (unidentified). Cookham had previously been held by Æthelbald, and after Offa's death, Cynethryth gained possession of Fladbury, which had been a foundation of King Æthelred's.[42]

Neither Æthelbald nor Offa was directly related to the previous king. The patrilineal succession, which had survived for three generations from Penda, was interrupted and became even more complicated in the ninth century. It is possible that the succession claims came from descent through the matrilineal line and, as we shall see in Chapter Six, at least one claimant attempted to strengthen his claim by marrying a female member of a powerful dynasty. Whether this idea can be extended to prove that the Mercian royal family had married into the Pictish, who were adherents of the matrilineal line, is debateable, and it might be stretching a point to say that Offa was in fact the consort of Cynethryth rather than the other way round,[43] but there is no doubt that Cynethryth was a queen in more than just name.

In 796 Charlemagne wrote to Offa and it looks as if the earlier animosity had at least been partly assuaged and that trade routes had opened up again. Further, he sent a gift of 'a belt, a Hunnish sword, and two silk palls' (mantles). The tone of the letter suggests that here Charlemagne is addressing an equal, and it is the only known occasion when Charlemagne addresses another ruler as 'Brother'.[44] Stenton certainly believed that Offa was able to deal on equal terms with Charlemagne. It might be, however, that the marriage fiasco may in fact have been the result of an attempt to put a salve on open wounds, and to effect, rather than maintain, good relations. The trade embargo might have been a demonstration of how insulted Charlemagne felt. Perhaps, rather than dealing on equal terms, Offa received what was in effect, a 'slap on the wrist'.[45]

In 781 Offa had become embroiled in a dispute with the Church over lands granted to Worcester. The estate at Ismere had been granted by 'Æthelbald, king of the Mercians to Cyneberht ... for the construction of a minster' and at some time after that, Cyneberht's son, Abbot Ceolfrith, granted the land, which he had inherited from his father, to the bishopric of St Peter's Worcester, 'by leave of King Offa'. Yet in 781 Heathored, bishop of the *Hwicce*, was forced to surrender the lands to Offa, 'the king having claimed them as heir of his kinsman, Æthelbald.' The only inference can be that in demanding land that had been legally granted by his predecessor, Offa showed that he was not overly concerned to acknowledge the law when it came to the matter of procuring land.[46] Archbishop Æthelheard referred to 'the rapacity of a certain king' and Archbishop Wulfred complained that Offa behaved as if 'Ecgberht [of Kent] had no right to bestow lands in hereditary right.'[47]

There are some aspects of Offa's reign for which he is better remembered, however. A possible date for his introduction of a reformed silver coinage is 765. The last quarter of the seventh century had seen a rapid rise in the circulation and use of coins, with increased minting. This was followed by an influx of foreign coins and then a rapid debasement, so that by the mid-eighth century the striking of coins all but ceased.[48] The broader, thinner pennies of Offa reversed this trend, and mirrored the reformed standards of the Frankish coinage by Pepin the Short (751–68), with the slight difference that they named the moneyer, rather than the mint. Offa had thirty-seven moneyers in total, one of whom was also moneyer to Beonna of East Anglia. It is not clear what happened to Beonna, who had been minting his own coins and whose actions in this regard may have represented a bid for independence following Æthelbald's death.

The East Anglians kept their independence long enough for coins to be minted for Æthelberht, but only a few of his pennies have been found, and these, with the scant details of his murder, are all we know about him, but it is clear the two things may well be linked. The fact that Beonna's moneyer also struck coins for Offa points to a potentially earlier date than the 790s for some of Offa's East Anglian coins.[49] Some time in the 790s, possibly around 792, there was a second reform of Offa's coinage, when the coins became larger, and more uniform in design.

The letter sent by Charlemagne to Offa in 796 mentions the trading of 'black stones and cloaks' and implies that merchants were under the kings' protection. The reference to customs evasion suggests merchants were paying for that privilege. Patrick Wormald suggested that the new coinage showed a desire by the kings to harness their subjects' wealth, probably because these subjects were becoming increasingly rich.[50]

Offa's queen, Cynethryth, was the only Anglo-Saxon queen to have coins issued in her name. Although she was only shown wearing a diadem on one of the coins issued in her name, her title is clear: *'regina M'*. Her coins probably predate the heavier pennies of the latter part of Offa's reign, but cannot be dated more specifically.[51]

Whether or not the Mercians exercised lordship over Wales between the battle of the Trent and the death of Offa is hard to determine. With less of a threat from Northumbria, it might be presumed there was less need for alliance, and perhaps the campaigns of Coenred, Æthelbald and Offa were symptomatic of nothing more than normal warring between border countries, but the Pillar of Eliseg, mentioned previously, suggests that at times this part of Wales was subject to Mercia. The papal legates who came in 786 divided their efforts between Canterbury, Northumbria and the 'parts of Britain' which could reasonably be taken to mean the parts of Britain under Offa's control.[52]

The *Annales Cambriae* has the entry for 795/6 of the 'devastation of Reinuch by Offa'. It has been suggested[53] that Reinuch refers to Brycheiniog, which was a kingdom in south Wales, roughly the area that later developed into Brecknockshire, now Brecon. Given its location, it is not surprising to see Offa of Mercia fighting the Britons on the Mercian border.

The record of a battle between English and Welsh at Hereford suggests the Welsh took advantage early on of the temporary collapse of the Mercian strength following the civil war upon Æthelbald's death.[54] If Æthelbald's reign was a time of Mercian attempts to make permanent territorial gains in Wales, precipitating Elisedd's uprising, then perhaps this gives added context to the construction of Offa's Dyke. It is interesting to note, however, that few historians dwell on the subject of the dyke, its dimensions or its significance, and yet often this is the only context in which Offa is known.

Of the dyke, Asser, Alfred the Great's biographer, said that 'there was in Mercia in recent times a certain valiant king, who was dreaded by all the neighbouring kings and states. His name was Offa, and it was he who had the great dyke made from sea to sea between Wales and Mercia.' While it may not be true that it stretched from coast to coast, there is no doubt that it was an impressive, and impressively long, construction. What it was for, whether it was defended, whether it was actually as big as originally supposed, are all questions which have been asked, answered, and the answers disputed.[55] Was it the demarcation of an agreed frontier? This seems unlikely, given the recorded hostilities between Welsh and Mercians during Offa's reign. It could have been a protection against Welsh incursions, or a base from which to launch Mercian offensives into Welsh territory. Offa would have had plenty of resources so the building itself would have presented no problem. Archaeologists continue to refine their conclusions about the dyke and a discussion of its construction and dimensions is for another book.

The dyke, though famous, yields little that reveals much about its architect. We have the letters of Alcuin, and Charlemagne, but not of Offa. What then, did Offa think of himself? There is, in his genealogy listed in the 757 entry of the *ASC*, mention of a previous Offa and in the Old English poem, *Widsith*:

Offa ruled Angles; Alewih Danes,—
of all mankind in mood the bravest,
yet never with Offa his earlship availed:
for Offa won, of all men first,
when still a boy the broadest empire:
none of his age showed earlship more
in stress of battle with single brand:
against the Myrgings marked he bounds
by Fifeldor: thenceforth 'twas held
by Sueve and Angle as Offa won it.

He appears in Beowulf as '*ealles moncynnes mine gefræge/þone selestan bi sæm tweonum*' (the best of all mankind between the seas) and as a spear-bold warrior who was praised for his fighting and who wisely ruled over his empire.

The inclusion of the earlier Offa in the genealogy might suggest an ambition to rule over a 'greater Anglia' and might even be the context for the *rex Anglorum* title on Offa's coins, but it may simply mean not king of the English but 'king of the Angles'. The title most commonly used by both Offa and his predecessor Æthelbald was *rex Merciorum*.[56]

Just as there is much debate and conjecture about the date of the *Tribal Hidage*, so too has there been much discussion about the dating of the epic poem, *Beowulf*. It was argued by Dorothy Whitelock that Offa's reign could provide a date for the poem,[57] and it seems apposite to sum up that proposal here.

Although it is usual to assign to *Beowulf* an early date, it should not be assumed that a later audience would not be interested, or understand, blood feud, for as late as 801 Alcuin wrote about the Northumbrian, Torhtmund, who had 'boldly avenged the blood of his lord'. There is also a point to be made that the audience was probably not merely an ecclesiastical one, therefore a widespread Christianity must be assumed, also pointing to a later date. On the other hand, a pre-Viking date is logical, for the praise of Danish rulers in the poem would otherwise not have been especially well-received. The suggestion is that it is reasonable then to suppose that the audience would be familiar with the valiant earlier Offa and tempting to posit that the poem's reference to the boundary in *Widsith* is a complimentary reminder that a greater Offa built a greater boundary, Offa's Dyke.

William of Malmesbury presents the story of Offa and St Alban thus: that the martyr's body was raised to the light and placed in a shrine by King Offa, 'who also honoured it by building a most beautiful church and establishing a large number of monks.' William says there is 'no doubt' that Offa acted upon instruction from a dream in which he was encouraged by the sight of a light like a huge torch, which hovered over St Alban's burial place.

The story of the ancient Offa defending his country on the River Eider was, according to Whitelock, preserved at St Alban's Abbey, the foundation of Offa the Great, and a place which had strong connections with Denmark, and thus another link to *Beowulf*. Is it possible then, that the poem was written in honour of, or even commissioned by, Offa himself?

He was certainly a powerful king. Stenton made a connection between the disappearance of the ruling house of the *Magonsæte* and Offa taking control of the area.[58] Excavation has been carried out at the possible site of Offa's palace in Herefordshire. It may be that the palace, which might also have been used by Æthelbald, stood to the west of Marden Church, on the River Lugg. Skeletons, some decapitated, have been found in a pit, which immediately brought to mind the story of Æthelberht, the murdered king of East Anglia whose body was said to have been thrown into the Lugg. Were these bodies the remains of members of his entourage? Two timber watermills have been excavated, providing further indication of extensive habitation. The excavations were carried out between 1999 and 2002, with the findings due to be published in late 2018.[59]

Herefordshire was not as affected by the Viking incursions but, generally, could the reason we know so little about such a king as Offa be a result of the Vikings having destroyed much of the written evidence?[60] The laws of King Alfred (871–899) record that 'I, Alfred, collected these [laws] together and ordered to be written many of them which our forefathers observed... those which I found ... which seemed to me most just, either of the time of my kinsman, King Ine, or of Offa, king of the Mercians, or of Æthelberht, who first among the English received baptism, I collected herein, and omitted the others.'[61] Whilst we still have Ine's laws – or at least, those which Alfred decided should be copied – Offa's have not survived.

On 29 July 796, Offa died. His wish came true and he was succeeded by his son, Ecgfrith. Ecgfrith, alas for his father's hopes for him, only reigned for 141 days and Alcuin wrote that he died because of the sins of his father. But Roger of Wendover has a great deal of good to say about Offa; he details the story about St Alban, that Offa had nearly completed his most noble monastery when he died, that he was buried in Bedford, and that Ecgfrith had ruled conjointly with him for eight years and 'walked in the steps of his pious father'.[62]

William of Malmesbury, on the other hand, seems ambivalent about Offa. He says he is unsure whether to 'censure or commend' him, accusing him of murdering Æthelberht, praising him for the business about St Alban, but reproving him for the founding of the archbishopric at Lichfield. Nor, apparently, did Offa's 'rapacity' stop there, for he 'showed himself a downright public pilferer, by converting to his own use the land of many churches, of which Malmesbury was one,' which may reflect some local bias, but he has nothing else to say about him.[63]

The details we have of Offa's reign suggest the story of a strong king who had beside him a powerful queen. Two of his daughters married other kings, although one, as we will see in Chapter Six, was to die in penury having been accused of murder. He dealt on equal terms – at least, in his eyes – with the mighty Charlemagne and was frequently victorious in battle. Alcuin knew that Offa had a copy of Bede. This suggests some level of literacy and we know that he was the promulgator of legal codes. Alfred said he had seen Offa's laws. This is no casual comment. There are two elements to this: the first is that Offa's laws must have been impressive indeed for Alfred to wish to include some of them when promulgating his own law codes. The second is the possibility of what else was lost to us. We only know about Offa from other people, those witnesses 'from without', but unlike the view of Penda, presented to us purely as a warlord, we get nuances with Offa of something more; a Frankish king addressing him as brother, suggestions of trade and commerce. It seems he was a shrewd businessman, and a ruthless foe. He was clearly a statesman and in his dealings with the Church, probably no more self-serving and pragmatic than other kings. He saw the importance of using other methods than warfare to secure the succession, so he was more than a barbarian warlord. Yet still he evades us.

If Æthelbald was almost the greatest king no one has heard of, then Offa must be one of the most famous and yet unknown. Despite our having little information about him, a glance at Mercian history might show him to be the last successful king of Mercia. But there was another, and he too reigned for a long time.

CHAPTER 6

The Forgotten Kings

The reigns of the kings who ruled between the death of Offa and the abdication of Burgred span half a century, with one king ruling for twenty-five years during that period. Either side of that reign, the rest add up to twelve in number, but include second, short-lived, and disputed reigns. These are the forgotten kings, the ones whose complicated names and troubled and troublesome family relationships hint, ostensibly, at nothing more than squabbling and a general disintegration of the powerful kingdom of Mercia. But this period, often overlooked, reveals two important facets of Mercian history: the reign of Cenwulf, and the dynastic disputes which had repercussions even in the later ninth and early tenth centuries. There is no reason to neglect this period, for there is a wealth of information, but unravelling it can be complicated.

The shadow of an insecure succession was not a new apparition. Offa had come to the throne after fighting Beornred, who had succeeded after Æthelbald had been murdered. There was instability and rarely only one claimant to the throne. Offa was obviously aware of the likelihood that there would be other contenders for his throne after he died, and this must have been one of the reasons he worked so hard to have his son anointed, to validate Ecgfrith's position as the legitimate son of a legitimate king. It was all for naught, however, as Ecgfrith reigned for a mere five months after Offa's death.

Virtually nothing is known of Ecgfrith's reign. Four charters survive, (S148–51), of which only the first is not to be treated with caution as spurious or of doubtful authenticity. We do not know how he died, but Alcuin considered Ecgfrith's untimely death to be a direct consequence of Offa's sins, 'For truly, as I think, that most noble young man has not died

for his own sins; but the vengeance for the blood shed by the father.'[1]
Is this to be taken, with the letter sent by Charlemagne concerning the
men of the dead lord, Hringstan, mentioned in Chapter Five, as evidence
that Offa worked hard to eradicate as many potential claimants to the
Mercian throne as possible?

Ecgfrith, during his brief reign, seems to have maintained a good
relationship with his brother-in-law in Wessex, Beorhtric. S149, a charter
of admittedly dubious authenticity, records: 'Wherefore, I, Ecgfrith,
king of the Mercians, in the first year of our reign granted by God, at
the request of Beorhtric, king of the West Saxons, and Archbishop
Æthelheard, have returned to Abbot Cuthbert and to the brethren of the
monastery of Malmesbury land of thirty hides in the place that is called
Pyrton, on the eastern side of the wood that is called Braydon, for the
remission of my sins and for the repose of the soul of my father, Offa,
which while he was alive he took from them.'[2]

Relations between Mercia and Wessex must have soured somewhat,
however, when in 802, Beorhtric, ally and son-in-law of Offa, died.[3]
Asser's *Life* of King Alfred gives the details, describing Offa's daughter
as a 'tyrant after the manner of her father' who decided systematically to
remove all those of her husband's advisers whom she detested. Beorhtric
accidentally drank the poison intended for one such advisor, and both he
and the young man died. She fled to the court of Charlemagne, where,
according to Asser, the emperor offered her the choice [in marriage?] of
him, or his son. She chose the son, 'as he is younger than you' to which
Charlemagne replied that had she chosen him, she could have had the
son, but since she had chosen the son, she could have neither. He did,
however, bestow upon her a convent, but her scandalous story did not
end with her taking the veil. Asser reported that she lived yet more
recklessly, and when 'at long last she was publicly caught in debauchery
with a man of her own race, she was ejected from the nunnery on
Charlemagne's orders.' Reduced to a life of poverty, she 'died a miserable
death in Pavia.'[4]

Already we have had the stories of Alhflæd (who murdered her husband
Peada), Osthryth (wife of King Æthelred, murdered by his household
troops) and Cynethryth, wife of Offa (accused of murdering Æthelberht
of East Anglia). Eadburh would not be the last Anglo-Saxon woman
to be excoriated by later chroniclers. Asser would certainly have been
writing with the knowledge of what happened to the Mercian succession
in the mid-ninth century, when the house of Wessex, or more specifically
when Alfred's grandfather, took control of Mercia. Later stories of
Cwoenthryth, of whom more in a moment, and Ælfgifu and Ælfthryth in
the tenth century, follow similar traditions, and we must remember that

Alfred's grandfather was Ecgberht, the West Saxon forced into exile by Beorhtric in alliance with Offa, so the Eadburh story might have come ready-laced with literary poison.

The *ASC* makes no mention of the story, only reporting the death of Beorhtric and the succession of Ecgberht. It does, however, record the antics of a Mercian ealdorman, Æthelmund, who 'rode from the province of the *Hwiccians* across the border at Kempsford.' He was met by Ealdorman Weohstan of Wiltshire and a 'great battle' ensued. The *ASC* records that both the ealdormen were killed and that the people of Wiltshire had the victory. This entry gives a glimpse of the turmoil which must have accompanied every succession, with loyal armed men ready to defend the status quo, or perhaps even to take advantage of the uncertainty.

Beorhtric was succeeded in Wessex by the former exile, Ecgberht. He never challenged Cenwulf of Mercia but, on the other hand, neither was he ever his subordinate.

Cenwulf, a distant relative who succeeded Ecgfrith, and his brother who ruled briefly after him, were reputedly descended from a brother of Penda and Eowa, a man named Cenwalh. There is no record of such a brother, but as we have learned with this period, we should not assume he didn't exist. On the other hand, it might be significant to recall that Penda married his unnamed sister to Cenwalh of Wessex. Of her fate, and any progeny, we have no information, but if she had children, then presumably they were born before she was repudiated in 645. If she and Cenwalh were married when the Mercians and the West Saxons 'came to terms' in 628, they had plenty of time to produce a number of children. As pointed out by Ann Williams, given the animosity between Wessex and Mercia, it would be ironic if one of the most successful kings of Mercia – Cenwulf – was in fact descended from a king of the West Saxons. Alternatively, he may have been connected to the *Hwiccian* kings, for he made strong claims to 'hereditary lands' in Winchcombe, in the heart of the territory of the *Hwicce*.[5]

Cenwulf did not witness any of Offa's charters, suggesting the likelihood that he, like others before him, had been in exile before he succeeded. Alcuin's letter regarding Ecgfrith's untimely death continued, pointing out that, 'You know very well how much blood his father shed to secure the kingdom on his son.' So it may well have been wise for Cenwulf to hide out, if indeed he had any choice in the matter. Cenwulf's ancestry is linked with Offa's, but their nearest shared ancestor is Penda's father, Pybba.

Of course, if the suggestion that Cenwulf and his brother were descended from Cenwalh of Wessex has any substance, they might

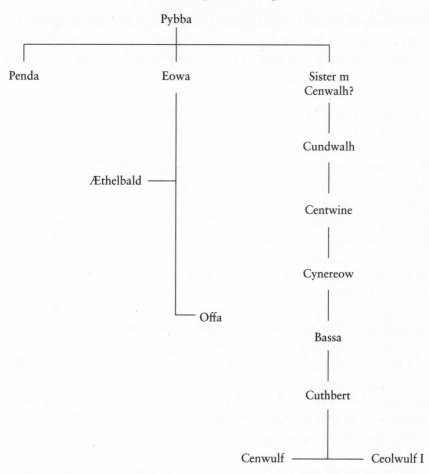

Cenwulf's relationship to Offa.

have wished to play this down. It is also possible, but pure conjecture, that Cenwalh's repudiated wife went back to Mercia, with her small children, who then grew up and lost any notion of connection to the West Saxons. Where Cenwulf and his brother grew up, though, might be more problematic for, at some point, as the charter evidence suggests, the family went into hiding.[6]

Cenwulf's achievement was 'scarcely less impressive' than Offa's. Patrick Wormald pointed out that from 798, Cenwulf's control of the South East was as real as Offa's, and although there is less evidence of his influence in Wessex or Northumbria, he increased Mercian pressure on the Welsh, and after his death his brother virtually overran Powys. He was the only English king before the tenth century to be styled 'emperor' and it has also been said that Cenwulf could be regarded as a 'respectable fifth in the line of Mercian overlords.'[7]

Alcuin pronounced that Ecgfrith's death was divine retribution for Offa's violent tendencies, but he does not appear to have welcomed the accession of Cenwulf. In his letter of 797 Alcuin wrote to an ealdorman of Mercia, Osbert, exhorting that both King Eardwulf of Northumbria and King Cenwulf of Mercia be reminded that they should hold themselves in 'godliness, avoiding adulteries.' He says his own king, Eardwulf, had dismissed his wife and taken a concubine and whilst he warns against this, saying, 'let your dearest king beware of this' there is no direct accusation that Cenwulf had put aside a wife. Yet Alcuin also urges the Mercians to observe 'the good and moderate and chaste customs which Offa of blessed memory established for them.'[8]

It is certainly possible that Cenwulf had two wives. A charter of 799 (S156) appears to show his wife, Cynegyth: *Ego Cenulf rex una cum coniuge mea Cenegiða regina*. This charter has been denounced as unreliable at best, but it might be worth noting that Cenwulf's son had the alliterative name *Cyne*helm and there was a kinsman, *Cyne*berht.[9] His – possibly – second wife, Ælfthryth, witnessed charters from perhaps as early as 804 to 817, attesting as *Ælfðryða regina Merciorum* in 814 (S173).

Like previous kings of Mercia, Cenwulf had dealings with the surrounding kingdoms. Examination of coinage suggests that there may have been East Anglian independence following Offa's death, with coins being minted by moneyers there in the name of Eadwald, although they cannot be dated with complete accuracy. This independence may not have lasted very long, however, as those same moneyers struck coins afterwards for Cenwulf.[10]

It is likely that, for a short while at least, the East Saxons also regained independence from Mercia following Offa's death, but this probably only lasted until 798. Cenwulf's relationship with the East Saxons is unclear. Sigeric, the king there after Offa's death, had gone to Rome in 798. Sigered witnessed charters of Cenwulf in 811 and 812 – as sub-king – and again in 814, but was styled *dux*. It seems safe to assume that this man is Sigered of the East Saxons, but we cannot know what the relationship was between Mercia and the kingdom of the East Saxons before 811. It clearly took Cenwulf a few years to 'find his feet' after Offa's death. Did he need to build up his power before he could take control of Essex, or had he come to some kind of arrangement with Sigered? Whatever the nature of the relationship, it was presumably achieved without violence, and Sigered was the last recorded East Saxon king.

In 801, Cenwulf was attacked by the Northumbrians, led by King Eardwulf, 'because of his harbouring of his enemies.' Simeon gives the background to this tale. King Æthelred of Northumbria, who had married Ælfflæd, Offa's daughter, in 792, had been murdered in the same year as Offa's death. During his reign he had already been deposed and exiled, before being reinstated, then he was murdered by a group of nobles. One of these men, Osbald, was appointed king but his reign lasted only twenty-seven days. Alcuin wrote him a letter in which he told Osbald, 'I am displeased with you ... consider how much blood of kings, princes and people has been shed through you or through your kinfolk.' Alcuin urged Osbald to change his ways and turn towards God.[11] Simeon reported that Osbald became an abbot. 'Osbald, once ealdorman ... and for a time king, then indeed abbot, reached his last day and his body was buried in the church of the city of York.'

While Osbald was clearly involved in the killing, it was a certain Ealdred who killed the king, and in a letter to Charlemagne in 801, Alcuin reveals that Torhtmund, 'the faithful servant of King Æthelred, a man proved in loyalty, strenuous in arms ... boldly avenged the blood of his lord.'[12]

In 798, there was a battle at Whalley, in modern-day Lancashire. Simeon of Durham explains that a conspiracy was formed by the murderers of King Æthelred, who were joined by an ealdorman named Wada, and these men fought against Eardwulf, Osbald's successor. Eardwulf had been the bitter enemy of the murdered Æthelred. Eardwulf won the battle and those who had fought against him – Wada is named – took flight. It was also in 798 that Cenwulf was ravaging Kent, in the area which Æthelweard the Chronicler called *Merscwari*, and he captured the king, Eadberht Præn.

If, as we know, Æthelred was married to Offa's daughter, it is not implausible that the Mercians would be sympathetic to the supporters of the murdered king. In fact, it seems as if these 'enemies', whom Simeon reports to have been harboured by Cenwulf, did indeed include Wada. A letter from Pope Leo III to Charlemagne in 808 mentions the '*dux*', Wada, in its discussion of Eardwulf's – later – exile and seems to confirm the accusation that Cenwulf had been harbouring Eardwulf's enemies.[13] Thus it can hardly be a surprise that Eardwulf attacked Mercia in 801. It was a long and ultimately indecisive campaign, the two sides eventually sealing a truce to hold for their lifetimes.

Kent had risen up in revolt against Mercia after Offa's death. Archbishop Æthelheard, known to have Mercian sympathies, fled his post, and Alcuin wrote to him saying, 'You are yourself aware for what cause you left your see; whether for fear of death or for the cruelty of torments of for the abomination of idolatry.'[14] Eadberht Præn, an exile at Charlemagne's court, returned to England around the time of Ecgfrith's death[15] and took over the kingdom of Kent.

Eadberht is likely to have been the Odberht mentioned in a letter of Charlemagne's as having sought refuge at Charlemagne's court. He is referred to in the letter as a priest, and it may be that he was forcibly tonsured as well as being forced into exile, to reduce his suitability to reign. If so, he renounced holy orders and when Offa died he returned to Kent, presumably forcing Æthelheard to flee Canterbury. Alcuin's denouncement of this action might have resulted from his anger at the archbishop's non-acceptance of Eadberht, as Charlemagne's protégé, for he seems to have been almost alone in his harsh judgement of Æthelheard.[16]

It seems as though Cenwulf waited until Eadberht had been excommunicated before he took action against him. According to the *ASC*, Cenwulf 'seized Præn and brought him in fetters into Mercia' where his eyes were put out and his hands cut off. Henry of Huntingdon refers to the capture, saying that the Mercians took Eadberht prisoner, but he makes no mention of the mutilations. It has been argued that the 'wanton act of barbarity' existed only in the imagination of the Norman interpolators of the annals.[17] William of Malmesbury called Cenwulf a 'truly great man' who 'surpassed his fame by his virtues, doing nothing that malice could justly find fault with.' His praise seems motivated by the latter's having restored Canterbury, and he goes on to say that Cenwulf released Eadberht Præn out of pity.

Cenwulf put his brother Cuthred into Kent, but initially as a puppet; a charter of 801 (S57), shows them together, 'Cenwulf, king of Mercia, and Cuthred, king of Kent', and Cuthred seems only to have been acting independently towards the end of his reign, where in a charter of 805 (S39) 'Cuthred, king of Kent', granted land with no reference to his brother. In 807 Cuthred died, and Cenwulf took direct control in Kent.

William of Malmesbury's observation that Cenwulf restored Canterbury belies the fractious nature of the king of Mercia's relationship with the Church, however. In 803 a council of Clofesho abolished the archbishopric at Lichfield. 'Cenwulf king of the Mercians, after an admonitory lesson [from the archbishops of Canterbury and York] about the great wrongs committed by his predecessor Offa, completely restored Canterbury to its former state.'[18] Jænberht and Offa had had an uneasy relationship, Offa's attempts to move the southern archbishopric to London having failed and his creation instead of the see of Lichfield under his direct control having been opposed by Jænberht. It had not been Jænberht who had anointed Offa's son Ecgfrith but Hygeberht, whom it seems Jænberht refused to acknowledge.

Mercian relations with the Church were not destined to improve. In 796, Æthelheard, Jænberht's successor, and an appointee of Offa, had fled when Eadberht Præn became king of Kent. When Cenwulf succeeded he sent letters to Pope Leo in 797 and 798 'humbly imploring' that a southern see in London replace both Canterbury and Lichfield, with Æthelheard as the incumbent.[19] The pope objected to the criticism of his predecessor's decision to establish the see at Lichfield and decreed that the southern see must remain at Canterbury: 'We pronounce it by our decree the first see.' The *ASC* records that Æthelheard went to Rome in 801, and in 802 Pope Leo wrote to him confirming his authority and that of his successors, and at the council of Clofesho in 803 Hygeberht was present, but as an abbot only.[20]

Cenwulf became embroiled in an argument with Æthelheard's successor, Wulfred, and there was a legal dispute over the Kentish minsters and the question of whether there should be lay control of ecclesiastical lands.[21] This dispute weakened Cenwulf's hold on Kent and the disputes continued until in 821 Cenwulf threatened to exile the archbishop unless certain estates were surrendered. The argument concerned not only Cenwulf, but his daughter, Cwoenthryth, too.

In 816 at the council of Chelsea, Wulfred attacked Cenwulf.[22] This argument involved Cenwulf's daughter, and the houses at Reculver and Minster-in-Thanet. The argument was not settled until the 825 council of Clofesho, which decided in Wulfred's favour.[23] When her father died in 821 and was succeeded first by his brother and then quickly by a man not directly related to the family, Cwoenthryth, Cenwulf's daughter, seems to have been regarded as his heir, although this would most likely mean to his property, rather than his kingdom.[24] She was by this time abbess of 'Southminster' (probably Minster-in-Thanet, in Kent) and in 824 she was in dispute with Wulfred who pressed the claim that he had been despoiled of his *domination* over the monasteries of Southminster and Reculver. In 827 she was compelled to surrender lands to Wulfred. Perhaps the main interest to this story is that it proves she was a powerful heiress, who also held the land-books of Winchcombe. Her argument with Wulfred necessitated the convening of a council at Clofesho in 825, and required the intervention of the then king, Beornwulf.[25] It may also add some context to the most famous story about this woman. She witnessed a charter of 811 (S165) which was also attested by other members of the royal clan: Cenwulf's brother's son, Coenwald and a 'kinsman' Cyneberht. Not present was Cenwulf's own son, Cynehelm (sometimes Kenelm). Clearly Cynehelm pre-deceased his father, but the tradition of his death is rather extraordinary.

The *ASC* entry for 821 states merely that Cenwulf, king of the Mercians, died, and Ceolwulf succeeded to the kingdom. Gaimar, an Anglo-Norman chronicler writing in the twelfth century, furnishes the detail that he died at Basingwerk. If true, it suggests that he might have been planning, or was already on, a campaign against Wales. He was buried at Winchcombe.[26]

Roger of Wendover takes up the story: 'He [Cenwulf] was succeeded by his son Kenelm, whom his father entrusted to his sister Cwoenthryth to bring up as he was but seven years old.' However, she was 'led astray by base ambition' and gave the boy to a 'certain officer' who took the child out on the pretext of going hunting and cut off his head. This story, according to Roger, would have gone undiscovered had it not been for a pigeon dropping a letter on the altar of St Peter in Rome. Thus the body was discovered and conveyed to Winchcombe, where the murderous sister chanted a psalm backwards, with 'a sort of jugglery'. When she got to the part which said, 'This is the work of those who malign me with the Lord' her eyes burst forth from their sockets and fell on the page she was reading. Roger added that in his day, the psalter was still stained 'with the gore of her eyes'. William of Malmesbury also blamed Cwoenthryth, and added that after this, the kingdom of the Mercians sank from its prosperity and, 'becoming nearly lifeless, produced nothing worthy to be mentioned in history.' In one version of the story, Cwoenthryth not only lost her eyes, but was then divinely punished by death.[27]

There is no contemporary evidence that Cynehelm/Kenelm ever ruled Mercia, but there is evidence for his existence. In 798 the Privileges of Pope Leo III granted Glastonbury to Cynehelm and his successors.[28] Charters of 799 (S156) and 821 (S184) are witnessed by Cynehelm – *Cenelm fillii regis, ego Kenelums filius regis consensi* – but are not considered authentic, although the witness list for the former may have a genuine basis.[29] There was a senior ealdorman called Cynehelm at the Mercian court, attesting charters until 812, although he is never described as the king's son, for example in S165 of 811: '*Ego Cynehelm dux consensi et subscripsi*'.

The earliest account of Cynehelm's life – and death – is contained in an eleventh-century *passio*.[30] It dates the murder to 819, although this would have been 821 if it was using the chronology of the *ASC* which at this time was two years out[31] and it is generally agreed that the person named in the charters would not have been a child in 821. There is no mention in the *ASC* of a Cynehelm succeeding his father.

The veracity of the story of Cynehelm's murder cannot be established, beyond saying that Cenwulf had a son who died before his father. Given the nature of the Mercian succession it is not unlikely that a king's son might have been done to death before he tried to take the throne, but the charter of 799 which mentions Cenwulf's first wife and Cynehelm is widely held to be a forgery. Known timelines do not give credence to the notion that Cynehelm was an infant at the time of his father's death and it is dangerous to assume that the story told in the *Vita S Kenelmi* bears much relation to the truth, although it is perfectly plausible that the son of Cenwulf would have been buried at Winchcombe.[32]

The point has been made that in Cynehelm and the cult associated with him, the family monastery had its family saint. Whatever the circumstances of it, Cynehelm's death allowed for the enhanced prestige of Cenwulf's house.[33]

As already noted, William of Malmesbury called Cenwulf a 'truly great man, [who] surpassed his fame by his virtues, doing nothing that malice could justly find fault with'. He said the king was 'religious at home, victorious abroad', and he conceded that 'taking up Offa's hatred against the Kentish people, he sorely afflicted that province' but he says that he released Eadberht soon afterwards 'moved with sentiments of pity.' William also said that after him the kingdom of the Mercians sank from its prosperity and, becoming nearly lifeless, 'produced nothing worthy to be mentioned in history.' He then sums up the years 821–875 in one paragraph. Similarly, Gaimar summed up the following years in a few short lines, making no mention of Cynehelm and saying that Cenwulf died in *Basewerce*.[34]

> And Ceolwulf reigned after him.
> Two years he held the land with much weariness
> At the end of two years he lost it.
> He was not beloved, therefore he fled.
> Such deeds had he done that all hated him.
> Many wished to kill him.
> We will leave him; and speak of him
> Of a brave king of another kingdom,
> Wessex. Ecgberht was his name.
> Beornwulf raised great strife against him.

In 816 Mercian armies had penetrated into Snowdonia; the *Annales Cambriae* reported that Saxons invaded the mountains of Eryri and the kingdom of Rhufoniog and in 818 Cenwulf 'devastated the *regio* of the Demetæ' (Dyfed).

T.M. Charles-Edwards[35] stated that Cenwulf's aggression towards Wales did not begin in 816 but at the beginning of his reign, asserting that Cenwulf, 'or his subordinates' slew Caradog, king of Gwynedd (*AC* 798 'killed by the Saxons'). Indeed the *Annales Cambriae* also records a Battle of Rhuddlan in 797, in which Cenwulf may have been involved.

It is difficult to discern the nature of these fights between the Mercians and the Welsh. The argument could be, possibly, that from the time of Penda onwards the Mercians were trying to keep control not only of the borders but of the Welsh themselves, and these recurring campaigns were attempts to deal with uprisings. Charles-Edwards postulated that once the threat from Northumbria was removed, so too was the need for alliance between Wales and Mercia. Certainly no other Mercian king had the same friendship with Wales as Penda had maintained. The recovery of Powys, commemorated on the Pillar of Eliseg, may represent the ending of a sustained period of Mercian rule over the area.

The *Annales Cambriae* recorded that the fortress of Deganwy was 'destroyed by the Saxons and they took the kingdom of Powys into their own control.' So perhaps William of Malmesbury's assessment that nothing else of note happened was a little wide of the mark? The entry in the *AC* also adds weight to the suggestion that Cenwulf had died whilst on campaign, and that his brother and successor, Ceolwulf, had continued or opened the campaign up again.[36]

However successful he might have been against the Welsh, Ceolwulf was less lucky in his own kingdom. The *ASC* entry for 823 reports not that he died, but confirms Gaimar's assertion, saying that he was 'deprived of his kingdom.' There are no further details for that year. Only two charters survive from his brief reign, and in both he is styled 'king of Mercia and Kent', and both are grants to Wulfred of Canterbury (S186, 187).

The next king, Beornwulf, may have been successful in deposing Ceolwulf, but a charter of 825 hints at a troublesome reign: 'After the death of Cenwulf, king of the Mercians, many disagreements and innumerable disputes arose among leading persons of every kind – kings, bishops, and ministers of the churches of God – concerning all manner of secular affairs, so that in various places the churches of Christ were greatly despoiled, in goods, lands, revenue and all matters.'[37] Coins issued at Canterbury were minted without a king's name between 821 and 823, as if the moneyers were unsure who was in charge.[38]

It was, perhaps, the inevitable outbreak of chaos which followed the passing of a strong ruler, a situation which would be echoed in 975 upon the death of Edgar.[39] A strong king had died, his son may have been murdered, and his brother had been deprived of the kingdom. All these things point to a period of great instability. In 824 the *ASC* recorded that two ealdormen, by the names of Burghelm and Muca, were killed. Muca appeared in those two charters of Ceolwulf's.

Conversely, Stenton pointed out that Beornwulf's authority was recognised in Essex, Middlesex, and Kent and that he was the dominant figure in southern England as late as 825, when he reached a settlement with Wulfred.[40] It is less clear whether he was dominant over the East Anglians.

In 825, however, the *ASC* records a battle between the forces of Ecgberht of Wessex and Beornwulf, 'king of the Mercians' at Wroughton (more usually called *Ellendun*) and 'Ecgberht had the victory.'[41] This was, according to Stenton, the moment when 'the ascendancy of the Mercian kings came to an end.' After 825, Kent, Surrey and Sussex were never again separated from the West Saxon monarchy.[42]

So who was Beornwulf, who seems to have been more dynamic than Ceolwulf, and whose name suggests no connection with the previous rulers? As well as having been defeated by Ecgberht, he had been the one who had to concede to Wulfred at the councils of Clofesho in 824 and 825 in the ongoing squabble with Cenwulf's daughter Cwoenthryth over the disputed Kentish minsters.

Beornwulf might be the same man who witnessed Cenwulf's charter of 821 and one of Ceolwulf's in 823, but if so, he occupied a low position on the witness list, suggesting that he was not a distinguished member of the nobility.[43] We know little else about Beornwulf, except that in 826, he was killed by the East Angles. The people of Surrey, the South and East Saxons had all submitted to Ecgberht of Wessex through 'fear of the Mercians.' Presumably any assumed happy or acquiescent subordination was no longer a fact. In Kent, coins were briefly produced in the name of Bealdred, who may have been a puppet king installed by Mercia[44] but in 825 he too had been driven out of Kent and his people submitted to Ecgberht. It is difficult to know whether he had reigned independently, and the similarity of his name to Beornwulf's hints at the possibility that he was a kinsman of the ill-fated Mercian king, installed in much the same way as Cenwulf had installed his brother Cuthred.

Beornwulf himself is not thought to have been related to the previous Mercian kings, whose names, Cenwulf and Ceolwulf, with their brother Cuthred, all alliterated. If we follow the alliteration theme though, it is possible to suppose that he might have been related to the Beornred who attempted to take power after Æthelbald's death in 757 but lost out to Offa.

In August 825, Ecgberht defeated the Britons at a place called *Creodantreow*. A late tenth-century letter mentions that the Cornish rose up against Ecgberht and that the king 'went thither and subdued them and gave a tenth of the land to God,' which may refer to this episode.[45]

The *ASC* entry for 784 notes that Ealhmund of Kent was Ecgberht's father, thus establishing the link between the two houses. When Bealdred was driven north out of Kent, the *ASC* says it was Ecgberht's son,

Æthelwulf, who drove him out. Thus we see powerful families in the south and southeast, dominant over the Britons of Cornwall, and only unsuccessful members of rival dynasties in Mercia. The tide was turning, for the son of Ecgberht, Æthelwulf, was the father of five sons, the youngest of whom was Alfred the Great.

Meanwhile, when Beornwulf of Mercia was killed by the East Angles, he was succeeded by a man named Ludeca. An awful lot appears to have happened in 825, and a charter (S1267), dated 826, suggests that Beornwulf was still alive and in power in 826. Whenever he died, his murder doesn't appear to have given the East Anglians full independence, for 'Ludeca [was] the last Mercian king to strike coins there.'[46] Ludeca doesn't appear to have been a member of any branch of the royal Mercian house. He was present at the 824 council of Clofesho: *Ego Ludeca dux consensi et subscribo* (S1434).

Whether he succeeded in 825, or in 826, he was dead by 827. We are not told by whom, but he was killed, according to the *ASC*, along with 'his five ealdormen'. John of Worcester said 'Ludeca, king of the Mercians, assembled his troops and marched his army into the province of the East Angles to avenge his predecessor King Beornwulf.'[47] His successor was Wiglaf.

Wiglaf was probably also not of royal stock, a fact which is indicated by his arranging for his son, Wigmund, to marry Ælfflæd, daughter of Ceolwulf, brother of Cenwulf, and the last king who could claim descent from the royal line.[48] Ælfflæd was remembered at Evesham as having descended from Coenred, grandson of Penda. It is possible that Wiglaf's wife, Cynethryth, might also have been a descendant of Penda. Wiglaf, and later his grandson, Wigstan, were buried at Repton, which might suggest a connection to Æthelbald.[49] Much good it appears to have done him though, for in 829, Ecgberht of Wessex conquered Mercia. Ecgberht is recorded as having conquered all the lands south of the Humber, and was listed as the eighth *Bretwalda*, added to Bede's original list, which omits any mention of Mercian kings.

According to Roger of Wendover, Ecgberht successfully led an army against the Northumbrians too. 'In the year of our Lord 829, Ecgberht, king of the West Saxons, after possessing himself of all of the southern kingdoms of England, led a mighty army into Northumberland, committing terrible ravages in that province and putting king Eanred under tribute.' But the *ASC* doesn't mention it and probably would have if it had been a noteworthy campaign.

Patrick Wormald pointed out that the success story of the first half of the ninth century was West Saxon, even if, 'by and large, we have only its own word for it.'[50]

In 830 though, it seems as though Wiglaf was back on the Mercian throne. Where he had been since being deposed, we can only guess. Stenton thought it more likely that Wiglaf was restored to power by a revolt and that a charter of 836 signalled Wiglaf's independence and the 'revival of Mercian authority over the southern episcopate'.[51] That charter from 836 shows Wiglaf granting the minster at Hanbury immunity from feeding the king, his officers and his messengers, reserving only 'the construction of ramparts and bridges.' It is witnessed not only by the archbishop of Canterbury, but almost all the southern bishops, which has been seen by some to suggest that Wiglaf was in control of southern England at this time, but Simon Keynes has pointed out that there was no currency minted in Mercia in the 830s.[52]

It seems hard to tally the idea of a rebellion with the fact that Ecgberht had led a successful campaign against the Welsh in that year, 'and he reduced them all to humble submission to him,'[53] which suggests that either he was on good terms with Mercia as he took his army through the land, or that he was in a position to stamp on any uprising. Roger of Wendover explains the restoration thus: 'Moved with compassion, [Ecgberht] granted to Wiglaf, king of the Mercians, that he should hold his kingdom of him under tribute.'

It should perhaps be remembered that Ecgberht had spent time in exile at the court of Charlemagne, and perhaps Frankish support had helped secure his position, and had now suddenly been withdrawn.[54]

A charter of 831 (S188) acknowledges that Wiglaf's reign had been interrupted, by declaring that it was issued 'in the first year of my second reign.'

Only three charters of Wiglaf's survive, dated 831, 833, and 836, (S188–190) and all show him granting land in Mercia – Hayes, Middlesex, Crowland and Worcestershire – without any mention of Ecgberht. Similarly, there are no grants by Ecgberht of land in Mercia during Wiglaf's brief exile[55] but, whilst not necessarily reduced to the role of sub-kings, the Mercian kings no longer enjoyed supremacy south of the Humber, and Ecgberht retained control of the southeast provinces, which changed the political landscape.

The last decade of Ecgberht's reign is a story of travails with Viking incursions, and when he died in 839 he was succeeded by his son, Æthelwulf.

Wiglaf himself died in the following year,[56] and was succeeded by Beorhtwulf, who presumably belonged to the same dynasty as the previous 'B' kings. Wiglaf's son, Wigmund, may have reigned briefly, or might in fact have pre-deceased his father. The – forged – *Chronicle of Crowland* said that he died of dysentery.[57] In any event, it seems that by

840 he was dead, for there was a scandal surrounding his widow and the opportunity for a story about yet another murdered saint. One almost imagines the later chroniclers rubbing their hands in glee when preparing to report these incidents.

Wiglaf's official successor, Beorhtwulf, had a son, Beorhtferth, and Roger of Wendover picks up the story. At Pentecost, 'Beorhtferth, son of Beorhtwulf, wickedly slew his kinsman St Wigstan, who was the grandson of two kings of the Mercians. The body of the deceased was carried to the monastery of Repton and is said to have been buried in the tomb of his grandsire Wiglaf.' Roger then describes heavenly miracles but gives no reason for the murder.

According to the earliest version of his *passio*[58] Wigstan was indeed the grandson of two kings, his father Wigmund being the son of King Wiglaf, and his mother, Ælfflæd, being the daughter of King Ceolwulf. The story goes that upon the death of Wigmund, Wigstan was offered the crown but demurred, being still only a boy and seeking a religious life. Beorhtferth sent envoys to ask for the hand of the widow Ælfflæd. Wigstan apparently forbade the match, his objection being that Beorhtferth was his father's kinsman (*cognatus*) and indeed, his [Wigstan's] own godfather. Thwarted in his plans, Beorhtferth slew Wigstan, whose body was taken to Repton. He was interred in the mausoleum of his grandfather, Wiglaf, and apparently a miraculous shaft of light shone down upon the site where the murder had taken place, much as it had done after the murder of King Æthelberht at Offa's court, mentioned in Chapter Five. There is no evil queen behind this tale of murder, but miracles are attached to it. Can the story be dismissed? There is an argument[59] for suggesting that there might be some truth in it.

We can recall that Wiglaf appeared not to be of royal stock and tried to legitimise his kingship by marrying his son Wigmund to Ælfflæd, daughter of Ceolwulf. His eventual successor, Beorhtwulf, was apparently a relative of Wigmund's, but more significantly, his name suggests a connection to the earlier king, Beornwulf, who ruled from 823–5 and possibly with Beornred who was deposed by Offa in 757. His sons both had names beginning with B. It looks as if there were two families staking claim to the Mercian kingship, what we might call the 'B' kings and the 'C' kings. If Wiglaf aligned himself to the 'C' branch, it is possible that Wigstan was the victim of a power struggle between these two houses. Cults do seem to have grown around dynastic disputes, and it would happen again in the tenth century.

The succession from Penda down to Offa is fairly straightforward, although the direct line from Penda was cut in 716, and the names of the following kings, Cenwulf, Ceolwulf and even their brother Cuthred, throw up no surprises. That the Cynehelm who attested Cenwulf's charters in the first years of the ninth century is unlikely to have been his son[60] suggests that along with the previously mentioned Cyneberht, there were quite a few members of the 'C' dynasty. However, the appearance of a proliferation of men with names beginning with B, and then apparently a royal family whose names alliterate on the prefix *Wig-*, ushers in a new period of dynastic rivalry.

The first probable member of this family to emerge was Beornred, who was deposed by Offa in 757, and perhaps Offa's son-in-law, Beorhtric of Wessex, was related to him. There is no proof that all the men whose name began with B were in any way related to each other and no way of knowing how they came to power, or where their power base lay.

Wigmund married, through Ælfflæd, into the family of Ceolwulf, and their son was killed by a member of the 'B' family, Beorhtferth. We are not told what happened to this murderer, save that the *passio* reports that once he had killed Wigstan and attacked his companions he was at once driven insane.[61] He appears in a charter of his father Beorhtwulf as *Berhtric filius regis* (S198) dated 844/845 and generally regarded as authentic.

There is no proof that any of these three families belonged to the ancient Mercian royal house, and there is nothing to say that they originated from the heartlands of the Trent Valley.[62] It may be that succession at this time depended on which local lord could muster the most support and troops.

It seems likely then, that Wigstan was the victim of a dynastic dispute but, like the earlier murder of Cynehelm, purchase could be made and the royal centre, this time at Repton, elevated, with the rise of a cult attached to yet another royal saint.

What doesn't seem clear is where Beorhtwulf himself came from. That his son murdered the heir of the previous king without there being any repercussions suggests that he had a solid army of supporters. He was strong enough, and secure enough, it seems to mint coins.

Beorhtwulf and Æthelwulf of Wessex minted coins by the same moneyers, with two of eleven of Beorhtwulf's moneyers also striking coins for the West Saxon king. The coins were almost identical, save for the inscription, so some kind of co-operation between the two kingdoms is indicated.[63]

In 849 the *Annales Cambriae* records that 'Meurig was killed by Saxon[s]', which might indicate the nature of Beorhtwulf's policy towards the west of his kingdom, and hostilities in 853 after his death suggest that he was exercising control over the Welsh.[64] And yet, in 851 the *ASC* entry says that 350 'heathen' ships stormed Canterbury and

London and 'put to flight' Beorhtwulf, king of the Mercians, with his army. It seems perhaps that the Mercian kings were no longer of the calibre of the previous warlord incumbents. And yet the invaders did not press their victory but went instead to Surrey.

Why was there no co-operation between the Mercians and the West Saxons? Was there no time? The *ASC* heaps praise upon Æthelwulf and his son Æthelbald, saying that they 'inflicted the greatest slaughter [on a heathen army] that we have ever heard of until this present day, and had the victory there.' Did Beorhtwulf in fact die when he was 'put to flight'? Alas, his fate is not recorded.[65]

It is possible that during Beorhtwulf's reign Berkshire passed out of Mercian hands, but this depends on how one interprets the evidence.[66]

A charter dated 28 March 840 shows Beorhtwulf agreeing to restore various estates to the Church of Worcester and confirming that they had been 'wrongly and illegally despoiled.'[67] This was not the only charter of this nature, and most of Beorhtwulf's surviving charters show him granting or returning land to the Church. A document from 849 saw the king promising not to rob the Church in future.[68] There may be an indication here that Beorhtwulf was taking land because there was a dearth of available acreage with which to reward his supporters, or that he didn't have enough lay support to fight the Church and hold onto lands he had seized.

It seems generally agreed that Beorhtwulf died in 852, and although his death is not recorded in the *ASC*, the entry for that year names Burgred as king of the Mercians. He is mentioned in connection with an uprising in Wales, suggesting that perhaps the Welsh had been subject to Mercia before Beorhtwulf's death. It seems unlikely, because Burgred needed the help of the West Saxons to subdue it. Or perhaps there was yet another disputed succession, which the Welsh used to their advantage?

The *ASC* has only seven entries on Offa's reign, and four on Cenwulf's, which include the accessions and deaths. It concentrates on the violence of the reigns, in contrast to the mentions of Ecgberht's conquests, which are more sympathetic in tone. Ecgfrith's death undid all the hard work which Offa had done to secure the succession[69] and Cenwulf's reign tends to be overlooked because of all the dynastic squabbles and short reigns which came after it. The disputes between the Mercians and Canterbury, and with Archbishop Wulfred in particular, must 'seriously have undermined confidence in the Mercian regime' and 'clearly something was rotten in the state of Mercia. The political disruption which followed the death of Æthelbald, and the deaths of Offa and Ecgfrith had been masked on those occasions by the rapid imposition of new regimes; and it is as if, in the 820s, the Mercians were simply unable to get their act together.'[70]

Ecgberht of Wessex turned the tide and reversed a situation which had been in place for centuries. Force of arms, and determination, brought Ecgberht success, but dynasty played a part. Penda's line had been good and strong, and so was Ecgberht's, as it turned out. The Mercian dynasty became weak and fragmented at the very time that Wessex seemed to find cohesion. Fate also played a huge part in this reversal of fortunes; that, and geography. This was not just a turning of the metaphorical tide, this was now a story of foreign ships sailing on real tides. The Viking age had begun.

CHAPTER 7

Burgred and Ceolwulf II: The Last Kings of Mercia

The next – indeed, the last – two kings of Mercia appear to have hailed from the 'B' and 'C' families. When Beorhtwulf of Mercia died around 852, he was succeeded by Burgred. There is no evidence of a disputed succession, nor of any short-lived reign by an otherwise unknown claimant, and since the only hint of disarray suggested is by the records of skirmishes with the Welsh as mentioned in the previous chapter, the assumption must be that it was a peaceful accession.

It is difficult now to produce a narrative of Mercian history without commenting on West Saxon activity. Not only do these two histories run together, but both are full and increasingly frenetic as the Viking raids became more frequent and sustained.

One of Burgred's first acts as king of Mercia was, with Æthelwulf of Wessex, to attack the Welsh. It is interesting to note how this was reported in the *ASC*, and how it introduces a theme, which reappears regularly in the chronicles for the mid-ninth century onwards. Dorothy Whitelock pointed out the differences between the versions of the chronicles. The C (incorporating A & B) *Chronicle* states that Burgred asked King Æthelwulf to help him to bring the Welsh under subjection to him. 'He then did so, and went with this army across Mercia against the Welsh and made them all submissive to him.' The D [E] *Chronicle* says that 'Burgred, king of the Mercians, subjected to himself the Welsh with King Æthelwulf's help.[1] Is the fact that Burgred asked for help indicative of the bias of the chronicles, or is it a sign of diminishing Mercian power? Perhaps Mercia itself was declining, or maybe Burgred was not of the calibre of the warrior kings who had gone before him.

Possibly he didn't have the support of the Mercians themselves; if we are correct in assuming that he came from the 'B' family then we might be equally sure that his successor Ceolwulf came from the rival 'C' family, and he seems to have been accepted, despite his epithet as foolish thegn, as we shall discover in a moment. Burgred's coinage was more numerous than any other previous king[2] but from 871, his pennies were reduced in diameter, as if Mercian wealth was somewhat diminished.

Asser's reporting of the Welsh campaign stresses the superiority of Æthelwulf and his forces. 'Burgred, king of the Mercians sent messengers to Æthelwulf, king of the West Saxons, asking him for help, so that he could subject to his authority the inland Welsh.' He goes on to say that as soon as the message arrived, Æthelwulf 'assembled an army and went with King Burgred to Wales, where immediately on entry he devastated that race and reduced it to Burgred's authority. When he had done this, he returned home.'[3]

In the same year, Burgred married Æthelswith, the daughter of King Æthelwulf. Roger of Wendover says that she was given the 'appellation of Queen'. Certainly, in a charter dated 868, she is styled 'queen of Mercia' (S1201).

The earlier history of Mercia showed its kings marrying their daughters to other kingdoms, and the inference is that it was the smaller kingdoms who hoped for elevated status and/or protection through these alliances. Policy seems to have moved in the opposite direction in the late ninth century, with marriage alliances apparently linking a Mercia much reduced in authority with the more powerful Wessex. These marriage alliances were not a new concept, of course; Beorhtric of Wessex had married Eadburh, Offa's daughter, but the conferring of royal association was in the other direction, with Mercians now marrying princesses from West Saxon families, rather than marrying off their own princesses.

The more widely known history of the late ninth and early tenth centuries is one of Alfred the Great's battles with the Viking invaders. With Wessex thus in the headlines and in the ascendancy, is it possible to piece together the last years of the Mercian kingdom?

A charter dated somewhere between 883 and 911 shows the renewal of a grant that had been made by King Burgred, 'the ancient land-book having been carried off by "pagans"' (S222) which, even though it is not wholly reliable, gives one example of how the historian's search for Mercian characters and events is hampered by not only the lack, but the loss, of written evidence.

The *ASC* leaves the impression that the Viking raids only caused problems from about 835, when 'in this year heathen men ravaged Sheppey', but several extant charters suggest that earlier incursions had caused problems.[4] The *ASC* leads readers to suppose that the West Saxons were the only effective leaders against the attacks. This may be bias but, of course, it may also be true.

William of Malmesbury said that by marrying Æthelswith, Burgred 'exonerated himself, by this affinity, from the payment of tribute and the depredations of the enemy, but after twenty-two years, driven by them from his country, he fled to Rome.'

This is to dismiss the whole of his reign, and there may be evidence of partnership, or at least co-operation between the kingdoms. A charter of Burgred's reign, dated somewhere between 852 and 874 and not extant in the original form, records a grant by Burgred to Eanwulf, an ealdorman, of land in Binegar, Somerset, which was in Wessex.[5]

Yet, from the 860s onwards, the bishops of London, in theory owing allegiance to Mercia, attested only charters of the West Saxon kings, suggesting a shift in ideas about who was in power.[6]

The transference of power from one kingdom to the other leads to an interesting aside and prompts consideration of Berkshire, and in particular, of Pangbourne.

Berkshire remains a region of some debate among historians, and discussion centres around a charter of 844.[7] The charter is preserved in the Abingdon archives and records that Ceolred, bishop of Leicester, gave fourteen hides at Pangbourne in Berkshire to King Beorhtwulf, and that Beorhtwulf then gave the same land to Ealdorman Æthelwulf, but it might be that by the end of the decade at least some part of the region was under West Saxon control, because according to Asser, Alfred was born at Wantage in 849 in what was then a West Saxon royal estate. The fact that Alfred was born, according to Asser, on 'the royal estate called Wantage in the district known as Berkshire; in 849 (or shortly before) has been thought to show that by the late 840s Berkshire as a whole had fallen into West Saxon hands. It may be that there was some kind of surrender or exchange of land, but it could also be the case that Wantage, to the south of the Thames, remained in West Saxon hands, while Pangbourne, situated on the Thames, remained under Mercian control.[8]

However, it does seem as though Ealdorman Æthelwulf, the recipient of the land, moved to the West Saxon court, for he attested Mercian charters in the early 840s, re-emerging in the court of Wessex in the 850s and 860s.[9]

Sir Frank Stenton's view of Berkshire was that it had been the dominion of Æthelbald, and that Offa, 'took away the monastery of Cookham and very many other towns from King Cynewulf, [of Wessex] and added them to the Mercian imperium.' He believed there was good reason for saying that the whole of Berkshire was annexed to Mercia at this time. He added that the Pangbourne charter did not stand alone, and that eight years beforehand, Bishop Heahbeorht of Worcester, by a similar grant, had obtained immunities for Hanbury monastery from Beorhtwulf's predecessor, Wiglaf. He was certain that the Pangbourne charter proved that 'Berkshire remained subject to the Mercian kings until within six years of the middle of the ninth century,' and that 'there can be no question that the king who grants immunity to a religious house within a shire is for the time being the accepted lord of that shire.'[10]

Ealdorman Æthelwulf has been identified as the person of that name who witnessed a Berkshire charter of Æthelswith, wife of Burgred of Mercia, in 868 and, as such, was therefore presumably a 'Mercian ealdorman set over Berkshire, who at some undefined date transferred his allegiance to the king of Wessex.'[11]

Patrick Wormald agreed that in 844 Berkshire must still have been in Mercian hands and that it probably had been so since at least the reign of Offa. He pointed out that the transaction by which Beorhtwulf of Mercia persuaded the bishop of Leicester to give him the estate 'in perpetuity, in exchange for an immunity for certain unnamed monasteries' and then transferred it, with a 'wholly unqualified immunity' to Æthelwulf, is 'typical of the Mercian kings of this period, and one wonders how the bishop of Leicester felt about royal "persuasion".'

In 862, Æthelwulf received ten hides at Wittenham from King Æthelred of Wessex (S335). In this charter there is no mention of the land having come from the Church, and the immunity is subject to the usual three duties of maintaining bridges, fortifications and fighting men. Wormald wondered if, in fact, the kings of Wessex were richer in land than the Mercians and thus could afford not to pressurise the Church and could be less generous when granting immunities to lay beneficiaries. If so, then a case may be made to show how, and why, Berkshire passed from Mercian to West Saxon control by the time Alfred was born at Wantage.[12]

Æthelwulf's death and burial adds further layers to this complicated state of affairs. In 871, three days after the Danish army established itself at Reading, Æthelwulf intercepted them on a road running south from Pangbourne, and he was killed in the ensuing fighting. Æthelweard the Chronicler seems to confirm the ealdorman's Mercian origins because he records that Æthelwulf's body was taken for burial to the town of '*Northweorthige*, in the tongue of the Danes, Derby.' It is difficult to propose any other reason for his being buried so deep in Mercia, unless he was still considered a Mercian.

Stenton argued that the story of Æthelwulf proved that for more than sixty years after the battle of Bensington, Berkshire remained a Mercian ealdormanry, 'subject … to the spiritual rule of the bishops of Leicester.' Further, he said that those sixty years were of significance because 'the Mercian retention of this county suggests that the permanent importance of the victory won by Ecgberht of Wessex over Beornwulf of Mercia at *Ellandune* in 825 has very materially been exaggerated.' However, he also conceded that after the assistance given to Burgred by Wessex against the Welsh, and the subsequent marriage of Burgred to Æthelswith, in 856 King Æthelwulf of Wessex granted land at Ashbury in Berkshire to his thegn[13] and it may be 'permissible' to suggest that Berkshire was the price Burgred had to pay for West Saxon assistance in 853.

In the winter of 854/5 Vikings, or as the *ASC* called them, the 'heathen', stayed in Sheppey for the first time. There was to be no long-lasting peace for many years to come.

In 855 King Æthelwulf left Wessex and went to Rome, leaving Wessex to his son Æthelbald and the eastern provinces to another son, Æthelberht. He returned with a new wife, Judith of Flanders, but did not live for long afterwards. Upon Æthelwulf's death in 858, the two brothers retained the areas they had been given, but only two years later, in 860, Æthelbald died, and Æthelberht took over all of Wessex.

In 860, a Viking force attacked Winchester and was defeated. In 864 Vikings camped at Thanet and 'made peace' with the people of Kent. The following year, in 865, Æthelberht of Wessex died and was succeeded by his brother, Æthelred.

Meanwhile, the *Annals of Ulster* reported that at that time 'the Britons were expelled from their country by Saxons so that they were held in subjection in *Maen-Conain* (Môn, or Anglesey). If this was an army from Mercia, which seems likely, then perhaps we should not assume that Burgred had no military strength. The tale of the Viking incursions into his eastern territories may in part have been the story of his eyes being drawn to his western borders. This was certainly not to be the end of hostilities on the Welsh border.

In 865/6 the Viking force known as the Great Heathen Army landed in East Anglia and overwintered there. The East Anglians were reported to have 'made peace.' In 866/7, the Great Heathen Army moved from East Anglia to Northumbria and took over the city of York and in 867/8 it moved from Northumbria to Nottingham in Mercia and overwintered there.

In 868 Alfred of Wessex married Ealhswith of the Mercians. Asser says that at the time, Alfred was 'heir-apparent' and that his wife – whom Asser does not name – was from Mercia, of 'noble family' and that she was the daughter of Æthelred *Mucil*, ealdorman of the *Gaini*.[14]

Ealhswith had a brother, Æthelwulf. The *ASC* entry for 901 records his death, stating that he was the 'brother of Ealhswith, King Edward [the Elder]'s mother'. Asser said that Ealhswith's mother was a lady named Eadburh. He states that she was of 'royal stock', and a charter dated 897 suggests that this brother, Æthelwulf, was related to the Mercian royal family.[15] In Chapter 74 of his *Life*, Asser describes the wedding, which he says took place 'ceremonially in Mercia in the presence of countless persons of both sexes' and he says the feasting lasted 'day and night'. There is no mention of this in the *ASC*, but it is possible that the memory of a West Saxon king, Beorhtric, having been poisoned by his Mercian wife, Offa's daughter, was still rather fresh.

Further evidence of co-operation between the kingdoms is provided by the issue of a 'single uniform coinage for both Wessex and Mercia.' However, between *c.* 865 and *c.* 875 Burgred of Mercia's *Lunettes* coinage, also adopted by Wessex, was being debased, and similar coins were being struck by Wessex, suggesting that by at least the end of Burgred's reign, Wessex had control of London.[16]

In 868 Burgred and Æthelred joined forces, and their combined armies besieged Nottingham. There was no pitched battle and the Mercians 'made peace.' It might be fair to say that at this point the two kingdoms were on a par, and that the alliance was one of equal partners, or at least that would perhaps have been the Mercian perspective.

The Great Heathen Army went back to York for a year, then in 869/70 marched across Mercia to overwinter at Thetford in East Anglia. During this period, King – later Saint – Edmund of East Anglia, was killed.

In 871 a force known as the Great Summer Army arrived in Reading, and presumably joined the Great Heathen Army of 865. There were battles that year at Reading, Ashdown, Basing and *Meretun*. The *ASC* gives far more detail about these than the attacks on Northumbria or Mercia. Whereas we hear simply that at Nottingham the English kings 'besieged them there,' here we have named casualties – 'Sidroc was killed there' – before we hear about King 'Æthelred and his brother Alfred' leading a great army to Reading where they 'fought against the army; and a great slaughter was made on both sides and Ealdorman Æthelwulf was killed, and the Danes had possession of the battlefield.' There is even more detail about the battle of Ashdown.

In late 871 Æthelred died and was succeeded by his brother, Alfred. The *ASC* sums up the year, listing nine battles, and only then do we see the oft-used phrase and hear that now it was the turn of the West Saxons to 'make peace.'

Over the winter of 871/2, the Vikings took up quarters in London. The Mercians 'made peace.' Roger of Wendover says that 'Burgred, king of the Mercians, purchased a truce of them for a sum of money.'

Ingulph's forged *Chronicle of Croyland* relates that in 871 Burgred was busy fighting the Welsh, but it is possible that this was based on fact, and that there was a Welsh raid in this year.[17] With the suggestion of fighting in 865 recorded in the *Annals of Ulster*, this entry by Ingulph, and the death of Rhodri Mawr in 878 and then the battle of Conwy in 880/881 with the 'vengeance for Rhodri at God's hand' (*AC*) it is clear that the Mercians had their hands full with the Welsh during this period. Is this why they developed a tendency to 'make peace' with the Danish invaders?

Asser also uses the phrase 'made peace' and a lease by Bishop Werferth of the *Hwicce* in 872 grants an estate to 'Eanwulf, a king's thegn', for him to 'possess happily for his life and to leave to three heirs after him such as he shall choose' but makes the point that 'the abovementioned bishop agreed to [the grant] chiefly because of the very pressing affliction and immense tribute of the barbarians, in that same year when the pagans stayed in London.'[18]

Æthelweard the Chronicler says of 872: 'After a year had elapsed from the time of their coming to Reading, they measured out their camp in the neighbourhood city of London. But the Mercians ratify [sic] a treatment with them and pay a stipend.' So it seems unanimous that the Mercians paid tribute.

Sure enough, in 872/3 the Vikings went to Northumbria, took winter quarters in Torksey in Lindsey and the Mercians 'made peace.'

So far, the story of a roaming army picking sites to pitch its tents and then holding its hand out for payment looks as if it might have gone on *ad infinitum* but in 873/4 the Vikings took winter quarters at Repton. Repton was highly significant to the rival Mercian royal house, the burial place of Æthelbald, Wiglaf and Wigstan, and suddenly the game changed.

Ceolwulf II was famously dismissed in the *ASC* as a 'foolish king's thegn' and there is every likelihood that he was facilitating the invaders at this point. Repton was the burial place of Æthelbald, but more pertinently it was the burial place of St Wigstan, whose mother, Ælfflæd, was the daughter of Ceolwulf I. If she was also the mother of Ceolwulf II, then this was no foolish king's thegn, but a rival claimant leading a successful coup with the aid of the Vikings. Burgred had the backing of the West Saxons, so unsurprisingly the *ASC* would have been ill-disposed to speak well of Ceolwulf.[19]

With the Vikings at Repton, in the heart of Mercia, Burgred was driven 'across the sea' (*ASC*). William of Malmesbury recorded that he died at Pavia. He said that 'the kingdom was next given by the Danes to one Ceolwulf, an attendant of Burgred's, who bound himself by oath that he would retain it only at their pleasure.' His stark summing up continues thus: 'After a few years it fell under the dominion of Alfred ... thus the sovereignty of the Mercians, which prematurely bloomed by the overweening ambition of an heathen, altogether withered away through the inactivity of a driveller king.'[20] It is interesting that, despite the marriage alliance and the fact that, as we've seen, Burgred and the West Saxons were working in concert at various points, no assistance appears to have been forthcoming from Wessex.

A charter of King Æthelred of Wessex, dated *c.* 868 is attested by 'Beorhtferd *filius regis*'. Was this a Mercian atheling visiting the West Saxon court? The alliterative name could, tentatively, be taken to show that this was a son of Burgred and Æthelswith.[21] If this witness was indeed a son of the Mercian king and queen, he could have been no older than fourteen in 868. In theory, he was old enough to succeed to the Mercian throne, but he did not. Presumably any unrecorded offspring either died early or fled with their parents when Repton was occupied. Upon their departure, Ceolwulf II became the last king of Mercia.

Was he really no more than a king's thegn, or was he a member of one of the royal dynasties? Ælfflæd, if indeed she was his mother, was of high status; her suitor was said to have murdered her son, Wigstan, and he was her suitor because he was attempting to strengthen his own claims. The name of Wiglaf's wife, Cynethryth, seems to suggest a kinship going back to Cenwulf if not earlier royal lines. The later *Life* of his grandson Wigstan gives the name of Wigstan's mother, wife of Wiglaf's son Wigmund, as Ælfflæd – a name borne by a ninth-century abbess of Winchcombe, a house on which descendants of Offa and of Ceolwulf I had claims.

Was he 'foolish'? In the years before Guthrum the Viking's arrival in Cirencester, possibly 875–878, a particular coinage, the *Cross and Lozenge*, was being struck, in what looks like a joint enterprise to reform the coinage, with Alfred and Ceolwulf working together.[22] It seems unlikely that Alfred would have had as a partner in this venture a 'foolish thegn'. Why then was the *ASC* so damning in its appraisal? The reason may be the indisputable fact that Ceolwulf was co-operating with the Danes, and/or the resultant removal of the brother-in-law of Alfred. Æthelweard the Chronicler passes no comment on Ceolwulf other than that he 'possessed the kingdom.' Alfred seems to have had no qualms working with this 'thegn' since coinage was issued jointly.

A charter of 875 shows Ceolwulf granting estates in Worcester to the community of St Mary's, a charter which is attested by Mercian bishops and laymen (S216). Therefore it appears he was acting independently, issuing charters and coins. But the *Cross and Lozenge* coinage throws up some interesting information, for it seems as if the coins of this type in London were not issued concurrently, but that Alfred's were minted first. Does this mean then that in 874/5 the people of London turned to Alfred, rather than to Ceolwulf, or the Vikings? If moneyers were issuing coins in Alfred's name, in London, before Burgred's flight, then this might shed new light on the situation in London.[23]

Certainly Ceolwulf seems to have assumed that not much in Mercia would change, and appears to have been acting as a king sure of his tenure. A charter of 875 grants to him an estate belonging to the bishop of Worcester, which he was free to leave to three heirs: 'The bishop grants to the king a four-life lease of 6 hides at Daylesford, Gloucs., with reversion to Worcester ... for the soul of King Ceolwulf and his successors.' (S215)

In 874/5 the army left Repton. In 1974, more than 250 skeletons were excavated in the grounds of Repton Vicarage, in Derbyshire. The initial assumption was that here was a gravesite related to the Viking takeover of Repton. The remains of 264 people, roughly twenty percent of whom were female, were surrounded by weapons, including an axe, several knives, and silver coins dated to between 872 and 875. The men, aged predominantly between eighteen and forty-five, had died from violent injury. But, radiocarbon dating revealed the grave to contain bones that had been placed there over centuries. However, in early 2018 it was announced that the original radiocarbon dating had produced confusing results because of a 'marine reservoir effect': 'The previous radiocarbon dates from this site were all affected by something called marine reservoir effects, which is what made them seem too old. When we eat fish or other marine foods, we incorporate carbon into our bones that is much older than in terrestrial foods. This confuses radiocarbon dates from archaeological bone material and we need to correct for it by estimating how much seafood each individual ate.'[24]

A Dane called Halfdan took part of the army from Repton to Northumbria and took up winter quarters by the Tyne. Leaders Guthrum, Oscetel and Anwend went to Cambridge. Perhaps this division saw the breaking up of the coalition of the Great Heathen Army and the Great Summer Army as they went their separate ways. In the summer of 875, Alfred of Wessex won a naval battle. The *ASC* reports that Halfdan began to plough the land in Northumbria and his men began to support themselves.

In the 'harvest season' (Asser says 'August') the Cambridge army went via Wareham and Exeter – where Alfred had engaged them and secured hostages from them and a 'firm' peace – into Mercia. This time there is no inference to be drawn regarding Ceolwulf's co-operation, because the *ASC* states clearly that of Mercia, 'they shared out some of it and gave some to Ceolwulf.'

The division of Mercia in 877 is seen as a triumph of treachery on the part of Ceolwulf, who seems to have invited the Vikings in. He was certainly working with them and put up no defence. Small wonder that the chroniclers dismissed him. Was he a 'shrewd negotiator'[25] or a quisling? Henry of Huntingdon simply called him a 'weak king', but obviously viewed him as more than a thegn. If he was a contender from the rival house to Burgred's, then it is easy to see how the invaders were able to move in on the back of a dynastic dispute. The arrangement would have suited both parties; the Vikings met no resistance, and Ceolwulf got his kingdom.

He was free to operate elsewhere. Ceolwulf was probably the leader of the Mercian force that killed the Welsh king, Rhodri Mawr, in a battle only mentioned in Irish and Welsh annals. Whilst not named, the English leader is more likely to have been Ceolwulf, since Alfred was busy elsewhere at this point.[26] The *Annales Cambriae* recorded that in 878 'Rhodri and his son Gwriad is killed by the Saxons'. Clearly Ceolwulf was untroubled by hostile incomers in Mercia if he was able to fight the Welsh. But what did the Mercians think of these developments?

There had been a short period of co-operation between the two kingdoms, with Æthelbald, Æthelred and Alfred all to varying degrees 'assisting' the Mercians. It may be that the emergence of Ceolwulf as a king acting independently of Wessex was welcomed by those in Mercia who did not appreciate the increasing reach of the West Saxons over their territory.[27]

The charters issued at this time give no indication that Ceolwulf regarded himself, and was regarded, as anything other than a legitimate king of Mercia. S216, as mentioned above, was witnessed by the bishops and shows Ceolwulf granting land to St Mary's at Worcester. S215, also from 875, is a grant to Werferth, bishop of Worcester, and carries the exemption of the burden of feeding the king's horses and servants, in return for liturgical services. In both these charters he is styled 'king of the Mercians' and these grants are not made by permission of Alfred. Whether things changed in 877, we cannot know.

In 2015 a coin hoard was discovered which adds credence to the notion that it would be wrong to dismiss Ceolwulf II as a puppet king, or a 'mere' king's thegn. The hoard comprised about 200 coins, not all complete, with several items of jewellery and fifteen silver ingots. Thirteen of the coins are of the rare *Two Emperors* type which show Alfred of Wessex and Ceolwulf of Mercia seated together beneath a winged figure. The finds also include a single *Two-Line* type penny which, it is known, was not produced until after the battle of Edington in 878.[28] The hoard indicates that the political landscape of the 870s might have been 'deliberately misrepresented in the 890s after Alfred had taken over the whole of Ceolwulf's kingdom.'[29] Of the *Two Emperors* coins, one which has Ceolwulf as *rex*, while Alfred is styled *rex Anglo(rum)*, it has been pointed out that it might be too little information to make an informed conclusion about the status of these two kings.[30]

It also should be considered that, not long after the division, Ceolwulf disappears from the record. It is not possible accurately to assess when he died, but a Worcester regnal list in *Hemming's cartulary* gives him a reign of five years, and an entry in the *Annales Cambriae* [880], which states that the battle of Conwy was 'vengeance for Rhodri at God's hand', suggests that if it were indeed Ceolwulf who killed Rhodri in 878, then it might well have been Ceolwulf who died at the battle of Conwy.

It is also possible that Ceolwulf was not active in Wales as late as 880 or even 878 and that his disappearance from the records and the arrival of the Dane, Guthrum, in Cirencester in the winter of 878/879 is something more than a coincidence.

It has been suggested that Alfred was able to exert greater influence over Mercia because Ceolwulf left no heirs,[31] but there was at least one member of the rival royal house left. In 902 at the battle of the Holme, the *ASC* recorded that among the fatalities was 'Brihtsige son of the atheling Beornoth', suggesting that there were still residual members of the 'B' dynasty active in Mercia. It may even be that this Brihtsige was fighting alongside a rebellious West Saxon atheling in the hope of having his claim recognised.[32] The charter of *c.* 868 with its record of 'Beorhtferd *filius Regis*' mentioned a possible son of Burgred's, and there may have been another contender for the throne of Mercia. There is every reason to suppose that the 'B' dynasty survived but, in the event, Ceolwulf was succeeded not by another king, but by an ealdorman. The administrative structure in Mercia differed from that in Wessex, in that ealdormen were not so much appointed by the king but were leaders of their own local peoples.[33] This may explain, firstly, the rise of the next leader, Æthelred, ealdorman of Mercia and, secondly, the rise of Wessex, because Mercia gradually collapsed, to leave Wessex standing clear of the shadow.

After Ceolwulf II's disappearance, there were no more serious contenders for the Mercian throne. We only know about the atheling Beornoth because of his son's rebellion. Of the only two charters which survive from Ceolwulf's reign, the first, S215, is witnessed by a Beorhtnoð *dux,* the second, S216, by a Beornoth *dux,* but there is no suggestion that this is the same person[34] nor that either is connected to the later statement about Beornoth atheling in the *ASC* entry for 902. Nor is there any name on either charter which could suggest the presence of the man who was to lead the kingdom after Ceolwulf's death.

However large or small his base of support, and however strong his links to the royal Mercian dynasty, Ceolwulf II was the last king of Mercia. But the story of this kingdom did not die with him, nor with Alfred the Great.

CHAPTER 8

The Lord and Lady of the Mercians

The next ruler of Mercia came, seemingly, from nowhere. Æthelred of Mercia left no discernible paper trail prior to becoming leader. A charter, purporting to renew an original grant of Burgred's because the original had been 'carried off by the pagans' seems to show Æthelred making the renewal, but it is witnessed by both Burgred and his queen, Æthelswith (S222). It is unlikely that such a charter would have been issued in an ealdorman's rather than the king's name, and the document has been declared not genuine in its extant form, so we cannot take it as proof that Æthelred was ever a leading ealdorman at Burgred's court.

It is possible that he is the Æthelred who attested two Mercian charters of the late 860s.[1] S212 is a grant by Burgred of two hides of land, in exchange for five hides 'on a single-lifetime lease, 400 silver *sicli* and various other items.' There is an Æthelred on the witness list, although he is quite near the bottom of that list. Another charter, S214, dated 869, shows Burgred, king of Mercia, and Æthelswith, queen, granting five hides of land in return for fifty mancuses of gold. Here, an Æthelred appears at the very bottom of the witness list, below a number of others who are styled *dux* while he is not.

Where, then, did he come from? And how did he assume control? If he was the same man who attested those charters he clearly was not a leading ealdorman.

Roger of Wendover said that he was 'of the royal stock of that nation' but elsewhere he lists the kings of Mercia and says: 'From Burgred, the kingdom of the Mercians was transferred to the kingdom of the West Saxons.' He does not even mention Ceolwulf II and neither does the regnal list in *Hemming's cartulary*.[2]

There doesn't seem to be any suggestion that it was Alfred who appointed Æthelred. He must have been acceptable to the Mercians; there was no power struggle – that we know of – and yet it seems certain that there were still members of the 'B' family alive. One rose up against the established Mercian/West Saxon alliance in 902, so it can't be assumed that they were all happy to let the title of king pass them by. Perhaps Æthelred had something that previous kings lacked: good generalship. It is also possible that he was at the battle of Conwy in which Anarawd of North Wales avenged his father Rhodri Mawr's death.[3] If indeed this is where Ceolwulf II met his death, is it possible that Æthelred was then in a prime position to take over English Mercia? Pure speculation, of course, but a believable scenario perhaps.

A later, by no means certainly reliable, source records that a man whom the Welsh called *Edryd Wallthir* – Edryd Long-hair – made 'great Preparations for the re-gaining of the said Countrey' yet it has also been suggested that the battle of Conwy was where Æthelred lost power, rather than gaining it.[4] His status as leader of Mercia is not clear and oft-debated.

Asser talked about the Welsh submitting to Alfred's overlordship, driven by 'the might and tyrannical behaviour of Ealdorman Æthelred.' Were they placing themselves under Alfred's protection, or complaining about his 'vassal'? Was he a sub-king reduced to the rank of ealdorman, much as kings of minor kingdoms had been in the past? Or were those chroniclers who called him king, and subsequently his wife, queen, simply unaware of the traditions of rulers in the English kingdoms and their status?[5]

When Asser mentions that Anarawd of Gwynedd submitted to Alfred, he says he did so 'on the condition, that he should be obedient to the king's will in all respects, in the same way as Æthelred.'

It has been suggested that Alfred undermined Mercian power over the Welsh and there was a danger for Wessex that these two subordinates might combine their forces.[6] It seems unlikely though, given that the southern Welsh, if Asser is to be believed, were railing against Æthelred's 'tyranny', and it is clear that the main threat to both Wessex and to Mercia was that of the Danish incursions.

Alfred's endeavours against the invaders are well documented. Is it possible to unravel Æthelred's contribution and come to any conclusions about his role and station?

In 886 Alfred occupied London. The assumption is that it was completely under Viking control at that point, although this can't necessarily be proved.[7] According to William of Malmesbury, Alfred granted London to 'a nobleman named Æthelred' who conducted himself with 'equal valour and fidelity'. Henry of Huntingdon says that London was *given* [my italics] to Æthelred the ealdorman. There is no suggestion of equal status, or autonomy.

Asser, in Chapter 83 of his *Life*, adds the detail that Alfred restored the city 'splendidly – after so many towns had been burned and so many people slaughtered.' He 'entrusted it to the care of Æthelred' and all the Angles and Saxons who had not been scattered or in captivity with the Vikings 'turned willingly to Alfred and submitted themselves to his lordship.'

The consensus therefore seems to be that London was under Viking control, Alfred fought them, ejected them, the Londoners submitted to him and he then gave his subordinate, Æthelred, the job of keeping hold of the city. But can we take this at face value?

Dorothy Whitelock thought it clear from Asser's addition, 'after the burning and massacre' that Alfred obtained London by warfare, but Simon Keynes has said that there is no suggestion from the *ASC* that there was any force required.[8] The interpretation depends on whether Asser's remark refers directly to the occupation of London, and it may be that Alfred made a strike on London in 883, not against Danes who had been settled there since the division of Mercia, but a fresh Viking incursion.

It is probably safe to assume that, whatever the nature of the occupation, the campaign was a combined Mercian/West Saxon affair. Whatever the circumstances, and however many years this took, the significance is that submission in 886 and whether this should be taken to mean all of the English people – Saxon, Kentish, Mercian – or the people who had been freed from subjection to Vikings by Alfred's retaking of the city. It is a point that could form the basis of a discussion about Alfred's status, generally, as king of the English people, but for the purposes of this study, the salient point is that Alfred respected London's status as a Mercian town.[9]

Whatever the status of the men involved, Mercia was not yet a province of Wessex. Æthelweard the Chronicler, a member of the West Saxon royal house and writing in the tenth century, calls Æthelred a king, and Mercia his kingdom.[10] Whether he was happy to remain as ealdorman, as F.T. Wainwright suggested,[11] might be a moot point. It is likely he had little choice.

In 890 Guthrum died[12] and in 892 the Great Danish Army returned from the Continent in 250 ships, Hasteinn came with eighty ships, and both armies made fortresses in Kent.

Somewhere between 893 and 896 the occupying armies of Northumbria and East Anglia broke their truces to join the newly arrived Vikings. Presumably these Northumbrians and East Anglians were the remnants of the Great Heathen and the Great Summer armies, so it is hardly a surprise that they joined forces, although in 896 they split up again.

In 893, Alfred had positioned himself between the forces and came to an agreement with Hasteinn, by which Hasteinn gave oaths and hostages, and Hasteinn's sons were baptised with the sponsorship of Alfred and the ealdorman Æthelred. Hasteinn broke the truce, however, and went to Benfleet and 'ravaged the province.' The other force, based at Appledore, ravaged Hampshire and Berkshire. On their return, they were halted at Farnham in Surrey by the army of Edward the Elder, Alfred's son.

Æthelweard the Chronicler recorded that after Farnham, the Danes were besieged in Thorney Isle and 'Earl Æthelred lent his aid to the prince [Edward].'

Meanwhile, the Vikings of Northumbria and East Anglia besieged Exeter, where Alfred fought them. Stuck in Exeter, Alfred sent part of his army to London, where, with reinforcements, they took Hasteinn's camp at Benfleet while he was away on a raid.

It is possible that this whole chronology might be wrong[13] but the point is, chronology aside, that the three leaders were clearly working in concert. It is a reversal of the report that Æthelwulf sent aid to Burgred, for now it shows Æthelred of Mercia coming to the aid of Edward of Wessex.

With Alfred still in Exeter, the other Viking armies gathered at Shoebury in Essex, building a fortress there, and then moving up the Thames where they met reinforcements from Northumbria and East Anglia. They continued along the Severn. They were met at Buttington on the River Severn in modern-day Powys by Æthelred, and the ealdormen of Wiltshire and Somerset. According to the *ASC* 'some portion' of the Welsh people were also there. There was no intense fighting; the combined forces starved the Vikings out until they emerged, weakened, and those who survived fled back to Essex.[14]

The Vikings gathered in Essex, with a large army from Northumbria and East Anglia, left their women, ships and property in East Anglia and occupied the deserted city of Chester. The English besieged them, seizing cattle and burning crops, and starved them out. Æthelred is not named as the leader of the English here, but it is hard to imagine who else it would have been, this far into Mercian territory.

In 894, the *ASC* records that the Vikings left Chester, raided Wales, and then, returning through Northumbria and East Anglia, made their way back to Essex. They then sailed up the Thames and up the Lea, built a fortress, and overwintered there. The army which Alfred had fought at Exeter went home in the same year.

In 895 the English from London and elsewhere marched on the fortress on the Lea but were repulsed. They then built two fortresses lower down the river so that the Vikings couldn't get their ships out, but the Vikings got round this by going overland to Bridgnorth on the Severn and building a fortress there. The Englishmen of London destroyed or removed the ships on the Lea. The Vikings overwintered at Bridgnorth.

Then in 896, the Viking armies all went either into East Anglia or Northumbria, or over the Channel to the Seine.

But, though the armies which had arrived in 892 left in 896, Northumbria and East Anglia were still Viking strongholds and they continued to attack the south coast. Alfred ordered the building of ships, and when six Viking ships harried the Isle of Wight, he sent nine new ships against them.

In 899 Alfred of Wessex died. In his will he left Æthelred a sword worth 100 mancuses, but there is no mention in the document that Æthelred was his son-in-law. This omission could, of course, be accounted for if the will was drawn up before the marriage took place, but then it seems unlikely that he would have bequeathed anything at that stage to a man whom he hardly knew. Probably around the time that Æthelred of Mercia was given control of London, he also married Alfred's daughter, Æthelflæd. It is safe to assume that she was younger than him, by some margin.

There is very little mention of her in the chronicles. Roger of Wendover only says of her marriage that she was 'united to Æthelred, earl of the Mercians.' Asser is clear that she was the firstborn, and it is assumed she was raised somewhere other than the court of Wessex, and this is inferred from Asser's statement about the youngest two children of Alfred and Ealhswith: 'Edward and Ælfthryth (a younger daughter) were at all times fostered at the royal court under the solicitous care of tutors and nurses.' But it is a large leap to assume that the other children were not brought up at the Wessex court, and nowhere does Asser specifically say that Æthelflæd was raised elsewhere. If she were, then Mercia would have been a possibility, since her paternal aunt and her maternal uncle were active at the Mercian court in the years immediately after her birth. One must assume, however, that had she been sent there, she would have returned to Wessex when Burgred and her aunt Æthelswith fled to the Continent in 875.

William of Malmesbury has barely ten lines about her. He says that she refused sex after a difficult labour with her only child, and that she was a spirited heroine who 'assisted' her brother with advice and was of equal service in building cities.

Henry of Huntington proclaimed:

Heroic Elflede! great in martial fame,
A man in valour, woman though in name:
Thee warlike hosts, thee, nature too obey'd,

Conqu'ror o'er both, though born by sex a maid.
Chang'd be thy name, such honour triumphs bring.
A queen by title, but in deeds a king.
Heroes before the Mercian heroine quail'd:
Caesar himself to win such glory fail'd.[15]

Henry was clearly rather taken with her, but he got somewhat muddled when talking about this family. He calls Æthelwold Edward's brother – he wasn't, he was his cousin – and he says that Ealhswith was Edward's wife, when she was his mother. He also seems to think that Æthelred was Æthelflæd's father and that Ælfwynn was her sister, when in fact they were her husband and her daughter respectively.[16]

What we do know about her is remarkable, yet barely remarked upon. Why? Henry of Huntingdon's confusion might be a good place to start. In the translation by Forester of 1853, the editor tells us that, '*The Saxon Chronicle* nowhere tells us who [Æthelflaed] was, except as it describes her to be the lady of the Mercians.' Thus, when Henry of Huntingdon found that she succeeded Æthelred, he had no idea why, and assumed that she was his daughter.[17] The *ASC* does describe her though, as Edward's sister, as does Æthelweard the Chronicler, but he only mentions her once, when he says that 'the king's sister' departed this life. There is no suggestion that she was anyone's wife, much less that she was at any time in charge of Mercia.

Henry of Huntingdon also mentions that Æthelred was infirm. Forester said there was no reason for him to have made this up as a way of explaining her acting as leader before his death, because no mention is made of her having done so. He seemed to think that the province of Mercia was granted to Æthelred and Æthelflæd jointly, à la William and Mary. We need to look for clues elsewhere, to see if she was in fact active politically before her husband's death.

Certainly, the pair had a reputation as joint and just rulers. A record of a court case of the late 890s concerning the rights of an estate showed the pair settling a land claim and respecting the rights of the dead, and it was recorded that 'there was no justice until Æthelred became lord of the Mercians.'[18]

Edward the Elder – though he was not known as such during his lifetime – succeeded Alfred. The first trial of his reign was the rebellion of his cousin, Æthelwold. He was the son of Alfred's elder brother, King Æthelred of Wessex. The assumption must be that he had been too young at the time of his father's death to inherit the kingdom, especially in such turbulent and dangerous times. Initially, Æthelwold took his forces to Wimborne, and holed up there with a nun whom he had kidnapped, stating that he would live there or die. What happened though was that he escaped in the night and went to join the Viking army in Northumbria, who swore allegiance to him as their king.

In 902 Æthelwold and his East Anglian Viking allies harried Mercia and went as far as Cricklade in Wiltshire. When he crossed the Thames into Wessex, Edward chased him, harrying in Essex and East Anglia, 'all their lands between the Dykes and the Ouse, as far north as the fens.' When Edward then ordered a withdrawal, he sent seven messengers to the men of Kent, who lingered behind, counter to his commands. The Danish army then overtook the men of Kent at the – unidentified – Holme. In the ensuing fighting, there were losses on both sides. Three are significant: one being the father of Edward's future wife[19] and the others being Æthelwold himself, and Brihtsige, 'son of the atheling Beornoth.'

As discussed in the previous chapter the alliterative names suggest that here we have members of the 'B' royal family. It might be that Beornoth was a relative of Burgred's but had neither the inclination or the wherewithal to make good his claim against Ceolwulf II and his Viking backers. If so, perhaps his son, Brihtsige, harboured some resentment against Æthelred and saw the chance, when Æthelwold rebelled against Edward, to gain the Mercian throne. This is all conjecture, but the fact that there were still members of the royal Mercian house of fighting age when Æthelred was ealdorman suggests one of two things: either Æthelred was a mighty warlord who kept control of Mercia by military strength, or he was Alfred's puppet. In which case, the timing of this rebellion is pertinent. Perhaps Brihtsige had not yet got the measure of Edward and sought to overthrow a perceived West Saxon yoke.

Coin finds add information to the activity at this time. The Silverdale Hoard, unearthed in 2011, supplemented the knowledge gleaned from studying the coinage of the Cuerdale Hoard. Both were found in Lancashire, and both contained Anglo-Viking coins.[20] The Silverdale Hoard was much smaller but contained two items of specific interest. One was a coin which carried the name *Airdeconut* with the words DNS (*Dominus*) *Rex* on the reverse, hinting that there had been some hitherto unknown – and Christian – Viking king in the closing years of the ninth century. More relevant to this story, though, is the other coin, a silver penny dated to about 900 to 902, and bearing the name ALVVALDVS (*Alwaldus*) Here, perhaps, is proof that Æthelwold really was recognised as king in the north, and that had he not been killed in the battle, he would have continued to remain a very large thorn in Edward's side, possibly installing Brihtsige on the Mercian throne as his under-king.

And what of Æthelred? Despite the *ASC* statement that Æthelwold and his Vikings harried Mercia, it says that it was Edward who chased them and faced them down at the battle of the Holme. Could this be the first indication that Æthelred had been taken ill?

In 906 Edward made peace with the Vikings 'from necessity'. In a few short years the English resistance had withered from a triumvirate to Edward working, seemingly, on his own. Gone are the comments along the lines of 'with the aid of Æthelred, earl of the Mercians' and in 907 an entry merely states that 'Chester was restored.'

By whom? If it was Edward, why not say so? Why, if Æthelred was incapacitated, was he not replaced, or Edward not take direct control? Was he simply too hard-pressed? It seems strange that at this pivotal time, a woman was allowed to lead. And yet, although we have little information, there are precedents for women having direct control of Anglo-Saxon kingdoms: Bebba, who gave her name to the mighty fortress at Bamburgh, Queen Seaxburh, who ruled for a year in Wessex after her husband Cenwalh had died, and Queen Æthelburh, who, according to the *ASC*, in 722 destroyed a fortress at Taunton, which King Ine of Wessex had built.

Æthelred might have been attempting to boost his claim to lead Mercia by marrying a woman who had Mercian royal blood, but this interpretation rests on whether or not it was his choice to marry her, or whether he was pressed upon to do so by Alfred. She was never called a queen by English sources, no coins were issued in her husband's name, or in hers when he died.[21]

The charter evidence shows first Æthelred, then the couple, and then Æthelflæd alone, issuing charters in their own names. S218 is a charter dated 883 in which Æthelred is 'by the inspiration of God's grace endowed and enriched with a portion of the realm of the Mercians.' In another charter, from 884, he is styled, 'by gift of divine grace supported in the rule and lordship of the Mercian people' and there is no reference to King Alfred (S219). This charter is of interest also because of the place where it was drawn up, Risborough in Buckinghamshire, suggesting that the English portion of Mercia extended to very near London, which may provide another hint that the Vikings didn't necessarily have complete control of London up to 886. It offers the possibility that after Ceolwulf's death, Æthelred might have been acknowledged as king, only to swiftly have to acknowledge Alfred's overlordship, much like other sub-kings had done under Mercian kings in previous generations.

S217 is attested by Alfred, Æthelred *dux* and Æthelflæd *conjux* and it confirms that land in Oxfordshire, a border area taken from Mercia by Ecgberht in 823, was back in Mercian control by the time of this grant.[22]

It is clear that Æthelred was more than a 'mere' ealdorman, but also that he was not completely independent of Alfred. We might consider the kings of the *Hwicce*, gradually reduced to the status of ealdormen, although we still have no real evidence that Æthelred was of royal stock. S346 styles him as a sub-king: 'Alfred, king of the English and the Saxons, and Æthelred, *subregulus et patricius Merciorum*' but is not generally considered to be authentic.

S221, dated 901 shows Æthelred and Æthelflæd, rulers of Mercia, granting to the community of the church of Much Wenlock land in Shropshire and a gold chalice weighing 30 mancuses in honour of Abbess Mildburg. It shows that the couple were still joint rulers in 901 and in the early years of Edward's reign, but Simon Keynes has argued that charter and coin evidence shows they were operating 'from the start' under Edward's overall control.[23] S367 is a charter of Edward's, stating that the couple held rulership and power over the people of the Mercians under the aforesaid king: '*qui tunc principatum et potestatem gentis Merciorum sub prædicto rege tenuerunt.*'

Yet other charters show the two of them transferring the 'rights and claims which would normally denote the regal status of the grantor, but only in those charters which show grants to the church of Worcester.'[24] The bishop of Worcester was Werferth, not only a close friend of the couple but a frequent visitor to the court at Wessex.

The extant charters provoke as many questions as they answer. Perhaps those charters which related to Worcester and did not need the endorsement of Wessex were in what might be termed 'free Mercia'.[25] In S224 Æthelflæd is termed 'Lady of the Mercians' and she is never accorded the title *regina*. Her status seems to have been an anomaly. Clearly she was in charge of Mercia, certainly after her husband's death if not beforehand, yet she was seemingly of a lower status than a king's wife. And whatever status she had was evidently not transferable to her daughter, at least not in the eyes of the West Saxons.

Charter evidence only takes us so far. It is clear, though, that for some time before his death, Æthelred was in some way incapacitated.

The Irish fragmentary annal known as the *Three Fragments* records that when Chester was overrun, messengers were sent to the 'King of the Saxons, who was in a disease and on the point of death.' It suggests it was his wife who held sway at this point.

For the year 908, Roger of Wendover says the city of Leicester was restored, 'by the care of Æthelred, duke of the Mercians, and his wife [Æthelflæd].'

Neither the *ASC* nor the *Mercian Register* records his illness, but there is no mention of him in 909 or 910; in 909 Edward gathered West Saxon and Mercian forces and went harrying into Northumbria. Again, there is no mention of Æthelred.

In 910 the *ASC* says the Northumbrians broke peace, although they may have been reacting to Edward's campaign of the previous year. They ravaged Mercia and he sent an army of West Saxons and Mercians. Æthelweard the Chronicler tells us that the Northumbrians had crossed the Severn at Bridgnorth when the combined English forces met them. There was a battle, either at Tettenhall or Wednesfield (the two locations are less than 4 miles apart, both equidistant from Wolverhampton). It is often assumed that the Mercian forces were led by Æthelred, and that his death the following year was the result of injuries sustained in the battle, which was a victory for the English. But his name disappears from all the sources long before this and is clearly mentioned in earlier campaigns. There would be no reason to exclude his name from Tettenhall, leading to the conclusion that he was not present at the battle.

For the sources are clear; Æthelred died in 911. And yet, the building of the fortress at the unidentified *Bremesbyrig* is attributed to Æthelflæd, his wife, and this appears to have taken place in 910. Henry of Huntingdon doesn't say who restored Chester, or fought at Tettenhall, but does credit Æthelflæd for *Bremesbyrig*.

When Æthelred died, Edward took London and Oxford under his direct control, according to the *ASC*. Why was he happy to leave Mercia 'proper' to his sister?

Perhaps it was taking him some time to secure his reign. Viking activity was strong, and early on in his reign he had been forced to counter a rival bid for his throne. Perhaps there were other similar incidents. It is possible that by taking Mercia under his direct control, he would have been spreading himself too thinly. But if that were the rationale, why not appoint an ealdorman to rule the province for him in his name? To have a woman leader was not unprecedented but it was still rare. Was it better to have his royal relative there until such time as he wanted to take over? Was he staking his claim and protecting his inheritance? He did not allow her daughter to succeed: Æthelflæd was the daughter and sister of kings but her daughter was not. It could also be that personal qualities came into play. Edward was clearly happy to work with his sister, and as has been so often the case, we cannot always know the family dynamics, the personalities of those involved.

Of the ealdormen of Mercia, we know that by the 890s only three signed charters: Æthelfrith, who also held lands in Wessex, and was to become the founder of a powerful family; Æthelwulf, and Ealhhelm. It is sometimes thought that Ealhhelm was the father of an eminent and somewhat notorious tenth-century ealdorman of Mercia, who came to prominence in the reign of King Edgar, but the connection cannot be proved. There was also a newcomer, Alfred.

It is hard to know how politically and militarily active Æthelflæd was, or to what degree men of the Mercian court were making decisions and taking action on her behalf. Her status is hard to establish, even when her husband was alive, but clearly she was considered a ruler in her own right, independent of a husband, although not necessarily independent of her brother's overall authority.[26]

We have had glimpses of 'warrior women' in Mercia over the preceding centuries. Whilst there is no evidence that she fought, Penda's wife was given the task of ensuring the safety of the young hostage Ecgfrith, son of Oswiu of Northumbria. The anonymous Lindisfarne *Life of Cuthbert* records the wife of that same Ecgfrith accompanying him on his campaign against the Picts, and awaiting news of the battle at Carlisle,[27] but there is nothing to suggest that these women actually took part in the fighting. Likewise we cannot know for sure that Æthelflæd wielded a sword, or even led Mercian troops. The *Mercian Register* focuses on her building programme, although the succinct reporting might suggest that this was nothing unusual for a lady of her status. While in the *ASC* she is described only as Edward's sister, in the *Mercian Register*, she is styled Lady of the Mercians (*Myrcna hlæfdige*) which, though not precisely definable, is the exact equivalent of her husband's status as lord of the Mercians (*Myrcna hlaford*).

So, what is the *Mercian Register*, sometimes known as the *Annals of Æthelflæd*? It is, or rather they, are a series of entries contained in three of the vernacular chronicles of the *ASC*[28] and it/they concentrate exclusively on Æthelflæd. The *Mercian Register* records her death with the words 'the eighth year in which she had held power with right lordship'. The same word, *anweald*, is used for the power of which her daughter was deprived in 918. There are only two references made of Æthelred, once at his death in 911, and once as Ælfwynn's father. Edward is barely mentioned, not with regard to his taking London and Oxford, or even in relation to removing Ælfwynn from power after her mother's death. The focus is on Æthelflæd's role as ruler.

The A *Chronicle* of the *ASC* is probably a 'court' chronicle. It contains strong references to Edward, and to his Mercian family, and may even have been designed in such a way as to issue a warning to those who might support the bloodline of Æthelwold; Brihtsige is called the *son* of an atheling, rather than an atheling. So it might not so much have been ignoring the Mercians, as justifying Edward's claims, and acknowledging Alfred's inheritance.

Æthelflæd's position, with a foot in both camps as it were, being the wife and widow of Mercia and the daughter and sister of Wessex, might distract from the fact that there were ongoing tensions between the two kingdoms. Mercia had not gone away, and those tensions were to come to the fore at least twice more upon royal deaths. The first of these was the occasion of Edward's death, when the Mercians supported Athelstan over his half-brother in Wessex.[29]

Pauline Stafford argued that the annals were probably contemporaneous and can be seen almost as a dialogue. Was the *Mercian Register* based on a longer chronicle, now lost? The reference to Æthelred's daughter might suggest that he was far more important and featured more heavily in the original text.[30]

In November 911 Edward built a fortress at Hertford and the following year he took an army into Essex and built a fortress at Witham. Æthelflæd, too, was building, at *Scergeat* (unidentified) and Bridgnorth. In 913 she built fortresses at Tamworth and Stafford.

The identity of the enemy was changing. As early as 855 Vikings had been campaigning in the Wrekin area, and since Anglesey was attacked at the same time, it seems likely that these raiders were Irish-Norse. Norse Vikings had been expelled from Dublin in 902. In 914 the battle of Corbridge took place, where the Dublin Viking, Ragnall, defeated the Scots and the English Northumbrians. In that same year an enemy fleet came from Brittany ravaging Wales and the Southwest. Edward built a fortress at Buckingham and received submissions from Bedford and Northampton, meanwhile his sister built fortresses at Eddisbury (in Cheshire) and Warwick. In 915 she built fortresses at Chirbury (modern-day Shropshire), *Wearburh* (unidentified) and Runcorn, thus strengthening the border against the Irish-Norse in Wirral and Lancashire. The following year she sent, or accompanied, an army into Brycheiniog. The *Mercian Register* tells us:

In this year before midsummer, on 16 June, the day of the festival of St Quiricus the Martyr, Abbot Ecgberht, who had done nothing to deserve it, was slain together with his companions. Three days later Æthelflæd sent an army into Wales and stormed *Brecenanmere* [at Llangorse Lake near Brecon] and there captured the wife of the king and thirty-three other persons.

There is no detail offered about the abbot, so we cannot know why he was so dear to her that she was prepared to avenge his life in such a forceful manner.

The king, whose wife was captured, was Tewdr, king of Brycheiniog. There are two contenders, and both are mentioned in Asser's *Life* of Alfred as having submitted to Alfred. Alfred died in 899 so either of these men could, in theory, have still been alive and militarily active in 916.

One is the father of Elise, while the other is listed as Tewdwr ap Griffi ab Elise, who, as Teowdor, *subregulus*, witnessed a charter of King Athelstan in 934 (S425). The Welsh system of patronymics suggests that he must have been the grandson of Elise, although Kari Maund names him as Tewdwr ab Elise, suggesting a closer consanguineal relationship.[31] It is unknown why the abbot should have been killed, or why a king who had submitted to Alfred the Great chose to anger Alfred's daughter in this way. Perhaps he fancied his chances against a perceived weak female ruler and perhaps there were hostilities between the English and the Welsh that have gone unrecorded.[32] Maybe these are separate to the main thrust of the hostilities and the antagonism between the Welsh and the Mercians was continuing, but going largely unrecorded by the *ASC*, which would have had little interest in such matters. We do know that 'a great raiding ship-army … raided in Wales … where it suited them and took Cameleac, bishop in Archenfield and then King Edward ransomed him back for forty pounds.'

In 917 Edward built fortresses at Towcester and *Wigingamere* (unidentified) and received submissions from Northampton, East Anglia and Cambridge. Meanwhile Æthelflæd took the borough of Derby – one of the Five Boroughs – and lost four thegns who were 'dear to her'. Details of this important retaking of one of the Five Boroughs are not recorded in the main part of the *ASC*.[33]

The activity was frenetic, and it is notable that this level of co-operation was not evident earlier. Had Æthelflæd been staying close to home while her husband was ill? There is no doubt that the pace of the building speeded up after 911.

In 918 the second battle of Corbridge saw Ragnall once more pitched against the Scots and the English Northumbrians. The *Three Fragments* says Æthelflæd directed the battle, ordering her troops to cut down the trees where the 'pagans' were hiding. 'In this manner did the queen kill all the pagans, so that her fame spread abroad in every direction.' Thus we are led to believe that as well as partnering her brother in an extensive and well-co-ordinated attack on the Danes, she was conducting her own campaign against the Norse.

Æthelflæd took Leicester 'peacefully' and received pledges of loyalty from the people of York, possibly in connection with the aggression of Ragnall, while Edward took Stamford and Nottingham.

Was she literally leading these armies; if so, where did she learn to do this? Is it conceivable that she was no more than a consort before her husband's death, or were they acting in concert? If so, it was unprecedented. Roger of Wendover claimed that Queen Seaxburh of the West Saxons was expelled because 'they would not go to war under the conduct of a woman,' and we don't hear of any other leaders' wives acting in this way. It is yet another aspect of her 'reign' which is difficult to interpret.

The building campaign was not random, though. Her fortifications at Tamworth, Stafford and Warwick would have been designed to defend eastern Mercia, but would also have put pressure on the Danish armies in the midlands, and probably led to the submission of those at Bedford to Edward. Likewise, Edward's assault on Northampton would have eased the way for her at Derby and Leicester, although the main *ASC* credits only Edward, and omits any mention of the Mercian contribution.

The situation was unique. Clearly Edward was the dominant partner, but there is no evidence to suggest that his sister was unhappy about the arrangement. He seemed disinclined to put another ealdorman in her husband's place. Could it be that the sibling bond was strong? If both believed, rightly, that the greatest priority was to regain Danish Mercia, then it is credible that they were happy to work in harmony towards a common goal. We can only speculate as to what her intentions might have been afterwards, had she survived.

On 12 June 918, Æthelflæd died at Tamworth. Her body was taken to Gloucester for burial, unsurprisingly, for this is where her husband was buried, and where she'd had the remains of St Oswald translated. Gloucester was clearly an important centre for her. It adds strength to the suggestion that her husband might have been from the territory of the *Hwicce*. It is also worth noting that her body was not sent back to Wessex for burial although Pauline Stafford suggested that she 'never lost her identity as a West Saxon princess' and was buried 'in the east porticos of a new minster founded on the model of her brother's foundation at Winchester.'[34] But how much of a statement is it, that she was buried in Mercia? It could equally be argued that it was natural to bury her in the territory where she had ruled, and where her husband had been laid to rest and it seems questionable that the practice was to send royal women back to their country of birth for burial. It is unlikely that her body was embalmed[35] so, and especially given the time of year, no doubt it was a speedy procession from Tamworth to Gloucester.

The *Annals of Ulster* recorded the death of the 'most famous queen of the Saxons' and the *Annales Cambriae* recorded that 'Queen Æthelflæd died'. Is it possible though that they used the royal title because they simply didn't know what else to call her? The *Mercian Register* says that the men of York offered their submission and their allegiance in return for protection against Ragnall. His seizure of York the year after her death suggests that they were right to be worried. Is this a measure of her authority, or just the recording of a threatened community pleading for help from a stronger one? Had the men of York asked Edward for aid, it would scarcely have been remarked upon. Perhaps the modern interpretation seeks to mark as unusual something which at the time was considered a simple fact.

In December 918, Æthelflæd's daughter was taken into Wessex. The *Mercian Register* complains that she was 'deprived of all authority'. Why was Edward content to let his sister govern Mercia, but not her daughter, and why did it take him six months to supplant her; was it a simple case that the daughter did not match the mother in terms of ability?

As Sir Frank Stenton pointed out, it cannot be assumed that the Mercian lords would just roll over and accept this.[36] As the Danish armies fell away, they might have felt free to give their allegiance somewhere other than Wessex; is this what prompted Edward to seize Tamworth?

F. T. Wainwright believed that Edward didn't dare upset the Mercian nationalists, and that Æthelflæd's achievements were watered down so as to keep the separatists from rising up.[37] But this does not explain what changed in the six months during which Edward left Mercia well alone. If there were, indeed, a Mercian separatist movement, removing their figurehead in June or December would presumably have been equally aggravating. The other side of the argument is that her victories overshadowed Edward's and that, in particular, John of Worcester's Mercian bias may have had the effect of highlighting her achievements and minimising Edward's.[38]

Was there overt hostility towards the Mercians? Interestingly it has been suggested that Edward might have been named after his maternal grandmother, Eadburh, of whom Asser wrote in glowing terms.[39] S1442 concerns the responsibilities of her son Æthelwulf towards the monastery at Winchcombe and might be an indication that she was connected to the Kings Cenwulf and Ceolwulf I who claimed Winchcombe as a royal possession. If Edward was named after her then it might confirm a tendency to nurture connections with Mercia.

And what of Athelstan, who ultimately succeeded his father Edward the Elder, initially in Mercia and then in Wessex? William of Malmesbury tells us that he was brought up in Mercia. Was there a clear statement of intent when Edward left Athelstan to be brought up there? If, as Wainwright suggested, Æthelflæd knew what Edward had in mind,[40] then she seems not to have been opposed to it, or was it the case that she was resigned to it? However, Athelstan was not Edward's recognised heir – his younger half-brother succeeded in Wessex – so was it a foregone conclusion that he would get the governorship of Mercia? Janet Nelson quoted Patrick Wormald who 'remained convinced' that the Second Ordo was first used for Athelstan's coronation and that the theme of two peoples was apt 'in the aftermath of Edward's vigorous suppression of Mercian (semi) independence.'[41]

What happened after Edward's death is well known to us. It does not explain, however, why Edward acted the way he did in 918. It has been suggested[42] that his sister's untimely death left much of the work undone and that Edward needed to move quickly to make sure of Mercian co-operation, and to prevent an upsurge of nationalism. The problem with pressing this argument is that there does not seem to have been anyone who would have led such a rebellion, as we shall see in Chapter Nine, unless the ealdormen were prepared to stand behind Ælfwynn. If so, why did they not make a stand in June 918, and indeed why acquiesce to Edward's actions in December?

It is clear that there is a bias towards the West Saxons in the *ASC*. But is it fair to say that it is therefore automatically anti-Mercian? It is possible that the chroniclers weren't so much anti-Mercian, as simply recording what they knew[43] and that as we've seen, the politics of Mercia might not have been quite so unified. The epithet of 'foolish king's thegn' given to Ceolwulf II might not have been so much anti-Mercian as pro-Burgred and Æthelred. Of course, we cannot expect Asser's *Life* of Alfred to be anything other than biased towards its subject; written by a Welshman, and during his patron's lifetime, it could hardly have been otherwise. He is not completely effusive though, dwelling on Alfred's illnesses, and seeming to disapprove of the West Saxon custom of not allowing kings' wives to be called 'queen'.

The *Mercian register*, of course, goes the other way. It records Æthelflæd's achievements, but doesn't really put them into the wider context, or relate them to the campaigns of Edward.[44]

With the *ASC* main chronicles and the *Mercian Register* offering such opposing insights, it would be easy to assume that, family connections aside, these two kingdoms of Mercia and the West Saxons had little to unify them. A centuries-old situation which saw the lack, or loss, of written evidence in Mercia adds to the notion that here was a country playing 'catch-up' when it came to religion and culture.

In fact, far from being a question of Mercian power slipping away under the dominance of a stronger Wessex, there is evidence that many leading Mercians were at Alfred's court. His wife, Ealhswith, a Mercian, would presumably have brought Mercian ladies and/or attendants with her, and Asser clearly knew her mother, Eadburh, which suggests that she too was a frequent visitor. Ealhswith's brother, Æthelwulf, was a leading Mercian ealdorman and with her son-in-law, Æthelred, would no doubt have attended when 'all the councillors of the *Gewisse* – West Saxons – and of the Mercians' were obliged to meet.[45]

But it was not only relatives who made up the Mercian visitors to the West Saxon court. Bishop Werferth of Worcester was granted his bishopric during the reign of King Burgred of Mercia, and in 874 he received a grant of privileges from Ceolwulf II, freeing the diocese from the 'charge of feeding the king's horses, in return for spiritual benefits and the lease of four lives of land at Daylesford, Worcestershire,'[46] yet he was also the recipient of a gift of 100 mancuses of gold in Alfred's will. He probably entered Alfred's entourage in the early 880s, and he translated the *Dialogues* of Pope Gregory into English at the king's command. Asser called him a man 'thoroughly learned in holy writings.' He was described as a 'friend' of Æthelred and Æthelflæd in a charter dated between 884 and 901 – *eac for Wærferðes biscopes bene heora freondas* (S223) – concerning the fortification of Worcester with which he was directly involved. William of Malmesbury noted that 'since there was no good scholar in his kingdom [Alfred] sent for Werferth.' He was not the only learned Mercian at Alfred's court, however.

Plegmund, archbishop of Canterbury, was one more in a long line of native Mercians to hold the archbishopric. He was instrumental in subdividing the huge dioceses of Wessex, Winchester and Sherborne.[47] The preface to the translation of Pope Gregory's *Pastoral Care* acknowledges the help of four men, including Plegmund. He is the man assumed to be responsible for improving standards of literacy, and in 898 he attended a meeting, the Conference of Chelsea[48] at which Æthelred, Æthelflæd and Bishop Werferth were also present, to discuss plans for London following its recovery in 886. Asser described him as an 'estimable man richly endowed with learning.' Along with others, he and Werferth were summoned by Alfred who 'showered them with many honours and entitlements' and 'the king's desire for knowledge increased steadily and was satisfied by the learning and wisdom of all four men.'[49]

It is not surprising that Alfred should have turned to Mercia; there is a suggestion that there was a tradition for what Simon Keynes calls 'intellectual achievement.'[50] It is clear that Alfred used Offa's laws when promulgating his own, but there is also poetry which dates from a similar time and may well be Mercian in origin. The name Cynewulf is spelled out in runes in the texts of four Old English poems, all concerned with religious themes, and apart from the works of Bede and Cædmon they are the only surviving works which can be attributed to a named author.[51]

The Old English translation of Bede is thought to have been made by a Mercian contemporary of Alfred's.

Æthelflæd was associated with more than a number of saints' cults, and perhaps revived them after the demise of the Mercian royal house.[52] As mentioned above, she and her husband gave a gold chalice to the house at Wenlock in honour of St Mildburg, daughter of Merewalh, king of the *Magonsæte*: 'Æthelred and Æthelflæd, rulers of Mercia, to the community of the church of Much Wenlock ... a grant of ten hides ... they also grant a gold chalice weighing 30 mancuses in honour of Abbess Mildburg' (S221) and she arranged for the translation of the bones of St Oswald from Bardney (where they had been placed under the instruction of Osthryth wife of King Æthelred). She was probably also responsible for the establishment of the relics of St Werburg, daughter of King Wulfhere, at Chester. There were other associations, but it is a nice closing of the circle that the last independent ruler of Mercia honoured the granddaughters of Penda.

It is an interesting point that we have little more evidence for the career of Æthelflæd than we do for earlier periods, but there seems to be a lot more to say. We wouldn't know anything about her achievements were it not for the *Mercian Register* and the odd oblique reference in the Irish and Welsh annals, but the pendulum should not swing too far the other way; it shouldn't take away from Edward's achievements.

We cannot know, but Æthelflæd must have been a remarkable woman of strong character. There may be earlier precedents for female rule, but not quite in such challenging circumstances. That Edward left her in charge, firstly after her husband's incapacitation, and then again after his death, when he could have marched in and brought Mercia under his direct control, surely tells us a lot about her and their relationship. Timing is frequently important, and Edward's reluctance to leave her daughter in charge, possibly suggesting that Ælfwynn was of a lower calibre, might also have been connected with the fact that by the time of his sister's death, he now had adult sons.

It is hard to discern whether his sister had anyone guiding her. Ealdorman Æthelfrith, who married into Æthelflæd's Mercian family, also held lands in Wessex. His son became one of King Athelstan's most trusted and influential advisors, so it may be safe to assume that Æthelfrith himself was influential. There was another prominent ealdorman, Ealhhelm, but Æthelflæd must surely have been making a lot of decisions herself, and her brother was clearly content to let her, if indeed he had a choice. He took London and Oxford away from her, but he left the rest. This may have been because of their strategic importance, and to take the rest might have been beyond his military capabilities at that juncture.

Wainwright was of the opinion that Mercia would have been rejuvenated under her and her husband after the failures of Burgred and Ceolwulf. So, if Æthelred was Alfred's puppet, can we assume that the Mercians were happy about that? Or does it strengthen the argument that he wasn't a puppet, but very much considered a leader in his own right? Whatever the 'lamentable failures' of Burgred and the 'national degradation' under Ceolwulf,[53] it is hard to think that Mercian nationalism would have just evaporated. Did London only submit to Alfred on the promise that Æthelred would govern there?

Depending on which historian one reads, Edward destroyed Mercian independence, Æthelflæd's contribution was deliberately suppressed, it shouldn't be assumed that Mercia was politically subordinate to Wessex, and that hers and her husband's sovereignty have been deliberately airbrushed from the history books.[54]

It is probably enough to say that while they acknowledged the overlordship of Wessex – as other kingdoms had done towards Mercia – Æthelred and Æthelflæd were operating fairly independently within Mercia. Whether and how much things changed with the succession of Edward is more a question for a book about the kings of Wessex and the debate about the nature of that kingship, be it of the Saxons, the Anglo-Saxons, or the English.

We will see in coming chapters that however the kings were styled, the notion of the kingdom of Mercia remained, if only as a training ground for future kings, and with divisions continuing into the eleventh century.

Finally, what of Ælfwynn? A charter of 904 (S1280) includes her as a third life on a lease of land from 'Werferth, bishop, and the community at Worcester, to Æthelred and Æthelflæd, their lords ... for their lives and that of Ælfwynn, their daughter' in Worcestershire, so perhaps she was based there in her teens.[55]

Charter evidence suggests that she moved up the witness list order considerably after her father's death. Maggie Bailey has pointed out that Athelstan did not witness the Mercian grants at this point, and thus perhaps was not being considered as a future Mercian leader.[56] We do not have any contemporary evidence that Athelstan was fostered at the Mercian court.

There is one other charter, S535, dated 948, which shows King Eadred granting to 'Ælfwynn, a religious woman' land in Kent. It has sometimes been assumed that this woman was the daughter of Æthelflæd, and further, that there is a connection with the son of Ealdorman Æthelfrith. His son became so powerful that he was known as Athelstan Half-king, and such was his closeness to the royal family that the future King Edgar was sent, when a small boy, to be fostered with the Half-king's wife, whose name was Ælfwynn. She was a woman of wealth, whose estates were gifted by her youngest son for the founding of Ramsey Abbey. Is it possible that she was named foster mother to Edgar because of her royal Mercian connections; that she was the daughter of Æthelflæd, Lady of the Mercians? Though not common, it is not an incredibly rare name, and it would be unwise to assume that Ælfwynn, daughter of Æthelflæd can be connected either with the wife of the Half-king or of the religious woman mentioned in the charter of 948.[57]

If the argument were to be pressed, it would be more likely that Ælfwynn ended her days in a nunnery, stripped of political power. The kingdom of Mercia ceased to exist, and this is usually where the tales of Mercia stop, but its history continued, and its leaders were to prove influential at pivotal points in the rest of the tenth and the first half of the eleventh centuries.

CHAPTER 9

The Formation of 'England': Mercia Fades

The last entry in the *Mercian Register* records that, in 924, 'King Edward died at Farndon, in Mercia, and his son Ælfweard died very soon after at Oxford ... and Athelstan was chosen by the Mercians as king and consecrated at Kingston.'[1] Athelstan would not be the last king of Wessex to begin his tenure in Mercia. Is it the case that Mercia was a 'training ground' for kings? In this instance, it is tempting to conclude that if there were any intent, it was that Athelstan was given Mercia and that Ælfweard was given the pick of the crop i.e. Wessex, because the latter was the legitimate son. The assumption is that Athelstan was living in Mercia; if so, we must wonder why. Was he fostered when Edward married again? There is no contemporary evidence that he grew up in Mercia.[2] It also wouldn't be the last time that one of two royal brothers met an untimely death, which allowed the other to accede to the other's territory, but as always, there is no suggestion in the chronicles of foul play.

But are we reading the chronicles correctly? The *Mercian Register* does not say that the country was split, only that the Mercians chose Athelstan after Ælfweard died. The fact that Athelstan then met resistance in Wessex might point to the fact that he was a claimant put forward as a rival to Ælfweard's successor and not that Wessex and Mercia were ruled separately for those brief few days after Edward the Elder's death.

The *ASC* says that Edward died and Athelstan succeeded him. Edward died in Farndon, which is 9 miles from Chester, deep in northwest Mercia. He had been conducting a campaign against the men of Chester, who had allied with the Welsh against him. Simeon of Durham said that Athelstan was with him when he died, and that Edward handed the kingdom over to him. Yet a charter of 901, recording an 'important gathering' at Southampton, shows Ælfweard taking precedence over Athelstan.[3]

151

Of course, we might know a great deal more about the succession arrangements, and the true strength of feeling in Mercia – and their 'fire power'– if Ælfweard had lived.

William of Malmesbury mentions virtually nothing about Ælfweard, though he does repeat the assertion that Athelstan was born of a concubine. He says that Athelstan's grandfather, Alfred, had given him 'a scarlet cloak, a belt studded with diamonds, and a Saxon sword with a golden scabbard. Next he had provided that he should be educated in the court of Æthelflæd his daughter, and of his son-in-law Æthelred; so that, having been brought up in expectations of succeeding to the kingdom, by the tender care of his aunt and of this celebrated prince[4] and, after the death of his father, and decease of his brother, he was crowned at Kingston.'

Mercian acceptance of Athelstan implies that the Mercians were happy with events post-918. This may not be the case. Although the two kingdoms of Mercia and Wessex had co-operated from the reigns of Æthelwulf and Burgred, and during the earlier alliance with Offa and his son-in-law Beorhtric, they had a much longer history of antipathy.

Perhaps Edward's takeover was not inevitable. In 918, the English position was strong, but by 919 the Dublin-York Vikings held Northumbria and perhaps Mercia chose between a rock and a hard place with Edward.[5]

In the first half of 918, Edward began building a fortress at Stamford and took back the town, the third of the Five Boroughs to go back into English hands. After his sister's death he took Nottingham. The *ASC* reported that 'all the people who had settled in Mercia, both Danish and English, submitted to him.' Coin evidence shows that Lincoln appears to have remained in Viking hands.[6]

Edward had been minting coins in Wessex and Mercia and it seems that as far as he was concerned, he was already king in Mercia. A charter of 903 (S367) shows that he had authority over the Lord and Lady of the Mercians: 'King Edward, with Æthelred and Æthelflæd of Mercia, at the request of Æthelfrith, *dux*, renews the charter of a grant ... at Monks Risborough, Bucks.' The Mercians seem to have had a different perspective, for, as we have seen in the previous chapter, the *Mercian Register* makes it clear that after her mother's death, Ælfwynn was deprived of her 'authority'.

The Welsh, no doubt, would have been delighted. If Edward was a king who could take over Mercia, then he was a man they could deal with. The leading Welsh princes submitted to Edward. The *ASC* says that the smaller princes followed suit: 'And all the race of the Welsh sought to have him as lord.' It has been suggested, on the other hand, that the Welsh were not necessarily so enamoured of Athelstan.[7]

Towards the end of 918 Edward ordered a Mercian army to build a fortress at Manchester. The Danelaw south of the Humber was under his control, but Ragnall attacked York in 919 and Sihtric, his brother, stormed Davenport in Cheshire in 920.

Whatever the Mercians felt about being ruled by Edward, no doubt Athelstan was a more palatable proposition. After all, if he had been fostered there, he would have been familiar with the Mercian nobility and it seems inconceivable that he would not have been present at some of the skirmishes between the Mercians and the Vikings during his aunt's 'reign' and then his father's operations in the north and west. Was he there, though? Do we have any evidence of this?

'In Mercia … Athelstan had become a familiar figure, thanks partly to his involvement in military campaigns against the Danes,'[8] yet there is no mention of him in the campaigns in the *ASC*. But if he was thirty when he became king, then it is reasonable to suppose that he would have been fighting, but whether that was alongside his father in his campaigns, or assisting the Mercians in theirs, we can't be sure.

Sarah Foot, writing in 2011, was of the opinion that in view of his father's new marriage, it would have made sense for him to go to Mercia, but then William of Malmesbury would have known that too, and was, as she cites David Dumville as saying, 'a treacherous witness'.[9] But the opposition Athelstan faced in Wessex – from his half-brother Edwin – would suggest that he was indeed an outsider.

Athelstan was not crowned until 925. It is possible that the delay hints at some unrest, even a revolt, but there is some evidence to suggest that later coronations in the tenth century were also delayed – Æthelred Unræd in 978/9, for example – and they weren't always even recorded, so we have no idea about some of them. Perhaps there was some resentment amongst those who were in support of Ælfwynn, and who felt that with Edward's passing here was a realistic chance for a successful uprising.

There were hints of conflict with Athelstan's half-brother, Edwin. William of Malmesbury records a conspiracy to have Athelstan blinded, because of objections to his illegitimacy, a conspiracy led by a certain Alfred and on behalf of Athelstan's half-brother, Edwin. It is not impossible that after Ælfweard's death, whilst the Mercians chose Athelstan, the West Saxons chose Edwin; as full brother of Ælfweard his legitimacy seems not to have been in doubt. Later in the century the Mercians would choose one king over his brother in Wessex, and it may have been that, for a time, the country was divided. Edwin died at sea, and Athelstan was allegedly to blame, for which William of Malmesbury claims he served a seven-year penance to atone for his wrongdoing in banishing Edwin, and put to death the man who had implicated Edwin, thus causing Athelstan to exile his brother.

Whatever the truth of this story, and even William of Malmesbury had his doubts about its authenticity, it is unlikely to have delayed the coronation. Edwin witnessed a charter of Athelstan's in 933,[10] so was alive for some time after Athelstan's succession. However, Folcwin, the deacon of St Bertin's, writing in the tenth century, referred to Edwin as a king, which may offer a clue to the succession struggles that might have been ongoing after Edward the Elder's death.[11]

In 926 Athelstan gave his sister in marriage to Sihtric of York, but Sihtric died the following year. The E version of the *Chronicle* notes that Athelstan drove one Guthfrith out, while D says that he succeeded to the kingdom of the Northumbrians and that he brought under his rule 'all the kings who were on this island.' This submission occurred during a meeting at Eamont in Cumbria. The *ASC* gives the date as 12 July. After this meeting, Athelstan began to be styled *rex Anglorum,* king of [all] the English. It may be, though, that rather than a submission, this meeting was Athelstan's attempt to receive recognition of his lordship over Northumbria.[12]

In 937 Athelstan and his brother, Edmund, won the battle of *Brunanburh*, commemorated by a poem in the *ASC*. *Brunanburh* has not been conclusively identified – Simeon of Durham called it *Wendun* – but we know that during the battle five young kings were slain, seven of the earls of Olaf, sometimes Anlaf, Guthfrithson were killed, Olaf was driven back to Dublin and Constantine returned to Scotland. Simeon says that Athelstan put to flight, 'Olaf with 615 ships, and also Constantine, king of the Scots, and the king of the Cumbrians with all their host.' Henry of Huntingdon added the curious detail that the Mercians 'hurled their sharp darts.' It was a decisive victory, but perhaps celebrations that Northumbria had been incorporated into the kingdom of England as easily as had apparently Mercia, were premature.

We must presume that there were Mercians among Athelstan's army, but there is little detail about the ealdormen of this period. In the ninth century, each shire of Wessex had an ealdorman, but by the reign of Athelstan the districts managed by each had grown larger.[13] Twenty-nine ealdormen witnessed his surviving charters, the names being a fairly even spread of English and Scandinavian,[14] but never more than fifteen appear on any given charter. A pattern was forming and continued, as the numbers of ealdormen grew smaller, their areas of land grew bigger, and their power increased accordingly. However, the heydays of the powerful earls would come later in the tenth century. During the reigns of Athelstan and his two successors, his half-brothers Edmund and Eadred, there were no significant ealdormen attesting charters.

The Lady Æthelflæd had probably been ably assisted by men such as Æthelfrith, who had lands in both Mercia and Wessex and was the founder of an influential dynasty. His son became so powerful during the reign of King Athelstan that he was known as Athelstan Half-king, but his power base was East Anglia. Of the Mercians, Ealhhelm appears to have faithfully served during the time of Æthelred and Æthelflæd and a man named Ealhhelm attested between 940 and 951. He was also the founder of a powerful dynasty, this time based in Mercia, but of Ealhhelm himself, we know little, save to say that he almost certainly is not, despite the rarity of the name, the same Ealhhelm who served Æthelflæd. For this man to have been active before her death in 918, yet also have a son who was probably aged around twenty in 956, seems implausible.[15]

The career of Athelstan Half-king will be explored in the next chapter, but it does seem that the creation of powerful ealdormen happened in King Athelstan's reign. It may be that it was his way of dealing with the greatly expanded kingdom. It is possible that he divided the area previously known as Mercia into two: the western province, incorporating the dioceses of Lichfield, Worcester and Hereford, and the eastern province, less easily defined in terms of dioceses, bordered by the Thames and reaching as far as Lincoln, and including Cambridge and Northampton. This area became known as East Anglia but was occasionally called East Mercia. This too, would have repercussions.[16]

Uhtred, an ealdorman of northwest Mercia, last witnessed a document in 934.[17] For the rest of Athelstan's reign, there are no surviving attestations of Mercian ealdormen of royal diplomas. The northern dioceses are also under-represented during this period, suggesting that perhaps in the last years of the reign there was a decrease in power over the area.

In a few short months after Athelstan's death in 939, the Northumbrians were, according to the *ASC*, 'false to their pledges' and led forces into Mercia, overrunning the Five Boroughs, occupying Tamworth and taking high-status prisoners.[18]

Athelstan had not married, and was succeeded by his half-brother, Edmund, who was the son of Edward the Elder and his third wife, Eadgifu of Kent. Edmund had fought alongside Athelstan at the battle of *Brunanburh* and had already proved his military skills. Now he would be forced to use them again and his reign would be an exhausting series of struggles to regain the territories so recently won back from the Vikings. As Sir Frank Stenton pointed out, Edward the Elder's achievements in winning the recognition of his overlordship 'from English and Danes between Thames and Humber' and from 'English, Danes and Northmen from Northumbria' was nearly undone by Olaf Guthfrithson's adding the shires between the Humber and Watling Street to his kingdom of York.[19]

Edmund was married twice, first to Ælfgifu, by whom he had two sons, who would each become kings in their time, and then to Æthelflæd of Damerham, whose will is extant and who went on to marry a leading Mercian ealdorman.[20]

When Edmund succeeded, he appointed three ealdormen, with Æthelwold, son of Athelstan Half-king, receiving Kent, Sussex and Surrey, Ealhhelm appointed to central Mercia, while a man named Æthelmund was appointed to northwest Mercia, staying in office until his death in 965. He regularly witnessed the charters of not only King Edmund but his successor Eadred, and after 952 he was the only Mercian ealdorman on the witness lists, apparently controlling those areas of Mercia not under the control of Athelstan Half-king. He dropped down to fifth or sixth place after 955. His last witnessing, ten years later, must have been as an old man, if he was the thegn who witnessed from 928 to 940 prior to his appointment as ealdorman.[21]

Olaf Guthfrithson, defeated at *Brunanburh*, returned almost immediately upon Athelstan's death in 939 and after he had taken Tamworth, Edmund besieged him at Leicester. Simeon of Durham records that there was no severe fighting, 'for the two archbishops, Oda and Wulfstan, reconciled the kings to one another and put an end to the battle.' He adds that a boundary line was agreed, with Watling Street marking the border between the two kingdoms.

Not long afterwards, Olaf Guthfrithson died, and was succeeded by Olaf Sihtricson, son of the King Sihtric who had briefly been married to Athelstan's sister, although he was presumably not her son.

In 942 Edmund defeated Idwal of Gwynedd but whilst the *Annales Cambriae* mentions the incident, the *ASC* doesn't. It was more concerned with the 942 recapture of the Five Boroughs. The *ASC* says that the Danes of the Five Boroughs were 'subjected by force under the Norsemen' while John of Worcester says that Edmund 'wrested completely out of Danish hands' the Five Boroughs and brought 'all Mercia under his control.'[22]

Æthelweard the Chronicler, writing in the tenth century, says that it was Wulfstan, [archbishop of York], and the 'duke [ealdorman] of the Mercians who expelled certain deserters, namely Ragnall and Olaf from the city of York and gave it into the king's [Edmund's] hand.'

Perhaps, as Stenton argued, the Northumbrian Norse were seen as a 'wild and lawless' bunch, adventurers, not to be trusted. But if the Danes already settled in the Five Boroughs were not disposed to support Olaf and his armies, then the question might be asked, how did Olaf manage to take over the towns so swiftly upon Athelstan's death? Is it credible that the Danes in this area were not capable of defending their territory?[23]

In 943 Edmund stood sponsor in baptism to Olaf, and then to Ragnall. It may be that he and Olaf were fighting over the Northumbrian kingship. Simeon records that Olaf was driven out in 943, so perhaps Ragnall took over, but Edmund drove Olaf out of Northumbria in 944, so it might have been the case that there were two kings there for a while.

Again, in 943, reports from the *Annales Cambriae* indicate cross-border troubles, when Idwal son of Rhodri and his son Elisedd were killed by the Saxons. The focus was not on Mercia during this time, for in 945 Edmund ravaged Strathclyde and gave it to Malcolm, king of the Scots. The *ASC* calls it Cumberland and the *Annales Cambriae* confirms the identification of Strathclyde with Cumberland.

In 946 Edmund died, stabbed in a brawl. According to John of Worcester, this occurred while Edmund was at Pucklechurch, Gloucestershire; while trying to rescue his steward from a renowned thief, named as Leofa, he was killed by this same Leofa, on 26 May. The *ASC* records that it was 'widely known' how he came to be killed, and also furnishes the information that he was married to Æthelflæd of Damerham at the time of his death.

Eadred was a full brother of Edmund, and most of his eleven-year reign was taken up with dealing with Northumbria. Famously, he was the one who drove Eric Bloodaxe out of York. He was not especially active during the last years of his life, and seems to have leaned heavily for administration on Dunstan. Dunstan was born around 910 and probably received his education at Glastonbury. His mentor – and kinsman – was Bishop Ælfheah of Winchester. In 940 he became the abbot of Glastonbury, but he was influential at the courts of both Edmund and Eadred. Dunstan is considered to be one of the leading lights of the monastic reformation of the tenth century, which was driven by a desire to establish and/or restore the religious houses as true monastic institutions, following the rule of St Benedict. Dunstan studied hard in the library at Glastonbury and there is reason to believe that in that library there was a copy of Bede's *Historia Ecclesiastica*.[24] The *Life* of St Dunstan tells us that, 'When King Edmund had been killed by a wicked robber, the next heir, Eadred … loved the blessed Father Dunstan with such warmth of love that he preferred hardly anyone of his chief men to him.' However, it also tells us that many at Edmund's court had begun to 'detest the man of God, with more bitter and foolish hatred, and to envy his prosperity even to wish him dead.'[25]

In November 955 Eadred died. There are hints in the *Life* of Dunstan that he was not well, afflicted in some way by a 'long sickness'. He mentioned Dunstan in his will and left him 200 pounds to keep at Glastonbury for the people of Somerset and Devon.[26]

He died childless, and the heir was the young son of his brother King Edmund. Eadred left a court in which his mother, Eadgifu, the abbot Dunstan, and Archbishop Oda, were prominent members. The new king would have to navigate his way through a court teeming with different factions, including not only his relatives, but the family of Athelstan Half-king, at whose home the king's younger brother had been fostered. Mercia was about to prove influential once more as the kingdom was split again.

CHAPTER 10

Ælfhere, the Mad Blast from the Western Provinces

In 955, Eadwig, eldest son of King Edmund, and nephew to King Eadred, acceded to the throne on 23 November, but was in all likelihood not crowned until the following year. It may be that the established 'old guard' at court sought to keep control over the young boy, who was probably about fifteen years old at the time. He married a young woman named Ælfgifu, and their union is the subject of scandalous legend.

As King Eadwig was probably fifteen years old, we can assume that his young bride, Ælfgifu, was of a similar age, although there is no evidence of her birth date. During the feast which followed the wedding, it was noted that the king had disappeared. Dunstan, abbot of Glastonbury and faithful servant of the previous king, was sent to find him. And find him he did; in bed, with his young wife and her mother.

From the earliest, almost contemporary, *Life* of Dunstan, written by an author identified only as 'B', we have this account:

A certain woman, foolish, though she was of noble birth, with her daughter, a girl of ripe age, attached herself to him, pursuing him and wickedly enticing him to intimacy, obviously in order to join and ally herself or else her daughter in lawful marriage. Shameful to relate, people say that in his turn he acted wantonly with them, with disgraceful caresses, without any decency on the part of either. And when at the time appointed by all the leading men of the English he was anointed and consecrated king by popular election, on that day after the kingly anointing at the holy ceremony the lustful man suddenly jumped up and left the happy banquet and the fitting company of his nobles, for the aforesaid caresses of loose women ... but when he did not wish to rise, Dunstan, after first rebuking the folly of the women, drew him by his hand from his licentious reclining by the women, replaced the crown, and brought him with him to the royal assembly, though dragged from the women by force.[1]

Of the scandal, it was also reported that Oda branded the woman's face with a white-hot iron and banished her, and when she returned she was hamstrung.[2] Henry of Huntingdon doesn't mention anything about the less savoury aspects of Eadwig's reign, and neither does the *ASC*.

What is certainly true is that the king argued with Dunstan, not least because of the matter of his grandmother's inheritance,[3] which Dunstan accused him of stealing, and Dunstan was banished. The *Life* goes on to say that as Dunstan boarded the ship which was to carry him to his exile on the Continent, messengers were sent from the king's mother-in-law, threatening that she would put out Dunstan's eyes if he ever returned to England.

Who was this 'mother-in-law'? She was the mother of Ælfgifu, and the mother-in-law of Eadwig.[4] Making allowances for the fanciful embellishments of the later chroniclers, and the expected bias of the writer of the *Life* of Dunstan, it is safe to assume that this story was embroidered, but there were real tensions between the rival factions at court and it is possible to put forward a number of reasons for this reported hostility.

The young royal couple was forcibly separated, the marriage annulled by Archbishop Oda. But it was not done immediately.

The young queen and her mother were probably women of high birth, and seemingly related to the royal family as well as to Mercian nobility. It is possible that they were descended on one side from Æthelwulf, ealdorman of the Mercian *Gaini* tribe, who was the brother of Alfred the Great's Mercian wife, Ealhswith. This would also link the women to the family of Athelstan Half-king, who was Æthelwulf's grandson.[5]

On the other side, it appears that the women were descended from royalty. The king's young wife bestowed land upon an Æthelweard, presumed to be Æthelweard the Chronicler, who stated that his great-great-grandfather was Alfred the Great's brother. If Æthelweard was the young queen's brother, this means that she and Eadwig were related other than by marriage, and shared a common ancestor, Alfred's father. Thus Eadwig and his wife would have been third cousins, once removed.[6]

The marriage was annulled on grounds of consanguinity. Legislation dating from 1008 – a law code of Æthelred the Unready – states that

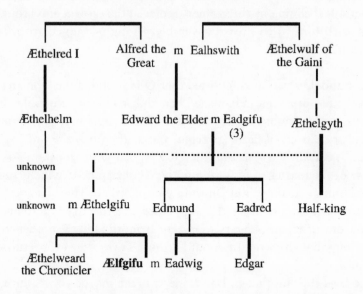

(Broken lines denote unknown connections)

Proposed genealogy for Queen Ælfgifu.

marriage is forbidden 'within six degrees, that is to say, four generations'[7] but if they were third cousins once removed, then this law, even if it was *de facto* prior to 1008, would still not apply.

The divorce was not initiated until 958, by which time Eadwig had lost most of his kingdom. In all likelihood it would have been Oda, the then archbishop of Canterbury, who conducted the marriage ceremony, the same archbishop who instigated the annulment. It seems inconceivable that he would have been unaware at the time that the couple was related.

The relationship, whilst not necessarily illegal, might nevertheless have caused concern. Through the proposed paternal descent, Eadwig's wife was a descendant of Alfred the Great's brother. His son, Æthelwold, too young to become king when his father died, later rebelled against his cousin, Alfred's son Edward the Elder, fighting alongside the Danish invaders at the battle of the Holme in 902. Significantly, it was at this battle that Eadgifu's father, fighting on the side of Edward the Elder, met his death. It is possible that the animosity towards Eadwig's marriage stemmed from Ælfgifu's being a member of the 'rival' line,[8] but the bloodline of Alfred the Great was long-established by this time. More plausible is the personal enmity, stemming from the loss of Eadgifu's father, and the fact that Eadgifu had status as the mother and grandmother of kings, status which would be rescinded were Queen Ælfgifu to have children of her own.

In 955, the young Eadwig had been named king because his uncle had died without issue. Eadwig and his younger brother Edgar had been raised separately, the latter at the palace of Athelstan Half-king of East Anglia.

Eadgifu had been the third wife of Edward the Elder and mother of the two previous kings. She attested charters as 'queen' during the reigns of both of her sons. In 949, she witnessed a grant by her son to Canterbury Cathedral, attesting as '*Eadgiua regina matre mea*, (S546). She was, indeed, officially the Queen Mother, and the family bond seems to have been tight, until Eadwig, the grandson, deprived his grandmother of her property.

Eadgifu was also closely linked to Athelstan Half-king. Whilst the proposed genealogy shows that the Half-king and King Eadwig's 'in-laws' might have been related, it seems that the Half-king had more reason to support Eadgifu's faction.

We cannot be sure who was charged with Eadwig's upbringing,[9] but Edgar grew up in the house of the man so powerful that his epithet was Half-King. Specifically, Edgar was entrusted to the Half-king's wife.

Athelstan Half-king, ealdorman of East Anglia, had served the three previous kings, amassing land and wielding influence during the reigns of all of Edward the Elder's sons. We cannot know the full extent of his land ownership because he died as a monk, and thus would not have left a will, but his epithet gives a fair indication of his wealth. In all, he was witness to more than 150 charters, *dux* at a time when kings of England achieved military success over the Danelaw and Strathclyde.[10] His influence must have been more than merely political; the families must have been close. When Eadwig and Edgar's mother died in 944, the infant Edgar went not to his stepmother, but to Ælfwynn, the Half-king's wife.

She was a wealthy woman, holding estates that were eventually gifted by her youngest son for the founding of Ramsey Abbey. Is it possible that she was named foster mother to Edgar because of her royal Mercian connections; that she was the daughter of Æthelflæd, Lady of the Mercians? This suggestion, discussed in Chapter Eight, only carries significance with the benefit of hindsight, demonstrating the importance of Mercia in Edgar's reign; only one lady with the name of Ælfwynn can be tenuously linked to the daughter of Æthelflæd, and there is no suggestion that this person, who was a religious woman at that time

(S535) was also the Half-king's wife. However, his wife was obviously a woman of means and the connections between the royal family and the house of East Anglia were strong.

So, it appears that on one side of the court the East Anglians constituted the 'old guard' who supported Eadgifu, and their family's fortunes changed with the accession of King Eadwig.

King Eadred bequeathed lands to his mother, and Eadgifu herself claimed in 959 that she had been despoiled of her property.[11] Was Eadwig being manipulated by courtiers who hadn't been advanced under Edmund and Eadred, or was he trying to create a new group of followers? He was accused of distributing the lands of churches to 'rapacious strangers'.[12]

Eadwig was certainly rich enough to reward his followers. By all accounts, bar one, Eadwig was ill-suited to the office of king. The huge number – more than sixty – of extant land charters suggest that he attempted to buy the support of the nobility and two years into his reign, he found himself having to share his kingdom with his younger brother. Eadwig was isolated, left with only the erstwhile kingdom of Wessex. His younger brother, Edgar, needed the support of the Church, and one of his first acts was to recall Dunstan.

It can be taken as read that he had the backing of the East Anglians, having grown up there, and he now courted the Mercians, whose support, with that of the Northumbrians, was crucial. For a time, there were two courts, with Eadwig's kingdom now restricted to the central heartland of Wessex.

John of Worcester wrote that in 957: 'The people of Mercia threw off their allegiance to Eadwig, king of England, disgusted at the folly of his government, and elected his cousin [sic] Edgar.' Roger of Wendover said that Eadwig, for his 'unwise administration of the government committed to him, was entirely forsaken by the Mercians and the Northmen; for, disgusting by his vanity all the wise men and the nobles of his kingdom, he, nevertheless, eagerly cherished the ignorant and the wicked. So that unanimously agreeing in deposing him, they, by the direction of God, chose his brother Edgar to be king.' William of Malmesbury stated that Eadwig was 'despoiled of the greatest part of his kingdom.'

We cannot know to what extent Edgar, at fourteen – if we can believe the chroniclers about his age – was himself being manipulated, but it would be difficult and probably inaccurate to describe what happened as a rebellion. The division of the kingdom was very neat and in 959 there was smooth reunion,[13] but division it certainly was. 'And thus in the witness of the whole people the state was divided between the kings as determined by wise men, so that the famous River Thames separated the realms of both.'[14]

Eadwig continued to issue charters as full king (*Rex Anglorum*),[15] but hardly any pertaining to land outside Wessex. None of Edgar's charters from 957 have survived, but those from 958–9 show him granting land and privileges from the West and East Midlands, Essex and Yorkshire, independently, and styled as king of Mercia.[16]

A charter of 955, when the boys were both still only princes, shows them attesting in identical fashion, as if they had equal status: '*Ego Eadwig cliton consensi et subscripsi. Ego Eadgar cliton consensi et subscripsi*' (S565). It is possible that the division, far from being a 'rising up', was pre-arranged, as might have happened before. Although full brothers rather than half-brothers, these boys were in a similar situation to that of the sons of Edward the Elder, who was succeeded in Mercia by his natural-born son Athelstan, and in Wessex, briefly, by his eldest legitimate son, Ælfweard.

That division had lasted a mere sixteen days, and this latest one, though longer, was nevertheless also a rather short-term arrangement. The suggestion that Mercia was seen as some kind of training ground for future kings falls down a little in this case, though, for even if it is accepted that Athelstan had been fostered in the court of Mercia, Edgar had been brought up in East Anglia.

The versions of the *ASC* differ over the dates of accession, with D stating that Edgar became king of the Mercians immediately upon Eadred's death in 955, while others state that Edgar succeeded to the kingdom of Mercia in 957, or that Eadwig ruled from 955 until his death, as if there were no division at all. Edgar attests Eadwig's charters until 957, after which we find him in Mercia, and Eadwig does not then attest any of Edgar's. Eadwig continued to issue coinage, the implication being that in so doing he retained overall control. It is unlikely that Edgar would have risen up in rebellion and allowed his brother to be the one to continue minting coins.[17]

Edgar is named as under-king in Mercia – *regulus* – in a Worcester charter drawn up in late 956 so we might speculate that it was always the plan for him to succeed, or perhaps that Eadwig was made to approve this plan from the very beginning of his reign. Abingdon appears to have remained part of Eadwig's sovereignty; Abbot Æthelwold began to witness royal diplomas continuing as the only abbot regularly to witness Edgar's charters until he became bishop of Winchester in 963. He seems genuinely to have had a connection to both the young princes and, along with Dunstan and later Bishop Oswald, was to play a pivotal role in Edgar's reign.[18]

Famously, one of Edgar's first actions when he became king of Mercia in 957 was to recall Dunstan, establishing him as bishop of Worcester, a see in the heart of Mercia. When Archbishop Oda, who had presided over Eadwig's enforced annulment, died, Dunstan must have hoped for elevation to the archbishopric of Canterbury, but if so, he was initially disappointed. Eadwig, still king of the English, nominated the bishop of Winchester instead, and Dunstan had to wait.

This bishop of Winchester, archbishop-elect, had not been a monk, but a married clerk. He had a son, and thus was not celibate, which would have earned the disapproval of the reformers who sought to bring strict monastic rules back to the Church. William of Malmesbury, in his *Gesta Pontificum*, accused this bishop of buying the see at Canterbury and of insulting Oda's grave by saying: 'At last you miserable old man you have breathed out your life and departed, making room, though late in the day, for a better man.' Depicted as virtually dancing on the old man's grave, the bishop of Winchester certainly had a bad press. Dunstan had studied under his predecessor at Winchester, who was possibly a relative of Dunstan's. So perhaps Dunstan took against him for personal as well as professional reasons.[19]

Of more significance was the bishop's closeness to the family of Ælfhere of Mercia, a family with kinship ties to the royal house. Ælfhere was granted his ealdordom in Mercia by Eadwig, in 956, as one of the 'new guard', and thus would have immediately earned the enmity of the East Anglians, whose patriarch the Half-king lost land with the granting of that ealdordom. The Half-king retired to Glastonbury early in Eadwig's reign. Perhaps this had always been his intention, but what of the timing? It might have been the result of his being ousted from power by Eadwig; it could be that the Half-king saw that his time of influence was over. Or possibly he waited until his foster son, Edgar, was securely on the throne of Mercia and then, having fulfilled the duty of a foster father, he retired. His eldest son, Æthelwold, became ealdorman of East Anglia. Powerful lay dynasties were being established in East Anglia and Mercia, and their rivalry during this period shows that while the old kingdoms had been swept away, regional differences had not.

It is perhaps from this point that we can chart the rise of the powerful families who would come to dominate the political landscape for the next hundred years; Ælfhere was called *princeps Merciorum gentis* rather than *dux*.

Ælfhere's father was a man called Ealhhelm, who was probably not the Ealhhelm who had served the Lady of the Mercians, but was an ealdorman of Mercia from 940–951, holding power in an area of central Mercia around the diocese of Worcester and coterminous with the old territory of the *Hwicce*. The name is not common, and of sixty-nine charters in which it appears, only two have the name duplicated in the lay section of the witness lists.[20] Ealhhelm, Ælfhere's father, first appears in 930, in a charter dated 3 April (CS 669) where he is sixteenth of twenty thegns. Throughout Athelstan's reign he stayed in that position, but in 940 when King Edmund succeeded to the throne, he promoted three men to the rank of ealdorman: Æthelmund, Æthelwold, and Ealhhelm. From this point until 951, Ealhhelm witnessed regularly, and was fourth or fifth of six or seven ealdormen who witnessed. However, the link to Ælfhere comes from a reference in the poem *The Battle of Maldon*, from which it is safe to infer that he was the father of Ælfhere and Ælfheah and the father-in-law of Ælfric *cild*, Ælfhere's successor in Mercia (*See* below, p 181).

There has been some difference of opinion about Ælfhere's siblings. Michael Lapidge and Cyril Hart both said that Ælfheah was his younger brother, but Ann Williams says that Ælfheah was the elder brother.[21] The likelihood that Ælfheah was, in fact, the eldest brother stems from the fact that by 940 he was married to a woman named Ælfswith and he and his wife were recipients of Eadwig's generosity.[22] This generosity was repaid when, after the country was divided in 957, Ælfheah remained with Eadwig in Wessex. He was not appointed as ealdorman until 959, but it has been suggested that rather than this being indicative of his being the younger brother, he was in fact serving Eadwig in some official capacity, that of seneschal.[23]

The connection to the royal family of Wessex may have been through marriage. Edgar's maternal grandmother, Wynflæd, might have been the wife of Ealhhelm.[24] Ælfheah had connections with the bishop of Winchester, Ælfsige, the same bishop who was accused of jumping on his predecessor's grave, and we know from his will that he entrusted the care of his son to Ælfheah. The fact that he was a married bishop with a son is possibly the reason for the animosity shown to him by the chroniclers. Ælfheah was also closely linked to Ælfthryth, Edgar's queen and mother of Æthelred Unræd. In his will, he referred to her as his *gefæðeran*, a word which might denote some kind of godparent relationship, and it is possible that he was godfather to one of her sons. Ælfheah's career and relationships show the family's wealth, power and connections. But it was his younger brother, Ælfhere, who was to ruffle the feathers of the religious establishment in the tenth century.

There is no suggestion that the family was Mercian. Ælfheah held land in Wiltshire, Berkshire, Surrey, Buckinghamshire, Somerset, Hampshire and Middlesex. His will mentions 'brothers' rather than 'brother', but only names Ælfhere. One of his brothers was perhaps an Eadric who held land in Hampshire, and another an Ælfwine, who might have been a monk at Glastonbury.[25]

Ælfhere was appointed ealdorman in 956, by King Eadwig, but he appears earlier, in a charter of King Eadred, who addressed him as *propinquus*, suggesting a kinship (S555). It is likely that Ælfhere received the ealdordom which his father had held. His father was ealdorman only until 951, and when Ælfhere began witnessing charters, he ranked lower than Athelstan Half-king, who may well have been ruling some or all of the territory, control over which Ælfhere was granted in 956. The disputed area of 'Eastern Mercia', mentioned briefly in Chapter Nine, was to become the scene of hostile action later in Ælfhere's career.

From Eadwig, Ælfhere received land in Oxfordshire and Warwickshire and in 957 he received land in Gloucestershire (S587, 588, 1747). It is likely that he held some of the land of Evesham Abbey, previously held by his father, and from King Edgar he received lands in Somerset, and from Æthelred Unræd, lands in Buckinghamshire. His brother Ælfheah bequeathed him land in Wiltshire, Berkshire and Somerset. Added up, the lands total about 200 hides, and this may have been only a portion of the land at his disposal but, unfortunately, his will has not survived. There is no record of his having married, but he owned land at Wormleighton, Warwickshire and after his death, a charter of Æthelred Unræd's concerns lands at Wormleighton, held by a woman named Eadflæd, who was deprived of the estates by Ælfhere's successor, Ælfric *cild*. It is possible, though not certain, that she was Ælfhere's widow (S896, 937). Nothing more is known of her.

When the kingdom was divided in 957, most of the new guard – Ælfhere, Athelstan *Rota*, Byrhtnoth (later to be of *Battle of Maldon* fame) and Æthelwold of East Anglia – all went with Edgar, even though appointed by Eadwig. But Ælfheah stayed in Wessex with Eadwig. These decisions possibly had more to do with where these men held land than with personal loyalty.

Dunstan had served two previous kings, the sons of royal grandmother Eadgifu, and, as previously noted, according to his hagiographer, 'B', 'When Edmund had been killed by a wicked robber, the next heir [Eadred]... loved the blessed Father Dunstan with such warmth of love that he preferred hardly anyone of his chief men to him.' This being the case, it is safe to assume that Dunstan would have been in Eadgifu's camp. He owed much to the Queen Mother, little to the louche Eadwig, and everything to the new king, Edgar, and yet he must have been frustrated to find enemies residing at the Mercian court. Nor was everything resolved with the reunification of the kingdom following Eadwig's death in 959.

At a tragically – or fortuitously, depending on the viewpoint of those concerned – young age of around nineteen, Eadwig 'breathed his last by a miserable death.'[26] And whatever the circumstances of the division of the country, it knitted back together seamlessly with Edgar's accession to the whole kingdom when he was, according to the *Liber Eliensis*, 'chosen by the whole people of England.' It also recorded that, 'King Edgar, having been properly instructed by the blessed Dunstan, enacted just laws for the kingdom of the English and kept control, all the time, over a kingdom that was in a most tranquil state. He restored the churches which had been destroyed.'[27]

Edgar's epithet 'The Peaceable' is a clear hint that his reign was not troubled by Viking incursions, although there was at least one act of violence during his time as king. But his reign is largely remembered for the monastic reform, and his imperial-style coronation. The monastic reform was spearheaded, in varying degrees, by Dunstan, Æthelwold of Abingdon, and Oswald of Worcester.

Æthelwold was roughly the same age as Dunstan, and he and Dunstan were ordained by Ælfheah of Winchester, Dunstan's kinsman, on the same day.[28] For a short while he was a monk at Glastonbury but considered going abroad to study. Instead, a royal gift of a monastic site at Abingdon persuaded him to stay in England, and he was abbot of Abingdon until he became bishop of Winchester in 963. He was the driving force behind the monastic reform of the tenth century, complaining in his work *Regularis Concordia* about past practices which saw monastic lands given away and the acknowledgement of the 'overlordship of secular persons'[29] and he seems to have considered that the collapse of monastic life had more to do with English, secular reasons than Viking destruction.[30] Æthelwold is thought to have been the man responsible for the education of Edgar between the death of his father and his fostering at the East Anglian house of Athelstan Half-king. Devout, even-handed, he was also seemingly canny with money, building up a vast treasury for Ely.

The third of the reforming trio was Oswald, probably a native of the eastern Danelaw. He was the nephew of Archbishop Oda of Canterbury and seemingly a relative of Oskytel, archbishop of York. He studied abroad, at Fleury, and returned to England to find that his uncle, Oda, had died. When Dunstan moved from the bishopric of Worcester to become archbishop of Canterbury, Oswald filled the vacant see and remained bishop of Worcester until his death, despite becoming archbishop of York in 972. He established several monasteries in his Worcester diocese, and turned Worcester into a monastic priory. The youngest son of Athelstan Half-king, Æthelwine, provided lands which had been part of his mother's estate to enable Oswald to found the abbey of Ramsey in 968. At Ramsey it was said that Oswald would 'feast royally, with plenty of wine drunk from horns chased with gold and silver.'[31]

The main source for Archbishop Oswald's activities is Byrhtferth of Ramsey's *Life* of Oswald, but it must be noted that there is obvious and expected bias, and that Byrhtferth does not give specific dates in his hagiography.

Byrhtferth says that 'in those days there were no proper monks.'[32] Æthelwold was troubled by 'lascivious clerks' and the reform saw the eviction of clerks at – among others – Winchester and Worcester, to be replaced by monks. The *Regularis Concordia* proscribed the making of wills, which protected the common endowment. The rule of celibacy was enforced and hereditary abbacies were forbidden, the aim being to prevent local men from seeking to enforce their hereditary rights. Both Æthelwold and Oswald were concerned that the ealdormen might have been tempted to take back what they thought was their own land, and the rights thereof. It was seen as some by an attack on local interest, and 'monasticism became high politics.'[33] 'The essential point to grasp is that the tenth-century reform was not just about monastic observance but about property rights and patronage as well.'[34]

'An Old English Account of King Edgar's Establishment of Monasteries' (*EHD*), widely believed to have been written by Æthelwold of Abingdon, says that Eadwig 'distributed the lands of the holy churches to rapacious strangers,' but an early Yorkshire charter shows King Eadwig giving land so that the archbishop of York could found the minster of Southwell (S659). Granting the land to the archbishop, the king says, 'He is to possess it profitably for as long as he lives and after his death to leave it to whomever he sees fit.'

Conversely, early on in his reign, reformation of the monasteries was not of pressing concern to Edgar. The St Werburg's charter of 958 (S667) sees him granting land to an unreformed house of secular clerks near Chester and can be seen as perhaps more of a move to empower Mercia than as any nod to reform.[35] But there may be another important point to be noted concerning the St Werburg's charter. Edgar issued a law code in which he appeared to acknowledge the debt he owed to the Danelaw.[36] A charter granting land at Kineton in 969 honours the old 'boundary of the Mercians', a charter of 958 mentions the *Magonsæte*, and in 963 a charter granting land at *Plesc* mentions the *Wreoconsæte*.[37] It looks as if Edgar was consciously recognising and respecting the old national identity of the Mercian kingdom and the peoples within it. The granting of land in the Werburg charter giving the minster a stake in half of the shire's twelve hundreds could have been part of this policy.[38]

John of Worcester called Edgar '*Rex Anglorum pacificus*' and it was certainly a peaceful reign, with one notable exception. The *ASC* accused Edgar of having 'loved unseemly foreign manners.' In 969 it recorded that he ordered all Thanet to be ravaged. According to Roger of Wendover, some merchants from York were taken prisoner by the islanders and 'spoiled of all their property', upon which Edgar moved against the islanders, deprived them of their goods and put some of them to death. Henry of Huntingdon adds that he did it 'not as a raging enemy, but by a king inflicting punishment of evil deeds.' Assuming that these merchants from York were of Danish rather than English extraction, it seems clear that Edgar was keen to show that all subject to his rule should expect the same rights under law.

The Mercian council was last heard of electing Athelstan as king in 924, but a lawsuit pertaining to Sunbury, Middlesex, begun in Eadwig's reign and continuing after the division of the kingdom, was 'then referred to Edgar for judgement and the Mercian council (*Myrcna witan*) upheld Eadwig's decision.'[39] This is important; even after so-called unity, even after fighting the Vikings together, these two 'kingdoms' were still very different. In 956 and 1035 Northumbria joined Mercia in supporting a rival claimant to the throne. The old allegiances were changing.

Among the Mercian ealdormen at the beginning of Edgar's reign were Athelstan *Rota*, husband of Æthelflæd of Damerham – who had previously been married to King Edmund –and Æthelmund of Chester. Byrhtferth of Ramsey has details of a funeral, possibly Æthelmund's: 'When all the officials of this land were gathered together with the king for the Easter celebration, it happened … that one of the king's distinguished ealdormen passed away. At his funeral the king ordered the ealdorman's retinue to carry the body honourably to its burial place.' Æthelmund was appointed at the same time as Ealhhelm, Athelstan *Rota* in 955.[40]

It seems that Athelstan *Rota*'s ealdordom may have been in southeast Mercia, since his wife, Æthelflæd of Damerham, held lands in Essex, Suffolk and Berkshire. Ælfhere's father Ealhhelm's career coincided with the recovery of the Five Boroughs by Edmund, but there is no evidence to suggest what part, if any, he played in this campaign. If Mercian troops were involved, and Æthelweard the Chronicler said that the 'duke of Mercia' was involved in the recovery of York, it is more likely that they were commanded by Æthelmund, whose sphere of influence seems to have been the north-western part of Mercia, including Chester.

From 957 onwards, Ælfhere outranked all other ealdormen. He became an ealdorman in 956 after attesting only two authentic charters, which suggests rather a meteoric rise.[41] There were two contributory factors at work here: the retirement of Athelstan Half-king and, more importantly, Ælfhere's area of control. After 970 he was the only ealdorman of Mercia, but beforehand he seems to have become senior to the others. Edgar as 'king of the Mercians' would have needed his support. Already in 962, he was witnessing a lease issued by Oswald, bishop of Worcester as 'ealdorman of the Mercians', two years or so before Æthelmund's death. He was described in the *Life* of Oswald as *princeps Merciorum gentis*, a title not recorded since the death of the Lady of the Mercians and the removal of her daughter in 918. It is possible that a thegn Ælfwine witnessing charters in the late 950s and early 960s is the same Ælfwine identified as Ælfhere's brother,[42] and if so, then it shows that the whole family had risen to power.

There were no successors to Æthelmund (d. *c.* 965) or Athelstan *Rota* (d. *c.* 970) and it is probably safe to assume that Ælfhere took over direct jurisdiction of their ealdordoms. In 971 or 972, when his brother Ælfheah died, he probably also administered his lands in Wessex. He was certainly present at a council in London in the latter part of Edgar's reign, where a suit was heard concerning land in Kent.[43] He must have had impressive leadership qualities and have proved himself a loyal servant to his king.

The king whom Ælfhere served had a complicated marital history. The traditional narrative for Edgar's women is that he married Æthelflæd *Candida* (or more usually *Eneda*) by whom he had a son, Edward. He then seduced a nun, Wulfthryth, by whom he had a daughter, Edith. Then he married Ælfthryth, by whom he had two sons, Edmund and Æthelred Unræd.[44]

It is usual to associate Edgar's first marriage with Æthelflæd *Eneda* (the White, or Duck). According to William of Malmesbury, she was the daughter of an Ealdorman Ordmaer. But there is only one other reference to him, in the *Liber Eliensis* (ii 7) and he is not an ealdorman. It is not unique that there is no contemporary reference to the first wife of a king; the lack of information about her father, however, does make it difficult to establish her existence.

Edgar's second 'woman' and possibly wife, was Wulfthryth, later St Wulfthryth, who might or might not have been promised to the Church before Edgar impregnated her. John of Worcester has little to say, beyond that Edgar 'Also had … a son named Edward… and by St Wulfthryth a daughter name Edith.' Osbern of Canterbury (*c.*1050–1090), a Benedictine monk and translator of Anglo-Saxon hagiographies, said that the baby Edward was the son of a professed nun of Wilton, whose seduction earned Edgar a seven-year penance, causing his coronation to be delayed. Whatever the truth of the seven-year penance, whether imposed or self-imposed, it was nothing to do with delaying the coronation. We know that Edgar was crowned in Bath in 973, probably not for the first time, and we know that seven years before that he was already married to his last wife. She, like Ælfgifu before her, was associated with a court faction ostensibly hostile to the leading churchmen, and Edward was not her son. He was even considered illegitimate.

In the New Minster charter of 966 (S745), the royal children are described differently, with only the son of Ælfthryth, Edgar's last wife, being described as heir, and not Edward. This point is pivotal to the events following Edgar's death.

Edgar married Ælfthryth, widow of his East Anglian foster brother, Æthelwold, in 964, so his son Edward must have been born before that.

Ælfthryth's status was to eclipse even that of Eadgifu, the doughty grandmother who had held sway for so long. Ælfthryth has come to be known as England's first anointed queen, and was the first queen to be given a formal dower: in 964, King Edgar gave to his queen, 'Ælfþryð regni', a grant of 10 hides at Aston Upthorpe, Berkshire (S725).

She was the daughter of a Devonshire nobleman. Her first husband was the son of the Half-king of East Anglia and various tales are recorded by the later chroniclers about how she and Edgar came to be married, with accusations that she practised witchcraft and that Edgar murdered her first husband.[45] It seems implausible that Edgar would have killed Æthelwold; he grew up with him, and of the Half-king's sons, two became ealdormen of East Anglia, and all prospered during Edgar's reign. Edgar was always keen to support the family, particularly the youngest brother, whom he promoted to ealdorman ahead of his two elder brothers after Æthelwold's death. We can but wonder, however, whether this family of East Anglians, who were later to turn against Ælfthryth openly, did so because she began the affair with Edgar while her first husband, Æthelwold of East Anglia, was still alive. Like the earlier tales of marriage and murder and how they might have affected the family dynamics, the nuances are not detectable from the written records.

The New Minster Charter of 966 reveals the queen's status, and that of her children. The frontispiece for this refoundation and grant of privileges of the New Minster at Winchester shows Edgar alone, but Ælfthryth attests as the king's 'lawful wife'. At this time, she had borne Edgar only one child, a boy named Edmund. Edward – the son by a previous liaison, or possible marriage – and Edmund both attest as athelings (*clitones*) but Edmund, whose attestation precedes that of his half-brother, is described as 'the king's legitimate son' (*clito legitimus*) whereas Edward is merely 'begotten by the same king'. Each member of the royal family – Edgar, Ælfthryth, Edmund, and the king's grandmother Eadgifu – all have gold crosses against their names. Edward's has only an outline of a cross. It seems irrefutable, then, that Ælfthryth's children were the designated athelings.

We have already seen some of Edgar's legislation and how he was keen to acknowledge and respect the differences in the ethnic make-up of his country. His law code of 962/3 contained specific instructions that Earl Oslac 'and all the host who dwell in his aldormanry [Northumbria]' were to enforce the law, and that copies concerning the decrees were to be sent to Ealdorman Ælfhere and Ealdorman Æthelwine.[46] This was a declaration that power in the outer reaches of his kingdom was held in the hands of three leading ealdormen.

It is really from this point onwards that we see the four old major kingdoms – Mercia, Northumbria, Wessex and East Anglia – becoming ealdordoms or earldoms, sometimes with multiple ealdormen, but generally with one man presiding over the whole territory, often with the king holding Wessex for himself.

Despite being named as one of the three leading noblemen, Oslac was banished in the year of Edgar's death; all we know is that he was 'exiled from England'. Since the *ASC* also tells us that in the year Edgar's son succeeded him, there came a 'very great famine and very manifold disturbances' it may be that Oslac's banishment was connected with this time of faction and dispute.

Oswald the reformer held York in plurality with Worcester, and Edgar had a policy of appointing southerners in the north, keeping a careful balance. Oslac himself was not a Deiran, but possibly an East Anglian – his son Thored was the holder of land in Cambridgeshire[47] – but he could easily have clashed with Oswald over local jurisdiction and privileges, in the same way that Ælfhere of Mercia did, with devastating consequences.

In 973, King Edgar was crowned, probably not for the first time, in Bath. The choice of setting was symbolic, in more ways than one. It was close to the border between Mercia and Wessex, it was a city which had associations with Empire (Roman) and it may be that his age was significant too, given that he was thirty, the age at which men could be ordained bishop.

After the ceremony he was reportedly rowed along the River Dee by several kings who all bowed in homage to him. The identities of those present have proved difficult to pinpoint[48] but it is agreed that two of those in attendance were Hywel ab Ieuaf and his uncle, Iago. Iago was the king of Gwynedd and one of the sons of Idwal, who were fighting each other for a share of their inheritance.[49] Iago had imprisoned one of his brothers, Ieuaf, an act which understandably earned him the hostility of his nephew Hywel. Iago was also facing raids from Norse Vikings in the Irish Sea. In return for submission, Edgar offered protection. However, this seems only to have applied to seaborne raiding.

The following year, in 974, Iago's nephew Hywel drove Iago – temporarily – out of Gwynedd. It is tempting to wonder whether some private discussions were conducted with the English while Hywel was in attendance in Chester the previous year.

In 978, Hywel attacked the monastery at Clynnog Fawr, a religious centre with strong links to St Beuno and to the ancient Welsh royal house, the line of Merfyn. The salient point here is that he did so with the aid of English levies, who were more than likely provided by Ælfhere.

Hywel asked for Ælfhere's help again, in 983, as he fought against Einion ab Owain, in an attempt to prevent Einion from annexing Brycheiniog and Morgannwg for the kingdom of Deheubarth. He was unsuccessful in this and Ælfhere died the same year. Though Roger of Wendover is adamant that the ealdorman died of worms, it is possible that he in fact died from wounds sustained in the campaign. Rarely are such deaths recorded in this way.

Hywel's alliance with Mercia must have been personal, for it did not survive after Ælfhere's death, and he was killed by the English in 985. The event is not noted in the ASC but was recorded in the Welsh annals as an act of treachery. Ælfhere's successor as ealdorman of Mercia was banished in the same year, also for treachery. Much clearly happened in that year which we will never be able to reconstruct, but it is clear that the friendship was between Hywel and Ælfhere, not necessarily between England and Wales. It is also a reminder that Ælfhere, despite the reputation he later earned from the chroniclers, was not just bent on destroying the churches, but that he was an energetic and capable military leader, and one who could forge and maintain good working partnerships.

Still a young man, in 975 Edgar died, at the age of about thirty-two. Yet again England had the choice of two young boys, both sons of a king, both too young to rule. The difference, though, was that these were not even full brothers, having different mothers. Ælfthryth's son, Edmund, had died as an infant in 971, so the choice of athelings was now between Edward, her stepson, and Æthelred Unræd, her youngest child. Whatever had been the arrangement in 957, there was to be no joint kingship this time. Neither, it seems, was there any consensus or suggestion that the succession had been decreed and approved.

The succession dispute following Edgar's death, if it can be so called, was similar to, but subtly different from, that which had followed the death of Edward the Elder. In that instance, Ælfweard was actually

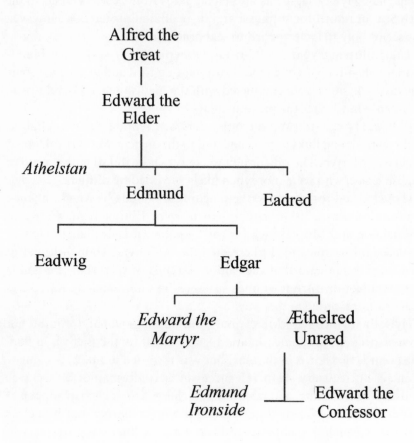

The Kings of Wessex, showing the position of Eadwig and Edgar.

the younger of the two, like Ælfthryth's son, but in 975 after Edgar's death it was the elder, and seemingly illegitimate, brother who initially succeeded.[50]

Byrhtferth of Ramsey in the *Life* of Oswald refers to Edward's tongue-lashings and cruel beatings and says that Æthelred was 'more gentle to everyone in word and deed'. He says that some nobles supported Edward, while others wanted to elect his younger half-brother.[51]

We might safely suppose that those supporting Edward's claim were Dunstan, Oswald, and the East Anglians, and that the champions of Æthelred were his mother, and Ælfhere of Mercia. Bishop Æthelwold also supported the younger boy, so the Church reformers did not stand as one on this issue. Æthelwold, when still abbot of Abingdon, had tutored Edgar, and was the leader of the Benedictine reformation, yet he had supported Eadwig's marriage and described Ælfgifu as '*thaes cininges wif*' (the king's wife, S1292) and he was also supportive of Ælfthryth,

Edgar's widow. Ælfthryth is mentioned by name in the *Regularis Concordia*. Although she is not called queen, her status is clear in the foreword: '[Edgar] most wisely ordered that his wife, Ælfthryth, should defend communities of nuns like a fearless sentinel, so that naturally a man might aid men and a woman might aid women without a breath of scandal.'

This period witnessed an inordinate number of land disputes and it may be that the death of Edgar was an opportunity to settle outstanding claims which still rankled, and perhaps hostilities between the nobility themselves, such as between Ælfhere and Æthelwine, of a less religious and more personal and/or political nature. Charters and chronicles do not speak to us of personal enmity, but there may have been an animosity between these two great men, possibly stretching back to the days of their fathers.

The family of Ælfhere had connections that allow us confidently to place them in the queen's camp. Ælfheah, the eldest brother and seneschal who fostered the son of Bishop Ælfsige was also close to Queen Ælfthryth and her predecessor. He died around the year 971, and his will (S1485) reveals the extent of his relationship with the royal family. He bequeathed an estate at Wycombe in Buckinghamshire to his 'kinsman', who has been identified as being the brother of Ælfgifu, Æthelweard the Chronicler.[52] Ælfheah also left an estate to Queen Ælfthryth, a gift of thirty mancuses, plus a sword to the elder atheling, Edmund, and an estate to Æthelred, the youngest son. More significant is the fact that he refers to the queen as his '*gefæðera*', the word indicating some kind of godparent/godchild relationship. If he was godfather to one of the princes, it suggests a close friendship indeed. There is no mention in the will of the other royal prince, Edward. Resentment was probably brewing long before 975.

It spilled over upon Edgar's death. Roger of Wendover wrote that, 'and so, after the death of the Pacific king, the kingdom was troubled and full of animosities; for a number of the nobles and great men thrust forth the abbats [sic] and monks from the monasteries in which King Edgar had placed them, and restored the clerks and their wives in their room, and one of them, named Ælfhere, with great insolence overthrew nearly all the monasteries which the revered Bishop Æthelwold had built in the province of Mercia.' This is one-sided, and only partly correct, for it was, in the main, the monasteries under Oswald's control which Ælfhere attacked.

The dispute over 'East Mercia' – the Fenland – was opened up again. One of the standoffs recorded during the so-called anti-monastic reaction following Edgar's death was at Peterborough, which had originally been part of Mercia. The eastern provinces, excepting the Five Boroughs, had become part of the ealdordom of East Anglia. The succession dispute, and the general attacks on the monastic institutions, may have precipitated a nationalist uprising among those who were against the shiring and wanted the territories back under Mercian control. Ramsey, Peterborough, Thorney and Ely all lay in this disputed territory. Evesham was attacked,[53] but it should be noted that the *Evesham Chronicle* also castigated Ealdulf of Worcester, former abbot of Peterborough, for his despoliation of Evesham.[54] The specific nature of Ælfhere's 'crime' at Evesham was, according to Florence of Worcester, that he put back the married priests and their wives.

At Peterborough, Ealdorman Æthelwine of East Anglia assembled an army and his brother Ælfwold killed one of the opponents who had seized land taken by the monastery. It is likely that these opponents included Ælfric *cild*, Ælfhere's brother-in-law and eventual successor in Mercia.[55]

The mention of the revival of the Mercian council and the acknowledgement of the geographical and legal differences between Mercia and Wessex during Edgar's reign might point to a sense of autonomy, whether officially recognised or not. Mercian law may not have been technically any different,[56] but it specifically operated in Cheshire, Shropshire, Herefordshire, Staffordshire, Worcestershire, Warwickshire, Gloucestershire and Oxfordshire. Was Alfred's incorporation of the – now lost – laws of Offa an attempt to amalgamate the two?[57] Edgar was accepted as king of the Mercians in 957 and styled thus. All these factors point to a continuing sense of otherness and perhaps a certain chafing under the West Saxon yoke. Whether Ælfhere was leading this nationalist surge, or whether he was just being carried along by it, is hard to say. By 970, significantly, Ælfhere was not only the sole ealdorman in Mercia, but his area of jurisdiction coincided exactly with that of Æthelred, Lord of the Mercians. If there was any nationalist sentiment among the Mercians, then Ælfhere would be a prime candidate for its figurehead, even had he not had personal scores to settle.

Whether or not it was Edward the Elder who was responsible for the dividing of Mercia into shires which showed 'no respect for the ancient divisions of Mercia',[58] Edward's actions towards Mercia must have led to resentment. The taking of London and Oxford under his direct control, the removal of Æthelflæd's daughter and, his final act, marching on Chester to replace the garrison which had rebelled in alliance with the Welsh, all these things would have ignited a spark of nationalist feeling.

Even without the suspicion of lingering Mercian resentment of West Saxon rule, the troubles cannot simply be dismissed by labelling what happened as being the clash between anti-monastic rabble rousers versus pious reformers.

Byrhtferth describes Æthelwine of East Anglia as 'outstanding for the probity of his morals', 'excellent in body and bearing' and being 'possessed of urbane eloquence' but there are examples of his family being less than honest when it came to matters of church land, described in the *Liber Eliensis*, which also shows a struggle for control in the area.[59]

All, layman and clergy alike, had lost out and many lawsuits were heard during this period. Asked to preside over a land settlement case at Horningsea, Æthelwine 'began for ever making fine promises to do this, but his words had no weight to them, and his promises never came to fruition.'[60] There was also a case at Hatfield, where it was claimed that, 'After the death of King Edgar, the aforesaid Æthelwine, and his brothers, laid claim to the estate of Hatfield. When, however, [his] claim had been narrated and made clear, they entered this estate and took possession of it for themselves.' It may be significant that Ælfhere was the recipient of the first grant by the young king, Æthelred Unræd, of land in Olney, Buckinghamshire, in the disputed territory (S834). He was succeeded in Mercia by a relation, while Æthelwine, despite having five of his own sons, was not.[61]

Roger of Wendover barely mentions Oswald and Æthelwold and may have gathered his information from the *Life* of Dunstan. William of Malmesbury has the same tales, almost word for word, of the spoliation of the monasteries, and of the manner of Ælfhere's death, except he says that he was eaten by lice. Henry of Huntingdon calls Ælfhere a 'dissolute noble', who with the 'consent and help of a powerful faction, destroyed some of the abbeys which King Edgar and Bishop Æthelwold had founded.' In fact, the monasteries involved were largely those in Mercia, which had been founded or refounded by Oswald.

Edgar's was a strong reign, probably owing as much to force of personality as the lack of invasion, and the political situation certainly unravelled once he was no longer at the helm. His working relationship with his leading ealdorman maintained a stable government throughout his reign.

Ælfhere's glittering career as a favourite of the king's had not been without the odd frustration, however. In the mid-960s a shipsoke[62] in the triple-hundred of Oswaldslow in the heart of Mercia would surely have stirred resentment. Oswald's leases, whilst acknowledging the consent of Ælfhere and of the king, nevertheless meant that the leaseholds of Worcester were thenceforth subject to the bishop. In addition, Ælfhere was forced to restore the lands to Evesham Abbey, which his father had held, and which was declared theft. Evesham may even have been the centre of another liberty of the same type as that of Oswaldslow and incorporated land which Ælfhere had previously controlled nearby at *Fisseburg*.[63] Another foundation, Pershore, which was perhaps a holder of a similar shipsoke, was hostile to Ælfhere, and while he and his family were patrons of Glastonbury and Abingdon (he was buried at Glastonbury) there was no grant made by him to the foundations associated with Oswald.

So why does the *ASC* say that he attacked the foundations of Æthelwold? This may have something to do with the dispute over the lands at Evesham, of which Æthelwold was considered the founder. Otherwise, it is clear that Ælfhere's family was on good terms with Æthelwold, and Abingdon was certainly a beneficiary of Ælfhere's generosity.

The *Evesham Chronicle* claimed that the abbey and its lands were seized in 976 by Ælfhere and given to a monk named Frithugar, who subsequently became abbot and gave the abbey to a powerful man called Godwine, in exchange for Towcester. However, charters show Abbot Osweard of Evesham witnessing from 970–974, then an Abbot Frithugar witnessing a reliable charter of King Edgar's later in 974. Since the so-called 'anti-monastic' reaction did not get underway until after Edgar's death in 975, the charter evidence seems to disprove the story in the *Evesham Chronicle*.[64]

Not only is it looking unlikely that Ælfhere was anti-monastic, it seems the situation might have been exaggerated in another way. Ælfhere was witnessing charters at Edward's court from 976, and so was clearly not in open rebellion. It may be that rather than a civil war, there was a brief interregnum, after which some kind of settlement was brokered. William of Malmesbury noted that Edward 'retained only the name of king, and gave them the power'.[65]

Byrhtferth of Ramsey wrote that Ælfhere, 'availing himself of enormous sums of money, cast out not only the sheep but also the shepherds' and that monks 'who were formerly accustomed to sit on caparisoned horses ... could then be seen carting a burden.' Certain 'devout men stood out against the blast of the raging wind which had come from the westernmost parts.' He says Ælfwold of East Anglia held out against the wrath of Ælfhere and that 'the wicked people said, "Let us overthrow the monks and the inheritance shall be ours".'

More likely is that Ælfhere simply objected to the encroachment on his territory and power and viewed the bishop of Worcester as no more than a rival landlord.[66] He was perhaps also unfortunate in receiving a bad press at a time when little else of note was happening. Edgar the Peaceable's reign threw up few 'headlines'.

The clerks who were replaced by the celibate monks were, according to the *Life* of St Oswald, of high birth, and the accusation was that they were frittering away the wealth of the Church on their wives. Of course, rich men have rich relatives, and it may be that the expectation was that these lands and offices would become hereditary. With this local power came authority over the local justice. The monastic reformation shifted power away from the local landed gentry into the hands of the Church. Thus, with the establishment of the triple-hundred and shipsoke, power was transferred from the laymen to the bishops, and the bishop exercised judicial power in the locality. Thegns and ealdormen who had previously held land by 'book' now lost the right to gift or sell it. In Mercia, it was still a relatively recent development that saw the king of Wessex controlling the midlands, and an interesting point to note is that Edgar would have inherited very little land in that area.

Bishop Werferth had referred to Æthelred and Æthelflæd as the Worcester community's lords, but by the time Oswald was bishop of Worcester, the lands were in the hands of a monk-bishop placed there by the king. This bishop, being celibate, could not found a dynasty. He did, however, establish seven monasteries in Mercia and, while he had no children, he still managed to give land to two of his brothers, a kinswoman and two further kinsmen. No wonder Ælfhere bridled at this new development. Worcester being at the very heart of old Mercia, deep in *Hwicce* territory, it would be surprising if other Mercians had not been similarly discontent. Nor was Ælfhere the only one, for a certain Edwin, ealdorman of Kent, was accused of seizing lands from the Rochester monks.[67]

Edgar had been canny in his policies, ensuring that none of his subjects became overly powerful, and his rule was one of balance. But whilst his ministers were all loyal to him, it seems that once he was gone, they were free to squabble, and a boy king, whichever one of them had succeeded their father, would have been unable to stop them, at least in the short term. Perhaps this also goes some way to explaining the sporadic and opportunistic Viking raiding which recommenced from 980.[68]

Edward reigned for three – plainly fairly unhappy – years. He died at his stepmother's house at Corfe in Dorset, on 18 March 978. Ælfthryth is accused variously of killing him herself or of instructing her servants to kill him. Roger of Wendover blamed her directly; Henry of Huntingdon recorded that she 'reportedly' stabbed him. Byrhtferth of Ramsey blamed 'magnates and armed men'. In the main it is the later chroniclers who set her up as wicked stepmother incarnate,[69] and Byrhtferth rehabilitates Ælfhere's reputation somewhat by saying that he was the 'renowned ealdorman' who ordered Edward's body to be exhumed for honourable reburial.

There was no other claimant and Æthelred, later to earn the epithet 'Unræd', became king at a time when he was still only a young boy. Some have it that he was crowned in 978, some in 979. There might have been a delay in his coronation or there may have been a misreading of the dates. If the former, it might show that it took some time to sort the country out, if the latter it would also indicate that there was little resistance to his succession if those in charge were confident enough not to have him crowned as soon as possible.

His youth inevitably meant a period of regency with his mother and Bishop Æthelwold taking charge. How much Ælfhere would have been involved is doubtful. Having 'exonerated' himself by reburying Edward's body, he was then busy in Wales, and died in 983. The *Annales Cambriae* recorded his attack on Dyfed. Roger of Wendover says he died, 'his whole body being eaten with worms.' Possibly this was ergot, a common infestation in grain, or it may be that the chroniclers thought this a suitably unpleasant death for such a man. Often people died soon after a conflict, and the chronicles rarely say 'died of wounds' but this must have been a common occurrence.

The fact that he was active in Wales in the last year of his life is a reminder that Ælfhere's career was not simply one of a powerful government minister locking horns with the Church. As ealdorman of Mercia he was in effect a Marcher Lord, and there were a number of occasions during his tenure when the Welsh and English clashed. It is safe to assume that, even when he is not mentioned specifically, he was responsible for the English muster.

The relationship between Mercia and Wales had always been something more complex than simply a history of bloody conflict. It is clear that, even as far back as the days of Penda, various Mercian leaders were as likely to form friendships with the Welsh as they were to attack them. In the case already mentioned of Ælfhere's activities in Wales in the 970s, it is clear that he was assisting Hwyel ab Ieuaf against his uncle, Iago. An entry in the *Annales Cambriae* for 967 records that the Saxons, led by Ælfhere, ravaged the kingdom of the sons of Idwal (i.e. Gwynedd). This could also have been on behalf of Hywel, or perhaps his father, who was later imprisoned by Iago. In 983 we hear of that attack on Dyfed, when the *Annales Cambriae* tells us that Ælfhere ravaged the lands of Einion ab Owain. Significantly though, here again he was campaigning alongside Hywel. Clearly these men had formed a bond. 'These raids suggest a pattern of alliance within the Welsh borderlands in which attacks were directed outward against other Welsh and Anglo-Saxon kingdoms.'[70] This appears to have continued in some capacity after Ælfhere's death, for in 992 the *Annales Cambriae* recorded an otherwise unmentioned Æthelsige working in partnership in a similar way.

Ælfhere of Mercia had no children. Odda of Deerhurst is named as Ælfhere's son in annals collected by John Leland (d. 1552), but this appears to be based on a statement in the Pershore annals that Odda restored the lands allegedly seized by Ælfhere. Given that he was still active in 1056 it seems implausible that he was the son of Ælfhere, and it is more likely that Odda was a kinsman of Ealdorman Æthelweard (d. 998), whom William of Malmesbury names as a patron of Pershore.[71]

Ælfhere's successor was Ælfric *cild*. Roger of Wendover calls him Ælfhere's son, as does John of Worcester, but he was probably his brother-in-law. In discussing his appointment, William casually remarks that he succeeded Ælfhere 'who had murdered the late king.' Henry of Huntingdon judged that Ælfric *cild* was 'harshly banished.' What we do know is that he was banished by Æthelred Unræd for 'committing many unheard-of offences against God and against my royal authority'(S896).

A letter survives, from Pope John to Ealdorman Ælfric, in which the pontiff says, 'We have learned ... that you commit many injuries against the church of Mary the holy Mother of God, which is called Glastonbury, and in your greedy cupidity have seized estates and villages from its rightful ownership, and you are constantly harmful to it because you cling to a dwelling close to the same place.'[72] It is not clear whether this letter was addressed to Ælfric *cild*, or to Ælfric, ealdorman of Hampshire, but if the charges concern Ælfhere's successor, it might go some way to explaining the nature of the offences which led to his dismissal and exile. But in some ways it also exonerates Ælfhere, giving further evidence that he was not the sole destroyer of abbeys and monasteries and nor was this practice confined to the period immediately following Edgar's death.[73]

It is unclear what happened to the Mercian ealdordom following the banishment of Ælfric *cild* in 985. It is certainly possible that it was held, until his death, by Æthelwine of East Anglia, just as his father, Athelstan Half-king, had held jurisdiction there between the death of Ealhhelm in 951 and the appointment of his son Ælfhere in 956.

Leofwine, whose career will be discussed in detail in Chapter Eleven, began witnessing as ealdorman in 994 and from that point until 998 there were only five ealdormen witnessing Æthelred Unræd's charters. These, in order of seniority, were: Æthelweard, ealdorman of the Western Provinces, who was also Æthelweard the Chronicler; Ælfric of Hampshire; Ælfhelm of Northumbria; Leofwine of the *Hwicce* and Leofsige of Essex. Titles aside, it must be assumed that between them, these men shared jurisdiction for the whole of England: Leofsige was responsible for East Anglia and Essex; Ælfric for Kent, Sussex, Surrey, Berkshire, as well as Hampshire and Wiltshire; and Leofwine was ealdorman not just of the territory of the *Hwicce*, but for the whole of Mercia.

Ælfhere was rich, with extensive landholdings across Mercia and Wessex. He governed an area which equated to the 'free Mercia' over which the Lord Æthelred had once held sway. He was energetic, campaigning in Wales until well into middle age and beyond and, judging by the number of charters he witnessed – in the region of 200 – ably carried out the duties of ealdorman, presumably attending all the shire and hundred courts which Edgar decreed should meet a certain number of times each year.[74] He operated at the heart of government, at one point being one of only three men with direct responsibility for spreading the word of the king. That it was he who arranged the reburial of Edward and received the first grant of the new king's reign, shows just how important he was. And yet, despite his reputation for despoiling the monasteries, even the most ardent apologist might concede that if the grounds were not sacrilegious then they were at best self-serving. Even so, he was never accused of being 'grasping' in the way one of his successors was. Edgar had chosen his ministers with discernment, and they had served him well, Ælfhere in particular.

William of Malmesbury's summation of Unræd's reign, in contrast, was that it was: 'Cruel in the beginning, wretched in the middle, and disgraceful in the end.'

CHAPTER 11

Wulfric, Eadric and Leofwine: Mercian Wealth and Power

Within the diminished kingdom, the nobility was rich and still powerful, and not just in terms of their own lands and jurisdiction; they also began to influence royal policymaking. Where Ælfhere had loyally served Edgar, he was like a dog let off a leash once his king died. Edgar had kept the country in balance, with the Church and aristocracy equally well-fed, literally and in terms of reward. This all unravelled after his death. There had been no Viking raids during his reign either, but there were many Danes who had settled in his kingdom. The identity of the inhabitants was changing, and roles were being redefined.

The case of Wulfric Spott is interesting. He didn't influence policy, as such, nor did he challenge for the throne, but his legacy is important. He left a will, which survives, and gives an opportunity to build up a picture of just how rich it was possible to become. His story shows how powerful families became interconnected, and how scheming and rivalry stopped being solely about kings, with the stories of the thegns and ealdormen coming to the fore.

Wulfric Spott was probably not an ealdorman. He was not an immediate member of the royal family,[1] but his wealth, power and connections are integral to the part that Mercians played in the history of the eleventh century up to the time of the Conquest. His wife was called Ealhswith, but nothing else is known of her. It has been assumed that his nickname came about because of some facial blemish.[2] He was the founder of an abbey, Burton-on-Trent, and in that, the act of a wealthy

183

layman endowing a religious foundation, he is not remarkable. But his story, the documentary evidence, and his descendants, are.

A man named Wulfric was granted an estate in Austrey, Warwickshire, by King Edgar in 958, and although Wulfric Spott was in possession of the estate at the time of the foundation of Burton, it may be that the original grant had been to his father, another Wulfric.[3] But it is his connection through his mother which is important.

Wulfric Spott's will reveals that he owned huge swathes of land, much of which was in land settled by the Danes.[4] A number of estates that lay in the middle Trent Valley can be studied through the Burton Charters,[5] and three of these estates were held by Wulfric Spott. One, Bromley (S878), was held by Wulfric's mother, Wulfrun.

As mentioned briefly in Chapter Nine, in 940, a year after King Athelstan's death, the Northumbrians were 'false to their pledges' and occupied Tamworth, taking high-status hostages. One of these hostages was named in the *ASC*: 'Wulfrun was taken captive in that raid.' The fact that this woman was named in the *Chronicle* suggests that she was, indeed, of high status. There are documents which indicate that she was Wulfric's mother, such as a charter of 995 in which Wulfric is described as her son: *Wuifric Wulfrune suuu hit siððan æt him gehwyrfde mid ðam* ðe him *gecweme waes be ðæs cynges lease* (S886).

Wulfric Spott might also have been related to another previous holder of the Bromley estate, a man named Wulfsige, possibly the same as one Wulfsige the Black, who was active in that area of the Midlands in the 940s but who disappears from the records around the time of the occupation of Tamworth.[6] Wulfsige may have been Wulfrun's father, for the estate at Bromley passed directly from him, to Wulfrun, and then to her son Wulfric (S878). But it is notable that Wulfric's patrimony is uncertain and that he is referred to as the son of Wulfrun. Either his father died young, or was disgraced, or both. Wulfrun was probably the founder of Wolverhampton Priory, and thus the person after whom the city was named.

Beyond this scant information we know little about Wulfric's antecedents.[7] Wulfsige the Black may have been his grandfather, and if he was active in the area around the time of Athelstan's accession, he might have been among those Mercians who reportedly chose Athelstan as king, although this can only be conjecture.[8] Because so little is known of the family, it is not possible to establish how they came by such wealth, but they held land on both sides of the Mercian/Northumbrian border.[9]

Wulfric's will mentions estates situated across the Midlands, from Gloucestershire to Yorkshire, but forty-eight of the seventy-four estates were in the North Midlands – Derbyshire, Staffordshire and

Shropshire – and the family fortunes may have sprung from a policy of establishing landowners loyal to the crown in areas of Danish settlement. Many of the estates line the route that Olaf might have taken in 940, and there may be a good reason why Wulfric's family was granted these lands after the retaking of the Five Boroughs by King Edmund.[10]

Wulfric had a brother, Ælfhelm, who became ealdorman of York. Olaf Guthfrithson had escaped from Tamworth and was later besieged in Leicester by King Edmund, and it was believed by later generations that he had been supported and accompanied by Archbishop Wulfstan of York. When Eric Bloodaxe, the last king of York, was killed in 954, Wulfstan was reinstated, but at the time it couldn't have been known that Scandinavian rule in York was over. After Wulfstan, kings were careful to appoint as archbishops of York men from south of the Humber, and in around 993, its earl, too, was a Mercian: Ælfhelm, son of the captured Wulfrun, and thus brother of Wulfric Spott.[11]

The exile of Ælfric *cild* in 985 and the deaths of Æthelwine and Byrhtnoth in the 990s along with the disappearance of Thored of York – possibly the son of Earl Oslac who was banished in 975, and who led a fleet, unsuccessfully, against Olaf Tryggvason in 992 and was not heard of afterwards – in about 993 had left the north without a single ealdorman, until the appointment of Ælfhelm, an arrangement which could be seen as a renewal of Edgar's policy of setting southerners in charge of the north. Although in this case, the incumbent was from a Mercian family. Ælfhelm was, however, murdered in 1006, and this was the catalyst for much of what was to follow. It seems that Wulfric Spott was part of a group closely associated with King Æthelred Unræd in the 990s, and it may be that, although Ælfhelm was accused of treason, his removal was part of a general 'cleansing' of one powerful group and the establishment of others, and of two families in particular, both based in the region of Mercia, and both destined to play pivotal roles in English politics in the eleventh century.

In his *History of the Ancient Abbies* the antiquarian William Dugdale called Wulfric the 'earl of Mercia and one of the Blood Royal', but there is no evidence that any of this statement is true, although he may have had some link to the royal house through his mother. Dugdale also says, erroneously, that Wulfric was slain in battle against the Danes in 1010 and was buried in the cloister at Burton Abbey. In fact, it is probable that he retired soon after the foundation of his abbey; he witnessed regularly from 980 onwards, usually appearing fourth or fifth in the list of thegns, but his signatures disappear after 1002.[12]

Wulfric Spott's will is dated 1002–1004 and a royal charter confirming the privileges of Burton Abbey was issued by King Æthelred

Unræd in 1004 (S906). In the will, Wulfric leaves land to his 'poor daughter' for her to enjoy without forfeit, but the land was to go to the abbey after her death. He also asks his brother Ælfhelm to protect her and her land, suggesting that she was unmarried, or perhaps widowed. Wulfric bequeathed land to his brother Ælfhelm, and to Ælfhelm's son, Wulfheah.

At the same time that Ælfhelm was murdered, his sons, Wulfheah and Ufegeat, were blinded, all on the king's orders. Those brothers had a sister, Ælfgifu, who became known as Ælfgifu of Northampton.

Another beneficiary of Wulfric's will was Morcar, who was married to Wulfric's niece, Ealdgyth.[13] Morcar was left a block of land in northeast Derbyshire and the adjacent parts of Yorkshire, and three of the Burton charters record land gifts by the king of yet more estates in Derbyshire.

Morcar had a brother, Sigeferth, and the pair moved in exalted circles. They were both beneficiaries of the atheling Athelstan (S1503), who predeceased his father, Æthelred Unræd. Morcar also received grants from the king himself, the estates were in northern Mercia[14] and all of them were near those left by Wulfric Spott. Sigeferth's ranking, high up the witness lists, is another indication of his importance.

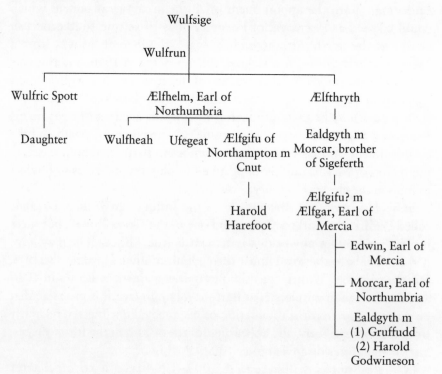

The Family of Wulfric Spott.

Rich and successful as they clearly were, these brothers were murdered in 1015, and Sigeferth's widow, another Ealdgyth,[15] was imprisoned by the king, an action which was to have far-reaching consequences later in the reign.

At the beginning of Æthelred Unræd's reign, the old order was dying off. In 983 Ælfhere of Mercia died, followed by Bishop Æthelwold in 984. It was a time of political instability; in 985 Ælfric *cild* was banished and was not replaced. The next ealdorman of Mercia was not appointed until 1007, and he was destined to be remembered for all the wrong reasons, being given an epithet which translates as 'the Grasper' or 'the Acquisitor'.

This was also a period of violence, with renewed raiding from abroad. In 986 the king laid waste to Rochester and the Vikings raided Iona. In 988 they ravaged Watchet in Somerset and in 991 the battle of Maldon took place, in which Ealdorman Byrhtnoth fought valiantly, but ultimately unsuccessfully, to repel the invaders.

In 992 the English fleet gathered at London, led by Ealdorman Ælfric and Earl Thored. The *ASC* recorded that the former sent someone to warn the enemy and then he absconded before the battle. It is probably this event which cost Earl Thored his earldom, to be replaced by Ælfhelm, brother of Wulfric Spott. Up to 990, Ælfhelm cannot be distinguished from other men of the same name but after this date, only one surviving charter of Æthelred Unræd's is witnessed by a thegn of this name. The earliest surviving charter which he witnessed as ealdorman is dated 993, which seems to confirm that he replaced Thored.[16]

If Thored was a local man then the appointment of Ælfhelm marked a change in royal strategy. Ælfhelm's lands may have been as similarly widespread as his brother Wulfric's, but it is known that he gave three estates in Northamptonshire to Peterborough.[17] His daughter, Ælfgifu, became known as Ælfgifu of Northampton, according to Florence of Worcester, so it makes sense to assume that his main holding was in this county. His appointment would mean that York would receive an earl familiar with the Anglo-Danish area, but who also had interests south of the Humber. He was given the English title of ealdorman, rather than earl, as his predecessor Thored had been known.

Ælfhelm's position may well have been strengthened by his brother's bequest to him of Conisbrough, Yorkshire. Wulfric also left to him and his son Wulfheah all his lands between 'Ribble and Mersey'. Ælfhelm was styled *dux Transhumbranæ Gentis* in a charter of 994 (S1380) but another man, Waltheof, witnessed as *dux* in 994 (S881), so it is probable that he was ealdorman of only the southern half of Northumbria.

In 993 the Vikings raided in Lindsey and Northumbria. In the same year, presumably in connection with the incident in 992, upon the king's orders Ælfgar, son of ealdorman Ælfric, was blinded. Viking raids continued on a yearly basis from 997 until 1002, when on St Brice's Day – 13 November – the king ordered all the Danish men in England to be slain.

Roger of Wendover says that in the St Brice's day massacre, 'Gunnhildr, sister of King Swein, was slain.' Roger relays the tale that this woman, who was married to a Dane named Pallig, had come to England with her husband and had embraced the Christian faith. She had mediated with the king for a peace between English and Danes and offered herself, her husband and her son as hostages. 'Having been committed to the custody of Earl Eadric, after a few days this traitor caused her husband and her son to be cruelly slain in her presence with four lances, and lastly ordered the noblewoman to be decapitated.'

There are two important names here: King Swein, who was henceforth to be a regular feature of the raiding,[18] and Earl Eadric.

Meanwhile in that same year, the king married Emma of Normandy. The frenetic pace of raiding continued, with Swein taking an army to Exeter in 1003 and harrying Wessex, particularly Wilton and Salisbury, before returning to sea. In 1004 he landed with a fleet in East Anglia and sacked Norwich and Thetford. In 1005 he returned to Denmark but was back the following year harrying Sandwich, the Isle of Wight, Hampshire, Berkshire, and Wiltshire. In 1007 tribute was paid. And in the same year, Eadric was appointed ealdorman of the Mercians.

Eadric Streona was recently voted the most evil man in British history.[19] William of Malmesbury called him 'the refuse of mankind, the reproach of the English; an abandoned glutton, a cunning miscreant; who had become opulent, not by nobility, but by specious language and impudence. The artful dissembler, capable of feigning anything, was accustomed, by pretended fidelity, to scent out the king's designs, that he might treacherously divulge them. Often, when despatched to the enemy as the mediator of peace, he inflamed them to battle.' His nickname, commonly held to mean 'the Grasper' or 'Acquisitor', might alternatively have been the shortened form of a compound personal name, such as *Streonwald*.[20]

Henry of Huntingdon says that he was 'appointed ealdorman over Mercia; a new traitor, but one of the highest class.' Leofwine, whose son Northman was executed in 1017, was already ealdorman of the *Hwicce*. More than one source connects Eadric Streona with Eadric the Wild, who had estates in Herefordshire and Shropshire, so it is probable that a presumed link with the area of the *Magonsæte* is correct, and that Eadric took charge of the northern shires. Eadric the Wild, or Eadric *Silvaticus*, has been identified as the son of Eadric Streona's brother, Ælfric.[21]

From 1012 onwards, Eadric headed the list of ealdormen witnessing Æthelred's charters. His predecessor Ælfhere had done this, of course, but Eadric consolidated his position of power by going one step further, and in an almost unprecedented move, he married the daughter of the king.[22]

Marriages of political alliance were nothing new. As far back as the seventh century the kings of Northumbria were making marriage alliances with the Mercians, for example, for joint rule, subjugation, or the promise of security and/or help, but these tended to be royal marriages. It may be that Æthelred, Lord of the Mercians, was something more than a mere ealdorman but, even so, his marriage to Alfred's daughter was the only other notable occasion when a royal princess married an ealdorman.[23]

Was Æthelred Unræd simply running out of royal kin? Or was he trying to assert his own authority by making new appointments? His mother disappears from the records shortly after the death of Bishop Æthelwold. Ælfhere, the previous ealdorman of Mercia who had been a kinsman of the kings of Wessex, died in 983; Æthelweard the Chronicler, brother of King Eadwig's wife, and descendant of King Alfred's brother, died in 998. The king was certainly gathering a new guard around him, and it may be that Eadric himself was of relatively low birth. His father has been tentatively identified as a thegn named Æthelric who was an attendant at court from the later 980s, and it may be that Eadric had several brothers, perhaps as many as five. Eadric himself headed the witness list in 1007[24] and his marriage to the king's daughter, Eadgyth, may have occurred at around this time. Roger of Wendover reported, perhaps rather sniffily, that Eadric was not noble, merely wealthy.

In 1006, around the time when Eadric came to prominence at court – and this may be no coincidence – Ælfhelm, ealdorman of York and brother of Wulfric Spott, was murdered, and his sons Wulfheah and Ufegeat blinded.[25] The *ASC* gives no reason for these acts, nor does the *Chronicle* apportion blame to any specific person. But the *ASC* does mention that the king spent the following Christmas in Shropshire, so John of Worcester's story, that Eadric Streona invited him to a feast at Shrewsbury and then, taking him hunting, led him into an ambush, may have some truth to it. That there might have been a general purge, or period of unrest at the very least, is suggested by the fact that one Wulfgeat was also deprived of his property, which Florence of Worcester blamed on 'unjust judgements and arrogant deeds which he had committed.'[26] Certainly, Eadric would have profited.

Eadric, and a man named Ulfcytel of East Anglia, were rising to power. The foundation of Burton Abbey by Wulfric Spott might be shown to be a sign of loyalty, generally, and Ælfhelm and Wulfheah, along with Wulfric, were regular attendants at court[27] but the forging of any links with the northern nobility might, as perhaps had been the case with others before him, such as Oslac, have been seen as disloyalty to the king.

In 1009 the *ASC* records an incident that happened around this time 'or a little earlier' when one of Eadric's brothers, Brihtric, accused a South Saxon, one Wulfnoth – presumably of treachery – and thus Wulfnoth 'went away and enticed ships to him until he had twenty, and then he ravaged everywhere along the south coast.' Brihtric took eighty ships, intent on defeating him, but his ships were dashed to pieces in a fierce wind, whereupon Wulfnoth came and burned them. Following this debacle, Thorkell's army landed at Sandwich, and the people of Kent 'made peace with that army and gave them 3,000 pounds.'

After this, Thorkell (a prominent Norwegian noble who was later to defect to the English) ravaged the Isle of Wight, Hampshire and Berkshire and 'on one occasion the king had intercepted them with all his army, when they wished to go to their ships, and the whole people was ready to attack them, but it was hindered by Ealdorman Eadric, then as it always was,' although this last remark might reflect the chronicler's knowledge of events which happened after this.[28]

A charter of 1014 concerns land which had been sold to Eadric by the bishop of Sherborne, land he had been forced to sell because of the attacks by the Danes; it is possible that the original transaction took place around this time, when the bishop needed to raise funds to pay tribute, and Eadric was in a position to buy the land.[29] If Eadric was profiting in such a way from the sale of land then it might explain his nickname of 'the Acquisitor'. A shrewd man could get very rich very quickly in such circumstances.

The *ASC* says that in 1012 the London Assembly was attended by 'Ealdorman Eadric and all the chief counsellors of England' so it is clear that Eadric was 'top dog' at this point. Also in this year, Thorkell swore allegiance to Æthelred Unræd. The catalyst for this was that during his army's campaign in Kent the archbishop of Canterbury had been captured and killed, seemingly counter to Thorkell's orders. Thorkell brought with him forty-five ships to put at the king's disposal.

While the Danes were away, it seems Eadric was not idle, and continued the tradition of the earls of Mercia always finding time to foray into Wales. The *Annales Cambriae* reports that Eadric ravaged *Menevia* (St David's) with another called Ubrich.

In 1013 the returning army was not that of Thorkell, but Swein Forkbeard, king of Denmark. Once Swein had made his way round East Anglia and up the Trent to Gainsborough, Earl Uhtred (of Bamburgh, appointed 995, and son of Waltheof) submitted to him, as did the people of Lindsey, and then all the inhabitants of the Five Boroughs. Once Swein had secured the north he turned southwards[30] but the *ASC* doesn't mention what, if any, part Eadric had to play in the defence of Mercia. This is notable because had Eadric submitted to Swein, the antipathy shown towards him by the *Chronicle* would have ensured mention of such an act. Therefore, we must assume that Eadric remained loyal to Æthelred, who had made use of Thorkell's ships and escaped to Normandy.[31] Swein was not king for long, dying in 1014, and Æthelred returned from exile in Normandy, called back by his councillors if he would 'govern them more justly than he did before.' Matters were not settled, however, and the struggle for England continued, this time with Swein's son, Cnut.

Meanwhile, Æthelred's eldest son, Athelstan, died and his younger brother Edmund, later known as Ironside, became atheling. Athelstan's will is extant and is an important document, providing much information about the friendships, connections and alliances between the young men at court at this time. Athelstan bequeathed land in Derbyshire to his brother Edmund, where Morcar of the Seven Boroughs held estates, and Morcar's brother Sigeferth is probably the man who was bequeathed land plus a sword, horse and shield. It is easy to picture these young men, the two princes and the two thegns, as close friends. If so, then Edmund would never have been kindly disposed towards Eadric, if Eadric had been responsible for the murder of Ealdorman Ælfhelm, the father of Morcar's wife.[32]

In 1015 a great assembly convened in Oxford where Eadric betrayed Sigeferth and Morcar, the chief thegns of the Seven Boroughs. He enticed them into his chamber, and they were 'basely killed' inside it. The king then took their property and ordered Sigeferth's widow to be seized and brought to Malmesbury. 'Then after a short interval, the atheling Edmund went and took the woman against the king's will and married her.' (*ASC*.)

In common parlance, one might say that things had escalated quickly. So what was going on here? Was Æthelred seeking retribution for the brothers' part in the capitulation of the north to Swein? Was he neutralising the perceived enemy in the ranks by removing them altogether and seizing their property?

The murders, unexplained, of Ælfhelm in 1006 and Sigeferth and Morcar in 1015, may have occurred because of a suspicion not only of disloyalty generally, but specifically because of a belief that they had invited Swein to England.[33]

Was Edmund making a bid for the throne? Did he suspect Emma of Normandy's intentions regarding her own sons? (The atheling Athelstan and Edmund Ironside were sons of the king's previous wife, while Emma of Normandy had given the king two more sons, Edward, and Alfred.)

Was Eadric envious of Sigeferth and Morcar's influence in court circles – clearly they had friends in high places, if we look at Athelstan's will – or was he simply carrying out punishment ordered by the king for the thegns' submission to Swein? This, we must recall, was the extended family of Wulfric Spott and the connections were about to become even more tangled when Cnut married the daughter of the murdered Ælfhelm,[34] whose sons Wulfheah and Ufegeat were blinded on the king's orders and perhaps – and it is a big perhaps – at Eadric's hand. It may explain, however, why he was later implicated in their blinding and their father's killing.

It may also be that Eadric supported the sons of Æthelred and his second wife, Emma of Normandy, and that Edmund felt that now was the time to make a bid for his claim as atheling.[35]

Æthelred Unræd may have been seeking to rid himself of those whom he thought disloyal, but he perhaps didn't anticipate that his son Edmund would react in the way he did. Perhaps he was unaware of, or dismissed, the close connection between the athelings and the family of Sigeferth and Morcar. But it may also be that the charge against the thegns was that they had been aiding Edmund's bid for the throne.[36] With his marriage to Sigeferth's widow, Edmund was able to secure the submission to him of the Seven Boroughs.

Eadric Streona was caught between the proverbial rock and a hard place. The king, whom he'd served loyally, was old and ailing. Edmund was in the north, Cnut was back and claiming the throne for himself, Eadric was in Mercia with the king's troops and probably about to be attacked by Edmund. Should he attack Edmund, or Cnut?

Eadric's eggs really were all in one basket and he had no one other than the ageing king in his corner. It is easy to see why Eadric was friendless, but not so obvious to see why he would be so keen to carry out the king's orders, thus ensuring that he only had the king on his side. It might help to understand his antipathy towards the family of the two murdered thegns by looking at their landholding and seeing it as something of a local rivalry.

The family of Wulfric Spott were holders of land in eastern Mercia, with estates lying mainly in Derbyshire, Nottinghamshire, Leicestershire, east Staffordshire, north Warwickshire and south Yorkshire. Eadric's power base was in western Mercia, in Herefordshire, Shropshire, Worcestershire and western Staffordshire.[37] He may have been acting

The River Trent, at Repton.

Sutton Hoo – The mound of the ship burial, of Rædwald, or perhaps one of Penda's victims.

Yeavering in Northumberland – the site of Edwin's palace.

Heavenfield – where Oswald prepared for battle against Cadwallon.

Rowley Burn – where Cadwallon met his death.

Bamburgh – seat of the Bernician Kings, attacked by Penda.

The Priory Chapel of
St Mary, Deerhurst,
Gloucestershire, in the
Hwicce heartland, showing a
double-headed Anglo-Saxon
window and a blocked-up
Anglo-Saxon doorway.

St Mary's, Deerhurst –
Anglo-Saxon carving of the
Virgin Mary with the child
Jesus in her womb.

Above: The River Severn at Tewkesbury, Gloucestershire.

Right: Lichfield Cathedral – carving of Peada of the Middle Angles. (Photo credit: Richard Tearle.)

Effigy of Osric, sub-king of the *Hwicce*, at Gloucester Cathedral, which he is said to have founded.

Chester – St Werburg, daughter of Wulfhere, is commemorated in the street name; she was the patron saint of Chester.

Repton, St Wystan's (Wigstan) Church – the crypt which housed the remains of Æthelbald, Wiglaf and Wigstan.

Repton, St Wystan's Church – the original Saxon door to the tower.

Above left: The Repton Stone in Derby Museum, retrieved from a broken cross at St Wystan's Church, believed to be a depiction of Æthelbald.

Above right: Lichfield Cathedral – carving of King Offa. (Photo credit: Richard Tearle.)

Below: Replica of a coin of King Offa, from author's own collection.

Offa's Dyke near Knighton in Shropshire.

Offa's Dyke plaque near Knighton in Shropshire.

Sarcophagus from St Alkmund's church, Derbyshire, dating from *c.* 800.

Pillar of Eliseg, Denbighshire.

Replica of a coin of King Cenwulf, from author's own collection.

A carving of King Cenwulf in St Peter's Church, Winchcombe.

Above: Stones from the abbey at Winchcombe, now housed at Sudeley Castle, Gloucs.

Left: Carving of St Kenelm at the well outside Winchcombe, where his funeral procession was said to have rested.

Above: The Repton Viking burial site.

Right: The Repton Viking burial site, showing the backfilled trench from the 2017 dig.

Above left: Lady Æthelflæd with Athelstan, statue at Tamworth, Staffordshire (photo credit: Richard Tearle.)

Left: A close-up picture of the statue, which was raised in 1918 on the millennial anniversary of Æthelflæd's death. (Courtesy of Humphrey Bolton under Creative Commons).

Above right: King Athelstan, the nephew of Æthelflæd, giving a book to St Cuthbert. Illuminated manuscript from Bede's *Life of St Cuthbert*.

The remains of St Oswald's Priory, Gloucester, the burial place of Æthelred and Æthelflæd, Lord and Lady of the Mercians.

This carved stone slab was found during excavations at St Oswald's. It is believed to have been the base of a cross and probably dates from the late ninth century, when the church was first established by the Lord and Lady of the Mercians but before it was rededicated to St Oswald, after his relics were interred there *c* 909. (Courtesy of Fæ under Creative Commons.)

Lady Godiva, statue in Coventry.

The River Wye from Yat Rock, Gloucestershire.

upon the king's orders, but Eadric had nothing to lose and everything to gain if he could acquire the additional land which neighboured his own. We should perhaps not underestimate how many squabbles were conducted away from court that were not necessarily all of national political importance.

Eadric obviously decided his needs would be better met by opposing Edmund, and when Cnut landed at Sandwich, Eadric defected, taking forty ships with him. Edmund, meanwhile, had joined forces with Uhtred of Northumbria.

In 1016 Cnut and Eadric went into Warwickshire, 'and ravaged and burnt, and killed all they came across,' this being an area where Eadric himself didn't hold land, but where Ealdorman Leofwine did. Uhtred of Northumbria and Edmund Ironside meanwhile ravaged the lands where Eadric might have been able to gather men and resources: Staffordshire, Shropshire and Cheshire.[38] Was this action a reluctance to meet the Danish army head on, or were they in fact taking the opportunity to destroy as much as they could of Eadric's power base? Florence of Worcester accused them of cowardice: 'The Mercians refused to engage ... unless they were joined by King Æthelred and the Londoners,' but it is just possible that they simply did not wish to act without the king.

Cnut withdrew from Mercia, a strategy which likewise drew Uhtred away from Mercia. When Uhtred heard that Cnut was heading 'into Northumbria towards York' he hastily turned north and 'submitted then out of necessity, and with him all the Northumbrians, and he gave hostages.' Nevertheless, the *ASC* says, he was killed 'by the advice of Ealdorman Eadric'. After that Cnut appointed Eric of Hlathir, his brother-in-law, earl of Northumbria.

It is perhaps not surprising that Eadric would be blamed, although it is only the C version of the *Chronicle* which names him as the perpetrator. Perhaps it was not enough for Cnut to receive his submission, and Eadric dripped a word or two in Cnut's ear about the damage done by Uhtred to his (Eadric's) lands. Perhaps Cnut wanted his own man in Northumbria, and Eadric was merely following orders.

A short tract, *De Obsessione Dunelmi*, written in the eleventh century, makes no mention at all of Eadric when describing the murder of Uhtred. The killing takes place in the context of Northumbrian politics, and after talking about the daughter of Bishop Ealdun, the author finds it necessary to retrace his steps and explain about the death of Uhtred, who, he says, was approached by Cnut to join him, but Uhtred refused. 'He replied that the worst thing is the man who does such things against his lord and father-in-law. "No reward" he said, "could persuade me to do what I ought not to do. I will serve the king as long as he lives."'

After Æthelred's death, the tract continues, Cnut sent to Uhtred and ordered him to come to him. Uhtred, having accepted promises of safe conduct, did so, but 'through the treachery of a powerful king's thegn, Thurbrand, known as Hold, the king's soldiers who had hidden behind a curtain spread across the width of the hall, suddenly sprang out in mail and slaughtered the earl and forty of his chief men who had entered with him.'[39]

Whether or not Eadric was complicit in the murder of Uhtred, on 23 April 1016, Æthelred Unræd died and Edmund was declared king. Therefore, what happened next is perhaps no terrible surprise; it would be fair to surmise that Eadric was probably not Edmund's favourite person.

Ironside, now officially King Edmund II, fought a series of five battles, the second being at Sherson near Malmesbury at which the *ASC* says, 'Ealdorman Eadric and Æthelmær Darling were supporting the Danish army against King Edmund.'[40] At this battle Eadric made Edmund's supporters think he was dead. Roger of Wendover accused Eadric, upon seeing that the English were prevailing, of cutting off the head of a certain man and holding it up, exclaiming, 'It is in vain for you English to fight, for you have lost your head; flee, then, with speed; for here I hold in my hands the head of King Edmund.'

A deadly serious game of chase was initiated. The *ASC* reported that the Danish army went into Mercia 'slaying and burning whatever was in their path, as is their custom' – although presumably not Eadric's lands – and after that there was a battle in London, and a fourth in Otford, in which the English had the upper hand. At this point Eadric met Edmund at Aylesford and this is when 'no greater folly was agreed to than that was.' Why did Edmund agree to take Eadric back? Eadric seems to have been one who could easily persuade, and it may also be that Edmund was feeling overconfident following the success at Otford, where the *ASC*, without mentioning the battle, says that the Danish army 'fled before him with their horses into Sheppey.' But if we are to take everything the chronicles say about Eadric at face value, it still seems incredible that Edmund should have been seduced by him at this point.

A fifth battle occurred, this time at *Assandun* – most likely Ashingdon – in Essex. This is when Eadric, with the *Magonsæte*, 'betrayed his liege lord'. How loyal had Eadric been in the first place? Was his return to Edmund genuine? The men of the *Magonsæte* had, only a few months earlier, seen their territory ravaged by Edmund's troops.[41] On the other hand, perhaps Edmund, confident after earlier successes, had underestimated the strength of Cnut's army.

The *ASC* for this period, written at a time when the collapse of the English defence was already known, is biased towards the place where it was written, East Anglia, and four of the six men mentioned as dying at Ashingdon had connections with this area.[42]

The *Liber Eliensis* says that Edmund 'played the part of an energetic soldier and good commander; he would have crushed all of them together, had it not been for the schemings of the treacherous Ealdorman Eadric. 'And there was a massacre in that place of almost the whole array of the nobility of the English, who never received a more wounding blow in war than there.'[43] Which makes what happened next rather odd.

Cnut went to Gloucester, having heard that Edmund was there, and they came to terms. The *Encomium Emmæ Reginæ* says that Eadric was the one who brokered the peace terms. 'Eadric, who had previously withdrawn from the fighting, now returned to his lord and his companions, and was received for he was an able counsellor.'[44] According to the *Encomiast*, Eadric talked his way out of his withdrawal from the fighting with consummate ease, claiming that he knew the enemy well enough to know that they could not have been beaten, and that he was doing the English a favour by surviving, arguing that it was better to withdraw whole than wounded.

Roger of Wendover has a rather splendid tale of the two kings engaged in single combat, after which the kings 'embraced each other amidst the rejoicings of both armies. They then exchanged garments' – presumably not unlike footballers after a match – in token of peace. Henry of Huntingdon adds that Cnut cried out, 'Bravest of youths, why should either of us risk his life for the sake of a crown? Let us be brothers by adoption, and divide the kingdom.'

Not long afterwards, Edmund conveniently died – providing yet another case of the kingdom not being shared by two kings for very long – although he could well have received ultimately fatal wounds in the battle. Roger of Wendover claimed that it was Eadric's son who murdered Edmund, concealing himself in the sink whilst the king was answering the call of nature, and thrusting 'a very sharp knife into the king's bowels, leaving the king mortally wounded.' Henry of Huntingdon has the same story.

In 1017, Cnut married Emma, the widow of Æthelred Unræd. After Edmund's death, it seems that Eadric got what was due to him. This, initially, was his appointment, or confirmed appointment, as ealdorman of Mercia. But, also in 1017, he was killed.

There are various versions of what happened. The *ASC* merely states that he was killed, along with various others, including Northman, son of Leofwine, ealdorman of the *Hwicce*. The F version of the *Chronicle* adds that he was 'very rightly killed'.[45] The *Encomium* gives the most detail, although it is not generally a wholly trustworthy source. Of the killing of Eadric, the *Encomiast* says that, 'the king said sadly: "Shall you, who have deceived your lord with guile, be capable of being true to me? I will return to you a worthy reward" ... and summoning Eirìkr [Eric], his commander, he said, "Pay this man what we owe him; that is to say kill him lest he play us false." He indeed, raised his axe without delay, and cut off his head with a mighty blow.'[46]

Roger of Wendover offers two options, saying that Cnut ordered Eadric to be suffocated and thrown through a window into the Thames, or that he had him beheaded. 'But whether the traitor ended his life one way or the other, it does not much matter; since this is sufficiently clear, that he, who had deceived so many, by the just judgement of God met with condign punishment.'[47]

Intriguingly, it is possible that Cnut was already exercising caution with Eadric even before ordering his execution. Hemming mentions an Earl Ranig and says that when the country was divided between Cnut and Edmund, Earl Ranig was appointed in charge of Hereford.[48] No doubt it would not have done Cnut any harm to have one of his own men keeping a watchful eye on Eadric.

Why then, was Eadric killed? The obvious answer is that he was a notorious turncoat and not to be trusted. John of Worcester said that Cnut 'feared that some day he would be entrapped by Eadric's treachery,' as had his predecessors, Edmund and Æthelred Unræd. Or perhaps, having no rivals to the kingship left, Cnut simply no longer needed Eadric. But other factors were at work. Cnut had married an Englishwoman, and her name was Ælfgifu of Northampton. Her father had been killed, and her brothers blinded, very possibly by Eadric. Presumably hovering in the shadows, waiting to emerge, was a certain Godwine, who was to rise to power so spectacularly over the next few years, as we shall see in Chapter Twelve. If Godwine was indeed the son of Wulfnoth, who had been provoked into rebellion by the accusations of Eadric's brother, Brihtric, in 1009, then here we see the beginnings of family rivalries which were to help rive the country apart over the next few decades.[49] The *Encomium* says that it was Eric of Hlathir who killed Eadric, and certainly Eric's son, Hakon, received some of Eadric's ealdordom. Hakon was also given control of Worcestershire,[50] an appointment which would have ousted Leofwine, ealdorman of the *Hwicce*, whose son Northman had been killed with Eadric.

Leofwine's territory had been ravaged in the fighting of 1015, and it seems that his grandson, Æthelwine, son of Godric, had his hands cut off, presumably whilst a hostage of the Danes.[51] In 1014, the *ASC* recorded that Cnut 'put ashore the hostages that had been given to his father, and he cut off their hands, ears and noses.' It is safe to assume, therefore, that Leofwine's family would not have been natural supporters of Cnut. He isn't mentioned by name during the fighting of 1015–1016, but it is probable that he was fighting for Edmund. Yet, in 1017, the *ASC* says that Northman, the son of Leofwine, was killed, as if part of the same purge which saw the removal of Eadric Streona. Was he an adherent of Eadric? It is hard to make sense of the loyalties here, for after Eadric's death, Leofwine was promoted, and held the earldom of Mercia until his death in 1023, whereupon he was succeeded by his son, Leofric.

Not much is known about Leofwine, beyond the fact that he was appointed ealdorman of the *Hwicce* in 994.[52] An Æthelsige was accused by King Æthelred Unræd of being 'an enemy of Almighty God and all the people' and of murder and theft. He was deprived of his land (S893) and his office, which seems to have involved an official position in Mercia.[53] It is tempting to connect this Æthelsige with the man who harried the Welsh in 992.[54] The confiscation of the land may be connected with Leofwine's appointment in 994. From 1002 to 1005 he was the last of only three ealdormen regularly to witness the charters of Æthelred Unræd, and it is likely that he held responsibility for the whole of Mercia during those years,[55] and when Eadric Streona was appointed in 1007, Leofwine's area of control was reduced to that of the territory of the *Hwicce*. He didn't regain all of Mercia upon Eadric's execution; in 1014 the king granted land to Leofwine in Herefordshire,[56] but when Eadric Streona died on Christmas Day 1017, his territory was given to Earl Eglaf and it would appear Leofwine was subordinate to him. Nevertheless, he was influential enough in Mercia that upon his death his authority passed to his son.

It is hard to imagine that Leofwine and Eadric were on friendly terms. If indeed Leofwine had been the only ealdorman between the Thames and Humber from 994 until 1007, then Eadric's presumed jurisdiction over Cheshire, Shropshire, Staffordshire and possibly Herefordshire[57] should have been enough, but Eadric appears to have made claims on Leofwine's territories, seizing Worcester lands.[58] A charter of 1013 shows Eadric at the top of the witness list, with Leofwine second (S931). Also on the witness list are the thegns Sigeferth and Morcar, those names being a reminder of another reason why the family would not have been kindly disposed towards Eadric.

If the family of Leofwine was connected to that of Ælfgifu of Northampton, then it would be no surprise to see him in Cnut's favour. But Cnut still put two of his Danish kinsmen into Leofwine's ealdordom, a third in Northumbria (in 1017 Cnut divided England into four, keeping Wessex for himself, Thorkell got East Anglia, Eadric – briefly – got

Mercia, and Northumbria went to Eric) and another Danish earl in Herefordshire.[59] But Leofwine still retained overall control of Mercia, and though Hakon was earl of Worcester, his deputy was Leofwine's son, Leofric, and another son, Eadwine, appears to have been his father's representative in Herefordshire. A Worcester charter dating from the period 1016 to 1023 shows the witness list order: Earls Hakon, Eglaf, and Leofwine, then Leofric and Eadwine. Eadwine was killed fighting the Welsh at Rhyd y Gores in 1039.[60]

Evidence can be pieced together which might give some clues as to Leofwine's origins. It is assumed that he was local to the territory of the *Hwicce*, he held land in Warwickshire granted by the king in 998 (S892) and in 1014 he was granted an estate in Herefordshire (S932). If his son, Northman, was the man named in receipt of an estate in Hampton-by-Evesham, in S873, then this would also point to *Hwiccian* origins, although this charter is regarded as spurious.[61]

Hugh Candidus mentions Leofwine's father. Giving details of 'Names of Certain Possessions [of the Monastery]', Hugh says, 'these are the lands: – Leofwine the Alderman [ealdorman] the son of Ælfwine gave unto God and S Peter [land at] Alwalton.' This is the only known reference to Leofwine's parentage.[62]

There has been a suggestion that this man, Ælfwine, is in fact Æthelwine, the ealdorman of East Anglia, son of Athelstan Half-king and nemesis of Ælfhere of Mercia.[63] Leofwine's grandson, Leofric, who died in 1066, held abbacies in Peterborough, Thorney and Crowland, all tenth-century foundations of Æthelwine's. It is no more than supposition, but if correct, it would add another dimension to the hostility between Leofric of Mercia, and the upstart Godwine. Æthelwine had a son named Leofwince, but it cannot be proved that this man was our Leofwine.

However, intriguingly, Ælfhere's successor, Ælfric *cild* had a son named Ælfwine, who was killed at the battle of Maldon in 991. 'Then the son of Ælfric, a warrior young in winters, chose his words and urged them on; Ælfwine said ... "I come from a mighty family of Mercian stock; my grandfather was Ealhhelm, a wise ealdorman..."'[64] However, the clue might be in that phrase, 'young in winters'; the impression is that Ælfwine was a young man when he died in battle. It has been suggested[65] that Leofwine came from the eastern, rather than the western, Midlands and that there might be a link with Wulfric Spott. Leofwine's son and grandson married women from the eastern shires, with Ælfgar, the grandson, marrying a woman named Ælfgifu, who may have been the daughter of Ealdgyth, Wulfric's niece, who was married to Morcar of the Seven Boroughs. Leofric was later to show support for Harold I, also known as Harefoot, son of Ælfgifu of Northampton, who was

Ealdgyth's cousin, suggesting a long-standing connection between the two families.[66]

Leofwine and Leofric, his son, appear to be the only Englishmen whose family remained in power during Cnut's reign.[67] Thus it would seem that the general purge was less along ethnic and more along personal lines.

Mercia was still important; Eadric had been able to bring large numbers of troops and with them influence the outcome of battles. For a long time, the north was still not secure, and Mercia was a useful buffer. Eadric, though, was clearly expendable. Can any defence be put forward for him?

It has been pointed out[68] that given his reputation it is remarkable that he was entrusted with high office by three successive kings. Indeed, if he was shown to be so untrustworthy so early on, why did Æthelred advance him? Perhaps, along with a willingness to do the king's 'dirty work',[69] he had qualities which now elude us, thanks to the commentary which survives. In 1006, the *ASC* says that the army from Wessex and Mercia was called out, yet it 'availed no whit more than it had often done before; for in spite of it all, the Danish army went about as it pleased.' Perhaps Eadric showed some kind of military and organisational skills, which appealed to a king whose country was being ravaged. And we know that in 1012 Eadric was busy harrying Wales, so he must have been at least halfway competent as a general. S1423 is a charter dated between 1016 and 1023 for a lease of land in Worcestershire which '*a ða hit weste læg*' (had been laid to waste) and hints at the devastation caused by Cnut and Eadric ravaging in not only Warwickshire, as claimed, but also Worcestershire.[70]

Of course, Eadric's reputation is sealed in the words of those who had cause to commit his deeds to writing. A brief look at the history of the shire of Winchcombe gives a clue as to how Eadric fared at the end of his life and provides another reason why he should have been so reviled by the chroniclers. Hemming has this to say about Eadric, 'whose cognomen was Streona, that is, "Acquisitor", first under King Æthelred and afterwards for a while under Cnut, [who] was set over the whole realm of the English and held dominion over it like an under-king.' This is no surprise. Plenty of other sources suggest the nature of Eadric's power, influence and wealth. But Hemming continues: 'He joined townships to townships and shires to shires at will; it was he who amalgamated the hitherto independent county of Winchcombe with the county of Gloucester.'

It seems that a redrawing of boundaries around the time of the partition of England between Cnut and Edmund resulted in the expansion of Gloucestershire at the expense of Herefordshire, and the complete subsummation of Winchcombeshire. Local men would have no cause to remember the architect of these changes with any fondness and regional sensibilities may still have been sharp enough to flavour the bias of the chronicles.[71] In 1009 the *ASC* reports that the army was 'hindered by Ealdorman Eadric, then as it always was.' But this is in relation to Kent, and perhaps Eadric was less inclined to commit his Mercian fyrd to the defence of the eastern counties.[72] It must also be remembered that we do not hear much about what was going on outside of the area of interest of the chronicler.

The vested interests of various landowners might help to explain why the raising of national levies failed so frequently during this period. But it doesn't explain why only Eadric is really singled out for mention. The *ASC* is the only one to name Eadric as complicit in Uhtred's murder and it may even be that Uhtred was trying to get back to his stronghold of Bamburgh when he was overtaken by Cnut's men and killed.

If Eadric was indeed the broker of peace between Cnut and Edmund, he had managed to maintain a position of chief advisor, to both kings. But he was on thin ice, for both Edmund and Cnut had married into the family of Wulfric Spott, and it is possible that his vacillation was the result of his not being able to decide which was the best side for him to support. He really had little choice but to play Edmund and Cnut off against each other, for he had burned bridges to both camps.

Much of his evil-doing can be explained away in terms of loyalty to Æthelred, but he would not be forgiven for his actions in 1016.

The *Encomium* has Eadric playing a pivotal role in the fall of the English, and thus gives a near contemporary account of his actions, but the whole thing is serving a distinct purpose; it was more concerned with showing what happened to those who deserted their lords, and it was aimed at an Anglo-Danish audience.[73]

The *ASC* complained about the lack of co-ordinated English defence. To put a man like Eadric in charge of Mercia might have been a solution to this, but the concentration of such power in the hands of a relative newcomer would inevitably fuel resentment.

The next earl of Mercia was a less colourful character, but the politics, intrigue, and family rivalries were no less intense, in the final chapter of English history before a conqueror from Normandy changed the landscape, both political and physical.

CHAPTER 12

The House of Leofric

Leofric was the son of Leofwine, the second of four generations of that family to govern in Mercia. It is likely, though, that Leofric did not replace Eadric Streona immediately as earl of all Mercia. He appeared on the witness list as earl in a charter of around 1023 (S979) but didn't sign again until 1032 (S964). It is possible that he began his career as Hakon's sheriff[1] with Eadwine, Leofric's brother, being his father's representative in Herefordshire. Earl Ranig seems to still have been active within Mercia at the time of Cnut's death. Northman's subordinate post under Leofwine probably went to Leofric after Northman's execution in 1017. Ingulph's forged history of Crowland gives details and says that the king greatly loved Leofric and gave him all of Northman's lands. A year after he inherited his father's earldom, Leofric may have also received the earldom of Earl Eglaf.[2]

Leofric had other brothers besides Northman. He was remembered at Worcester as a despoiler of the abbey's estates for the benefit of his thegns and his brothers Godwine and Eadwine. The family was presumably in a position to buy, or commandeer, profitable land. Hemming shows Eadwine acquiring church lands in Worcester by paying the tax due on them.[3] On the other hand, Leofric, whilst not being quite so famous as his wife, Godiva, was remembered as being a generous benefactor not only to Coventry, which he apparently founded, but also to Worcester, Evesham, Chester, Wenlock, Leominster and others.

Leofric followed his father as earl of Mercia, and his son and grandson would follow him, and they were the only comital family of this period to achieve this. However, his was not the only powerful family active during this period. Godwine, who had been a beneficiary of the atheling Athelstan's will, might reasonably be supposed to have been a supporter of Edmund, but his star rose to its apogee through his service to Cnut.

A charter of 1019 (S956) shows Godwine ahead of Leofwine on the witness list, and from 1023 Godwine headed the witness lists on all Cnut's extant charters after 1023, signing as *Godwine dux* (S959, 960) or *Godwinus dux* (S976). In 1033 Siward first signs as *dux*. He was possibly the immediate successor to Eric of Hlathir as earl of Northumbria, or a man named Eadulf *Cudel* (Cuttlefish) may have been earl of the whole region for a time.[4]

In 1035 Cnut died. An assembly at Oxford agreed yet another joint rule; this time between Cnut's sons Harthaknut and Harold Harefoot. Harthaknut was the son of Cnut and his second wife Emma of Normandy. Harold was the son of Cnut and Ælfgifu of Northampton, although the ASC is doubtful of his parentage.[5] Just as with the joint rules of 957, the discord in 975, and possibly the earlier division of 924, this situation left the country polarised, with the aristocracy in two distinct camps.

It might say something about the nature of the two leading earls that Godwine was confident, or rash, enough to support an absent king, while Leofric proposed a regency until things could be more finally settled, albeit that the nature of this regency was experimental, involving not a parent of a young monarch, but the adult half-brother of the 'king'.

Harthaknut was ruling in Denmark at this point, and Leofric and most of the nobles north of the Thames wanted Harold to rule for both, as both king and regent. Godwine and the nobles of Wessex were opposed to this. It would have been bucking a trend had Mercia and Wessex supported the same candidate in a succession dispute, but family ties must also have been a factor. Leofric's son married an Ælfgifu, possibly the relative of the murdered Ælfhelm, and wife of Morcar of the Seven Boroughs. If the family tree on page 186 is correct, then Leofric was related by marriage to Harold's family.

Initially it might be assumed that Godwine's and Leofric's families were friends, given that Godwine was in the same camp as Edmund and the thegns of the Seven Boroughs, and not in that of Eadric. He might have been expected to support Ælfgifu of Northampton rather than Queen Emma, although there is no definitive evidence as to the nature of the way in which he came into Cnut's favour.[6] But while on paper it looks as if, for whatever reason, he and Leofric ended up in different factions, there was no great level of recorded hostility between the two men. The chasm was to open up when their sons came to maturity.

Harold Harefoot remained in Mercia after Cnut's death, safe in his heartland and away from the control of Emma and Godwine. Emma stayed in Winchester with Harthaknut's housecarls and kept Wessex. But the *ASC* says that Harold was full king and seized many of her treasures.

In 1036 Emma decided to support her sons by Æthelred Unræd instead, who were at this point both in Normandy. This *volte-face* cannot have been a welcome development for Godwine, who had relied on Cnut's favour. As something of a parvenu, he would have nothing to gain from the restoration of the native dynasty. So he switched to supporting Harold. In the period 1036–37 more and more coins were issued in Harold's name, even in Harthknut's territory, and this might have been partly what persuaded Emma and Godwine to give up their waiting for Harthaknut.

Edward and Alfred returned from Normandy but Edward was turned away and in 1037 Alfred was captured and blinded, a deed for which Godwine was almost universally blamed.[7]

The *ASC* seems not to have been in favour of Harold generally, recording that support for him was 'not right'. It was, in the main, pro-Edward the Confessor, although the E version tends to favour Godwine.

The *Encomium* has a different perspective on the events of 1036. It should be borne in mind that it was written, essentially, as a piece of propaganda in support of Emma and her championing of Harthaknut. The *Encomiast* has a detailed story about Harold Harefoot forging a letter, supposedly from Emma, urging Edward and Alfred to return to England, in order that Harold could then lure them into a fatal trap. Was there ever such a letter? And was it a forgery, or was it genuine? Was the story made up to cast a slur on Harold, or to excuse Emma's decision to switch support to her sons in Normandy?[8]

Whatever the truth, the *Encomium* must, at any rate, be regarded as hugely biased. It does not call Edmund Ironside a king's son, but merely a 'youth',[9] and it treats Edward and Harthaknut as full brothers, as if Æthelred Unræd had never existed. But it does give one intriguing insight into the regard in which the extended family of Wulfric Spott were held, and of their status. In *Book III* it denies that Harold is Cnut's son. This in itself is not enough to refute Harold's claims, and the *Encomium* further denies that he is Ælfgifu of Northampton's son. Clearly his position as her son is important. If Emma denies that he is of this family, then she is not attacking them. The importance of Ælfgifu's kinship is clear, and Emma does not wish to offend this great family.[10]

In 1037 Harold Harefoot became full king of England and Emma was driven into exile. In 1040 Harold died and Harthaknut became king. It was not to prove an especially popular reign. In 1041 two of Harthaknut's housecarls were killed by the citizens of Worcester as they tried to collect tax, which resulted in the ravaging of Worcestershire. In that same year, Harthaknut invited his half-brother Edward to share the kingship with him, and in 1042, upon Harthaknut's death, Edward became full king of England.

An integral part of his kingship was the relationship he had with the powerful Godwines. Almost immediately he made Godwine's eldest son, Swein, an earl, and it wasn't long before Harold, the second eldest, was also elevated to this rank. Swein held two shires from within his father's earldom, those of Somerset and Berkshire, and three from Mercia, being Herefordshire, Gloucestershire and Oxfordshire. Meanwhile Harold became earl of East Anglia.

With these appointments the power of Godwine, elevated during the Danish rule, and his family, was confirmed. Had Cnut been wise to allow the concentration of power to rest in the hands of so few men? In many ways he was only doing what Edgar had done and, like Edgar, he cannot have known that he was going to leave two sons who would both die young. In Godwine we can see an Eadric-type figure, but whether Cnut would have seen this at the time, we cannot know.[11]

In November 1043 Edward seized his mother's lands and property. He rode with Leofric, Godwine and Siward, and his attack on his mother is hardly surprising, given that she doesn't seem to have supported him fully at any point. It is also interesting to note that, at this stage anyway, Leofric and Godwine were acting in tandem, any personal enmity presumably having been subordinate to their duty as the king's servants.

In 1045 Edward appointed Beorn Estrithson, the Danish nephew of Godwine, as earl in eastern Mercia, which bordered Leofric's territory. Edward married Godwine's daughter, and Godwine became an in-law to the king, just like Uhtred of Bamburgh and Eadric Streona before him. And, just like Eadric Streona, Godwine's loyalties appeared not to be fixed.

The year 1046 saw the first acts of disobedience from the Godwine family, as Swein teamed up with Gruffudd ap Llywelyn, king of Gwynedd and Powys, and went into South Wales. On the way back, according to the *ASC*, he 'ordered the abbess of Leominster to be brought to him, and he kept her as long as he pleased, and then let her go home.' In revenge for being forced to give her up,[12] he deprived the church of Worcester of a number of estates.

From John of Worcester: 'Meanwhile, Earl Swein, son of Earl Godwine and Gytha who had left England earlier because he was not permitted to marry Eadgifu, abbess of the convent at Leominster, whom he had seduced, went to Denmark, and returned with eight ships, saying dishonestly that he would henceforth remain faithful to the king.' Beorn, who was Swein's cousin – Beorn's father and Swein's mother were siblings – apparently promised to intercede on his behalf with the king, and Swein came to Pevensey and asked Beorn to make good his promise of help, and with this mission in mind, to go with him to Sandwich. But Swein led the trusting Beorn instead to Bosham, 'where his ships lay and, when he had brought him aboard, ordered him to be bound at once with cruel bonds and he held him until he came to Dartmouth where he killed him, and threw him into a deep ditch, and covered his body with earth.'[13]

Gruffudd ap Llywelyn's cross-border alliances did not end with his ill-fated association with Swein Godwineson. It seems he was looking for a more reliable partner, and he looked now to a family with whom he came into more frequent contact. Although he had been responsible for the death in 1039 of Earl Leofric's brother, Eadwine,[14] it seemed there was a mutual benefit in allying with Ælfgar, Leofric's son, who would have been feeling isolated as the Godwines gained more and more land and power.

At the start of 1051, Godwine's earldom stretched from Kent to Cornwall. He was father-in-law to the king of England, his son Swein had been re-admitted to the fold and given an appointment which included Oxford, Gloucester and Hereford – Mercian shires – and Berkshire and Somerset in Wessex. Harold Godwineson was earl of Essex, East Anglia, Cambridgeshire and Huntingdonshire. But he did not have complete sway. Leofric and Siward had thwarted a proposal to support Swein Estrithson (Beorn's brother) with English ships. Magnus, king of Norway, and Swein Estrithson of Denmark were locked in conflict for control of Denmark. Swein was the nephew of Godwine's wife Gytha. In 1047 Swein had asked for fifty English ships to be sent to his aid, but as Florence of Worcester recorded, whilst Godwine counselled the king to send the ships, the proposal was objected to by 'Earl Leofric and all the people'.

In 1051 Eustace II, count of Boulogne, a former brother-in-law of King Edward, landed at Dover on an official visit to England. Godwine's son Tostig had married the half-sister of Eustace's rival, the count of Flanders, and Swein Godwineson appears to have been embroiled in some animosity with the stepson of Eustace. Whether or not this informed the incident at Dover, what occurred was that Eustace and his men were attacked, Edward ordered Godwine to ravage Dover in retaliation, and Godwine refused. Godwine and his sons Swein and Harold came together, with the intention of going to the council. Leofric, Siward and Ralf answered Edward's call to join him with their armed forces. Those on the king's side advised that hostages should be given and that they would again in London to consider the charges against Godwine. But the Godwines fled and Edward outlawed them. Harold's earldom of East Anglia went to Ælfgar, Leofric's son. The Mercians now had control of the middle strip of the country, from west to east, and a friend in the north in Earl Siward.

Whilst the punishment seems perhaps a little harsh, it is likely that Edward had never forgiven Godwine for what happened to his brother Alfred. Godwine had also stirred up trouble at a time of danger, for Harald Hardrada of Norway had set his sights on England. The advice of Leofric and Siward to take hostages rather than engage in hostilities indicates that they were pragmatists, politicians in a way that Godwine could never be.[15]

In any event, their banishment was short-lived, and by 1052 they were back, which meant that Ælfgar Leofricson was displaced from East Anglia. However, in 1053, Godwine died, and his son Harold became earl of Wessex in his place. Ælfgar was back in East Anglia and suddenly the Godwinesons were isolated.

The pendulum swung again, just two years later. In 1055 Siward of Northumbria died and Tostig Godwineson became earl of Northumbria. Siward's son Waltheof was too young to succeed him, and there was something of a precedent for placing southerners in positions of authority in the north (Edgar, for example, with Earl Oslac, and Ælfhelm, brother of Wulfric Spott) but it was not usual for the lands north of the Tyne to be ruled by anyone from outside the local family of Bamburgh.[16]

In the same year, Ælfgar Leofricson was outlawed. John of Worcester echoes the *ASC* in saying that he was 'guiltless' but version E of the *Chronicle* has him admitting his guilt 'before all the men assembled'. It was at this assembly that Edward gave the earldom of Northumbria to Tostig.[17] Had Ælfgar wanted Northumbria for himself? Or would he have been worried that Tostig would then get the vacant East Anglian earldom and leave the Mercians split? Possibly it was difficult for Ælfgar to establish himself in an area which would have been loyal to Harold Godwineson. At around this time, Edward put another of Godwine's sons, Gyrth, in charge of Norfolk, a shire within Ælfgar's earldom. It is difficult to piece together; did Ælfgar bridle against the appointments, or did the new appointees trump up some charges to get rid of him? Certainly, Ælfgar's actions after his banishment show a high level of disaffection, but whether this proved the charges or was spurred by them cannot now be known.

John of Worcester explains what happened next. Ælfgar 'soon went to Ireland, and returned when he had acquired eighteen pirate ships, and approached Gruffudd, king of the Welsh, to request his help against King Edward.' They advanced on Hereford and were met by the son of the king's sister, the 'timorous' Earl Ralf, who ordered the English 'contrary to custom' to fight on horseback, but before battle was joined, the earl took flight.

Roger of Wendover says that upon sight of the rebels, Earl Ralf fled, and was pursued by Ælfgar and Gruffudd, who slew 500 men, before slaying seven clergymen who were defending the doors of the cathedral, and then burning the town. Harold made peace, and Ælfgar was re-established in East Anglia.

In the autumn of 1057 Leofric died and on 21 December Ralf of Hereford died. This raised the question of what to do about the territories and how to deal with the Welsh. Leofric may not have been the most charismatic of men but his loyalty to Edward was never in question. Ælfgar was a bit of a troublemaker, and Ralf's son was still a child. In the end, Edward permitted Ælfgar to succeed his father, while the Godwines carved up the remaining territory among themselves. Gyrth took over in East Anglia and another brother, Leofwine, became responsible for the shires around the mouth of the Thames. Harold took Herefordshire, part of Gloucestershire and perhaps Shropshire.[18]

What can be said, then, of Leofric and his career? The *Vision of Earl Leofric* dates from the late eleventh century and speaks of Leofric's piety, that he had a vision of St Paul, that he was 'but a moderate drinker', and that he prayed in secret when all his drunken companions were asleep.[19]

The impression of Leofric is that of a steady and sensible man, protective of his lands but lacking the overweening ambition displayed by his predecessor, Eadric Streona, and of his rival, Godwine. He was himself the son of an ealdorman and was in power for more than twenty years 'without violence or aggression'.[20] Of his wife Godgifu, or Godiva, much has been written but little can actually be said with certainty.

A Godgifu who appears in the *Liber Eliensis*, the widow of an earl distributing her goods among the churches, is not her. The entry says that she was a widow in the reign of Cnut, and Leofric was alive until 1057.[21]

Lady Godiva is probably a deal more famous than her – apparently – rather staid, conformist husband. While he maintained his earldom with little fuss, and contended only with a wayward son, she notoriously took all her clothes off and rode naked through the streets of Coventry to protest against the taxes levied by her husband.

The story goes that Leofric founded the monastery at Coventry on the advice of his wife. We know that he and she were in fact generous patrons of the church – in one example Leofric and Godgifu asked Bishop Wulfwig[22] for permission to endow the monastery of Stow St Mary and assign lands to it. The bishop granted their request. Slightly later they furnished it with priests and desired that divine service should be celebrated there 'as it is in St Paul's, London.' (S 478) – but at Coventry he endowed the foundation with so much land, woods and ornaments that 'there was not found in all England a monastery with such an abundance of gold and silver, gems and costly garments.' Godgifu was keen to free the town of Coventry from such a financial burden, and yet when she spoke to her husband about it, he rebuked her, saying, 'Mount your horse, and ride naked, before all the people, through the market of the town, from one end to the other, and on your return you shall have your request.' Whereupon, she 'loosed her hair and let down her tresses, which covered the whole of her body like a veil, she rode through the marketplace, without being seen, except her fair legs, and having completed the journey, returned with gladness to her astonished husband,' who then freed the town from the aforesaid service, and confirmed what he had done by a charter.[23]

By this stage, the *ASC* is full of detail, such that we don't have to pick apart scant charter information as with earlier centuries, and yet there is nothing in the *ASC* about this incident, or indeed anywhere else. Only Roger of Wendover has the story.

Ingulph's forged history of Crowland says that Leofric was a 'very devout man, and remarkable for his numerous alms-deeds ... at the suggestion of his wife, Godiva by name, both the most beauteous of all the woman of her time, as well as the most holy in heart.' This is a long way from Roger's story, however.

William Dugdale said of Coventry that the church was 'so richly adorned with gold and silver and precious stones, that the walls seem'd too narrow to contain all the treasure.' Dugdale says of the foundation charter that in it Leofric gave 'twenty-four villages, with the moiety of the town of Coventry in which it stands, with all liberties and customs which he himself enjoy'd in the said estate and that the abbot of the said house should be subject to none but the king.'[24]

William of Malmesbury wrote that: 'In two porches at Coventry lie the bodies of the builders of the monastery, an excellent married couple, though the wife, Godiva, has the greater fame. In her lifetime she contributed all her wealth to the church and when she was on the point of death, she gave orders for a circlet of gems to be hung round the neck of a statue of the blessed Mary.' He noted that these gems were worth 100 marks of silver.[25]

Charters relating to Leofric's gift to Coventry are spurious, for example, S1226, which records his granting land to Coventry in 1043, and S1098, a writ of King Edward's declaring that he confirms the gifts made by Earl Leofric and Godgifu to Abbot Leofwine and the brethren at Coventry Minster. S1000, dated 1043 showing King Edward confirming to Coventry Abbey privileges and land, as granted by Leofric, *dux*, is also considered to be spurious.

Since the charters relating to Leofric's foundation of Coventry are forgeries, can we be sure that he, never mind Godgifu, had any hand in the endowment of the monastery, or the granting of the twenty-four villages? Henry of Huntingdon said, when writing of the death of

Leofric, that he was 'the renowned earl of Chester, whose wife Godgifu, a name meriting endless fame, was of distinguished worth, and founded an abbey at Coventry, which she enriched with immense treasures of silver and gold.' Henry seems sure that the foundation of Coventry was attributable to the lady alone, and what of his comment that her name merited endless fame?

Florence of Worcester, which is only just over 40 miles from Coventry, and writing before 1118, stated that Leofric and Godgifu were jointly responsible, saying that Leofric 'was buried with all pomp at Coventry; which monastery, among the other good deeds of his life, he and his wife … had founded.'

A possible suggestion is that it was Leofric who made the grant, but that the land belonged to Godgifu. It has been pointed out that in the writ where Edward supposedly confirms the gift, the exemptions listed are anachronistic. There is no evidence that the original charters were lost, and Joan Lancaster[26] thought it more likely that the forgeries were made anyway, for other reasons. The prior's right to half of Coventry is not listed in the Domesday survey, and the suggestion is that the forgers added lands which were not granted by Leofric to lands which were. It is possible that the five hides of Coventry held by Godgifu in the Domesday Warwickshire survey represent Coventry, intact, proving that at this time, it did not form part of the abbey's possessions. Lancaster's conclusion seemed to be not that Leofric didn't found the abbey, but that the charters were forged to suit the needs of later priors.

Estates at Wolverley and Blackwell, Worcestershire, were said to have been taken from the monastery of Worcester. Earl Leofric is alleged to have held them unjustly for a long time.[27] He retained certain other estates, which were claimed by the church of Worcester, but rather than their being returned upon his death, the grant was extended to Godgifu. They were then seized, with her other possessions, by her grandsons.[28] As a result, according to Hemming, one grandson, Edwin, perished, abandoned by his friends. The other, Morcar, died in captivity. It was perhaps not quite so simple. Dubious relationship with certain Church lands aside, Leofric comes across as a politician not prone to impulsive action, and it might be said that his son and grandsons were impetuous, even traitorous,[29] but it is surely more a question of their having been provoked. The changes which occurred following Leofric's death, whilst allowing his son to succeed him, nevertheless actually left Ælfgar isolated.

The *ASC* reports that in 1058 Ælfgar was banished for a second time. 'But he soon returned with violence through the help of Gruffudd.' It was possibly around this time that Ælfgar's daughter, Ealdgyth, married, or was given in marriage to, Gruffudd. Just as he had in 1055, Ælfgar had returned with the Welsh king's assistance, only this time they were also aided by a Viking fleet, commanded by Harald Hardrada of Norway. Whether or not it was the intention, this was no invasion fleet, but merely succeeded in restoring Ælfgar to his earldom in Mercia. We can't be sure, because at this point the *ASC* unhelpfully says that it was all 'too tedious to relate'. But it was probably no small matter, for the Irish *Annals of Tigernach* entry for 1058 reports the sailing of 'a fleet led by the son of the king of Norway, with the foreigners of the Orkneys and the Hebrides and Dublin, to seize the kingdom of England, but to this God did not consent.'

Despite the lack of evidence, it is tempting to suppose that Ælfgar's exile in 1058 can be linked to his expulsion three years earlier, in 1055. The alliance between Gruffudd and Ælfgar was beneficial to both, but had it really been forged in 1055? Gruffudd had proved his strength as far back as 1039, and perhaps Ælfgar would have been taking a gamble had he arrived, as he did, on Welsh shores with his Hiberno-Scandinavian pirate ships. It has been suggested[30] that Ælfgar, whose father Leofric was growing old, and who was being squeezed by avaricious Godwines, might have made overtures towards Gruffudd prior to 1055, and that this friendship might in fact have been the reason for his exile in 1055 and his being accused of treason. The impetus may well have sprung from his being displaced in 1052 when the Godwines were brought back into the fold and Ælfgar had to give up his earldom.

Had Ælfgar lived, it is unlikely that he would have supported Harold Godwineson's election to the throne. He, far more than his father, had reason to resent the Godwines. He had been banished twice, and both times Harold had been involved.

We are not given the date of Ælfgar's death, but it must have been around the year 1062. His – presumably – eldest son, Burgheard, had predeceased his father. We know of him through a charter of 1061, in which Ælfgar granted land to the abbey of Rheims, in honour of Burgheard, who was buried there, and also the gift of a richly decorated gospel book. It is likely that Burgheard was on his way back from Rome when he died, having accompanied Bishop Wulfwig of Dorchester on a mission to press mutual interests in Lincolnshire against the escalating power of the Godwines.[31] Ælfgar's surviving sons must have been quite young, probably only in their teens, when their father died. The eldest, Edwin, succeeded as earl of Mercia. In 1063 the Welsh raiding began and Harold – who had been in charge of Hereford since 1057 – decided to retaliate.[32] In May he sailed from Bristol while his brother Tostig invaded North Wales. Gruffudd escaped from this two-pronged attack but was killed by his own men and 'his head and the prow of his ship with its ornaments were sent to Earl Harold, who at once sent them to King

210

Edward.' After this, according to Geoffrey Gaimar, 'there was no more care about the Welsh.'[33]

In 1064 Harold went to Normandy, where he famously either swore, or did not swear, an oath to support Duke William's claim to the English throne. Meanwhile in England, his brother Tostig was stirring up resentment.

In 1065 John of Worcester's record says the northerners rose up in rebellion to avenge the deaths of three northern thegns, including Earl Uhtred's son, Gospatric, who died on 28 December 1058, and for whose killing Queen Eadgyth was blamed, said to be acting in the interests of her brother Tostig. John also said that they were objecting to a huge tribute which Tostig had unjustly levied on the whole of Northumbria.

The rebels went to York where they seized two of Tostig's housecarls and killed them, before breaking open Tostig's treasury. The following day they killed another 200 of Tostig's men. The *ASC* adds that the rebels called for Morcar, the younger brother of Edwin, to replace Tostig.[34]

Tostig was unlikely ever to have been accepted by the Northumbrians. The Mercian isolation when surrounded by Godwines might have been geographical, rather than political, for the Northumbrians would not take kindly to Tostig, who, unlike Siward before him – a Dane by birth and married to a Northumbrian woman – had no local connection to the area. And Harold's influence in the south must have been subject to the fact that his lands were somewhat scattered.

The Mercians, even sandwiched as they were, north and south, by the Godwines, still had a solid power bloc. At this stage it would hardly have seemed feasible that in a few short years, Harold would reign supreme.[35]

So now, the natural alliance was the Mercians and the Northumbrians against Wessex, an almost complete reversal from where the story of Mercia began.

Morcar was able to join the rebels incredibly quickly, suggesting that this had been some while in the planning.[36] Once on the march, they were joined by Morcar's brother Earl Edwin at Northampton, who had with him men from Wales as well as Mercia.

Discussions were held at Northampton and then at Oxford. The rebel demands were for the renewal of Cnut's law in the north, and the dismissal of Tostig. Tostig accused Harold of fomenting the rebellion against him and Harold had to swear an oath to clear himself of this charge. Edward wanted to use force to crush the rebellion, but his counsellors were against the idea, it was late in the year and so they gave in to the demands. It was said that Edward never really recovered from the stress of this incident.[37] Just before Christmas, Tostig and his wife

Judith left for Flanders, where her half-brother Count Baldwin gave them welcome.

At some point, but it must have been after 1063, Harold married Ealdgyth, sister of the earls Edwin and Morcar, and widow of Gruffudd. There is no reason why Harold would have moved to marry her before Edward's death. Afterwards, it may have been a way of keeping the earls of the north 'onside'. There is no evidence that Edwin and Morcar opposed Harold's election in 1066, following the death of King Edward, but it is fairly certain that they were both young, and inexperienced.

It need not be stated that 1066 was a significant year, but the battle at Hastings was not the only conflict. In May, the ousted Tostig Godwineson harried the Isle of Wight, Sandwich, and continued to cause a nuisance as far north as the Humber. Edwin and Morcar drove him into Scotland.

Roger of Wendover's account seems to get a little confused. After the expulsion of Tostig he says that *Mercher*, son of Ælfgar, was made earl of Northumbria. He says that when Tostig landed at the mouth of the Humber he was driven back by the brothers Edwin[38] and *Mercard*, and then as he was committing 'ravages in Northumberland' he was opposed by Earl *Mercher* and the men of that region. He says that among those who fled to Scotland were the brothers Edwin and *Morcar*, as well as the nobles *Mercher* and Waltheof. In 1071, he says, Edwin, *Mercher* and Siward took refuge in the woods at Ely where all but Hereward perished. He may have thought that these were different people, but even so, his account is confused, for it seems that Edwin was not at Ely.

Safe to say that Edwin and Morcar were working together when Tostig returned in alliance with Harald Hardrada of Norway. Harald anchored his fleet at Riccall on the Ouse, and before King Harold could get there from the south, Edwin and Morcar had to face the might of the Norwegian forces. It seems they managed to assemble their fighting forces with relative speed. At Gate Fulford, outside York, battle was joined. For most of a day, they blocked the road and stopped the Norwegians advancing, but they finally gave way and their men were cut down or drowned. The men of York made terms, which probably shows that Harold's recent progress north had failed to win them over to his cause. Edwin and Morcar survived the battle. They would barely have had time to regroup in order to provide any assistance at Stamford Bridge, and it is not certain whether they were at Hastings,[39] but it can probably be said in their defence that they would have had few troops to bring with them, having suffered such heavy losses at Fulford.

By March 1067 those who had sworn to William included Archbishop Stigand of Canterbury, Edgar the Atheling (grandson of Edmund Ironside), Edwin, Morcar and Waltheof, son of Siward of Northumbria.

William sailed to Normandy, expediently taking these five with him, effectively as hostages. Perhaps he knew that the submissions were made under duress, with no sincerity. Returning at the end of 1067, William faced rebellion from Devon.

In the summer of 1068, Edgar, Edwin and Morcar left the court and went north, where the Northumbrians were making ready to rebel. Their leader was Earl Cospatric. Early in 1069 William appointed a man by the name of Robert de Comines as the new earl of York, but he was attacked by the rebels and burned alive in the bishop's house at Durham. The men of York declared for Edgar, but William rode north, relieved the new castle, and suppressed the rebellion.

In that same year there was a Mercian revolt led by a Herefordshire thegn, Eadric the Wild, who was in alliance with the Welsh princes. The rebellion spread as far as Cheshire and Stafford. The king went to Stafford where he defeated the rebels, but he was called to York by an attempt by the Danes to retake the city. To reinforce his control, William harried the north, and the only pocket of resistance left was the remnant of the Mercian host, which had been defeated at Stafford. William marched against them and crushed them. Castles were erected at Chester and Stafford, and William returned to Wessex. He had made sure that the devastation would mean that Mercia and Northumbria would never again rise up against his rule.

There is no evidence that the brothers Edwin and Morcar had been involved in the uprising, but Edwin's death came about when he was on his way to Scotland, presumably in flight, although it seems his demise was brought about by his own followers under circumstances which are lost to us now. The *ASC* records merely that in 1072 [1071] 'Earl Edwin and Earl Morcar took to flight, and went different ways through woods and across open country, until Edwin was slain by his own men, and Morcar went by ship to Ely.' Here, Morcar joined Hereward the Wake.

Hereward, the legendary resistance fighter from the fenlands, was alleged by some sources to be the son of Leofric and Godiva. Could Morcar really have been fighting alongside his uncle?

According to a twelfth-century source, the *De Gestis Herewardi Saxonis*, Hereward was the son of Leofric, kinsman of Ralph the Staller, and Eadgifu, the great-great-granddaughter of Earl Oslac of Northumbria, banished in 975.[40] Ingulph's spurious history of Crowland says that this Leofric was the kinsman of Earl Ralf of Hereford, but still says Leofric's wife was called Ediva (Godiva?).[41] So where does the suggestion come from that Leofric was the father of Hereward; is it merely a confusion over names?

A fifteenth-century genealogy of the Wake family, setting out the descent of the Barony of Bourne, states that Hereward was the son of Earl Leofric and Lady Godiva. It has been suggested that if this was not a guess by the compiler of the Wake genealogy, then it was probably an attempt to give Edmund Holland, earl of Kent, for whom the work was written, a more noble lineage. Interestingly though, according to Domesday Book, the estate was held by Earl Morcar in 1066. Although he is recorded as having held a large number of estates in Lincolnshire, it seems Morcar did not hold the full rights to all of them. He may have held Lincolnshire as part of his earldom or it might have been a separate earldom held by his brother Edwin.[42]

The standoff at Ely was fated to fail. When William learned what was happening, he summoned land and naval levies, surrounded the area, and ordered a causeway to be built. The rebels surrendered; the *ASC* names Morcar among them, and says that Hereward escaped. It further states that William dealt with the prisoners as he pleased, but gives no further detail of Morcar's fate.

For more information we need to turn to Orderic Vitalis, who says that William flung Morcar into fetters 'without any open charge' and kept him in prison under Roger, castellan of Beaumont. According to this version, it was when Edwin heard of this that he vowed to free or avenge his brother. So for six months he tried to gather support from the Scots, Welsh and English, and it was at this time that three – unnamed – brothers betrayed him to the Normans. He was slain with 'twenty knights'. His killers' success was partly due to a high tide, which kept Edwin trapped beside a tidal stream.[43] Here we are told that all – Norman and English – mourned Edwin, for he had devoted his life to good causes, was born of pious parents, and was handsome to boot. Even William was appalled, and exiled his killers. 'Edwin being dead, and Morcar languishing in prison', William divided up the chief English provinces among his followers. In 1087 William was in Normandy and, according to Florence of Worcester, on perceiving that 'death was approaching', he liberated, among others, Morcar and Wulfnoth, Harold Godwineson's brother.

His successor, William Rufus, went in great haste to England, taking those two with him, but as soon as he reached Winchester he 'placed them in confinement as before'. William was crowned king on 26 September and Florence makes no further mention of Morcar's fate, so it must be assumed that he died in captivity.[44]

Edwin and Morcar had been young men at the time of the Conquest, as far as we know, unmarried and without issue. Of their sister's children by Harold Godwineson, Florence of Worcester remarked that at the same time as William Rufus went back to England to become king, his brother

Robert also distributed treasures for the good of their father's soul, and released from prison 'Ulf, son of Harold, formerly king of England'. It cannot be stated with certainty that this Ulf was Ealdgyth's son. After the Battle of Hastings, Ealdgyth, apparently pregnant[45] was, according to John of Worcester, sent by her brothers to Chester.

It seems she gave birth to a son there, named Harold after his father, and perhaps she had twins, the other possibly being Ulf. But it is hard to reconcile this with the knowledge that Ulf was imprisoned and Harold, as far as we know, was not.

There is no further mention in the records of Ealdgyth. Harold 'Haroldson' is recorded as having been with Magnus III of Norway on a tour of the Orkneys and Hebrides in 1098. William of Malmesbury: 'In his eleventh year, Magnus, king of Norway, with Harold, son of Harold, formerly king of England, subdued the Orkney, Mevanian, and other circumjacent isles.'[46] Sailing south, they encountered Hugh, earl of Chester and after a skirmish, they sailed away. Nothing else, and this not much, was heard of Harold Haroldson.

He would have been, as far as we know, the last surviving member of the house of Leofric, earls of Mercia.

EPILOGUE

From Supremacy to Obscurity

The earliest Mercian king mentioned by Bede is Cearl, but beyond that tantalising comment, that he married his daughter to King Edwin, we have no further evidence of his reign, however much we might guess his role at the battle of Chester, or his authority over the southern kingdoms at the time. The kings which followed traced their lineage from his presumed brother Pybba, through Penda, or his brothers, and yet we know virtually nothing about these brothers, and hardly much more about Penda. The sources are even confused about the dates of his reign. What we do know about the man described as being of royal stock, and a gifted warrior, is that he successfully gathered an army which included the East Anglians, the Mercian tribes and not a few British kings, all prepared to march with him against Northumbria.

The Mercians secured their overlordship of the southern kingdoms by leading the opposition to Northumbrian ambition. The Northumbrian hold over the British kingdoms was fragile, a fact which Penda was able to use to his advantage by his alliance with Cadwallon. The stages by which the smaller kingdoms were gathered under the Mercian 'umbrella' are unknown to us, but by the end of the seventh century they were no longer simply the Marcher people, the folk on the boundary, but had client or satellite states from the Cheshire Plain through the Severn Valley and down as far as the Wye.

The relationship with Gwynedd seems to have been based on a friendship between the two men, Penda and Cadwallon. Mercian policy was fluid and it seems that Eowa, either by inclination or coercion, was a supporter of the Northumbrians. Wales itself was not a cohesive unit, British and English kingdoms were still developing, their borders and allegiances shifting. Penda was not fully successful, but his victories and alliances set Mercia on the road to domination over the south.

The marriage alliances between his children and the Northumbrians remind us of how selective the information is regarding Mercia. Bede tells us that Æthelburh, daughter of the king of Kent, married the pagan Edwin and was instrumental in the latter's conversion to Christianity. Her cousin, Domne Eafe, was given to one of Penda's sons in marriage. They separated, both to pursue a monastic life. But Bede tells us nothing of this.

Early in the period, the *ASC* and surviving evidence such as Ine's law codes lend Wessex the appearance of power, calm, and structure, whilst at the same time, all information about Mercia comes from their enemies, rivals and victims, perceived or otherwise. Mercia is presented as a violent, uncultured regime. But we have no corroborative evidence, and it may have been no more violent or less cultured than other kingdoms. Offa's laws, had they survived, would have confirmed this. The attempts at establishing an archbishopric at Lichfield are reported only because the pope thwarted it, and the spat between Cenwulf and Wulfred is handed down to us via Canterbury, not Mercia. Bede's history, it must be remembered, is an ecclesiastical and not a political history. Felix's *Life* of Guthlac and Hugh Candidus' *Chronicle of Peterborough* are notable in mentioning the Mercian kings in a good light, the latter particularly in terms of the foundation and endowment of Medeshamstede.

If there is some doubt as to whether Merewalh was Penda's son, there is no disputing that Wulfhere was both his son and heir. While the kingdom of the Middle Angles under Peada survived only for a short time, greater Mercia was still a force to be reckoned with. Within twenty years of Penda's death, his sons had established themselves as overlords of southern England. Wulfhere was not listed among the *Bretwaldas*, but his power is in no doubt. By 665 Essex was under his control, and his kingdom had extended to the middle Thames area. He was free to dispose of the bishopric of London and he married a Kentish princess. By the time of Oswiu of Northumbria's death, the whole of southern England appears to have been under Wulfhere's lordship, and in 674 he led an army drawn from all the southern nations, albeit to defeat.

Perhaps Ecgfrith was an overlord of Mercia for a short while, but there are no records of this and at the battle of the Trent, Wulfhere's brother Æthelred, whose reign is often overlooked, sounded the death knell for Northumbrian supremacy, which was killed off completely by the Picts at *Nechtanesmere*. Lindsey again became a Mercian province, and after the Trent, Ecgfrith never again attempted to conquer any southern kingdoms, nor did his successors, who were kept busy by new threats from their northern border. Northumbria ceased to be a threat to the Southumbrian hegemony. No longer did the Welsh and the Mercians make common cause in order to withstand Northumbrian invasion. Æthelred reigned for twenty-nine years, his friendship with Wilfrid earned him the respect of Rome, and he was able to abdicate his throne in favour of his nephew. We are fortunate to have favourable accounts of him from the *Vita Ecgwine* as well as the *Vita Wilfridi*.

Æthelred and his successors, his son Coenred and his nephew Ceolred, were overlords between the Humber and the Thames, but faced challenges from Wihtred of Kent, and Cadwalla and Ine of Wessex.

Bede, summing up the political situation in 731, stated that all the southern kingdoms were subject to Æthelbald, but again, stopped short of calling him *Bretwalda*. Æthelbald and his successor, Offa, ruled for almost a century between them, and aside from their client kingdoms it is worth noting the size of Mercia itself by the middle of the eighth century.

The relationship between Mercia and its neighbour, the kingdom of the West Saxons, is highlighted by the story of Berkshire. Records from Clofesho in 798 (S1258) show Æthelbald taking control of the monastery at Cookham, only for Cynewulf of Wessex to take it back, along with the region of the Upper Thames. Cynewulf and Offa then fought at Bensington, Offa won, and took the area back. It may be though, that Offa's power over Wessex was not as strong as the victory might suggest, because the papal legates in 787 met him and Cynewulf jointly.

Æthelbald's reign, though difficult to piece together, was surely impressive. He was popular, or strong, or both, enough to take the throne having been an exile. We know he attacked the Welsh, the West Saxons, and the Northumbrians, and charter evidence shows that he had control of London and the East Saxons, who lost Middlesex and Hertfordshire. In the Ismere charter, we see that he claimed kingship in the style of *Bretwalda*, and Clofesho records show his interest in reforming some aspects of the Church, even though Boniface saw fit to castigate him.

In our search for information, it is necessary to look further afield than the English chronicles. The Welsh annals supplement the scant details we have for the Mercians and tell us about the westernmost campaigns of the Mercian kings. The *ASC* tells us little of Offa's reign, beyond his violent acts – the murder of Æthelberht being the notable example – and is, in contrast, far more sympathetic to Ecgberht of Wessex. William of Malmesbury merely pronounced that Offa 'murdered many persons'.

Offa seems to have considered himself an equal of Charlemagne, and yet the documentary and chronicle evidence for the latter is far greater. Can we really suppose that there were no royal charters preserved in Lichfield, Repton, Crowland, St Albans? And yet it wasn't even known until the thirteenth century where he had been buried. Clearly, even if there had been a Mercian equivalent of the Northumbrian annals, they went the same way as any royal charters. Such chronicles, and historical traditions of the great churches, were interrupted.

Alcuin spoke of the good, moderate and chaste customs of Offa and we know that Alfred the Great imported Mercian scholars to his court and copied some of Offa's laws. The fact that Charlemagne was prepared to deal with Offa should tell us something about the man, and his level of learning. Offa probably thought himself Charlemagne's equal, for not only did he style himself 'king of the English', he revoked a charter of the king of Kent on the grounds that a client king had no authority to make such a grant. Nor should we forget that he persuaded the pope to make Lichfield an archbishopric and that he had his son anointed.

During Offa's highly successful reign, the once-independent rulers of the *Hwicce*, of Sussex and Kent, came under his overlordship, he extended his reach over Lindsey, Surrey, Essex and East Anglia, and whilst he did not achieve suzerainty of Wessex and Northumbria he still managed to marry his daughters to their kings.

Beorhtric of Wessex owed his position to Offa, and his marriage to Offa's daughter sealed the alliance. Together they were able to oust Ecgberht, but ultimately not permanently and when Ecgberht came back he founded the dynasty that produced Alfred the Great. Slowly, the balance of power began to shift in favour of Wessex.

But not immediately: on his succession, Cenwulf crushed a Kentish rebellion, maintained authority over Sussex, Essex, and East Anglia and, although his relationship with the Church was perhaps less successful, with his pleas for a London archbishopric refused, he forced Archbishop Wulfred to back down after their dispute over the monasteries, and he kept his throne for a quarter of a century.

However, while Wessex was overshadowed by Mercia, it was never completely subordinated and when Ecgberht defeated Beornwulf at *Ellendun*, he was able to secure the submission of Kent, Surrey, Sussex, Essex and East Anglia. By 829 he held sway over Mercia too, and became the eighth recorded *Bretwalda*.

Whether Wiglaf regained Mercia by force, or with Ecgberht's acquiescence, remains unclear. But relations between the two kingdoms began to take on a new dynamic as the scales tipped. Coin evidence shows Beorhtwulf and Æthelwulf issuing the same coinage and using the same moneyers.

Alliance seems to be confirmed by the evidence that Burgred sought, and obtained, assistance against the Welsh in 853 and that in the same year, he married Æthelwulf's daughter. A spirit of co-operation is further indicated by Burgred and Æthelred issuing a joint coinage in the 860s.

When the Viking raiding began in earnest, some kingdoms collapsed, and one did not. The reasons are difficult to explain, since by the very nature of what happened, the written evidence largely survives only in the one kingdom which was able to endure.

Later innovations, such as the building of the fleet and *burhs*, give a partial explanation, but why was Wessex able to weather the crises of 871–8? Geography played a part, and the Danish centre seemed to be in an area defined on the outer edges by York, Thetford, Reading and Repton. They were not able to establish a permanent presence in either Bernicia or Wessex. They must have been aware of the importance of Repton, it being the resting place of at least two kings, Æthelbald and Wiglaf. So, obviously, must Ceolwulf II have been aware of its religious and political importance. And herein lies the key to another reason for the downward spiral of Mercian fortunes.

After the generations immediately following Penda, sons rarely succeeded their fathers. Kings often had no known relationship at all to their predecessors. Royal marriages were hugely significant, as demonstrated by the events which led to the murder of the other person famously interred at Repton.

The murder of Wigstan seems to have resulted from one such power struggle and an attempt to garner extra regal credentials through marriage. As Offa understood, the continuing fortunes of a kingdom depended on stability of succession, and the ability of a king to leave his kingdom in the hands of a son, or brother of adult age. This undoubtedly helped Northumbrian supremacy in the seventh century, but was not to be part of Mercian success in the eighth, where only the long reigns of two brutal, ruthless and resourceful kings, Æthelbald and Offa, ensured the continuation of Mercian supremacy. At the same time, the beginnings of a strong and fruitful dynasty in Wessex presaged the transfer of power from Mercia to the West Saxons. A 'perfect storm' saw the Mercian dynasty collapse, the West Saxon dynasty burgeon, and the increase in frequency and severity of the Viking raids.

In amongst all the chaos though, it should be noted that at times the Mercian kings went efficiently about their business, with charters such as S204 from the reign of Beorhtwulf and S214 from the reign of Burgred, showing the kings granting land in the presence of ealdormen and bishops. Ceolwulf II, the foolish king's thegn, also issued charters at odds with his epithet. The English annals give us very little information about this period of the 'forgotten kings'. Had more charters survived then, again, we might not be so quick to assume that this was a kingdom in inevitable decline. It would appear, though, that Burgred's initial response to the incursions was to panic, appealing for help and then attempting to buy off the invaders.

Is this completely fair? Burgred, it should be remembered, was only just back from a successful campaign against Wales, and was not able to beat back the invaders, even with West Saxon help.

Here, too, we might consider that question of how Alfred weathered the storm during that period of 871–78 by noting that even when he met the Great Heathen Army in 871, it had quite probably left behind contingents in Northumbria and East Anglia. Mercia was not ready quite yet to lie down and die, the West Saxons were happy enough to sue for peace, despite the *ASC* not always being happy to mention it, and it is significant that the army never returned to Wessex. Having subjugated Mercia in 874/5, it broke up, dispersing to York and to Cambridge. Those who attacked Chippenham were not heard of again and might have represented only a small part of the Cambridge army.

The *ASC* does not furnish us with the details of Ceolwulf II's demise, and it seems as though Alfred was able to step into a political vacuum. But what are we to make of Æthelred? Was he merely a puppet of Alfred's, installed by him and there to do the bidding of Wessex? His status and titles hint at something more, although we can do no more than guess at his origins and the circumstances which brought him to power.

The political structure of Mercia seems to have been different from the outset, with ealdormen being the leaders of tribes and local areas, rather than being appointed by the king. Indeed, for much of the ninth century, kings seem to have come from among, rather than above, this group of leaders, emerging from groups of local leaders, rather than from a royal dynasty served by government appointees. Perhaps part of the problem was simply that there were too many of these contenders.

And yet it is clear that Alfred achieved overlordship of Mercia, even if the route he took is not so obvious. He continued the policy of issuing joint coinage, with Burgred and then with Ceolwulf. He then entrusted London to Æthelred, apparently respecting its status as a former Mercian town. Shortly afterwards, his daughter was married to Æthelred, and we hear from the *ASC* that all of England not under Danish rule submitted to Alfred.

The marriage alliance was still an important diplomatic device. Married women retained their identity as members of their birth family, and support was certainly forthcoming if we are to believe that Penda attacked Cenwalh of Wessex because he had put aside Penda's sister. Eadburh's reputation at the court of Wessex was based solely on her being a treacherous Mercian, and the legend served as a reminder, no doubt, that the resurgence of Mercian power must be avoided. Local customs came into play, despite the women's origins. Æthelswith, a West Saxon in the Mercian court, was able to attest charters as *regina*, whereas

Ealhswith, a Mercian in the Wessex court, was not accorded the title of queen.

Alfred's daughter, on the other hand, half-Mercian and half-West Saxon, was not called queen, but was allowed to behave like one. She does not appear to have been governing Mercia for Wessex, but striving for some kind of autonomy, working alongside, rather than for, her brother. Was Edward threatened by this, and was this one of the reasons he moved against her daughter, or did his actions have more to do with the personal qualities of said daughter? Again, we are unlikely ever to know.

Æthelflæd is perhaps the best known of the Mercian women, and it is interesting that the last two independent leaders of Mercia were female, but there was a series of remarkable and powerful women in Mercia: Penda's wife, left as regent and in charge of a high-status hostage, Offa's wife Cynethryth, issuing coins in her own name, and Abbess Cwoenthryth who, far from arranging the murder of her brother, should be remembered for taking on the might of the Church and being named heir to her father's lands and estates. Ælfgifu, whose inclusion in the records is primarily a device to show the debauchery of Eadwig and the integrity of Dunstan, was very possibly a Mercian whose presence at court ruffled the feathers of the old guard. The easy way in which the country split back into Wessex and Mercia with Edgar's accession suggests that the glue had barely set from Alfred's joining together of the two kingdoms.

Yet his was no heavy-handed takeover. We can see from the siege at Buttington that Mercians, the Welsh, and the West Saxons were working in concert against the Vikings. Again, it may be that the perception of the relationship in Mercia was different from that in Wessex.

Perhaps we should be wary of viewing the disintegration of the independent kingdom of Mercia as a tragedy. We do not know how much cohesion there was; who considered themselves to be 'Mercian'. A look back at the problems presented by the *Tribal Hidage* will remind anyone studying this period that a definition of 'Mercia' is almost impossible. Perhaps the successes of Æthelbald and Offa have been overplayed, and that Mercia remained a confederation of states rather than a united kingdom. Bearing that in mind, it might have taken little more than a weak leader for all to unravel.

And unravel it certainly did, from the time of the Viking raids onwards. But it was to resurface in the tenth century as a political force.

There is no doubt that Mercia and Wessex were operating in a co-ordinated campaign during the latter years of Alfred's reign and the early years of Edward the Elder's. Political unity became more of a reality again under the reigns of Athelstan and Edgar. It seems that to a greater or lesser extent, both these kings began their careers in Mercia, and thus would have been more welcome to Mercians than other West Saxons.

However, the unity displayed in the early part of the tenth century should not be exaggerated. Succession disputes upon the deaths of Edward the Elder, Eadred, and Edgar, showed that separatist resentment flourished. Noblemen with vested interests were not necessarily happy to be governed by Wessex. National loyalty, or lack thereof, was to prove a constant headache for subsequent kings, right up until the Conquest. For Mercia, and especially Northumbria, Wessex was a long way away. The ealdormen were expected both to represent national authority and safeguard local interests. These men were powerful, yet they were also too easily and often suspected of treachery when local interests appeared to clash with national.

For there is no question that the history of Mercia did not stop in 918. Ælfhere, Eadric, Leofwine, Leofric, and Edwin all played significant parts in national politics. The nobles who challenged royal authority in 1065 showed support for local interest and their actions can in some ways be compared to those involved in the struggles for the throne in the preceding centuries.

The appointment of Eadric Streona, reported by a chronicler who used the phrase 'throughout the kingdom of the Mercians' shows not only that the old sensibilities and sense of nation survived, but how powerful the office was, and what could be done when it was administered by one who was noble in name but not deed. The recorded history remained that of the deeds of kings, so we only really hear of the ealdormen who went 'bad'. With the *ASC* becoming more contemporary, its West Saxon origins nevertheless ensured that Mercian history remained obscure.

The ealdormanries in the later tenth and early eleventh centuries were comparable in area to the eighth-century kingdoms, and with families being enriched by grants of land, and the office becoming *de facto* hereditary, these were powerful men indeed. The families were, as we can see from the wills of Ælfheah, brother of Ælfhere, and Wulfric Spott, hugely wealthy and interconnected, even across the regions. The Ælfwine in the poem of *The Battle of Maldon* who referred to his grandfather as Ealhhelm also refers to Byrhtnoth of Essex as his kinsman. The charter S911 implies some kinship between Ælfhere, Byrhtnoth and Æthelweard the Chronicler who, as we've seen, was related to King Eadwig through marriage.

Overmighty ealdormen who had the power to dictate policy and even affect the outcome of battles were not to be found exclusively in Mercia. There is perhaps little to choose between Eadric Streona and Godwine.

The conclusion has to be that Mercia, no more or less than the other kingdoms, was subject to the ebb and flow which affected all monarchies, the chance factor which dictated the number of heirs who lived to succeed their fathers, the geography that meant some regions were hit harder than others by invasion, and the relative strength of the neighbouring dynasties and fighting forces. Ultimately, what singles Mercia out is the lack of written evidence that existed, or survived. The story of Mercia is one where so often its leaders stand accused by those who wrote the history, and are not able to defend themselves.

The Kings of Mercia

Penda c. 626–655

Eowa c. 633–642?

Oswiu of Northumbria 655–658

Wulfhere 658–675

Æthelred I 675–704

Cœnred 704–709

Ceolred 709–716

Æthelbald 716–757

Beornred 757

Offa 757–796

Ecgfrith –796

Cenwulf 796–821

Ceolwulf I 821–823

Beornwulf 823–826

Ludeca 826–827

Wiglaf (1st reign) 827–829

Ecgberht of Wessex 829–830

Wiglaf (2nd reign) 830–839

Wigmund c. 839–c. 840

Wigstan 840?

Ælfflæd 840?

Beorhtwulf 840–852

Burgred 852–874

Ceolwulf II 874–879 or c. 883

Æthelred II (Lord) c. 883–911

Æthelflæd (Lady) 911–918

Ælfwynn (Lady) 918

APPENDIX I

The Danes in Mercia

It was in 787, during the reign of Beorhtric of Wessex, Offa's son-in-law, that the first Viking raid occurred. Three ships arrived, and the local reeve assumed that they were traders 'for he did not know what they were; and they slew him. Those were the first ships of Danish men which came to the land of the English.'

Just over half a century later, the *ASC* reports destruction in Lindsey and East Anglia, and the next year, in 842, Southampton was plundered, while a Mercian charter of 855 records the presence of the heathen around the Wrekin, '*Quando feurunt pagani in Wreocensetum*'.[1]

The mention of the heathen has been called a 'puzzling reference'[2] and is assumed to refer to a Dublin- or Irish-based expedition, or perhaps a collaboration between these Vikings and the Welsh, which would provide the explanation as to how they managed to penetrate so far 'up-country'. This must remain conjecture though, and it should be noted that the Welsh were not pagans and are not referred to as such in the English chronicles.

By 874, the Danes had come to Repton, and it is likely that Ceolwulf II was actively supporting them. In 877 Mercia was partitioned, with the invaders keeping the eastern lands for themselves whilst, according to the *ASC*, they 'gave some to Ceolwulf'. Æthelweard the Chronicler adds the detail that they built booths (erected their huts) in Gloucester and drove all the free men from Mercia.

If Ceolwulf II was accepted as king, and he seems to have been – as discussed in Chapter Seven – then this must raise questions about the nature of the relationship between the Danes and the Mercian 'locals', and how it developed over the next century and a half.

Sir Frank Stenton said that the partitioned regions of Mercia cannot be closely defined. In the south of the old kingdom there was 'much fighting' between Danes and English over the next thirty years, and there is no surviving evidence for the condition of Mercia immediately after 877. He pointed out that in the north, the medieval shires of Lincoln, Nottingham, Derby and Leicester have local nomenclature which is Scandinavian, and mirrors Yorkshire in containing Danish personal names not found elsewhere in England. He concluded that there is no evidence to suggest large-scale Scandinavian immigration later than 877, and it is most probable that the division of 877 covered the whole eastern half of old Mercia. He added that the earliest document showing its social organisation – a code of Æthelred Unræd – shows that 'in language and legal custom it was then a Danish rather than an English land.'[3]

In 878 Guthrum's army went from Cirencester to East Anglia, where Guthrum stayed until his death. Were any Danes left behind? What sort of vacuum was created, if the Danes left an area from which all the free men had been driven away?

The see of Hereford appears not to have suffered much disruption by the Danish wars[4] but in Repton, after the Vikings left, there is no evidence that monastic life there was restored. St Wigstan's relics were translated to Evesham in Cnut's reign, and it seems reasonable to suppose that there would have been no need for this had Repton been thriving again as a monastery.[5]

It seems that the Vikings were no more successful in establishing a permanent presence in Bernicia or West Mercia than they were in Wessex, and Ceolwulf II's charter of 875 (S215) mentioned in Chapter Seven, is an indicator that much at grass-roots level survived.[6] Bernicia, so far north, was not settled in the same way as the southern kingdom of Deira, with its centre at York, and it may be that by the tenth century the two kingdoms were still using predominantly different languages.

Much information is lost to us now. For an example of just how little we know about such details, we can look to the discussion regarding Alfred's retaking of London, and whether he was fighting Danes who had already settled there, or a fresh incursion, discussed in Chapter Eight.

In the early years of the tenth century, Norwegian and Irish-Norwegian settlers began to arrive in northwest England and southwest Scotland. The only clues to this are the place names of the areas concerned, and if this did indeed amount to a 'mass-migration in scale and intensity'[7] and went unrecorded by the English annalists, then does this suggest a level of peaceful settlement? Perhaps not, for the *Three Fragments* records an attack on the city of Chester. Of course, there was always the danger that these new invader-settlers would join forces with the Danes already in eastern England, but the *Mercian Register* records that in 918 the men of York offered their submission and their allegiance to the Lady of the Mercians, if she would lead an anti-Norse coalition.

So now there were different cultures and nationalities, and perhaps it didn't necessarily follow that the Norse and the Danes would make common cause against the English. From this point on, might there have been a subtle shift?

In the first half of 918, Edward the Elder had begun building a fortress at Stamford and took back the town, it being the third of the Five Boroughs to be thus restored. After his sister's death that same year, according to the *ASC*, he took Nottingham and 'all the people who had settled in Mercia, *both Danish and English* [my italics], submitted to him.'

A law code of Edward's makes provision for punishment for harbouring a fugitive, 'but if in the east or north, compensation shall be paid according to what the peace treaties say.'[8]

So, were the Danes of the Danelaw actually settling and integrating? Those who had overwintered in 865/866 were involved in military campaigns. At Repton, whence Burgred had been forced to flee, excavation is still ongoing, in an attempt to ascertain and understand the make-up of the population of the Viking camp there. The findings published in 2018 confirm that the skeletons found at Repton date from the period of Viking occupation, but have not so far answered questions about how, if, or when occupation might have become settlement.

There is evidence of a policy whereby land was bought from Danes in the northeast Midlands to establish English land ownership in Danish areas, although it wasn't until the reign of Edgar that the separate laws and customs of the Danelaw were fully acknowledged: 'And it is my will that secular rights be in force among the Danes according to as good laws as they can best decide on.'[9]

Dorothy Whitelock wondered 'whether Athelstan and his successor encouraged such infiltrations into Danish areas, as it is known Edward the Elder did. It would clearly be in their interest to break down the isolation of the north by such means.'[10] It seems so. Two charters of Athelstan's show Englishmen being encouraged to buy land from the Danes. Both bear the date 926, and one is preserved in the Abingdon archive, the other in the Burton. The Burton charter confirms to the king's *fidelis*, Uhtred, land at Hope and Ashford, which Uhtred had bought with his own money from the pagans by order of King Edward and Lord Æthelred, suggesting that the practice went even further back than Athelstan's reign, and that the land purchase must have taken place before 911, the year of Æthelred's death. With relatively so few surviving charters showing land grants in the midlands and the north, it is not possible to make up a list of those men whose loyalty was bought or rewarded by the English kings. Those which do survive show witnesses with Scandinavian names.[11] What we do know, such as in the case of Wulfric Spott, is that there were English thegns who, by the end of the tenth century at least, held estates in both English areas and those districts where the Danes had settled.

Before the death of Edward the Elder, all the Danish lands south of the Humber had been brought under the control of Wessex. But during his reign there were signs that loyalties were already moving away from purely ethnic divisions. Edward's cousin, Æthelwold, was recognised as king by the Danes and among the fallen at the battle of the Holme was Beornoth the atheling, who can probably be identified as being a member, albeit a minor, landless member, of the 'B' dynasty of Mercia. The episode did little to change the course of events, but it shows a son of an English king utilising a Danish army in pursuit of his own personal claim, and rendering the concept of 'enemy' fluid, only a generation after the time of Ceolwulf II's alliance with the invaders.

It seems unlikely that the two charters issued by Athelstan were the only ones of their nature and would therefore provide a further insight into the battle of the Holme and the concept of who were the 'local' armies and where their loyalties might have lain. With the two charters showing the land purchase policy stretching from Derbyshire in the north to Bedfordshire in the south, it is conceivable that Edward pursued this policy.

It also seems that this policy was continued in the reign of King Edmund, who granted in 942 to Wulfsige the Black land which had been 'recovered' from the Danes (S484). Wulfsige, introduced in Chapter Eleven, was likely to have been related to Wulfrun, mother of Wulfric Spott whose family was probably settled around Tamworth, for it was from here that she was abducted in 940. The lands granted to Wulfsige lay on either side of the River Trent and controlled the route from Derby and Nottingham to Lichfield and Tamworth and were thus strategically important. Although it is not known exactly how and when the estates were created, it may be that Wulfric Spott's landholdings were accumulated under a similar policy and with the frontier similarly in mind.[12]

If Wulfric's family was entrusted with property in northern Mercia as part of a deliberate policy, then it may be significant to note that the estates which Morcar subsequently received in grants from Æthelred Unræd between 1009 and 1012 (S922, 924, 927) were all in north Derbyshire, close to the lands bequeathed by Wulfric.

So, whose side were the 'settled' Danes of Mercia on during the 940s, during Edmund's struggles to regain the Five Boroughs and his fight with the Northumbrian Norse Vikings? Cyril Hart said that above the line of Watling Street, the English landlords were 'dispossessed of their estates, their land-books destroyed, and the fiscal system built up over the centuries by the English rulers was swept away.' Instead of the English system of the hide, the Danes introduced the ploughland, and it has been estimated that 'each Danish army settler ... received between eight and twelve ploughlands.'[13] So, a new system for new inhabitants, and presumably the existing people who dwelled in the area were subject to it.

The entry for 942 in the *ASC* says that the Danes of the Five Boroughs were 'subjected by force under the Norsemen (*Dæne wæran ær under Norðmannum nyde gebedgde).*' There has been some debate over the word *Dæne* and how the entry in the *ASC* should be interpreted. Were the Danes the oppressed, or the oppressors? If they were the oppressed, then it is plausible that Edmund was welcomed as a 'deliverer' by the Danish inhabitants of the Five Boroughs.[14]

Henry of Huntingdon though, seems not to have made the same distinction, for in describing the campaign he said that King Edmund led his army into that part of Mercia 'which had long been subject to the heathens ... recovering the Five Boroughs ... and utterly extirpating the Danes, who even at that time were called Normans (Norsemen)' while John of Worcester said that Edmund 'wrested completely out of Danish hands' the Five Boroughs and brought 'all Mercia under his control'.

Northumbrian independence had been reinforced by the Hiberno-Norse kings of York, but the English kings made continuous attempts to force the northerners to acknowledge their rule, and the independence of Northumbria ended when Eric Bloodaxe, the last king of York, was driven out in 954, during the reign of Edmund's brother, Eadred. But was loyalty to the English crown thereafter guaranteed?

Archbishop Wulfstan was accused of disloyalty by the *ASC*, which stated that he and the Northumbrians had pledged themselves to Eadred in 947 and 'within a short space they were false to it all.' If it is true, then it adds clarity to the later policy of archbishops of York holding the see in plurality with one in the south. (Oswald was bishop of Worcester and archbishop of York in Edgar's reign). While the *ASC* with its southern perspective may have considered the actions to be treacherous, it seems clear that many in the north, be they English or Dane, may have disliked being subject to a southern king.[15] With the fall of York it might be supposed that northern England became part of the kingdom of the English, but charter evidence shows an absence, generally, of northerners attesting. S939, dated between 995 and 999, refers to thegns gathered there from 'both Wessex and Mercia, English and Danish' but does not mention Northumbria.

There is other charter evidence which suggests strained relations between the kings in the south and the Northumbrians. In a grant of 949 (S550) the king is styled 'king of the English and ruler of the Northumbrians and emperor of the pagans and defender of the Britons': *Eadredus rex Anglorum gloriossimus rectorque Nor˘anhymbra et paganorum imperator Brittonumque*, whereas charters pertaining to the south style him much more simply and authoritatively *rex Anglorum* (S522).[16]

Edgar's law code known as Edgar IV, or the Wihtbordesstan Code, tacitly acknowledged the Danelaw, but it has been argued that there was little difference in the laws of the Danelaw area and those of Wessex, and that Edgar may have granted similar laws to the Mercians.[17] Further, there has been an argument made that it was powerful and independent northern (Danish) magnates who withdrew their support for Eadwig and made Edgar king of the Mercians and Northumbria in order to further their own separatist agenda[18] and thus the Danelaw remained separate rather than integrated.

The suggestion is that Edgar's Wihtbordesstan code, recognising Danish autonomy, was a setback for unification. Lesley Abrams summed up the arguments for and against this proposal, citing Patrick Wormald, who described it as an 'entente', and Simon Keynes who pronounced it an admission that Edgar was not in a position to legislate in the Danelaw. Abrams argued that, in fact, the Danes had no 'factional voice' in 957, although there are no extant charters for that year. Stenton spoke of 'distinctiveness and mass migration' while Sawyer said rather that it was a 'military elite.' Perhaps the 'Danishness' should be downplayed, and the allegiances were political, not ethnic. York had not long been free from Scandinavian rule, and the 'Danes' are unlikely to have been one cohesive 'pressure group.' Their interests may have merged after conquest by the West Saxons, but it cannot be stated with certainty how long it took. Abrams pointed out that it might be a case of differences of vocabulary rather than substance, that we should be wary of Stenton's 'over-exaggeration' but accept the idea of military settlement and that the Danes continued to arrive and settle in the tenth century. Edgar's code could be a reflection of a Scandinavian 'way of doing things' or indeed that by that time, 'Dane' might simply have meant 'not West Saxon'.[19]

The *ASC* records that in the next reign, in 993, a very large English army was collected, and 'when they should have joined battle, the leaders, namely Fræna, Godwine and Frythegyst, first started the flight.' Florence of Worcester added the explanation that it was on account of their 'being Danes on the father's side'. It is interesting to note this appraisal which was written from a post-Conquest perspective. It might have been coloured by the general assumption by this point that most cowardice and treachery was born of partisan interests, and that by the time of writing, the vacillations of Eadric Streona were common knowledge.

Treachery was certainly on the mind of Æthelred Unræd in 1002 when he ordered the slaughter which became known as the St Brice's Day massacre, and it is clear from the reporting of the incident that ethnic differences were still noteworthy.

In 1013 Swein had found allies in the north, and perhaps the land-buying policy ultimately backfired, for the will of Wulfric Spott 'reveals how there were by the end of the tenth century thegns in English areas who possessed also large estates in the districts settled by the Danes.' Members of his family were later to be accused of treason.[20]

Ælfhelm, earl of Northumbria from 993, was not local to the area, being a Mercian. His appointment may have been a deliberate policy, as with the archbishops, to have a non-Northumbrian keeping watch. Yet he owned land in Yorkshire and it seems he was suspected of treachery nevertheless, and after Ælfhelm's murder the practice of appointing members of the house of Bamburgh as earls of Northumbria was revived. But it was Northumbrians, even so, who submitted to Swein in 1013 at Gainsborough, and on his march south his army held back from any ravaging until they had crossed Watling Street.

Swein's actions pose interesting questions. Was he avoiding the Danelaw because it was loyal to England? Was he avoiding Thorkell the Tall, who had allied himself with the English? Finally, why did Uhtred of Northumbria submit to Swein; he was son-in-law to the king, Æthelred Unræd, and completely English.[21]

Assuming the most obvious reason for their executions, it is fairly easy to work out the part played by Sigeferth and Morcar in the submission of the north, albeit they are not named by the *ASC*. They may not have needed much persuading, Morcar's wife being the niece of Ælfhelm, a Mercian appointed as ealdorman of Northumbria, and murdered on the king's orders. We know from the will of Wulfric how extensive the family's landholdings were, so it would be a boon to Swein to gain their allegiance.[22]

It is not known precisely when Cnut married into this influential family, taking as his wife Ælfgifu of Northampton, but if it was 1013 then this would give another reason why Swein's army avoided the lands north east of Watling Street, thus sparing the estates of his new 'in-laws'.[23]

In 1016 it is said that Æthelred Unræd left his levies because he was led to believe that betrayal was imminent. He was not a popular king, and he owed his throne to the assassination of the previous incumbent, so he may well have been cautious about joining large assemblies of men who were armed.[24]

Talk of treachery is a reminder that the lines of loyalty were becoming ever more blurred, with no clear division now between Dane and English. Danes were fighting for the English, as can be seen in the cases of Pallig and Thorkell, and meanwhile Eadric Streona, an Englishman, fought for the Danes, and presumably had no problem persuading his Mercian subordinates to join him in this enterprise.

It has been argued that the Danish settlers were 'not numerous enough to change the customs and traditions of the region in which they settled' in the wake of Cnut's conquest but alternatively that there was 'widespread destruction' and 'decimation of thegnly aristocracy ... and a widespread distribution of aristocratic lands' after Cnut's succession.[25]

Ethnic loyalties were certainly becoming blurred; Godwine, son of Wulfnoth, but married to a Danish woman, gave his sons Scandinavian names: Swein, Harold, Gyrth, Tostig. Æthelred Unræd had himself played a part in this erasing of clear ethnic lines, firstly by marrying in 1002 Emma, the granddaughter of a Viking adventurer, and secondly by recruiting Viking forces such as those led by Thorkell. It has been noted that Harthaknut, having no personal following in England relied on support from his mother Emma's dower lands.[26]

Politics aside, what was going on at ground level? Hemming, with, it must be said, obvious bias towards Worcester, said that many Englishmen, noble and ignoble, rich and poor, were deprived of their estates.[27] He also said that the monks of Worcester were deprived of property in Herefordshire, Worcestershire and Oxfordshire – Herefordshire being controlled by Earl Ranig. With Eglaf connected to Gloucestershire and Earl Hakon's association with Worcestershire during this period, it begins to look as if by the early eleventh century, Cnut's men had settled in large numbers in the Welsh border shires, and thus in English Mercia.[28]

It was Sir Frank Stenton's belief that the Danish element in the Anglo-Danish state had been underestimated by historians and he considered the possibility that within Mercia there may have been subordinate governments held, with an earl's title, by men whose influence was purely local, but he admitted to a paucity of information, making confirmation impossible. Furthermore, the authorities for Cnut's reign were, he said, so 'meagre' that any list of earls is certain to be incomplete. Whilst the traditions of local government may well have remained unaffected, the earls appointed to oversee this link between crown and shire were almost exclusively new men, English or otherwise. Leofwine, and then Leofric, whom Cnut appointed earl of Mercia, were members of the only English

family who remained in power during these years.[29] This power must
have been limited, however, by the appointment of two of Cnut's Danish
kinsmen in the area, Ranig and Eglaf, discussed in Chapter Eleven, and
Cnut's 'interweaving of interests, royal and local, English and Danish'.[30]

It is difficult for historians to define the area which became known as
the Danelaw and who it was who could now be classed as a 'Dane'. The
armies which overwintered towards the end of the ninth century cannot
be thought of as settling, and until excavation delivers more answers,
the same must probably be said of Repton, despite what Paul Hill called
its 'overt symbolism'[31] but it seems clear that by the time of Edgar's
Wihtbordesstan Code of 962–3 the Danelaw was not only recognised,
but that the king acknowledged the help he had received from people
living in the area: 'Further, it is my will that there should be in force
among the Danes such good laws as they best decide on, and I have ever
allowed them this and will allow it as long as my life lasts, because of
your loyalty, which you have always shown me.' It was his son's law code,
however, (Æthelred VI), which made the first use of the term 'Danelaw'
and Cnut who decreed that the autonomy of the Danelaw would not
extend to the keeping of the peace there.[32]

So what can be said of the moment when the line was officially drawn?
The treaty between Alfred and Guthrum was not the partition merely of
Mercia, which had already been achieved in 877, but was the partition
of England, along a line which went 'up the Thames, then up the Lea,
and along the Lea to its sources, then in a straight line to Bedford, then
up the Ouse to Watling Street'. By the time of Alfred's death, therefore,
Wessex included all England south of the Thames and Bristol Avon,
while north of the Tees and west of the Pennines the surviving fragment
of the Northumbrian kingdom was ruled in 'virtual independence' by
ealdormen such as Eadwulf of Bamburgh.[33]

There is no surviving mention of the boundary running all the way
along Watling Street to Chester, so it might be pertinent to ask what
happened in northwest Mercia?[34] To the south of the Mersey, along the
Welsh border, Æthelred remained Lord of the Mercians from Cheshire
in the north to Gloucestershire and Oxfordshire in the south and his
jurisdiction included Buckinghamshire (CS 603). Watling Street, dividing
Mercian Warwickshire from Danish Leicestershire, formed the boundary
of the southern Midlands until it entered the region of London.[35]

Mercia ceased to exist, as a kingdom and then as an earldom, but the
boundary of the Danelaw still exists. The old boundary is an isogloss used
by modern-day linguists, and the linguistic influences of the Danelaw,
including not only accent but grammatical structure, can still be detected
in areas such as the Derbyshire Dales.[36]

APPENDIX II

The Shiring of Mercia

Gloucestershire, Oxfordshire, Warwickshire, Leicestershire ... These names are so familiar and so easy to pinpoint on a map. But when and how did these neat divisions come into being? The received view was, for a long time, that of Sir Frank Stenton who said that the shires of the west Midlands were created by Edward the Elder, with a 'ruthless disregard for local traditions'. It is clear that the boundaries of the newly created shires overrode those of the former kingdoms. The former kingdom of the *Magonsæte*[1] was divided into Herefordshire and Shropshire, that of the *Hwicce* into Gloucestershire and Worcestershire, apart from the most easterly area which became part of Warwickshire. Bedford, Huntingdon, Cambridge, Northampton, Nottingham and Leicester appear to have fallen more easily into the system, with each new shire containing roughly 1,200 hides or twice that number.

It has been suggested that in fact it was the 990s when 'the first concrete evidence for the Mercian shires appears'[2] and that it was a gradual process, rather than a single administrative edict.

The shires of both Wessex and Mercia – English and Danish – are generally agreed to have come into being as administrative districts deriving their names from a defensive town. In Wessex, the relationship between the two is sometimes less obvious, but it seems that Dorset (*Dornsæte*) and Somerset (*Sumorsæte*) derived from Dorchester and Somerton. Stenton was clear that no corresponding system existed in independent Mercia and that the shiring of western Mercia was a deliberate imitation of West Saxon systems of government, established between Alfred's reign and 980, the point at which Cheshire was first named in the *ASC*.[3]

Much earlier, C.S. Taylor attributed the shiring to Eadric Streona. Eadric's tenure appeared to coincide with the period when the shires began to take on their final form, with Shropshire being mentioned for the first time in 1006, Oxfordshire, Cambridgeshire and Buckinghamshire in 1010, Herefordshire, Bedfordshire, Huntingdonshire and Northamptonshire in 1011 and Warwickshire, Gloucestershire, Staffordshire, Lincolnshire and Nottinghamshire in 1016.[4]

In 827, King Ludeca of Mercia was killed and, according to the *ASC*, 'his five ealdormen with him'. It is thought that these five ealdordoms coincided with the Mercian dioceses of Lichfield, Worcester, Hereford, Lindsey and Leicester. But the secular organisation did not survive the Danish incursions.[5]

The origins of the shires of the western Midlands– the eastern Midlands have a different history – can probably be found in the territories which centred around the *burhs* built by Alfred and his children and son-in-law.

The *burhs* were initially garrisoned fortresses, built with the sole purpose of holding off the invaders. The surrounding land was obligated to provide the necessary resources to build, maintain and then garrison the *burhs*. The land was in some cases very large; the Domesday entry for Worcestershire suggests a whole shire attached to the *burh* of Worcester with an assessment of 1,200 hides.[6] The policy of *burh*-building may have been the key, but it should be remembered that the shires were crucial to administration, and so of control generally, and thus part of a drive by Alfred and Edward to bring the peoples of the separate kingdoms together.[7]

The shires were subdivided into hundreds – or wapentakes in the Danelaw – and many have associations with pagan meeting places. The hundred courts dealt with local administration and justice but by the tenth century, the hundred court was beginning to be used as a means of increasing royal government and authority to the more remote areas.[8]

In the ninth century the shires of Wessex each had their own ealdorman, but during Athelstan's reign this ceased to be standard practice and the administrative districts given over to the ealdormen grew larger. By the middle of Edgar's reign, western Mercia was a single ealdordom, reaching from Cheshire down to Gloucestershire.

Edgar's third law code stipulated that the *burh* court should meet three times a year and the shire court twice, so it would seem that only some of the burghal territories developed into shires, and it can be shown that even those did not immediately supersede the older Mercian regions. The *Magonsæte* appear in a diploma of 958 (S677), the *Pecsæte* and *Wreoconsæte* in 963 (S712a, 723), while Leofwine became ealdorman of the *Hwicce* in 996 and the men of the *Magonsæte* are recorded as being led by Eadric Streona in 1016.[9] A charter of Edgar's dated 969 shows that even at that late date, there was an awareness of the distinction between Mercia proper and the territory of the *Hwicce*. The boundary mentioned is the line separating the original Mercians from those who had settled in the Severn Valley (S773).[10]

During Edward the Elder's reign a system was in place by which territory was subordinated to a *burh*, or town. Between 911 and 918 (the dates when Æthelflæd was in control of Mercia) the *ASC* refers to London, Oxford, Bedford, Northampton, Derby, Cambridge and Stamford, and to the men, or the army, or the lands which 'belonged' to the towns, with the annals referring to military operations.[11] But the verb used, *hyran*, means 'hear and obey' and in the case of Winchcombe it was used to denote a district subordinated to a town in a sense which predated the Danish invasions. A record employing the word, and dated 897, refers to charters in which King Cenwulf forbade his heirs to grant leases of his hereditary lands belonging to Winchcombe for more than one lifetime (CS 575) and the district attached to Winchcombe is a unit of royal estate management.[12] It may be that Winchcombe was important because as well as being near the other royal centres such as Wellesbourne and Tamworth, it controlled the northern approaches to the Cotswolds.

The *Liber Wigorniensis* listed the Church's estates in the order of the territories in which they lay: Gloucester, Oxford, Winchcombe, Warwick and Worcester, with the suffix *-scire* added to the first three, 'probably soon afterwards'. The suggestion that Eadric was responsible for the shiring may stem from his being remembered by Hemming as having 'presided over the whole kingdom of the English and was in all things as powerful as an under-king, so that he joined vills to vills and provinces to provinces'.[13]

The entry in the *Liber Wigorniensis* would seem to reinforce Taylor's assertion that the midland territories dependent on towns were reorganised in 1007, and that the documents of Worcester would appear to have been compiled between 996 and 1016. According to Finberg, the addition of the suffix *-scire* should be dated at around 1007.[14] Why then did Winchcombe lose its county status? It is possible that an extensive redrawing of boundaries occurred around the time of the partition of the country between Edmund Ironside and Cnut, and probably in or about 1017, Gloucestershire was enlarged, with Herefordshire losing vast acreage (Finberg put the figure at 85,000 acres) and Winchcombeshire being swallowed whole.

Even if Hemming can be believed, and Eadric was responsible for the eradication of Winchcombeshire, it is not certain that he had any direct influence over the construction of other west Mercian shires. He was associated with the *Magonsæte,* as evidenced by the *ASC* entry of 1016. The territory included Herefordshire east of the Wye, southern Shropshire as far as Wenlock, and Gloucestershire west of the Severn. The bishops of Hereford were still known as bishops of the *Magonsæte* in the early 1100s.[15] Northern Shropshire was part of the territory of the *Wreoconsæte*, which is mentioned by name in the tenth century (S723: *in provincia Wrocensetna*).

Shrewsbury, which lay between the two districts, gave its name to the county of Shropshire, and was described as a city in a charter of 901 (S221: *in civitate Scrobbensis*). Shrewsbury 'articulates the structure of its dependent shire [so] the two must have developed hand in hand'.[16] Shropshire appears by name in the *ASC* entry for 1006, while Herefordshire does not appear until Cnut's reign, so it is by no means proven that Eadric was the architect of all the west Mercian shires. Stenton maintained that the shiring of the west Midlands was the work of a king 'who had no respect for the ancient divisions of Mercia' and that Shropshire represented an 'artificial union of lands which had once been divided between the *Magonsætan* and the *Wreocensætan*.' And he was of the opinion that Winchcombe had been created at the same time, i.e. in the last years of his reign, so Winchcombe had but a short time as an independent shire.[17]

Warwickshire was created by adding the eastern portion of the kingdom of the *Hwicce* to Mercian lands in and to the south of Arden, Warwick itself being similar to Shrewsbury and lying on the boundary of the *Hwicce* and Mercia proper. Eadric may have been the one who joined Warwick and Tamworth to form Warwickshire; on the other hand, there is the fact that the shire-boundary cuts through the ancient centre of Tamworth,[18] which adds weight to Stenton's argument that Edward the Elder was responsible, showing no regard for ancient boundaries.[19]

Even if it can be established that it was Eadric who was responsible for the shiring of the west Midlands, and it seems still largely open to debate, then there is much less basis for assuming that he had anything to do with the shiring of the eastern and northern Midlands. Did he carry out the re-organisation after the murder (at his hand) of Sigeferth and Morcar, thegns of the Seven Boroughs?

It seems that the shires of the eastern Midlands were created artificially, but here the process saw the shires developing from the areas of Danish army occupation and subsequent settlement: Leicester, Northampton, Huntingdon, Bedford and Cambridge. The town was the place where the army met. A list of sureties for Peterborough estates includes a transaction conducted at a 'meeting of the whole host at Northampton'.[20] In Derbyshire and Nottinghamshire, it appears that the middle of the tenth century saw the development of administrative structures which have no parallels elsewhere, and seem to have transferred responsibility for law and order to the individual communities as opposed to the lords and landowners, a system which must have been introduced after 942 and the reconquest of the east Midlands.[21]

Similar legislation was drawn up for Wessex and West Mercia by either Eadred or Edgar, and it is probable that the reforms of local government in the northern Danelaw can be attributed to one of these kings. Given that some aspects of the system were also operating in Yorkshire, it is reasonable to argue that it was after 954 when York submitted to Eadred.[22]

The *Hundred Ordinance* is a document which sets out how the hundred courts should be conducted, how often they should be held, and who should attend. There is debate over its date, but it is usually ascribed to Edgar or Eadred.[23]

From an early twelfth-century compilation, the *Laws of Henry I*, we learn that the English shires were divided not just into hundreds but also shipsokes, the latter being groups of three hundreds, or triple-hundreds, each group being required to provide a ship and a crew of sixty men.[24] The *ASC* entry for 1008 records that the king ordered ships to be built with a warship from every 310 hides, but it is likely that the shipsoke had its origins in the reign of Edgar. The Church of Worcester was granted a liberty of three hundreds. This liberty became known as the triple-hundred of Oswaldslow, and it was exempt from certain obligations and responsibilities under the law.

Sixty local charters survive from late tenth-century Worcester and show that the recipients of such charters had submitted to the bishop – Oswald – as their lord. Some, if not all, of these men had once held land by royal charter, with the tenure being hereditary and thus the new arrangements saw them become tenants of the Church, with the loss of their rights of inheritance. The *burh* of Worcester was the responsibility of the ealdorman, and as such would have been one of the sources of his power. With the *burh* now surrounded by Oswaldslow, where fighting men were subject to the bishop not the ealdorman, it becomes clear that the uprising in Mercia following the death of Edgar was less an anti-monastic reaction and more a drive to restore the status quo, by lord and commoners of Mercia alike.

Notes

Sources and Abbreviations

1. Jane Roberts in Brown/Farr p 70: She argues that Felix may well have been Mercian despite the connection to Ælfwald of East Anglia and thinks the impetus for the *Life* came from Mercia. Although Felix is often described as a monk of Crowland, there is no convincing evidence for a settlement at Crowland before the Benedictine revival of the tenth century.
2. Wendy Davies, in *Mercian Studies* pp 18–19, says sources may have existed that are already lost, and Florence was not always using dates, unlike the *ASC*, but seems to be independent of *ASC*.
3. Forester, *The Chronicle of Henry of Huntingdon*, pp xiv –xv, says that 'the earlier books being, as he informs us in the Preface, a compilation from Bede's *HE* and the *ASC*, they are of little worth' and that his works had been overrated. But his third book, though wholly compiled from Bede, has the merit of omitting the miraculous accounts and reserving them for a separate book, and that his works in general, being interspersed with very few of the sacred legends, means that 'he contrasts favourably not only with Bede but with Roger de Wendover and most other chroniclers, not excepting William of Malmesbury.'

Chapter 1 – Penda the Pagan King

1. *LE* i preface; i 15
2. *HB*: trans Giles p27
3. *Historia de Sancto Cuthberto* p 45
4. This genealogy has been erased from the A *Chronicle*.
5. *Chronicle of Henry of Huntingdon* p 56 Bk ii 616 and footnote: Florence of Worcester makes Cearl the same person as Crida, but as the name of Cearl does not appear in the genealogies of the kings, Henry considers him a different person, and not a son of Pybba.
6. Sims-Williams, *Religion and Literature in Western England 600–800* p 25
7. Stenton, *Anglo-Saxon England* p45; *HE* ii 20
8. *Life* of Guthlac p 73 Ch 1

9. Cynegils, Cwichelm, and Cenwalh were all members of the West Saxon royal house.

10. *See* Barbara Yorke, *Kings and Kingdoms of Early Anglo-Saxon England* pp 67–68: Bede says Sigeberht and Eorpwald were brothers, while William of Malmesbury and Florence of Worcester say that they were related only through their mother.

11. Kirby, *The Earliest English Kings* p 79

12. She married Alhfrith of Northumbria.

13. Cyneburh and Cyneswith both witnessed Wulfhere's charter of 664 (S68) as his sisters; William of Malmesbury *Gesta Pontificum* p 214 Ch 180 says that Penda had daughters named Cynethryth and Cyneswith. In his *Chronicle of the Kings* p 72 Bk i Ch 4, he asserts that Merewalh was Wulfhere's brother.

14. Thacker, *Kings, Saints and Monasteries in Pre-Viking Mercia* p 7

15. *Vita Ecgwine* iii.2 p 255

16. From Æthelweard the Chronicler, for example: From the years 604–655 the only mention of Penda is that in 655 he died and the Mercians were baptised.

17. Florence of Worcester, Giles in Archive.org p 9 gives the year as 603. Some background to this might be the Battle of Catraeth, commemorated in *Y Gododdin*. Dumville in Bassett's *The Origins of the English Kingdoms* p 216 points out that the poem only mentions the Deirans, not the Bernicians as the enemy, and that a major defeat of the Gododdin by the Deirans would have opened the way for a Bernician settlement in that area.

18. *HE* i 34

19. *EHD* 152 p 687

20. Presumably Bebba: *HE* iii 6, iii 16, tells us that Bamburgh was named after a former Northumbrian queen and Nennius names her as the wife of Æthelfrith *HB* Ch 63

21. Kirby, p 60

22. *See* Higham, *King Cearl, the Battle of Chester and the Origins of the Mercian Overkingship*: if Cearl sheltered Edwin for a decade and we know he was in East Anglia before 616.

23. We only know her name from Bede *HE* ii 14.

24. P 69; he also gets the date of Edwin's expulsion wrong p 55.

25. *HE* ii 5: 'Not only had he refused to receive the faith of Christ but he was polluted with such fornication ... in that he took his father's wife.'

26. *HE* iv 23; Nennius tells of Edwin's conquest of Elmet *EHD* 2, p 237; Also Barbara Yorke, *Kings and Kingdoms* p 84 says that the *HB* dates the end of Elmet independence to 616 but that it is an independent unit in the *Tribal Hidage*, suggesting that it had detached itself from Northumbria by the second half of seventh century and moved into the Mercian Sphere.

27. *HE* ii 9

28. Molly Miller, *The Dates of Deira*, p 50, has Edwin as an oppressor of Anglesey which was part of Cadwallon's kingdom of Gwynedd.

29. *HE* ii 20; Henry of Huntingdon adds the detail on p 95 that Hatfield 'reeked with red streams of noble blood.'

30. Wallace-Hadrill, *Early Germanic Kingship in England and on the Continent* p 81
31. *HE* iii 21
32. Geoffrey of Monmouth Book XIII Ch 1; also *see* Molly Miller pp 49–50 for more on the Welsh Triad poems and the *Moliant Cadwallon.*
33. Roger of Wendover *Flowers of History* p 80
34. *HE* ii 20
35. Brooks in Bassett p 167 and *ASC* (*EHD* pp150–151) '633 In this year King Edwin was slain by Cadwallon and Penda at Hatfield on 14 October ... and then Cadwallon and Penda afterwards advanced and laid waste all the land of the Northumbrians.' (E only. C (A, B) only say that Edwin was slain.)
36. Kirby p 79 refers to Penda's son Peada and his baptism, and says it is striking that Peada turned not to Canterbury, but to the Irishman, Finan; *HE* iii 13
37. *EHD* pp 149–150 and *see* Kirby p 68 for more discussion on the dates.
38. Sims-Williams, p 27 n.49; Brooks in Bassett, pp 165–166
39. Stenton said there was 'every reason to believe that the under-kingdom of the *Hwicce* was Penda's creation' in *Anglo-Saxon England* p 45 and n.1 but Kirby argued that 'there is no evidence that he was responsible for the formation of the *Hwiccian* kingdom' (p68) and that it is more likely that Mercian rulers were gradually extending their influence over once independent dynasties.' Sims-Williams p 27: 'Perhaps the battle of Cirencester gave the Mercians control over the *Hwiccian* kingdom' however, it may be that Mercian overlordship of the *Hwicce* and *Magonsæte* had to wait until the reign of Penda's son Wulfhere; *see* more on the origins of the *Hwicce* in Chapter Two of this book.
40. Sims-Williams p28
41. For more on this theory, *see* Kirby p 73
42. Stenton, *Anglo-Saxon England* p 38
43. Kirby held that the minor kingdom of Lindsey was key, because Oswald had established himself as a conqueror there, the monks at Bardney remembering him as an aggressor (*HE* iii 11). Further, that there is no evidence (p 74) that Oswald gained dominance over North Wales in the same way which Edwin had, and that when Penda 'fled before Oswald' and took refuge among the Welsh Oswald advanced no further than the vicinity of – possibly – Old Oswestry p 208 n. 30 cites *Vita Oswaldi* and *Symeonis Monachi Opera Omnia* Vol I p 350
44. *HE* iii 16 This must have been during Oswald's reign, if it was during Aidan's tenure. See Fisher, *The Anglo-Saxon Age* p 118
45. *EHD* p 238
46. *See* Brooks in Bassett p 169
47. *See* Sims-Williams p 29 and p 29 n. 60
48. *HE* ii 20
49. Charles-Edwards in *Kings, Currency and Alliances* p 60
50. Fisher p 117
51. *HE* iii 7

52. *HE* iii 18
53. Barbara Yorke, *Kings and Kingdoms* pp 62–63
54. *HE* iii 22
55. Kirby p 81 suggests that the invading army was on the way home and perhaps disenchanted.
56. *HE* iii 24; Henry of Huntingdon said that Oswiu offered an 'enormous tribute' pp 102–3
57. *HE* iii 24
58. *EHD* p 12; Hart in *Mercian Studies* p 45
59. Brooks, *Anglo-Saxon Myths*, p 62; Featherstone, *The Tribal Hidage and the Ealdormen of Mercia,* p. 30
60. Brooks, in *Anglo-Saxon Myths* p 74
61. *HE* ii 2 and *see* Geoffrey of Monmouth Ch13 Book XI for his account of the battle of Chester.
62. Stenton, *Anglo-Saxon England* p 202
63. *See* Higham *King Cearl and the Battle of Chester.*
64. Brooks in Basset pp 167–8; Finberg *ECWM* p 167 ff; Margaret Gelling in Bassett p 191; Barbara Yorke in *Kings and Kingdoms* pp 11–12
65. Barbara Yorke, *Kings and Kingdoms* p 84
66. Brooks in Bassett p 169
67. Fisher p 159
68. Ann Williams, *Kingship and Government in Pre-Conquest England 500–1066* p 16
69. Fisher pp 117–118 But *see* Margaret Gelling Signposts pp 186–187: Warburton developed from *Wærburg's* farm or estate, where the religious house was dedicated to St Werburg, probably because the name suggested it, and the same logic should, according to Gelling, be applied to Oswestry, where the dedication of St Oswald probably arose from a place name which did not originally refer to the saint.
70. *HE* iii 14; Barbara Yorke, *Kings and Kingdoms* pp 78–79 'Œthelwald was 'following an independent line and recognising the authority of Penda.'; William of Malmesbury, *Chronicle of the Kings* p 89 Bk i Ch 5: 'Æthelhere was justly slain by Oswiu, together with Penda, because he was an auxiliary to him, and was actually supporting the very army which had destroyed his brother and his kinsman.'
71. *HE* i 34, ii 20, iii 1, iii 9, iii14, iii 17; Molly Miller *Dates of Deira* p 44
72. *HE* iii 21
73. Fisher p 118
74. *HE* iii 21
75. *Marwnad Cynddylan* line 28 and *see* Sims-Williams pp 27–28 for the importance to Penda of the Welsh alliances.
76. Brooks in Bassett p 168
77. Ann Williams, *Kingship* p 19: She points out that Oswiu was not able to appoint a bishop to the Middle Angles until after the death of Penda.
78. Wallace-Hadrill p 81

78. *HE* iii 24
79. Brooks in Bassett p 166; but Sims-Williams p 28 'the *HB*, perhaps correctly, puts this in stark terms.'
80. Fisher p 118: Penda was driven by two things: to maintain independence from Northumbria and to expand his lands south of the Humber. But the main concern was with Northumbria.
81. *HE* ii 16

Chapter 2 – The Origins of The Mercian Kingdom

1. *See* Barbara Yorke, *Origins of Mercia* in Brown/Farr p 13 for more on the fact that the origins fell outside Bede's historical narrative and that there is still 'discord and confusion'; Sims-Williams p 7 who thought it unlikely that the Anglo-Saxons settled the area in any numbers before the sixth century, and there is no reason to ascribe a Celtic origin to the kingdoms although *see* Kessler and Dawson, *Mercia's British Alliance* for the idea that there was intermarriage; Kirby p 4 and Hart in *Mercian Studies* pp 43–44 for more on the boundaries and whether they were fixed.
2. Barbra Yorke in Brown/Farr p 21: dress finds suggest Anglian origin.
3. Barbara Yorke in Brown/Farr p 15. But *see* also Kessler & Dawson 2016
4. Fisher p 109
5. *HE* iv 13; Sims-Williams p 16
6. Barbara Yorke in Brown/Farr p 19
7. Brooks in *Anglo-Saxon Myths* p 64
8. Dorothy Whitelock *EHD* p 18 and *see* footnotes.
9. Barbara Yorke in Brown/Farr p 18
10. Ann Williams, *Kingship and Government* p 15
11. Barbara Yorke in Brown/Farr p 15
12. *Life of Guthlac* Ch II p 74; David Dumville, in *Anglo-Saxon England* Vol 5 p 33
13. Ann Williams, *Kingship and Government* p 15 n.14 for the first mention of the *Tomsæte* she says *see* her Chapter Five.
14. Stenton, *Anglo-Saxon England* p 41 CS 455, CS 454
15. Dorothy Whitelock, *EHD* pp 7–8
16. Although there is still debate about when and how the kingdom of the *Hwicce* came under direct Mercian control. Dorothy Whitelock p 18 *EHD*: 'The *Hwicce*, in the valley of the lower Severn presumably submitted to them after Penda's victory at Cirencester in 628, and the other peoples along the Welsh border can hardly have maintained independence after that time.'
17. *See* Appendix II on shiring and *see* Hart in Dornier p 49 for more discussion about the boundaries and the fact that they are coterminous with the diocesan boundaries.
18. An interesting side note is the theory that Bede was using a similar document. *See* the *Medieval Histories* link in the bibliography.
19. Featherstone in Brown/Farr p 23

20. *Ibid*

21. *HE* iv 6, iv 19

22. James Campbell, *The First Christian Kings*, in Campbell, p 59–61

23. Stenton, in *Anglo-Saxon England* p 295 declared it 'extremely corrupt'.

24. *See* Featherstone pp 23–25 and Barbara Yorke p 20 in Brown/Farr.

25. Stenton, *Anglo-Saxon England* p 295

26. Barbara Yorke, *Kings and Kingdoms* p 13: we should not assume that all the provinces in the *Tribal Hidage* had rulers of Germanic birth and she cites Elmet. She also points out that Bede was anti-British.

27. Ann Williams, *Kingship and Government* p 16, and her n.19 citing Brooks, *The Formation of the Mercian Kingdom* pp 16–19 and Margaret Gelling, *The Early History of Western Mercia* pp 184–91

28. Although as already noted, *see* note 26 above, this is an ongoing debate – how, when and how much the people of Elmet, known as the British Loides, came under Mercian control.

29. Barbara Yorke in Brown/Farr p 21

30. Dumville in *Anglo-Saxon England* Vol 5 p 37

31. Stenton, *Anglo-Saxon England* p 48

32. Thacker, *Kings, Saints and Monasteries in Pre-Viking Mercia* p 4

33. *See* Stenton Preparatory *Lindsey and its Kings* pp 127–135 for possible evidence of the importance of the king of Lindsey even at this late stage. But *see* also Barbara Yorke, *Early Kings and Kingdoms* p 113

34. Stenton, *Anglo-Saxon England* p 44

35. *See* Barbara Yorke in Brown/Farr p 19 and Hart in Dornier p 47

36. Featherstone in Brown/Farr pp 27–34

37. Kirby p 9. He cites Margaret Gelling in Bassett p 192 and Dumville pp 131–2 says that the Middle Angles were not mentioned as such in the *Tribal Hidage* and that it must have been a short-lived Mercian creation.

38. *See* Ann Williams, *Kingship and Government* p 16, and her n.23; *see* also Kirby pp 58–9

39. *See* Sims-Williams p 30 cf Old Icelandic *hvikari* – coward.

40. CS 432; Stenton, *Anglo-Saxon England* p 44

41. *HE* ii 2, v 23; Kirby p 6 cites Bassett in Bassett, who cites the Florence of Worcester reference from 680 about the creation of the bishopric. 'Presumably coterminous with the kingdom, in fact it probably helped to define the boundaries.'

42. Sims-Williams p 5: the kingdom of the *Hwicce* 'corresponded almost exactly with the medieval diocese of Worcester.'

43. *See* more in Sims-Williams p 3 and *ECWM* for charters and below, Chapter Ten p 167 and p 177 ff

44. *HE* iv 13 Bede makes the only mention of Eanfrith. Eafe is mentioned in the *Vita Wilfridi* and William of Malmesbury's *Gesta Pont*. She could be the Eafe in charters S1782, S1824; *HE* iv 23; The *Vita Wilfridi* Ch 21 says that Wilfrid was bishop of the Saxons, demonstrating Dorothy Whitelock's

point that Bede was the only one to distinguish Angles, Saxons, etc., *see* note 15 above.

45. Sims-Williams p 31 n.71
46. Finberg *ECWM* p 171 and *see* Stenton *Anglo-Saxon England* p 45 n.1 where he says that the dual origin of the *Hwicce* makes it very unlikely that any local family can have possessed an inherent right to rule over the whole people, and the later *reges, reguli* and *duces* were set in power by the Mercian kings.
47. *See* Sims-Williams p 33
48. *ECWM: see* his discussion of the careers of Oslaf and Oswudu pp 169–170
49. Sims-Williams p 33
50. *See ECWM* pp 172, 174–5; Sims-Williams p35 n. 99
51. *EHD* no 74 p 462
52. *EHD* 81 pp 471–473 & 84 pp 476–477
53. *See* Kirby pp 68–69 who cites Bassett p 6 and Dumville in Bassett pp 128–9
54. CS 332; Stenton Preparatory *Pre-Conquest Herefordshire* p 194
55. Sims-Williams p 5, & pp 43–44 for discussion about the boundaries.
56. *HE* v 23
57. *See* Kate Pretty in Bassett pp 171 ff and Sims-Williams p39 ff
58. Finberg *ECWM* p 217: there is no reference to the Eastern *Hecani,* and no explanation of the name has yet been offered; Sims-Williams p 41 gives the text of the rubric HACANA, *see* his n.1
59. For place name *see* Margaret Gelling *Signposts to the Past* pp 102–3
60. For more on her family *see* Chapter Three pp 60-1
61. Stenton Preparatory, *Pre-Conquest Herefordshire*, p 195
62. *Ibid* p 196
63. Sean Miller on Anglo-Saxons.net says Bede was probably unwilling to admit how big a part the British played in the conversion of the English. He refers to Sims-Williams pp 75–79 and the suggestion that the *Hwicce* & *Magonsæte* were already Christian when Bede first mentioned them; they were close to the Welsh borders.
64. *See* Finberg *ECWM* p 219 n.2
65. Stenton *Anglo-Saxon England* p 21
66. Sims-Williams p 40
67. *See* Margaret Gelling, *Signposts* p 93
68. But *see* Sims-Williams, p 26, who says this argument cannot be pressed.
69. *Gesta Pont* Ch 171 p 207
70. *ECWM* p 147
71. *ECWM* p 221 n.1 gives the full Latin inscription, taken from William of Malmesbury's *Gesta Pont.*
72. For discussion of this story, *see ECWM* p 223. It may be that initially Hereford was attached to the see of Lichfield.
73. Sims-Williams p 51
74. *EHD* pp 62, 250, 318, and pp 557–8
75. Sims-Williams p 6
76. *Ibid* p 22

77. Sims-Williams on p 25 n.41 'It is not true that all extant Mercian regnal lists begin with Crida and the extension back to him may be very late.'
78. Stenton, *Anglo-Saxon England* pp 38–39
79. Higham, *King Cearl and the Battle of Chester*, n.57
80. Stenton, *Anglo-Saxon England* pp 38–49

Chapter 3 – The Sons of Penda

1. CS 45; Stenton Preparatory *Medeshamstede and its Colonies* p 179 n.3
2. Chronicle of Hugh Candidus, Mellows & Mellows pp 2–3
3. *LE* i 17
4. *HE* iv, 19; Tim Pestrell, *Landscapes of Monastic Foundation* p 132, n. 148
5. Garmonsway's translation for E says that this chronicle laid the blame on Peada's wife.
6. Mellows & Mellows p 3; *HE* iii 24
7. Sharon M. Rowley, *The Old English Version of Bede's Historia Ecclesiastica* pp 119–120
8. *See* Kirby p 94 for discussion of dates.
9. *HE* iii 24
10. *EHD* p 19 n.20; 54 p 440
11. *HE* iv 13
12. *See* Charles-Edwards in *Kings, Currency & Alliances*, p 59, who believes that the baptism may have been later, as does Kirby, pp 115–6.
13. *HE* iii 7
14. Miller, Anglo-Saxons.net
15. *HE* iii 7, 30; Ann Williams, *Kingship and Government*, p 20 n.66: it was probably only at this point that the middle Saxons – first recorded by that name in 704 – gained a separate identity; Dumville, *Essex, Middle Anglia and the Expansion of Mercia* p 134 and Keith Bailey, *The Middle Saxons*, p 111 in Bassett.
16. *HE* iii 21, 24, iv 3 and *see* Kirby p 95
17. Ann Williams, *Kingship and Government* p 20 n.69 citing Ann Dornier, pp 157–8, and Alex Rumble, in Mercian Studies pp 169–71. Frithuwald may indeed have been married to Wulfhere's sister Wilburg n.70 John Blair 'Frithuwald's Kingdom and the Origins of Surrey' in *Origins*, esp. pp 105–7. *See* also Kirby p 96 for the possibility that Frithuwald was a Middle Angle.
18. Barbara Yorke in *Anglo-Saxon England* Vol 14 p 32 'His datable activities in East Saxon territory all come from the latter part of his reign i.e. 688–704.'
19. *Life* of Wilfrid, Ch 20 p 128
20. *HE* iv 12; Kirby, p 97
21. *Historia de Sancto Cuthberto*, p 29
22. *Life* of Wilfrid Ch 20 p 128
23. William of Malmesbury *Chronicle of the Kings* Bk ii Ch 7 p 146
24. Stenton, *Anglo-Saxon England* p 202
25. Dorothy Whitelock, *EHD* p 20

26. Dugdale, *Monasticon Anglicanum* p 143 Stone, Staffordshire

27. *The Chronicle of Hugh Candidus,* Mellows & Mellows pp 4–5

28. D.W. Rollason, *The Cults of Murdered Royal Saints in Anglo-Saxon England* Anglo-Saxon England Vol 11 p 11

29. Thacker, *Kings, Saints and Monasteries* p 4

30. *HE* iii 30: another clear demonstration that the East Saxons had come under Mercian domination; *HE* iv 16 (14)

31. *Gesta Pont* Ch 18 p 215

32. Richard Fletcher, *Roman Britain & Anglo-Saxon England* p 50

33. *Gesta Pont* Ch 100 p 144

34. *Vita Wilfridi* Chapter 16 'When Wilfrid was installed at York during Wulfhere's reign …'

35. *Ibid* Ch 40

36. *Gesta Pont* Ch 203 p 239; Barbara Yorke *Kings and Kingdoms* p 108; S1166, *see* also S71 and S73

37. *HE* iv 19 (17)

38. I am indebted to Ann Williams for the information gathered from David Rollason, *The Mildryth Legend: a Study in Early Medieval Hagiography in England,* Leicester 1982, pp. 39–40 and from S. Kelly, *Charters of St Augustine's Abbey, Canterbury,* Oxford 1995, no. 10 when I embarked upon my mission to unravel this confusion.

39. *LE* i 17

40. Finberg *ECWM* p 220

41. But *see EWCM* p 219 n.2 for more discussion on the likelihood that Penda was his father.

42. *HE* iv 12, 21

43. Kirby p 98

44. *Ibid* p 103

45. Colgrave, *Life* of Guthlac pp 3, 178

46. Kirby, p 107: Osric ruled the *Hwicce* as king (*HE* iv 23) (S51) in 676 (or 675 Nov) and Oshere granted land as king (S53) in 693 but Æthelred's consent was being sought (S51) and 'there can be no doubt' that he regarded Oshere as his sub-king (S1429 736 or 737, S1255 774).

47. Dumville in Bassett, p 135

48. Hugh Candidus, Mellows & Mellows p 8

49. *Vita Wilfridi* Ch 43, 44, 54, 57

50. *Vita Ecgwine* i 10 p 223, ii 2 p 239

51. Lapidge, Byrhtferth of Ramsey p 253 n.3: There is no other evidence to corroborate this.

52. *Ibid* p 254 n.7 'There is no independent evidence recording the grant by Osweard to Ecgwine of the estate at Twyford. Osweard's relationship to Byrhtferth and the spurious charters which derive from him. *See* p 252 n.2 and above Chapter One p 15)

53. *Gesta Pont* Ch 100 p 147, Ch 102 p 153

54. *ECWM* p 170, p 176 citing Tangl, 1916, *S Bonifatii et Lullie Epistolae*: A letter from Boniface to a lady named Egburg mentions her brother's 'tragic death; Kirby, p 107

55. *HE* iv 22

56. *Vita Ecgwine* iii 2 p 255

57. *HE* v 13, v 19

58. *Life* of Guthlac Ch 34 p 109

58. *Vita Ecgwine* iii 1 p 255: Lapidge says the amount is probably wrong.

59. *Ibid See* Lapidge's notes p 256–257: It is not entirely clear who this refers to. If it is Æthelred, then Byrhtferth was mistaken, for Coenred was the nephew. Concerning Æthelric: the manuscript here reads Æthelwulf, but Oshere of the *Hwicce* had four sons, who all seem to have been regarded as *sub-reguli*: Æthelheard, Æthelweard, Æthelberht, and Æthelric (*see* Sims Williams p 35–6). But no son of Oshere named Æthelwulf is known.

60. There was no king of East Anglia by that name, although there was an Offa, king of the East Saxons, who went to Rome with Coenred.

61. *Vita Wilfridi* Ch 57 p 172

62. Barbara Yorke, *Kings and Kingdoms* p 50

63. Here Byrhtferth makes the same mistake *see* note 60 above; Offa was king of the East Saxons.

64. *Vita Ecgwine* iii 3 p257 and n.17; iii 4 p 259

65. *EHD* 177 p 755

66. *Hemingi Chartularium Ecclesiae Wigorniensis*, ed T Hearne Vol II p 369: 'Ceolwaldus'; Barbara Yorke, *Kings and Kingdoms* p 111 n.82; *ASC* Chronicle B&C EHD 716: Whitelock says simply that they have it 'wrongly'.

67. *See* Barbara Yorke, *Kings and Kingdoms* p 111 & n.84

68. It was devastating to be shunned, *see* Stephen Pollington, *The Mead-Hall* p 29

69. Thomas Fuller, 1608–61 *The History of the Worthies of England* ed P.A. Nuttall, 3 vols, (London 1840) i. p 194, quoted in Rosalind Love, *Vita Sancti Rumwoldi*

70. *Ibid* p cxliv

71. Thacker, *Kings, Saints and Monasteries* p 4

72. *Gesta Pont* Ch 180 p 214. It seems unlikely that they would have been given to the Church in their infancy, given that their father was a pagan. William of Malmesbury said that the younger of the two was consecrated to celibacy, although King Offa of the East Angles – he makes the same mistake here as Byrhtferth – had hoped to marry her. He went to Rome with Coenred.

73. Thacker p 1 only says that these last two were Penda's 'supposed' daughters; p 7.

74. *Ibid See* n.46 for yet more supposed descendants of Penda: 'Elftreda' and 'Elgida' who may have been St Elfthryth of Repton and St Aldgyth of Bishop's Stortford.

75. *See* Bailey and Hohler in *Records of Buckinghamshire* vols 18 and 31; *Gesta Pont* Ch 73

Chapter 4 – Æthelbald the Elusive King

1. Dumville *Anglo-Saxon England* Vol 5 pp 32–34
2. *See* Pauline Stafford in Brown/Farr p 37 on changing interpretations of queenship in this period.
3. Bertram Colgrave: Introduction to the *Life* of Guthlac p 16
4. *Life* of Guthlac Ch xlv pp 139–141
5. Colgrave: Introduction to the *Life* of Guthlac p 8; William Dugdale *Monasticon Anglicanum* 'Croyland' No.164 p 16 'Æthelbald king of Mercia, by his charter dated in the year 716, gave ... the whole Isle of Croyland ... for the erecting of a monastery under the rule of St Benedict.'
6. Dorothy Whitelock, *EHD* p 21; Colgrave p 6; both citing Tangl No. 10 *S. Bonifatii et Lulli epistolæ* Berlin 1916
7. *Hemingi Chartularium Ecclesiae Wigorniensis*, ed T Hearne Vol II p 369
8. Life of Guthlac Ch li p 163, lii p 165
9. *HE* v 23
10. Miller on Anglo-Saxons.net. The charter certainly shows Æthelheard of Wessex confirming the grant.
11. Although, David Hill, *The Dwellers on the Boundary* in Brown/Farr p 175 suggests that this could have happened in Offa's reign, so perhaps they took it back after Æthelbald died?
12. S89 *EHD* 67 p 453
13. Stenton Preparatory *The Supremacy of the Mercian Kings* p 56 ff and p 56 n.3
14. Barbara Yorke, *Kings and Kingdoms* p 113
15. Kirby pp 111–113; Wormald in Campbell p 99
16. Barbara Yorke, *Kings and Kingdoms* p 63
17. Dumville in Basset p 135
18. Bede continuations p 296
19. Miller on Anglo-Saxons.net; T.M. Charles-Edwards, *Wales and the Britons* p 435
20. *EHD* p 241; Bede continuations 297
21. William of Malmesbury, *Chronicle of the Kings* Bk 1 Ch 4 p 73
22. Henry of Huntingdon Bk iv AD737
23. *EHD* 177 p 751
24. The location has never been established, but there were several councils of Clofesho, and it is assumed that it must have been somewhere in Mercia, and that perhaps it was Brixworth, Northamptonshire, or possibly Hitchin, Herts. 'The most famous lost place in England,' according to Slater & Goose, *A County of Small Towns* p 191.
25. *Gesta Pont* Ch 5 p 8; Kevin Leahy *Anglo-Saxon Crafts* p 75: The council banned clerics from wearing ostentatious clothing. He says that if this was how priests, monks and nuns dressed, one can only wonder what the rest of the population looked like.
26. S1258; *EHD* 79 p 468

27. *See* Stenton, *Early History of the Abbey of Abingdon* pp 22–23
28. Fletcher, *Roman Britain & Anglo-Saxon England* pp 98–99 considers that he might have been trying to harness the 'enormous resources of the Church to some secular purpose'.
29. *See* Wormald in Campbell p 100
30. *The English Correspondence of Boniface* – archive.org
31. S1782: This translation from *PASE* but *see* Stenton, *Anglo-Saxon England* p 205 who says 'stabbed' or 'smitten.'
32. S102, *EHD* 64 p 449 An interesting side note: this charter was witnessed by Ofa, Æthelbald's friend who shared his exile and who was helped by Guthlac after standing on a thorn.
33. Fletcher, *Roman Britain & Anglo-Saxon England* p 98
34. Kirby, p 115; Archibald/Fenwick/Cowell *A Sceat of Ethelbert I of East Anglia and Recent Finds of Coins of Beonna.*
35. *See* Chapter Five p 85 for more on Beonna and his possible identity.
36. D.M. Metcalf, *Monetary Affairs in Mercia in the time of Æthelbald* in *Mercian Studies* p 91: no sceattas have been unearthed from Droitwich, despite its importance as a salt workings, or along the line of Wat's Dyke, an earthworking probably constructed in Æthelbald's time. But excavations in the 1990s unearthed Romano-British pottery, which puts this dating in doubt. *See* British Archaeology Magazine issue 49 November 1999.

Chapter 5 – Offa the Great

1. Archibald/Fenwick/Cowell *A Sceat of Ethelbert I of East Anglia and Recent Finds of Coins of Beonna*
2. Barbara Yorke, *Kings and kingdoms* p 112 n.88
3. *ECWM* 31, 208; S116, 117, 146; Barbara Yorke, *Kings and Kingdoms* p 112; Vanessa King, *The Early History of Bredon*, p 80; S116 & 117 show Offa granting land to the church at Bredon.
4. S62: Ealdred, *subregulus* of the *Hwicce*, with the permission of Bishop Tilhere, to Æthelburh, his kinswoman; lease, for life, of the minster at Fladbury, Worcs., with reversion to the bishopric of Worcester; S127: *Ego Ethelburga abbatissa consensi. See* Kirby, p 134
5. Fletcher, *Roman Britain & Anglo-Saxon England* p 110: 'There is, as yet (2002) no modern book on him.'
6. Stenton, *Anglo-Saxon England* p 206
7. Williams/Smyth/Kirby *Biographical Dictionary of Dark Age Britain* p 189
8. *EHD* p 221 n.8; S108: *Ego Osuualdus dux Suðsax' consensi .+ Ego Osmund dux confirmavi.*
9. *See* Kirby, p 136
10. S25: Æthelberht II, king of Kent, to the minster of SS Peter and Paul (St Augustine's) Canterbury; exchange whereby the minster cedes the half-use of a mill to the royal vill at Wye, Kent, in return for pasture rights in the Weald for its tenant at Chart, Kent; S32: 'Sigered, king of Kent, to Eardwulf,

bishop, to augment his monastery; grant of 1.5 iugera in the northern part of the city of Rochester.'

11. S1264 and *see* Stenton, *Anglo-Saxon England* p 35 n.1; S155 Cenwulf, king of Mercia, to Christ Church, Canterbury; restoration of 30 sulungs (aratra) at Charing, 10 at Seleberhtes cert or Bryning lond (Chart) and 4 at Humbinglond in Barham, Kent, previously seized and redistributed by King Offa.

12. *See* Kirby, p 136

13. Henry of Huntingdon p 134–135 but n.3: Forester suggests that it might have been Orford, in Kent. One Ms reads 'Oxenford', Oxford.

14. Stenton, *Anglo-Saxon England* p 206

15. This may only have been temporary; *see* Wormald in Campbell p 111 and *EHD* 80 p 470 S155 for a charter which shows how the king of Kent has granted lands to a subject, only to have them seized by Offa on his return to power, saying it was wrong that the king presumed to give the land without his permission; S1264 *see* above, n. 11.

16. Stenton, *Anglo-Saxon England* p 209

17. Stenton, *Early History of the Abbey of Abingdon* p 24; CS 291

18. S123: Offa, king of Mercia, to Ealdbeorht, minister, and Selethryth, his sister; grant of 14 sulungs (aratra) at Ickham and Palmstead, Kent, with woodland in the Weald and other appurtenances; S125 Offa, king of Mercia, to Ealdbeorht, minister, and his sister, Selethryth, abbess; grant of 15 sulungs (aratra) at Ickham, Palmstead and Ruckinge, Kent, with swine-pastures, woodland and other appurtenances, including an urban tenement (vicus) at Curringtun in Canterbury; S128: Offa, king of Mercia, to Osberht, his minister, and Osberht's wife; grant of 1 sulung (aratrum) at Duningcland in the Eastry district, Kent; S134: (Clofesho) Offa, king of Mercia, to the churches of Kent; confirmation and grant of privileges.

19. Roger of Wendover adds the detail that he was buried at Repton.

20. *See* R. Woolf, *The Ideal of Men Dying with their Lord in the Germania and in the Battle of Maldon* Anglo-Saxon England Vol 5 pp 70–71 in ASE Vol 5 for discussion.

21. *EHD* 191 p 770

22. Stenton, *Anglo-Saxon England* p 218

23. *EHD* 203 pp 788–790

24. *Ibid* 204 p 792

25. *Ibid* 202 p 787

26. William of Malmesbury *Chronicles of the Kings* Bk ii Ch 1 pp 94–96 has details of his early adventures not mentioned elsewhere.

27. *EHD* 192 p 774–775

28. *Ibid* 20 p 313

29. *Ibid* 196 p 780

30. Thacker, *Kings, Saints and Monasteries* p 15

31. *Ibid* p 17

32. David Rollason, *The Cults of Murdered Royal Saints* Anglo-Saxon England Vol 11 p 9 and *see* his n.41; ASC 1055

33. *Ibid* p 17
34. *Gesta Pont* Ch 170 p 206
35. Roger of Wendover *Flowers of History* pp 158–159
36. Chronicle of John of Worcester p 225
37. S59, dated 770: *Ego Cyneðryð regina Merciorum consensi ei subscripsi . + Ego Ecgferð filius amborum consensi et subscripsi.* As seen in Chapter Ten, p 160-61, a king's wife's status was significantly enhanced by being the mother of an atheling.
38. Pauline Stafford in Brown/Farr p 38
39. This too was a scene to be repeated during the early years of Æthelred Unræd's reign in the late tenth century, when his mother was dominant at court.
40. Stephen Allott, *Alcuin of York*, letters 35, 36; Pauline Stafford in Brown/Farr p 39 n.2. This is not confined to her appearances with Ecgfrith; Wormald in Campbell p 110 makes the point that Alcuin, like Bede, was an important witness 'from without'.
41. Pauline Stafford in Brown/Farr p 39; Grierson & Blackburn, *Medieval European Coinage Volume 1* pp 279–281
42. S1258, S76
43. *See* Kessler & Dawson, *Mercia's British Alliance.*
44. *EHD* 197 p 781; Wormald in Campbell p101
45. *See* Kirby, p 144 who references the involvement of Charlemagne in the harbouring of Offa's enemies.
46. S89; *ECWM* CS 220, 241
47. CS 319; CS 332 – *see* Wormald in Campbell p 111
48. Grierson & Blackburn, p 157; Anna Gannon, *The Iconography of Anglo-Saxon Coinage* p 12
49. Kirby, p 137; Miller on Anglo-Saxons.net: Offa started to issue an East Anglian coinage in the later 760s/early 770s.
50. *EHD* 197 p 782; Wormald in Campbell p 106
51. Pauline Stafford in Brown /Farr p 39
52. Charles-Edwards in Brown/Farr pp 99–100
53. Sims-Williams, p 53
54. Fisher, p 163
55. Keynes/Lapidge *Alfred the Great*, Asser's *Life of King Alfred* Ch 14; For the most up to date information on this, and other archaeological sites, visit the Council for British Archaeology http://new.archaeologyuk.org/discover/
56. *See* Kirby, pp 174–175; *See* Ann Williams, *Kingship & Government* p 12
57. Dorothy Whitelock, *The Audience of Beowulf*
58. *See* Stenton Preparatory *Pre-Conquest Herefordshire* pp 193–196
59. *Ledbury Reporter*
60. Wormald in Campbell p 147 wonders how else to explain the lack of material from all kingdoms bar Wessex.
61. *EHD* 33 p 372
62. Roger of Wendover, *Flowers of History* pp 160–165
63. William of Malmesbury's *Chronicle of the Kings* Bk i Ch 4 pp 77–78

Chapter 6 – The Forgotten Kings

1. Letter to Osbert, ealdorman of Mercia, *EHD* 202 p 787
2. It will be recalled that William of Malmesbury accused Offa of stealing from the Church at Malmesbury: *see* above Chapter Five n.63.
3. *See* Keynes in *Kings, Currency and Alliances* p 3 n.8 where he cites S154 as perhaps implying that Ecgberht was recognised as king before the death of Beorhtric and a possible line of descent from the kings of Kent.
4. Asser's *Life* of Alfred Chs 14–15 (in Keynes/Lapidge pp 71–72)
5. Ann Williams, *Kingship & Government*, p 29; Bassett in Bassett p 8
6. Kirby, p 148 and n.103: a letter of Alcuin's to the people of Kent in 797 which suggests that Cenwulf was not of particularly high-quality stock.
7. CS289; Wormald in Campbell p 101; Keynes in Brown/Farr p 310
8. *See* above n.1; Kirby, p 148 says that he accused him of compounding his deficiencies by putting away his wife.
9. *See* Pauline Stafford in Brown/Farr p 42
10. Grierson & Blackburn, p 293
11. *EHD* 200 p 785
12. *Ibid* 206 p 795
13. Haddan & Stubbs, *Councils and Ecclesiastical Documents* Vol III p 564
14. *EHD* 203 p 789; also in or before that pivotal year of 798, the archbishopric of Canterbury was returned to Mercian hands. A charter of that year (S1258) shows Æthelheard (originally appointed by Offa) granting land to the abbess Cynethryth, in his role as archbishop of Canterbury.
15. Kirby, p 148 thought Frankish support for Eadberht would have been more forthcoming on Ecgfrith's death, but Brooks, *Early History of the Church of Canterbury* p 122 suggested that he established himself in Kent while Ecgfrith was still alive.
16. *EHD* 197 p 781; Kirby, p 149
17. Forester's translation of Henry of Huntingdon p 140 n.1: Henry, 'to his credit', rejects the story.
18. *Gesta Pont* Ch 8 p 13; *EHD* 210 p 799 Decree of the synod of Clofesho 803 abolishing the see of Lichfield.
19. *EHD* 204 p 791 Letter of Cenwulf to Pope Leo III
20. *EHD* 205 pp 793–794; the *ASC* says 799 but the chronology was two years behind the true dates for the late eighth and early ninth centuries – *see* Rollason in *Anglo-Saxon England* Vol 11 p 10; *EHD* 209 p 798; Brooks, *Early History of the Church of Canterbury* pp 120–132
21. *See* Kirby, pp 152–153 and Brooks, *Canterbury* pp 132–142
22. *See* Haddan & Stubbs, Vol III p 564 footnote: The letter shows that this argument was 'notorious'.
23. Kirby, p 153; S1435; For more on the dispute between Cenwulf and Wulfred, *see* Brooks 1984 cited in Keynes, Brown/Farr p 311 n.4; Wormald in Campbell pp 127–8
24. *See* Pauline Stafford in Brown/Farr p 41

25. Thacker, pp 10–11
26. *Ibid* p 10 and n.80: Winchcombe was a place of royal significance. Cynehelm/Kenelm was buried there, 'Offa probably founded a nunnery there and Cenwulf added a male community in 798'; Sims-Williams, pp 166–167: it was the subject of papal privileges. Documents pertaining to Cenwulf's rights over Winchcombe and other monasteries, which he claimed to have 'justly acquired', were held there, as was the captured Eadberht Præn.
27. Thacker, n.55
28. Armitage Robinson, *Somerset Historical Essays* p 38 n.2 and *see* S152 but Sims-Williams, pp 165–166 thought S152 unreliable.
29. Thacker, n. 62
30. Rollason, *Anglo-Saxon England* Vol 11 p 10: The writer claimed among his informants Queen Edith and a disciple of Archbishop Oswald (d.992).
31. *See* n.20 above.
32. Matt Firth, *Wicked Queens and Martyred Kings*; Sims-Williams, p 167
33. Thacker, p 12; Fletcher, *Roman Britain & Anglo-Saxon England* p 111: The Winchcombe psalter, produced in the about 1050, 'furnishes further evidence of the cult.'
34. Line 2239; Stenton, *Anglo-Saxon England* p 230 n.3: 'The statement is unlikely to be an invention, and may well come from the version of the *Chronicle* which Gaimar is known to have possessed.'
35. Brown/Farr p 100
36. AC 822; although Kirby, p 154 argued that it was in fact Beornwulf who led the attack.
37. S1435 translated Keynes in Brown/Farr p 311
38. Kirby, p 154 n.17
39. Keynes in Brown/Farr p 311 and *see* below Chapter Ten p 175 ff
40. Stenton, *Anglo-Saxon England* p 231 C 384/ S1435; Kirby p 154
41. *See* Keynes in Brown/Farr p 313 n.10 for reference to a possible fragment of a lost vernacular poem on the subject of battles, culminating with the battle of *Ellendun*.
42. Stenton, *Anglo-Saxon England* p 231; p 233 especially n.1
43. *Ibid* p 231: CS 340 and CS 373.
44. *See* Kirby, p 154
45. S273: *Principium autem huius scedulæ scriptum est in hoste quando Ecgbertus rex Geuuissorum movet contra Brittones ubi dicitur Creodantreow*; EHD 229 pp 822–823
46. Grierson & Blackburn, pp 293–4
47. Keynes in Brown/Farr p 313 n.11 gives possibilities for these five ealdormen and notes that John of Worcester's assertion might have been no more than a construction put upon the *ASC* by a Worcester chronicler in the later eleventh or early twelfth century.
48. Williams/Smyth/Kirby *Dictionary* p 6
49. Kirby, p 157
50. In Campbell, p 139

51. Stenton, *Anglo-Saxon England* p 233; S190 *EHD* 85 pp 477–479
52. *Kings, Currency and Alliances* p 4
53. *ASC*, although the *Annales Cambriae* doesn't mention it.
54. Kirby, pp 158–159
55. S278 is a grant by Ecgberht dated 835, of land in Berkshire to Abingdon Abbey. *See* below Chapter Seven for more on Berkshire going out of Mercian control.
56. Kirby p 160 says he died in 839.
57. Ingulph's *Chronicle of Croyland* p 23 but this has been denounced as a forgery.
58. Thacker, p 12
59. *Ibid* p 13
60. Keynes in Brown/Farr p 315
61. Greer Fein, *De martirio sancti Wistani*
62. Keynes in Brown/Farr p 319: there is no sign in Burgred's reign of Ceolwulf II and only two occurrences of Æthelred, the last ruler of Mercia. Whatever was happening, it doesn't look as if these men were necessarily coming up through the ranks.
63. Grierson & Blackburn, pp 292–293
64. *ASC* 853; Keynes/Lapidge p 69
65. James Booth in *Kings, Currency and Alliances* p 66
66. As n.55 *See* Chapter Seven p 122 ff for Berkshire, Æthelwulf & Pangbourne.
67. *EHD* 86 pp 479–80
68. Birch 445 *see* Wormald in Campbell p 139
69. Kirby, p 148
70. Keynes in Brown/Farr p 311, p 314

Chapter 7 – Burgred and Ceolwulf II: The Last Kings of Mercia

1. *EHD* p174 n.1, 2: Dorothy Whitelock pointed out that in the A version the verb is plural, 'allowing Burgred some share in the campaign'; *see* her comment about the 'varying sympathies betrayed by the different emphasis of the two versions.'
2. Wormald in Campbell p 138
3. Keynes & Lapidge Asser, Ch 7 p 69; in 855 Vikings were campaigning in the Wrekin area, and since Anglesey was attacked at the same time, it is likely that these raiders came from the Irish-Norse settlements.
4. S160, 1264, 186, 190 and *see* Kirby, pp 171–172
5. S1701: For discussion on this and more on Eanwulf, *see* Keynes in *Kings, Currency & Alliances* p 8 n.25.
6. *Ibid* p 9: Keynes also points out that very few Mercian coins were minted in the 850s, as a result of the Viking occupation of London in 851.
7. S1271 *EHD* p 25 n.10, p 177 n.10, 87 pp 480–481; Kirby p157: This shows Berkshire moving into Mercian control, whereas Keynes *Kings, Currency &*

Alliances p 6: the immediate gift of the land elsewhere is a sign that Berkshire moved at this point out of Mercian control.

8. Keynes and Lapidge, p 28; Booth in *Kings, Currency & Alliances* p 65

9. Keynes, *Kings, Currency & Alliances* p 6: A unique penny combining the obverses of King Beorhtwulf and King Æthelwulf was formerly regarded as a special issue struck to commemorate the transfer of Berkshire from Mercia to Wessex, but the coin is now more plausibly regarded as an aberration.

10. CS 291; Stenton, *The Early History of the Abbey of Abingdon* pp 24–25

11. *Ibid* p 26; but in *Anglo-Saxon England* p 234 he said that 'In later years, when Berkshire had at last become a West Saxon province, Æthelwulf continued to govern it on behalf of its new lords,' which is subtly different.

12. Wormald in Campbell p 141; Keynes in *Kings, Currency & Alliance* p 6 n.19

13. Stenton, *The Early History of the Abbey of Abingdon* pp 28–29; S317: Æthelwulf, king of Wessex, to Ealdred, his minister; grant of 20 hides (*cassati*) at Æscesbyrig (i.e. Woolstone), Berks.

14. *See* Keynes & Lapidge in Alfred the Great, Asser's *Life* of Alfred p 241 n.57 for discussion on the name *Mucil/Mucel*.

15. S1442 and *Ibid* n.58

16. Keynes in *Kings, Currency & Alliances* p 9; p 11; and *see* Grierson & Blackburn, p 311

17. David Hill, *The Dwellers on the Border* in Brown/Farr p 175

18. *EHD* 94 p 490

19. Paul Hill, *The Age of Athelstan* p 67: Alfred may have looked north with 'alarm' to see Ceolwulf allied with the Vikings.

20. *Chronicle of the Kings* Bk i Ch 4 p 88

21. S539; *See* Keynes, *Kings, Currency & Alliances* p 11 n.40

22. *Ibid* pp 17–18

23. Blackburn in *Kings, Currency and Alliances* pp 118–119

24. Cat Jarman, archaeologist, digventures.com

25. Miller on Anglo-Saxons.net

26. Charles-Edwards in Brown/Farr p 101

27. Keynes, *Kings, Currency & Alliances* p 35

28. ashmolean.org/watlington-hoard

29. Dr Gareth Williams, telegraph.co.uk

30. Keynes in *Kings, Currency & Alliances* p 16

31. Kirby, p 178

32. *See* more on the battle of the Holme in Chapter Eight p 136 ff

33. Cf discussion of the *Tribal Hidage* in Chapter Two p 43; Keynes in *Kings, Currency & Alliances* p 5

34. *PASE*

Chapter 8 – The Lord and Lady of the Mercians

1. Keynes in *Kings, Currency & Alliances* p 19

2. Hemming's Cartulary, Hearne p 369. While there is an Æthelred listed, coming after Æthelwulf, Æthelbald and Æthelberht and before Alfred, he surely must be Æthelred, king of Wessex.
3. Keynes, *Kings, Currency & Alliances* p 19 n.74
4. *Ibid* n.84; Charles Edwards in Brown/Farr p 101
5. The Fragmentary Annals of Ireland, *The Three Fragments* p 227 call his wife the 'Queen of the Saxons.'
6. T.M. Charles-Edwards in Brown/Farr p 102
7. Keynes, *Kings, Currency & Alliances* p 13
8. *EHD* p 886 n.2; Keynes *Ibid* p 21
9. Stenton in *Anglo-Saxon England* p 259: 'Alfred was respecting traditions by leaving London as part of Mercia' so, perhaps this was an official recognition of an already accepted fact.
10. Ann Williams, *Kingship & Government* p 74
11. Æthelflæd Lady of the Mercians in Clemoes, *The Anglo-Saxons: Studies in Some Aspects of their History and Culture Presented to Bruce Dickens* p 55
12. Guthrum and Alfred had famously come to terms and the country had been divided along Watling Street in the so-called Treaty of Wedmore in 878.
13. *See EHD* p 186 n.4, for the possibility that these events took place in 885.
14. Roger of Wendover said that it was Alfred who met them at Buttington, and that it was Alfred's army which had driven the Vikings away at Benfleet. A tree known as the Buttington Oak fell down in February 2018. It has been shown to be 1,000 years old, and pollarded, suggesting that it had been planted there deliberately, perhaps to commemorate the site of the battle: http://www.bbc.co.uk/news/uk-wales-mid-wales-43084088
15. Henry of Huntingdon Book v p 168
16. Keynes in *Edward the Elder* p 42: Henry of Huntingdon was hampered by having the *Mercian Register* but not the 'West Saxon' account for the years 914–20; hence his confusion about her family, generally.
17. Forester, *The Chronicle of Henry of Huntingdon*, p 166 n.1, remarks attributed to a Mr Petrie.
18. Victoria Thomson, *Dying and Death in Later Anglo-Saxon England* pp 22–23
19. She was Eadgifu and she was to play a major role at court later in the century.
20. Blackburn & Grierson, p 321 but note that their book was published in 1986 before the Silverdale Hoard had been unearthed.
21. For discussion of her status and that of queens generally, *see* Pauline Stafford in Brown/Farr pp 44–46
22. Maggie Bailey in *Edward the Elder* p 113
23. Keynes in *Kings, Currency & Alliances* p 38
24. S221, 225, and 224; Pauline Stafford in Brown/Farr p 46
25. *Ibid*
26. See Victoria Thomson, *Death and Dying* p 8
27. Stephanie Hollis, *Anglo-Saxon Women and the Church* p 86

28. Pauline Stafford, *The Annals of Æthelflæd: Annals, History and Politics in Early Tenth-Century England* p 101

29. *Ibid* p 113: Stafford says there is no contemporary evidence for Athelstan's having grown up in Mercia.

30. *Ibid* p 114

31. Kari Maund, *The Welsh Kings*, p 55, p 61

32. Whitehead, *The Attack on Llangorse*, English Historical Fiction Authors Blog.

33. The 'Five Boroughs' of the Danelaw, which were important strategic centres, the five being: Derby, Leicester, Lincoln, Nottingham and Stamford; Victoria Thomson *Dying and Death* p 11: the word used in the *Mercian Register* for 'dear' is *besorge*, which carries implications of care and anxiety, as well as love and value, instead of the more common *leof*. Is this a nod to her femininity?

34. Pauline Stafford, *Queen Edith and Queen Emma* p 92

35. Victoria Thomson, *Dying and Death* p 21: Bishop Werferth considered it a foreign practice.

36. Stenton, *Anglo-Saxon England* pp 325–329

37. *Æthelflæd Lady of the Mercians* p 68

38. Higham, p 3 and Keynes, p 42 in *Edward the Elder*; John of Worcester p 366: *Ætheredus dux et patricius dominus et subregulus Merciorum* and *Ægelfleda Merciorum domina.*

39. Barbara Yorke in *Edward the Elder* p 26

40. Wainwright, p 68

41. *The First Use of the Second Anglo-Saxon Ordo* p 117; Whitehead, *Rioting in the Harlot's Embrace* p 16

42. Paul Hill, *The Age of Athelstan* p 97

43. Keynes, *Kings, Currency & Alliances* p 41

44. Pauline Stafford in Brown/Farr p 48 points out that the *Mercian Register*, impossible to date accurately, does make much of Divine aid. She says it focuses on her 'regal' activity, whereas others have said the focus is military.

45. Keynes, *Kings, Currency & Alliances* p 31 n.140, p 39 n.168

46. *EHD* 95 p 491

47. Fletcher, *Roman Britain & Anglo-Saxon England* p 138

48. *See* Derek Keene in *Alfred the Great: Papers from the Eleventh-Centenary Conferences* edited by Timothy Reuter pp 243–244

49. Asser's *Life* of Alfred Ch 77

50. Keynes & Lapidge, *Alfred the Great*, p 259 n.167

51. Fletcher, *Roman Britain & Anglo-Saxon England* pp 111–113

52. Thacker, *Kings, Saints and Monasteries* p 18

53. Wainwright, p 55

54. Keynes in *Edward the Elder* p 42

55. Maggie Bailey, *Ibid* p 115

56. *Ibid* p 120

57. Whitehead, *Rioting in the Harlot's Embrace*, p 24

Chapter 9 – The Formation of 'England': Mercia Fades

1. The D *Chronicle* adds 'after 16 days', chronicles A, E, F don't mention Ælfweard.
2. *See* Pauline Stafford, *The Annals of Æthelflæd* 113 n.49
3. Williams/Smyth/Kirby *Dictionary of Dark Age Britain* p 128; Ted Johnson South, *Historia de Sancto Cuthberto* p 25; S365; Keynes in *Edward the Elder* pp 50–51
4. The implication is that Alfred wished his grandson to succeed. *Note* also that William only mentions Athelstan's aunt and uncle on the way to praising Athelstan.
5. Eric John in Campbell p161
6. Grierson & Blackburn, p 323; also *see* Appendix on Danes in this book for more about those who had 'settled' in Mercia.
7. Paul Hill, *The Age of Athelstan* p 56 suggests that Hywel Dda, whose grandfather was killed in 878, and who submitted to Athelstan in 927, named his son Edwin, as a deliberate insult to Athelstan.
8. Sarah Foot, *Athelstan: The First King of England* p 18
9. *Ibid* pp 33–34
10. S1417: Æðelstan *rex* + Eadwine *cliton*
11. *EHD* 26 p 318
12. Charles Insley, *The Family of Wulfric Spott* p 119
13. For more on this, *see* Appendix II in this book on the Shiring of Mercia.
14. Ann Williams, *Kingship & Government* p 89
15. Ælfhere, ealdorman of Mercia, 956–983 *see* Chapter Ten in this book.
16. Ann Williams, *Kingship & Government* p 172 and *see* also Chapter Ten in this book.
17. However *see* Hart, *ECNE&NM*, p 363 where he is said to have been ealdorman from 930 to *c.* 949.
18. For more on this *see* Chapter Eleven p 184
19. Stenton, Preparatory, *The Danes in England* pp 161–162
20. Athelstan *Rota*, appointed to the vacant southeast Mercian ealdordom by King Eadwig in 955. Not to be confused with an Athelstan who was appointed in 940, *See* Williams/Smyth/Kirby *Dictionary* p 52
21. Hart, *ECNE&NM* p 287
22. *See* Appendix on the Danes p 229
23. Stenton, Preparatory, *The Danes in England* pp 161–162; *see* Kevin Halloran *The War for Mercia, 942–943* p 105 for more on this topic.
24. *EHD* 234 *Life* of Dunstan p 826; Fletcher, *Roman Britain & Anglo-Saxon England* p 170
25. *See* Eric John, *Kings & Monks* p 64 n.5: 'Dr. Whitelock, *EHD* p 46, thinks that the *Vita Dunstani*'s claim that Dunstan occupied an especially important place in Eadred's counsels exaggerated. But the *Vita*, in my opinion, gives details of what its claim was based on which seem entirely credible.'
26. S1515, also *EHD* 107 pp 511–512

Chapter 10 – Ælfhere, the Mad Blast from the Western Provinces

1. *EHD* 234 p 829
2. Lapidge, Byrhtferth of Ramsey, *Vita Oswaldi* p 13 n.33
3. S1211 issued by Eadgifu in 959 notes that she was deprived of her property.
4. Her name is recorded once, on S1292 as *Æþelgifu þæs cyninges wifes modur* – the king's wife's mother.
5. The link is through the maternal line; in her will, Eadwig's queen left an estate at Risborough, which has been connected to a charter of 903 (S367) and which confirms the owner of the estate as the Half-king's mother, given to her by her father, Æthelwulf of the *Gaini*.
6. Æthelweard's chronicle says of Eadwig that 'on account of his great personal beauty, [he] was called All-Fair [*Pankalus*] by the people.' He held the sovereignty for four years, and was much beloved.' Given that this is the only chronicle to praise rather than damn Eadwig, it strongly suggests that there was a kinship.
7. VI Æthelred 12
8. Shashi Jayakumar, *Eadwig and Edgar* in Scragg pp 88–89
9. There is a charter, S597, which seems to suggest an Ælfric as adoptive parent. I'm indebted to Ann Williams who confirms that this is not what it means and cites: 'Susan Kelly, 'Charters of Abingdon Abbey', Oxford, 2000, 2v, v. 2 no. 55, pp. 230–8. She suggests (p. 236) that the beneficiary is Ælfric *cild*, the future ealdorman (983–5); he married Ælfhere's sister Æthelflæd, and since Ælfhere was a royal kinsman, this status came to Ælfric as well after his marriage. The word *'parens'* in this sense means 'kinsman', rather than 'parent' (father, foster-father); Ælfric was *adoptivus* because he was a kinsman by marriage rather than blood.
10. *See* Cyril Hart, *Athelstan 'Half-King' and his Family* for the career of Athelstan Half-king.
11. S1515; S1211: 'When Eadred died and Eadgifu was deprived of all her property, then two of Goda's sons, Leofstan and Leofric, took from Eadgifu the two aforementioned estates at Cooling and Osterland, and said to the young prince Eadwig who was then chosen [king] that they had more right to them than she. That then remained so until Edgar came of age and he [and] his witan judged that they had done criminal robbery, and they adjudged and restored the property to her.'
12. *EHD* 238 p 847
13. Florence of Worcester said that 'Edgar was chosen by the unanimous voice of the Anglo-Britons ... and the divided kingdoms were thus reunited.'
14. 'B' in the *Life* of Dunstan *EHD* 234 p 830; it has been suggested (Miller Anglo-Saxons.net) that the division is rather too neat to believe the popular uprising suggested by the *Life* of Dunstan.
15. Hart, *ECNE&NM* p 323: 'he continued to claim sovereignty over the whole of England just as if nothing had happened.'

16. For example, S676, 958: 'Edgar, king of Mercia, to … his *comes*; grant of 5 hides at Ham, Essex.'

17. Keynes in Scragg p 9; Frederick Biggs in Scragg p 138: Coin finds are too many in Eadwig's case to have been minted only over a two-year period … there are no finds of Edgar's that would support a suggestion of joint kingship.

18. CS 937, 1030, 1045 Hart, *ECNE&NM* pp 293–294

19. The married bishop of Winchester, archbishop-elect, died on his way to Rome to receive the pallium (the vestment symbolising the office of archbishop) from the pope, leaving the way clear for Dunstan to become archbishop of Canterbury.

20. CS 677, CS 765 *ECNE&NM* p 328

21. *ECNE&NM* p 260, Lapidge, *Byrhtferth of Ramsey* p 123 n.109, Ann Williams, *Princeps Merciorum gentis: The Family, Career and Connections of Ælfhere, Ealdorman of Mercia, 956–83* p 145 and n.6

22. S 462: 'A.D. 940. King Edmund to Elswithe [Ælfswith], his *kinsman* [my italics] and faithful minister … grant of 20 hides at Batcombe, Somerset.' Dorothy Whitelock in *Anglo-Saxon Wills* p 125 pointed out that since Ælfheah bequeathed this estate to his wife, he was probably a joint recipient of this grant and that his name was omitted by the copyist; S585, S 586, S639, and S662, which describes Ælfswith as Eadwig's kinswoman.

23. Ann Williams, *Princeps Merciorum gentis* p148 although *see* n.29 and Dorothy Whitelock, *Anglo-Saxon Wills* pp 121–2 for counter argument.

24. Pauline Stafford, *Limitations on Royal Policy* p 19 n.23 and *see* Dorothy Whitelock, *Wills* no 3. Such a relationship would mean that the brothers were Edgar's maternal uncles.

25. Hart in *ECNE&NM* p 261 thought Eadric was Ælfhere's son. *See* Ann Williams, *Princeps Merciorum gentis* pp 151–155 for discussion of these two brothers. While Hart said that 'Ælfhere's son, Eadric, is described as *major regiæ domus* in *Chron Abingd.* where he is said to have purchased the abbey of Abingdon for his brother Eadwine', Williams establishes that Eadric was a fourth brother.

26. 'B', *Life* of Dustan *EHD* 234 p 830

27. *LE* i 50

28. Fletcher, *Roman Britain & Anglo-Saxon England* p 173

29. Literally 'Agreement about the Rule.' It is a work drawn up by him to regulate and standardise monastic observance according to the rule of St Benedict; Thomas Symons, *Regularis Concordia* p 7

30. Eric John, *The King and the Monks in the Tenth Century Reformation* pp 61–62. John also makes the point that Æthelwold was alive in the reign of Edward the Elder so his silence on the incursions is significant. He obviously thought of monastic decline in more than the material sense.

31. Fletcher, *Roman Britain & Anglo-Saxon England* p 178

32. Lapidge, *Byrhtferth of Ramsey* p 77 n.120: Byrhtferth exaggerates the number of monasteries founded by Edgar.

33. For more detail on this generally *see* Eric John's article cited in n.30 above.

34. Fletcher, *Roman Britain & Anglo-Saxon England* p 179

35. C.P. Lewis in Scragg p 117 notes the use of the phrase 'for the salvation of my soul and [the souls] of my predecessors Edmund and Athelstan', positioning him as Edmund and Athelstan's heir, excluding Edward the Elder, Alfred, and Eadred and placing himself in the line of kings of *all* the English, even though he wasn't at the time, as if he expected to be king. Lewis says that perhaps the charter was paving the way for Mercia to play a greater role in England once Edward was gone. But it probably wasn't anticipating Benedictine Reform.

36. *EHD* 41 p 397 and *see* Appendix I The Danes.

37. S773, 677, 723 and *see* Sims-Williams, p 44

38. Lewis in Scragg p 112 says it looks deliberate.

39. A.J. Robertson, *Anglo-Saxon Charters* p 90 quoted from Ann Williams, *Princeps Merciorum gentis* p 163; Pauline Stafford, *Limitations* p 24: in 924/5, 956, 975 and 1035 Mercia supported a different candidate from Wessex.

40. Byrhtferth, *Vita Oswaldi* p 81; Ann Williams *Princeps Merciorum gentis*, p 146

41. Jayakumar in Scragg p 84

42. Ann Williams, *Princeps Merciorum gentis* p 158

43. *Ibid* n.74 Charters of Rochester.

44. For more detail on these complicated relationships, *see* Whitehead *Rioting in the Harlot's Embrace* pp 30–33

45. *Ibid* p 36

46. The term 'earl' was used for those in the Danelaw, but would gradually replace the title 'ealdorman'. It is a linguistic difference, but the function/office remained the same; those who lived in the Danish settlements, *see* *EHD* p 400 n.2; *see* Appendix I The Danes.

47. Williams/Smyth/Kirby *Dictionary of Dark Age Britain* p 223

48. *See* Ann Williams, *An Outing on the Dee*; Whitehead, *On the Trail of Dunmail*.

49. Idwal Foel was the son of Anarawd, who submitted to Alfred the Great, and whose father Rhodri Mawr's death had been avenged at the battle of Conwy.

50. Edgar was not unusual in having a complicated married life, for so had Edward the Elder. As Pauline Stafford put it in *Limitations* p 21, the later Saxon kings were serial monogamists, not always waiting for the death of a first wife before marrying again.

51. *EHD* 236 p 841

52. *See* Whitehead, *Rioting in the Harlot's Embrace* p 42 for identity of this recipient. *PASE* identifies Æthelweard 36 as the recipient of the land in Buckinghamshire and as the beneficiary of Ælfgifu's will S1484, thus confirming his identity as Æthelweard the Chronicler.

53. It was said that at Evesham, at this time, the remains of St Ecgwine were unearthed when the building collapsed and found to be uncorrupted. (Byrhtferth, *Vita Ecgwine* iv 11 p 301)

54. *See* Pauline Stafford, *Limitations* p 23 n.36

55. Ann Williams, *Princeps Merciorum gentis* p 166
56. Stenton, *Anglo-Saxon England* p 505 and *see* Chris Monk for a new translation of Mercian laws which suggests that at some point, they were indeed different.
57. Ann Williams, *Princeps Merciorum gentis* p 163 n.102
58. Stenton, *Anglo-Saxon England* p 337; Ann Williams, *Princeps Merciorum gentis* p 162 and *see* Appendix II The Shiring of Mercia.
59. Byrhtferth of Ramsey, iii 14 p 83; Ann Williams, *Ibid* p 165
60. *LE* ii 49
61. Pauline Stafford, *Limitations* p 26
62. Groups of three hundreds, each group being required to produce a ship and a crew of sixty men. The bishop who held the soke replaced the ealdorman as head of the contingent to the *fyrd. See* also Appendix II The Shiring of Mercia.
63. Ann Williams, *Princeps Merciorum gentis* p 159
64. *ECNE&NM* p 260. However, Hart said that Ælfhere had a son named Godwine, and he was tempted to speculate that this was the same man mentioned in the Evesham story. It seems clear though that Godwine was not Ælfhere's son. For the relationship, *see* Ann Williams, *Princeps Merciorum gentis* pp 169–170
65. *See* Shashi Jayakumar, '*Reform and Retribution: the 'anti-monastic reaction' in the reign of Edward the Martyr*' Studies in Memory of Patrick Wormald pp 349–50
66. Stenton, *Anglo-Saxon England* p 373
67. For more on this, *see* Eric John, *The King and the Monks in the Tenth Century Reformation* pp 77–86
68. Pauline Stafford, *Limitations* p 25: alternatively it might just show a renewed interest for recording such events.
69. For more on her reputation for witchcraft and murder, *see* Whitehead *Rioting in the Harlot's Embrace* p 40
70. *See* Lindy Brady, *Writing the Welsh Borderlands in Anglo-Saxon England* p 114
71. *Gesta Pont* Ch 162 pp 201–202
72. *EHD* 231 p 824
73. *See* Jayakumar *Reform and Retribution: the 'anti-monastic reaction' in the reign of Edward the Martyr* in Studies in Memory of Patrick Wormald p 351
74. *See* Appendix II The Shiring of Mercia.

Chapter 11 – Wulfric, Eadric and Leofwine: Mercian Wealth and Power

1. *ECNE&NM* p 373: 'Probably related through his mother to the English royal line.'
2. *Ibid*
3. *Ibid*

4. Dorothy Whitelock, *The Dealings of the Kings of England with Northumbria in the Tenth and Eleventh Centuries* p 81; *See* also Appendix I, The Danes.

5. P.H. Sawyer, *The Charters of Burton Abbey and the Unification of England* p 34

6. *Ibid* p 37

7. *See* Pauline Stafford, *Queen Emma and Queen Edith* p 219 n.51 for a possible link with this family not only to Queen Ælfthryth but also to Æthelred Unræd's first wife and that their fall was linked to the change of queens.

8. *See* Insley, *The Family of Wulfric Spott* p 123 who refers to this incident as the 'somewhat shady West Saxon takeover of Mercia'.

9. *See* Appendix I The Danes.

10. Insley, p 122; Appendix I; Insley, p 125

11. For more on Wulfstan's 'treachery', *see* Dorothy Whitelock, *Dealings* p 72

12. *See* n.7 above; Dugdale, p 27; *ECNE&NM* p 373

13. Hart in *ECNE&NM* p 323 said that Ealdgyth was the wife of Morcar and that her husband was the thegn of the Seven Boroughs killed in 1015. He wrote that 'probably her daughter was related to Wulfric Spott, but whether through her mother or her father does not appear.' He also says that Morcar was the son of Earngrim, and closely related to Wulfric, but that the precise nature of this relationship has not been determined.

14. Insley, p 126: Weston, Morley, Smalley, Kidsley, Crich, Ingleby, Eckington and *Ufre* which he says Sawyer identified as Mickleover (Sawyer, p 67).

15. According to John of Worcester. He may have made a mistake, or it may be that both brothers were married to women who bore the same, fairly common, name.

16. *ECNE&NM* p 258

17. Dorothy Whitelock, *Anglo-Saxon Wills*, no 17

18. The *ASC* records Swein and Olaf raiding in 994

19. BBC News Online December 2005 http://news.bbc.co.uk/1/hi/uk/4561624.stm

20. William of Malmesbury's *Chronicle of the Kings* Chapter x p 169; Stenton, *Anglo-Saxon England* p 381

21. Ann Williams, *Cockles Amongst the Wheat* p 3 and n.17; Keynes, *Eadric Streona* ONDB

22. Ann Williams points out in *Cockles* pp 3–4 that Uhtred of Bamburgh did the same but confined his interests to his own earldom.

23. In this period. The seventh-century princess of East Anglia had married Tondberht of the south *Gyrwe*, though again, his status may have been more than 'mere' ealdorman.

24. Keynes, *Eadric Streona*, ONDB; S916: Leofwine attests in second place.

25. The *ASC* doesn't name them specifically as his sons, but Dorothy Whitelock, *Anglo-Saxon Wills* p 153 gives supporting evidence and John of Worcester names them as his sons p 459.

26. Ann Williams, *Æthelred the Unready: The Ill-Counselled King* pp 71–2; *EHD* p 218 n.2; Roger of Wendover has a garbled story (entry for 1006) about a noble earl, Athelstan, being lured to a feast at Shrewsbury by the 'perfidious Eadric'

where he was slain by a murderer named Godwin, paid by Eadric, and that in revenge, the king ordered Eadric's two sons to be deprived of their sight.

27. Pauline Stafford, *Limitations* p 33
28. *See* Ann Williams, *The Ill-Counselled King* pp 116–117 and n.40 for suggestions about the motivation for Brihtric's accusation. Wulfnoth's son, Godwine, who may have been the future Earl Godwine of Wessex, was a beneficiary of the atheling Athelstan's will, which hints at yet more political faction and hostility to Eadric's family among Edmund Ironside's party.
29. S933 and Keynes in ONDB; Hugh Candidus p 34 wrote of those who could not pay tribute losing their lands and possessions.
30. Florence of Worcester: 'against the Mercians' *EHD* p 223 n.3
31. Roger of Wendover says that Eadric went with his king to exile in Normandy. It may be, of course, that he had little choice, being otherwise completely friendless.
32. The additional two boroughs making seven out of the original Five Boroughs are likely to have been Torksey and York – *see* Stenton, *Anglo-Saxon England* p 388; *See* n.28 above: Godwine, Wulfnoth's son, was also left a bequest.
33. Dorothy Whitelock, *Dealings* p 88: *La Vie Seint Edmund le Rei.*
34. We don't know the precise date of this marriage – *see* Appendix I, The Danes – but it wouldn't have made the brothers any more popular with Æthelred if it had already happened at this point.
35. As noted above, n.31, Roger of Wendover has Eadric sailing to Normandy with them, but this can only ever be supposition.
36. Pauline Stafford, *Limitations* p 36: Athelings were usually discouraged from marriage before the death of their father or reigning brother, *see* her n.118 where she says that the atheling Athelstan, whose will was extensive, makes no provision for wife or family.
37. Richard Fletcher, *Bloodfeud* pp 81–82
38. Keynes, ONDB
39. Christopher J. Morris, *Marriage and Murder in Eleventh-Century Northumbria* p 3
40. It is not possible certainly to identify 'Darling', although a minister called Æthelmær (24 in pase.uk) held land in Worcestershire in 991 according to S1365, although this seems a little early. No 25 in *PASE* also received land in Norton, Worcs, in a charter dated between 1016 and 1023. If this was him, then he obviously survived the battle(s).
41. Ann Williams, *Cockles Amongst the Wheat* p 5
42. Pauline Stafford, *Limitations* p 16
43. *LE* ii 79
44. Campbell & Keynes, *Encomium* p 29
45. *EHD* p 227 n.14
46. Campbell & Keynes, *Encomium* p 31–33
47. *Flowers of History* p 293
48. Hearne, Hemming's Cartulary p 274; Ann Williams, *Cockles* p 5

49. Æthelweard the Chronicler's son was Æthelmær, father of Wulfnoth. If this is the same Wulfnoth who was Godwine's father, then king Eadwig's disgraced queen, Ælfgifu, being the sister of Æthelweard, was Godwine's great-great-aunt.

50. Ann Williams, *Cockles*, p 5

51. *Ibid* p 7, citing Hemming.

52. But *see* Chapter Ten p 182 where it has been suggested that he was in fact ealdorman of the whole of Mercia; *ECNE&NM* p 344 and Stephen Baxter, *The Earls of Mercia: Lordship and Power in Later Anglo-Saxon England* p 16

53. Ann Williams, *The Ill-Counselled King* p 27

54. But this man is listed in *PASE* as Æthelsige 22 and the only incident recorded in his entry is the attack on Wales. The man who was deprived of his land and office was a landowner in Kent and Gloucestershire, and he is listed as Æthelsige 25. There is no suggestion that they are the same man, but it seems likely to me.

55. *ECNE&NM* p 345

56. *ECWM* pp 143–5

57. Baxter, p 23

58. *See* Appendix II, The Shiring of Mercia.

59. Ann Williams, *Cockles* p 9

60. S1423 and *see* S1460; *ASC*; Ann Williams, *Cockles* p 8 and *see* S1462; Baxter, p 32: if Eadwine were a shire reeve of Shropshire, this would give context for his death at the hands of the Welsh.

61. John of Worcester claimed that Northman was an ealdorman in 1017, but *see* Mark Lawson, *Cnut: England's Viking King* p 162 n.62 who agrees with Freeman's assessment in *The History of the Norman Conquest of England* in dismissing the claim.

62. Mellows & Mellows, *The Peterborough Chronicle of Hugh Candidus* p 36

63. Ann Williams *Cockles*, p 8 but *see* also Pauline Stafford *Limitations* p 43 n.71

64. Translation by K. Crossley Holland in *The Anglo-Saxon World* p 14

65. Ann Williams, *Cockles* p 8

66. *See* Wulfric's family tree on p 186 and Chapter Twelve for more on Leofric and Harold I (Harefoot)

67. *See* Stenton, *Anglo-Saxon England* pp 414–416 and Appendix I The Danes.

68. Keynes, ONDB

69. Ann Williams, *The Ill-Counselled King* p 77

70. Ann Williams, *Cockles*, p 5

71. Hearne, Hemming's Cartulary p 280; *ECWM* pp 234–5 and *see* Appendix II 'Shiring'.

72. Ann Williams, *The Ill-Counselled King* p 205

73. Campbell & Keynes, *Encomium*, p ix

Chapter 12 – The House of Leofric

1. Ann Williams, *Cockles Amongst the Wheat* p 8

2. Ingulph's *Chronicle of Croyland* p 115; *ECNE&NM* p 342

3. *Vita Wulfstani* cited in *ECNE&NM* p 342 but note that subsequently Leofric was noted for restoring estates to Evesham and building a church at Bengeworth, Worcs.; Mark Lawson, *Cnut* p 162 n.64; Pauline Stafford, *Queen Emma and Queen Edith* p 40 n.234

4. Dorothy Whitelock, *The Dealings of the Kings of England with Northumbria in the Tenth and Eleventh Centuries* p 83

5. *See EHD* p 232 n.4 the chronicler uses a rare word which avoids any word implying kingly authority.

6. Stenton, *Anglo-Saxon England* p 417

7. Apart from one version of the *ASC* which doesn't mention the death of Alfred at all.

8. *See* Campbell & Keynes, *Encomium* p ixx for the implications of the death of Harold Harefoot and the need for Emma to secure the loyalty of Godwine and Leofric, but also to clear herself of any charges that she encouraged Alfred to come to England and was thus in any way complicit in his death.

9. Although, further on, it does refer to him as the 'fugitive prince' p 27.

10. I am indebted to Ann Williams for her insight into this oblique reference to the family's status.

11. *See* Lawson, p 197 for discussion on this.

12. According to Worcester tradition, *see* Frank Barlow, *The Godwins* p 53 especially n. 23

13. Darlington, *Chronicle of John of Worcester* pp 549–553. John is the only one to give Swein's parentage p 549 n.9.

14. For Eadwine's death, *see* Chapter Eleven, (p 198) and *above* Chapter Eleven notes, n.60

15. *See* Stenton, *Anglo-Saxon England* pp 568–569

16. Dorothy Whitelock, *The Dealings of the Kings of England with Northumbria in the Tenth and Eleventh Centuries* p 83

17. Barlow, *The Godwins* p 74

18. *Ibid* p 83 quotes Freeman n.34: 'the whole kingdom, save a few shires in the middle, was in [the Godwines'] hands.'

19. Stephen Baxter, *The Earls of Mercia* pp 1–4

20. Stenton, *Anglo-Saxon England* p 417

21. *LE* ii 81. If she is the same woman, she is found again bequeathing land at Barking (*LE* ii 83) I am grateful to Ann Williams for the additional comments here: 'An extract from her will in the form of a letter is addressed to Bishop Aelfric (1023–38) and Abbot Leofric (*c.* 1022–1029), so about the same time as the gift of the "small but outstanding" estates at [Good] Easter, Fambridge and Terling (*LE* ii, cap 80). Only in the latter case is she called "widow of a certain earl." Her name is preserved in that of "Good Easter" (Goda's Easter). The will itself doesn't survive. Godgifu is a common name, and I suspect the idea that this lady's husband was an earl simply crept in during various copyings, by confusion with Earl Leofric's wife.'

22. Bishop of Dorchester-on-Thames 1053–1067

23. Roger of Wendover, *Flowers of History* pp 314–315

24. Dugdale, *Monasticon Anglicanum* p 31
25. *Gesta Pont* p 210 Ch 175. Clearly, by William's time she was already 'famous'.
26. Joan Lancaster, *The Forged Charters of Coventry*, especially p 122
27. Hearne, *Hemming's Cartulary* i p 261
28. Robertson, *Anglo-Saxon Charters* pp 211 & 461
29. Baxter p 5 quotes Freeman who said that they were little better than Eadric Streona.
30. Kari Maund, *The Welsh Kings* p 93
31 *PASE* Domesday Burgheard 6
32. Dugdale, *Monasticon Anglicanum* on Hereford p 288: 'King William the Conqueror restored to this Church divers Mannors unjustly taken from it by Earl Harold.'
33. Darlington, *Chronicle of John of Worcester* p 597; Hardy & Martin, Gaimar's *Estoires des Engleis* line 5084 p 161
34. Dorothy Whitelock in *Dealings* p 83 n.2 says that no connection can be made between this Morcar and Morcar of the Seven Boroughs, though the repetition of the name suggests a connection through marriage and that through the maternal line this younger Morcar was the grandson of the elder Morcar.
35. Stenton, *Anglo-Saxon England* p 572
36. Richard Fletcher, *Bloodfeud* p 161
37. *Vita Edwardi see* Barlow, *The Godwins* p 122 who says there is no evidence for his immediate decline in health.
38. Stenton, *Anglo-Saxon England* p 587 says that Edwin defeated him with the Lindsey militia.
39. Florence of Worcester says that they were there, and that they withdrew their troops upon hearing that Harold was dead.
40. David Roffe, *Hereward the Wake and the Barony of Bourne* p 1
41. Ingulph's *Chronicle of Croyland* p 134
42. Roffe, *Hereward and the Barony of Bourne* n.13: Michel, F, *Chroniques Anglo-Normandes Rouen*; Roffe p 2 quoting Lincolnshire Domesday 42/1, but also *see* the same article p 4 where he says that the Domesday survey does not prove Morcar's tenure of the estate and that it is 'famously imprecise' in its record of pre-Conquest lords and tenants.
43. Marjorie Chibnall, *Orderic Vitalis* pp 257–261. This version appears to contradict the implied timeline of the *ASC*, which reads as if Edwin died while Morcar was still hiding out at Ely.
44. For more on this, *see* Barlow, *William Rufus* p 65
45. Barlow, *The Godwins* p 170
46. *See* also Barlow, *William Rufus* pp 389–90

Appendix I – The Danes in Mercia

1. CS 487; *See* also B. Thorpe, *Diplomatarium Anglicum Aevi Saxonici* p 113
2. David Hill, *The Dwellers on the Boundary* in Brown/Farr p 175
3. Stenton, *Anglo-Saxon England* pp 254–55

4. Stenton, Preparatory, *Pre-Conquest Herefordshire* p 193

5. Martin Biddle & Birthe Kjølbye-Biddle, *The Repton Stone* pp 234–236

6. Kirby, pp 177–178

7. Wainwright, pp 62–63

8. Lesley Abrams, *King Edgar and the Men of the Danelaw* p 175 and *see* n.20

9. Edgar IV the 'Wihtbordesstan' Code *EHD* 41 p 397

10. Dorothy Whitelock, *Dealings* p 81

11. S397; Sawyer pp 29–31 suggested that the estates such as those mentioned in S397 lay in areas over which the grantors had, at the time, little authority and there is therefore a strong suspicion that it was left to the beneficiaries themselves to take and hold what they had been given.

12. *Ibid* p 37; and Insley, p 124 who thinks that the policy was initiated after the events of 940–2

13. *ECNE&NM* pp 14–15

14. *See* Halloran, p 98 for this discussion; Finberg, *The Formation of England* p 155: 'Edmund bided his time, knowing that the Danish population had no love for their Norse masters.'

15. Dorothy Whitelock, *Dealings* p 72–73

16. For a discussion of the Mercian 'alliterative' charters of this period *see* Insley, p 121.

17. Ann Williams, *Princeps Merciorum gentis* p 164

18. Niels Lund, *King Edgar and the Danelaw*, Med. Scand. 9

19. Lesley Abrams, pp 171– 177

20. Dorothy Whitelock, *Dealings* p 81; Ælfhelm, ealdorman of Northumbria, and thegns Sigeferth and Morcar, of the Seven Boroughs, discussed in Chapter Eleven p 186, p 191

21. For discussion of this, *see* Ann Williams, *The Ill-Counselled King* pp 117–20

22. *Ibid* p 120 n.5

23. Lawson, p 123: Her high status is evidenced by the fact that in 1023 one of her sons was offered in exchange for one of Thorkell's when he was reconciled with Cnut, so Cnut must have openly acknowledged his son.

24. *Ibid* p 51

25. Lucy Marten, *Meet the Swarts* p 18 citing Ann Williams, *Cockles* and *see* her n.7

26. Barlow, *The Godwins* pp 25–26; Pauline Stafford, *Emma and Edith* p 244

27. Hearne, *Hemming's Cartulary* i p 251

28. For more on this and more on land ownership *see* Lawson, pp 153–55

29. Stenton, *Anglo-Saxon England* pp 414–416

30. *See* Ann Williams, *Cockles* p 9 for the suggestion that these appointments were a product of the political events of 1015–17 and show Cnut's 'atypical treatment of the Mercian ealdordom' and his talent for 'shrewd practicality'.

31. Paul Hill, p 163

32. *Ibid* p 165 n.3

33. *EHD* 34 p 380; Stenton Anglo-Saxon England p 320

34. Paul Hill, p 164

35. Stenton, *Anglo-Saxon England* p 321
36. I am indebted to Gerry Lyons and Jennifer Robinson for these insights.

Appendix II – The Shiring of Mercia

1. Finberg, *The Formation of England* p 147 (He uses the term West Angles for *Magonsæte*).
2. Pauline Stafford, *Limitations* p 29
3. Stenton, *Anglo-Saxon England* p 337
4. Ann Williams, *The Ill-Counselled King* p 77
5. *ECWM* p 228
6. Eric John in Campbell p 176
7. Keynes in *Edward the Elder* p 59
8. Eric John in Campbell p 172
9. Ann Williams, *The Ill-Counselled King* p 78 n.71
10. Dorothy Whitelock *EHD* 113 p 519: 'The administrative reorganization which created the counties of the Midlands ignored this division.'
11. *ECWM* p 228 and *EHD* pp 193–8
12. *ECWM* p 229
13. Ann Williams, *The Ill-Counselled King* p 78; Hearne, Hemming's Cartulary i p 280
14. *ECWM* p 230
15. Sims-Williams, pp 43–47
16. Ann Williams, *The Ill-Counselled King* p 79 and n.78
17. Stenton, *Anglo-Saxon England* p 337
18. Tamworth was clearly an important centre, with recorded Christmas and Easter festivals there in 781, 814, 841 and 845 – Hart, in Mercian Studies p 58.
19. Ann Williams, *The Ill-Counselled King* p 80
20. Robertson, *Anglo-Saxon Charters* pp 76–77
21. For more of this *see* Roffe, *The Origins of Derbyshire* pp 110–116
22. *Ibid*, specifically p 110
23. *EHD* 39 p 393; Insley, p 121
24. Source is Eric John in Campbell p 173

Bibliography

Abrams, Lesley, 'King Edgar and the Men of the Danelaw' from Scragg, Donald (ed), *Edgar King of the English, 959–975* (Woodbridge: Boydell Press, 2008)

Allott, Stephen, *Alcuin of York* (York: Ebor Press, 1974)

Armitage Robinson, J, *Somerset Historical Essays* (Oxford: Oxford University Press, 1921/Leopold Classic Library Reprint)

Bailey, Maggie, 'Ælfwynn, second lady of the Mercians' from Higham N.J. (ed) & Hill, D.H. (ed) *Edward the Elder* (Abingdon: Routledge, 2001)

Barlow, Frank, *The Feudal kingdom of England 1042–1216* (London: Longman Group Ltd, 1980)

Barlow, Frank, *William Rufus* (California: California University Press, 1983)

Barlow, Frank, *The Godwins* (Abingdon: Routledge, 2002)

Bassett, Steven, 'In Search of the origins of Anglo-Saxon Kingdoms' from Bassett, Steven (ed), *The Origins of the Anglo-Saxon Kingdoms* (Leicester: Leicester University Press, 1989)

Baxter, Stephen, *The Earls of Mercia: Lordship and Power in Later Anglo-Saxon England* (Oxford: Oxford University Press, 2007)

Biddle, Martin, & Kjølbye-Biddle, Birthe, 'The Repton Stone' from Clemoes, P, (ed), *Anglo-Saxon England Volume 14* (Cambridge: Cambridge University Press, 1985)

Blackburn, Mark, 'The London mint in the Reign of Alfred' from Blackburn, Mark A.S., & Dumville, David, N., *Kings, Currency and Alliances* (Woodbridge: Boydell, 1998)

Blackburn, Mark, & Keynes, Simon, 'A Corpus of the Cross-and-Lozenge and Related Coinages of Alfred, Ceolwulf II and Archbishop Æthelred' from Blackburn, Mark A.S., & Dumville, David, N., *Kings, Currency and Alliances* (Woodbridge: Boydell, 1998)

Brady, Lindy, *Writing the Welsh Borderlands in Anglo-Saxon England* (Manchester: Manchester University Press, 2017)

Brooks, Nicholas, 'The Formation of the Mercian Kingdom' from Bassett, Steven (ed), *The Origins of the Anglo-Saxon Kingdoms* (Leicester: Leicester University Press, 1989)

Brooks, Nicholas, *Early History of the Church of Canterbury* (Leicester: Leicester University Press, 1996)

Brooks, Nicholas, *Anglo-Saxon Myths: State and Church 400–1066* (London: Hambledon Press, 2000)

Campbell, Alistair, (ed) & Keynes, Simon, *Encomium Emmæ Reginæ* (Cambridge: Cambridge University Press, 1998)

Campbell, James, 'The First Christian Kings' from Campbell J. (ed) *The Anglo-Saxons* (London: Penguin Books, 1991)

Campbell, James, 'What is Not Known About the Reign of Edward the Elder' from Higham N.J. (ed), & Hill, D.H. (ed), *Edward the Elder* (Abingdon: Routledge, 2001)

Charles-Edwards, Thomas, 'Early Medieval Kingships in the British Isles' from Bassett, Steven (ed), *The Origins of the Anglo-Saxon Kingdoms* (Leicester: Leicester University Press, 1989)

Charles-Edwards, T.M., *Wales and the Britons, 350–1064* (Oxford: Oxford University Press, 2013)

Chibnall, Marjorie, (ed & trans), *The Gesta Guillelmi of William of Poitiers* (Oxford: Oxford University Press, 1998)

Chibnall, Marjorie, (ed & trans), *The Ecclesiastical History of Orderic Vitalis: Volume II: Books III & IV: Bks.3 & 4 Vol 2* (Oxford: Oxford University Press, 1969 (1999))

Colgrave, Bertram, (trans), *Felix's Life of St Guthlac* (Cambridge: Cambridge University Press, 1985)

Crossley-Holland, Kevin, *The Anglo-Saxon World* (Woodbridge: The Boydell Press, 1982/2002)

Darlington R.R., (ed), McGurk, P., (ed), Bray, Jennifer, (transl), *The Chronicle of John of Worcester* (Oxford: Clarendon Press, 1995)

Davies, Wendy, 'Annals and the Origin of Mercia' from Dornier, Ann, (ed), *Mercian Studies* (Leicester: Leicester University Press, 1977)

Duffus Hardy, Thomas, & Trice Martin, Charles, (ed), *Lestorie des Engles Solum la Translacion Maistre Geffrei Gaimar Vol 2 Translation* (Cambridge: Cambridge University Press, 1889/2012)

Dugdale, William, *Monasticon Anglicanum, or the History of the Ancient Abbies, and other Monasteries, Hospitals, Cathedral and Collegiate Churches in England and Wales* (London: Keble, 1693/Forgotten Books, 2015)

Dumville, David, 'The Anglian Collection of Royal Genealogies and Regnal Lists' Clemoes, P., (ed), *Anglo-Saxon England Volume 5* (Cambridge: Cambridge University Press, 1976)

Dumville, David, 'Essex, Middle Anglia and the Expansion of Mercia in the South-East Midlands' from Bassett, Steven, (ed), *The Origins of the Anglo-Saxon Kingdoms* (Leicester: Leicester University Press, 1989)

Dumville, David, 'The Tribal Hidage: An Introduction to its Texts and their History' from Bassett, Steven, (ed), *The Origins of the Anglo-Saxon Kingdoms* (Leicester: Leicester University Press, 1989)

Eagles, Bruce, 'Lindsey' from Bassett, Steven, (ed), *The Origins of the Anglo-Saxon Kingdoms* (Leicester: Leicester University Press, 1989)

Fairweather, Janet, (trans), *Liber Eliensis* (Woodbridge: Boydell Press, 2005)

Featherstone, Peter, 'The Tribal Hidage and the Ealdormen of Mercia' from Brown, Michelle P., & Farr, Carol Ann, (ed), *Mercia: An Anglo-Saxon Kingdom in Europe* (Leicester: Leicester University Press, 2001)

Finberg, H.P.R., *The Early Charters of the West Midlands* (Leicester: Leicester University Press, 1972)

Finberg, H.P.R., *The Formation of England 550–1042* (St Albans: Paladin, 1977)

Fisher, D.J.V., *The Anglo-Saxon Age* (Harlow: Longman, 1973)

Fletcher, Richard, *Roman Britain & Anglo-Saxon England 55BC–AD1066* (Mechanicsburg: Stackpole, 1989)

Fletcher, Richard, *Bloodfeud: Murder and Revenge in Anglo-Saxon England* (London: BCA by arrangement with Allen Lane, Penguin Press, 2002)

Foot, Sarah, *Athelstan, the First king of England* (Yale University Press, 2012 (Reprint)

Forester, Thomas, (trans & Ed) *The Chronicle of Henry of Huntingdon* (London: Bohn, 1853/Nabu Public Domain Reprints)

Gannon, Anna, *The Iconography of Anglo-Saxon Coinage* (Oxford: Oxford University Press, 2003)

Garmonsway, G.N., (trans), *The Anglo-Saxon Chronicle* (London: JM. Dent & Sons, 1984)

Gelling, Margaret, *Signposts to the Past* (Chichester: Phillimore, 1978)

Gelling, Margaret, 'The Early History of Western Mercia' from Bassett, Steven, (ed), *The Origins of the Anglo-Saxon Kingdoms* (Leicester: Leicester University Press, 1989)

Giles, J.A., (trans), William of Malmesbury, *Chronicle of the Kings of England* (London: Bohn, 1847/Forgotten Books, 2015)

Giles, J.A., (trans), Roger of Wendover, *Flowers of History* (London: Bohn, 1849/Forgotten Books, 2012)

Grierson, Philip, & Blackburn, Mark, *Medieval European Coinage Volume 1* (Cambridge: Cambridge University Press, 1986)

Hart, Cyril, 'Athelstan 'Half-King' and his Family' from Clemoes, P, (ed), *Anglo-Saxon England Volume 2* (Cambridge: Cambridge University Press, 1973)

Hart, C.R., *The Early Charters of Northern England and the North Midlands* (Leicester: Leicester University Press, 1975)

Hart, Cyril, 'The Kingdom of Mercia' from Dornier, Ann, (ed), *Mercian Studies* (Leicester: Leicester University Press, 1977)

Henson, Donald, *A Guide to Late Anglo-Saxon England* (Thetford: Anglo-Saxon Books, 1998)

Higham, N.J., 'Edward the Elder's Reputation' from Higham N.J., (ed) & Hill, D.H., (ed) *Edward the Elder* (Abingdon: Routledge, 2001)

Higham, Nicholas J., 'King Cearl, the Battle of Chester and the Origins of the Mercian Overkingship' from *Midland History, Volume 17, – Issue 1* (Felpham: Phillimore, 1992)

Hill, David, *An Atlas of Anglo-Saxon England* (Oxford: Basil Blackwell, 1981)

Hill, David, 'Mercians: The Dwellers on the Boundary' from Brown, Michelle P., & Farr, Carol Ann, (ed), *Mercia: An Anglo-Saxon Kingdom in Europe* (Leicester: Leicester University Press, 2001)

Hill, Paul, *The Age of Athelstan: Britain's Forgotten History* (Stroud: Tempus, 2004)

Hollis, Stephanie, *Anglo-Saxon Women and the Church* (Woodbridge: Boydell Press, 1992)

Humble, Richard, *The Fall of Saxon England* (London: BCA by arrangement with Arthur Barker Ltd, 1975)

Insley, Charles, 'The Family of Wulfric Spott: an Anglo-Saxon Mercian Marcher Dynasty?' from Roffe, David, (ed), *The English and their Legacy 900–1200: Essays in Honour of Ann Williams* (Woodbridge: The Boydell Press, 2012)

Jayakumar, Shashi, 'Eadwig and Edgar: Politics, Propaganda, Faction' from Scragg, Donald, (ed), *Edgar King of the English, 959–975* Woodbridge: Boydell Press, 2008)

Jayakumar, Shashi, 'Reform and Retribution: the "anti-monastic reaction" in the Reign of Edward the Martyr' from Baxter, S., Karkov C., Nelson Janet L., Pelteret, D., (ed), *Early Medieval Studies in Memory of Patrick Wormald* (Abingdon: Routledge, 2016)

John, Eric, 'The Age of Edgar', 'The Return of the Vikings' and 'The End of Anglo-Saxon England' from Campbell J., (ed) *The Anglo-Saxons* (London: Penguin Books, 1991)

Johnson South, Ted, *Historia de Sancto Cuthberto* (Woodbridge: Boydell & Brewer, 2002)

Keene, Derek, 'Alfred and London' from Reuter, Timothy, (ed), *Alfred the Great: Papers from the Eleventh-Centenary Conferences* (Abingdon: Routledge, 2003)

Keynes, S., & Lapidge, M., *Alfred the Great* (London: Penguin Books, 1983)

Keynes, Simon, 'King Alfred and the Mercians' from Blackburn, Mark A.S., & Dumville, David, N., *Kings, Currency and Alliances* (Woodbridge: Boydell, 1998)

Keynes, Simon, 'Mercia and Wessex in the Ninth Century' from Brown, Michelle P., & Farr, Carol Ann, (ed), *Mercia: An Anglo-Saxon Kingdom in Europe* (Leicester: Leicester University Press, 2001)

Keynes, Simon, 'Edgar, *Rex Admirabilis*' from Scragg, Donald (ed), *Edgar King of the English, 959–975* (Woodbridge: Boydell Press, 2008)

King, Vanessa 'From Minster to Manor: The Early History of Bredon' from Roffe, David, (ed), *The English and their Legacy 900–1200: Essays in Honour of Ann Williams* (Woodbridge: The Boydell Press, 2012)

Kirby D.P., *The Earliest English Kings* (Abingdon: Routledge, 1992)

Koch, John T., (trans) *Cunedda, Cynan, Cadwallon, Cynddylan Four Welsh Poems and Britain 383–655* (Aberystwyth: University of Wales, 2013)

Lancaster, Joan C., *The Coventry Forged Charters: A Reconsideration* in Historical Research Volume 27, Issue 76, pages 113–140, November, 1954

Lapidge, Michael, (trans & ed), Byrhtferth of Ramsey, *The Lives of St Oswald and St Ecgwine* (Oxford: Oxford University Press, 2010)

Lawson, MK, *Cnut: England's Viking King* (Stroud: Tempus, 2004)

Leahy, Kevin, *Anglo-Saxon Crafts* (Stroud: Tempus, 2003)

Lewis, C.P., 'Edgar, Chester, and the Kingdom of the Mercians, 957–9' from Scragg, Donald (Ed), *Edgar King of the English, 959–975* (Woodbridge: Boydell Press, 2008)

Love, Rosalind C., (ed & trans), *Three Eleventh-Century Anglo-Latin Saints' Lives: Vita S Birini, Vita et Miracula S Kenelmi, Vita S Rumwoldi* (Oxford: Clarendon Press, 1996)

Love, Rosalind, C., (ed & trans), *Goscelin of Saint-Bertin: The Hagiography of the Female Saints of Ely* (Oxford: Clarendon/Oxford University Press, 2004)

Lund, Niels, 'King Edgar and the Danelaw' from *Medieval Scandinavian Studies* 9, 1976

Marren, Peter, *Battles of the Dark Ages* (Barnsley: Pen & Sword, 2006)

Marten, Lucy 'Meet the Swarts: Tracing a Thegnly Family in late Anglo-Saxon England' from Roffe, David, (ed), *The English and their Legacy 900–1200: Essays in Honour of Ann Williams* (Woodbridge: The Boydell Press, 2012)

Maund, Kari, *The Welsh Kings* (Stroud: Tempus, 2000)

McClure, Judith, & Collins Roger, (ed) *Bede: The Ecclesiastical History of the English People* (Oxford: Oxford University Press, 1994)

Mellows, Charles, & Mellows, William Thomas, *The Peterborough Chronicle of Hugh Candidus* (Peterborough: Peterborough Museum Society, 1980)

Metcalf, DM, 'Monetary Affairs in Mercia in the time of Æthelbald' from Dornier, Ann, (ed), *Mercian Studies* (Leicester: Leicester University Press, 1977)

Miller, Molly, 'The Dates of Deira' from Clemoes, P., (ed), *Anglo-Saxon England Volume 8* (Cambridge: Cambridge University Press, 1979)

Morris, Christopher J., *Marriage and Murder in Eleventh-Century Northumbria* (York: Borthwick Institute Publications, 1992)

Nelson, Janet, 'The First Use of the Second Anglo-Saxon Ordo' from Barrow, Julia & Wareham Andrew, *Myth, Rulership, Church and Charters: Essays in Honour of Nicholas Brooks* (Abingdon: Routledge, 2016)

Owen-Crocker, Gale R., *Dress in Anglo-Saxon England* (Woodbridge: The Boydell Press, 2004)

Pestell, Tim, *Landscapes of Monastic Foundation: The Establishment of Religious Houses in East Anglia, c.650–1200* (Woodbridge: Boydell & Brewer, 2004)

Preest, David, (trans), William of Malmesbury, *Gesta Pontificum Anglorum* (Woodbridge: Boydell Press, 2002)

Pollington, Stephen, *The Mead-Hall* (Thetford: Anglo-Saxon Books, 2003)

Pretty, Kate, 'Defining the Magonsæte' from Bassett, Steven, (ed), *The Origins of the Anglo-Saxon Kingdoms* (Leicester: Leicester University Press, 1989)

Robertson, A.J., *Anglo-Saxon Charters* (Cambridge: Cambridge University Press, 1956)

Rollason, D.W., 'The Cults of Murdered Royal Saints in Anglo-Saxon England', from Clemoes, P., (ed), *Anglo-Saxon England Volume 11* (Cambridge: Cambridge University Press, 1983)

Ronay, Gabriel, *The Lost king of England* (Woodbridge: The Boydell Press, 1989)

Rowley, Sharon M., *The Old English Version of Bede's Historia Ecclesiastica* (Cambridge: D.S. Brewer, 2011)

Sawyer, P.H., 'The Charters of Burton Abbey and the Unification of England' from *Northern History 10* (1975)

Sims-Williams, Patrick, *Religion and Literature in Western England 600–800* (Cambridge: Cambridge University Press, 1990)

Slater, Terry, & Goose, Nigel, *A County of Small Towns: The Development of Hertfordshire's Urban Landscape to 1800* (Hatfield: University of Hertfordshire Press, 2008)

Stafford, Pauline, 'The Reign of Æthelred II, A Study in the Limitations on Royal Policy and Actions' from Hill, David, (ed), *Ethelred the Unready: Papers from the Millenary Conference* (Oxford: BAR, 1978)

Stafford, Pauline, *Queen Emma and Queen Edith* (Oxford: Blackwell Publishers, 1997)

Stafford, Pauline, 'Political Women in Mercia, Eighth to Early Tenth Centuries' from Brown, Michelle P., & Farr, Carol Ann, (ed), *Mercia: An Anglo-Saxon Kingdom in Europe* (Leicester: Leicester University Press, 2001)

Stafford, Pauline, 'The Annals of Æthelflæd: Annals, History and Politics in Early Tenth-Century England' from Barrow, Julia & Wareham Andrew, *Myth, Rulership, Church and Charters: Essays in Honour of Nicholas Brooks* (Abingdon: Routledge, 2016)

Stenton, Frank, *Early History of the Abbey of Abingdon* (Reading: University College Press, 1913/Leopold Classic Library Reprint)

Stenton, Frank, 'Medeshamstede and its Colonies' from Stenton, Doris Mary, (ed), *Preparatory to Anglo-Saxon England: Being the Collected Papers of Frank Merry Stenton* (Oxford: Oxford University Press, 1970)

Stenton, Frank, 'The Danes in England' from Stenton, Doris Mary, (ed), *Preparatory to Anglo-Saxon England: Being the Collected Papers of Frank Merry Stenton* (Oxford: Oxford University Press, 1970)

Stenton, Frank, 'Pre-Conquest Herefordshire' from Stenton, Doris Mary, (ed), *Preparatory to Anglo-Saxon England: Being the Collected Papers of Frank Merry Stenton* (Oxford: Oxford University Press, 1970)

Stenton, Frank, 'Lindsey and its Kings' from Stenton, Doris Mary, (ed), *Preparatory to Anglo-Saxon England: Being the Collected Papers of Frank Merry Stenton* (Oxford: Oxford University Press, 1970)

Stenton, Frank, 'The Supremacy of the Mercian Kings' from Stenton, Doris Mary, (ed), *Preparatory to Anglo-Saxon England: Being the Collected Papers of Frank Merry Stenton* (Oxford: Oxford University Press, 1970)

Stenton, Frank, *Anglo-Saxon England* (Oxford: Oxford University Press, 1971 (1989))

Symons, Thomas, (trans), *Regularis Concordia* (Oxford: Oxford University Press, 1983)

Thacker, Alan, 'Kings, Saints and Monasteries in Pre-Viking Mercia' from *Midland History Vol 10, Issue 1* (Felpham: Phillimore, 1985)

Thompson, Victoria, *Dying and Death in Later Anglo-Saxon England* (Woodbridge: Boydell Press, 2004)

Thorpe, B., *Diplomatarium Anglicum Aevi Saxonici: A Collection of English Charters, from the Reign of King Aethelberht of Kent, A. D. Dc.v. to That of William the Conqueror* (London: Macmillan, 1865/2008)

Wainwright, F.T., 'Æthelflæd Lady of the Mercians' from Clemoes, Peter, (ed), *The Anglo-Saxons: Studies in Some Aspects of their History and Culture Presented to Bruce Dickens* (London: Bowes & Bowes, 1959)

Wallace-Hadrill, J.M., *Early Germanic Kingship in England and on the Continent* (Oxford: Oxford University Press, 1971)

Webb, J.F., & Farmer, D.H., 'Eddius Stephanus: Life of Wilfrid' from *The Age of Bede* (London: Penguin Books, 1983/1998)

Whitehead Annie, 'In Search of Dunmail' from *Cumbria Magazine Vol 66, No 1*, April, 2016

Whitehead, Annie, 'Rioting in the Harlot's Embrace: Matrimony and Sanctimony in Anglo-Saxon England' from *Sexuality and its Impact on History: The British Stripped Bare* (Barnsley: Pen & Sword, 2018)

Whitelock, Dorothy, *Anglo-Saxon Wills* (Cambridge: Cambridge University Press, 1930/2011)

Whitelock, Dorothy, *The Audience of Beowulf* (Oxford: Clarendon Press, 1951 [1964])

Whitelock, Dorothy, *English Historical Documents Volume I c. 500–1042* (Oxford: Oxford University Press, 1955)

Whitelock, Dorothy, 'The Dealings of the Kings of England with Northumbria in the Tenth and Eleventh Centuries' from Clemoes, Peter (ed), *The Anglo-Saxons: Studies in Some Aspects of their History and Culture Presented to Bruce Dickens* (London: Bowes & Bowes, 1959)

Williams, Ann, 'Princeps Merciorum gentis: The Family, Career and Connections of Ælfhere, Ealdorman of Mercia, 956–83' from Clemoes, P, (ed), *Anglo-Saxon England Volume 10* (Cambridge: Cambridge University Press, 1982)

Williams, Ann, 'Cockles Amongst the Wheat: Danes and English in the Western Midlands in the First Half of the Eleventh Century' from *Midland History 11*, 1985 – pre-publication personal copy

Williams, Ann, Smyth, A.P., Kirby, D.P., *A Biographical Dictionary of Dark Age Britain: England, Scotland and Wales, c.500–c. 1050* (London: B.A. Seaby, 1991)

Williams, Ann, *Kingship and Government in Pre-Conquest England 500–1066* (Basingstoke: Macmillan Press, 1999)

Williams, Ann, Æthelred the Unready: The Ill-Counselled King (London: Hambledon and London, 2003)

Williams, Ann 'An Outing on the Dee: King Edgar at Chester, AD 973' from Medieaval Scandinavia 14 (Belgium: Brepols, 2004) pre-publication personal copy

Woolf, R, 'The Ideal of Men Dying with their Lord in the Germania and in the Battle of Maldon' from Clemoes, P, (ed), *Anglo-Saxon England Volume 5* (Cambridge: Cambridge University Press, 1976)

Wormald, Patrick, 'The Age of Bede and Æthelbald', 'The Age of Offa and Alcuin' and 'The Ninth Century' from Campbell J., (ed) *The Anglo-Saxons* (London: Penguin Books, 1991)

Yorke, Barbara, 'The Kingdom of the East Saxons' from Clemoes, P, (ed), *Anglo-Saxon England Volume 14* (Cambridge: Cambridge University Press, 1985)

Yorke, Barbara, *Kings and Kingdoms of Early Anglo-Saxon England* (Abingdon: Routledge, 1990)

Yorke, Barbara, 'Edward as Ætheling' from Higham N.J., (ed), & Hill, D.H., (ed), *Edward the Elder* (Abingdon: Routledge, 2001)

Yorke, Barbara, 'The Origins of Mercia' from Brown, Michelle P., & Farr, Carol Ann, (ed), *Mercia: An Anglo-Saxon Kingdom in Europe* (Leicester: Leicester University Press, 2001)

Yorke, Barbara, 'The Women in Edgar's Life' from Scragg, Donald, (ed), *Edgar King of the English, 959–975* (Woodbridge: Boydell Press, 2008)

Online Sources:

Archibald, Marion M, Fenwick Valerie, with Cowell, M.R., *A Sceat of Ethelbert I of East Anglia and Recent Finds of Coins of Beonna* https://www.britnumsoc.org/publications/Digital%20BNJ/pdfs/1995_BNJ_65_3.pdf

BBC News Wales http://www.bbc.co.uk/news/uk-wales-mid-wales-43084088

BBC News Wales http://www.bbc.co.uk/news/uk-wales-mid-wales-26921202

Constitutiones Et Alia Ad Historiam Ecclesiae Anglicanae Spectantia' https://books.google.co.uk/

Dig Ventures. Com, https://digventures.com/2018/02/radiocarbon-dating-confirms-skeletons-found-in-vicarage-garden-are-probably-viking/

Dugdale, William, Sir, *The antiquities of Warwickshire illustrated : from records, leiger-books, manuscripts, charters, evidences, tombes, and armes : beautified with maps, prospects, and portraictures* https://archive.org/details/antiquitiesofwar00dugd

Firth, Matt, '*Wicked Queens and Martyred Kings: the 794 Beheading of St Æthelberht of East Anglia*', The Postgrad Chronicles June 5 2017 https://thepostgradchroniclessite.wordpress.com/2017/06/05/a-brief-biography-of-aethelberht-of-east-anglia/

Bibliography

Firth, Matt, Wicked Queens and Martyred Kings: the 891 murder of St Kenelm of Mercia https://thepostgradchroniclessite.wordpress.com/2017/03/27/a-brief-biography-of-kenelm-of-mercia/

Forester, Thomas, *The chronicle of Florence of Worcester with the two continuations; comprising annals of English history, from the departure of the Romans to the reign of Edward I* (London: H.G. Bohn 1854) https://archive.org/details/chronicleofflore00flor

Forsman, Deanna '*An Appeal to Rome: Anglo-Saxon Dispute Settlement, 800–810*' The Heroic Age Issue 6 Spring 2003 University of California, Los Angeles http://www.heroicage.org/issues/6/forsman.html

Furness, Hannah, '*Viking hoard discovery reveals little-known king 'airbrushed from history*" The Telegraph, 10 December 2015 http://www.telegraph.co.uk/news/earth/environment/archaeology/12043749/British-Museum-unveils-unique-hoard-of-Viking-coins.html

Giles, JA, *Old English chronicles: including Ethelwerd's chronicle, Asser's Life of Alfred, Geoffrey of Monmouth's British history, Gildas, Nennius, together with the spurious Chronicle of Richard of Cirencester* (London: George Bell & Sons 1906) via https://archive.org

Greer Fein, Susanna, *Art. 116, De martirio sancti Wistani* University of Rochester http://d.lib.rochester.edu/teams/text/fein-harley2253-volume-3-article-116

Haddan, Arthur West, & Stubbs, William *Councils and ecclesiastical documents relating to Great Britain and Ireland Volume III* (Oxford: Oxford University Press, 1871) https://archive.org/details/councilsecclesia03hadduoft

Halloran, Kevin, 'The War for Mercia, 942–943' from *Midland History Volume 41* http://www.tandfonline.com/doi/abs/10.1080/0047729X.2016.1159855

Hearne T, *Hemingi chartularium ecclesiæ Wigorniensis, descripsit ediditque Volume 2* https://play.google.com/store/books/details?id=0FAVAAAAQAAJ&rdid=book-0FAVAAAAQAAJ&rdot=1

Ingulph's chronicle of the abbey of Croyland with the continuations by Peter of Blois and anonymous writers (London: Bohn 1854) https://archive.org/details/ingulphschronic00ingu

Irish Archaeological and Celtic Society, Dublin; MacFirbis, Duald, O'Donovan, John, *Annals of Ireland. Three fragments, copied from ancient sources by Dubhaltach MacFirbisigh; and edited, with a translation and notes, from a manuscript preserved in the Burgundian Library at Brussels* (Dublin: Irish Archaeological and Celtic Society, 1860) https://archive.org/details/annalsofirelandt00irisuoft

John, Eric, *The King and the Monks in the Tenth Century Reformation* https://www.escholar.manchester.ac.uk/api/datastream?publicationPid=uk-ac-man-scw:1m2044&datastreamId=POST-PEER-REVIEW-PUBLISHERS-DOCUMENT.PDF

Jones, Mary, '*Annales Cambriae*' http://www.maryjones.us/ctexts/annales.html

Kessler, Peter, & Dawson, Edward, '*Mercia's British Alliance*' Anglo-Saxon England, The History Files, 11 March 2016 http://www.historyfiles.co.uk/FeaturesBritain/EnglandMercia01.htm

Keynes, Simon, Eadric Streona, ONDB http://www.oxforddnb.
com/view/10.1093/ref:odnb/9780198614128.001.0001/odnb-
9780198614128-e-8511

King's College London & University of Cambridge. Prosopography of Anglo-
Saxon England. http://www.pase.ac.uk/index.html

King's College London & University of Cambridge. The Electronic Sawyer.
http://www.esawyer.org.uk/about/index.html

Kylie, Edward, *The English Correspondence of St Boniface* Microform https://
archive.org/details/cihm_84747

Liebermann, Felix *Die Heiligen Englands: Angelsächsisch und Lateinisch*
(Hanover: Hahn 1889) https://archive.org/details/dieheiligenengl00liebgoog

Medieval Histories: The 'Lost' Tribal Hidage: http://www.medievalhistories.
com/lost-tribal-hidage/

Miller, Sean, Anglo-Saxon Charters (Anglo-Saxons.net) http://www.anglo-
saxons.net/hwaet/

Monk, C. (2018) *The anonymous tract known as Be Mircna Laga ('Concerning
Laws of the Mercians')*, Textus Roffensis, *f. 39v;* Translated from Old English
and edited. Rochester: Rochester Cathedral Research Guild. http://www.
rochestercathedralresearchguild.org/

Morris, Ian, Ledbury Reporter, *'Archaeologist enters debate over exact site
of King Offa's Herefordshire palace'* http://www.ledburyreporter.co.uk/
news/15711439.Archaeologist_enters_debate_over_exact_site_of_King_
Offa___s_Herefordshire_palace/

Records of Buckinghamshire Vols 18 and 31, Bailey and Hohler http://www.
bucksas.org.uk/offprintsbyvolume.html#1995

Roffe, David, *The Origins of Derbyshire* (Derbyshire Archaeological
Journal 106) http://archaeologydataservice.ac.uk/archiveDS/
archiveDownload?t=arch-2300-1/dissemination/pdf/106/DAJ_
v106_1986_102–122.pdf

Roffe, David, 'Hereward "the Wake" and the Barony of Bourne: a Reassessment
of a Fenland Legend' from *Lincolnshire History and Archaeology* 29 (1994)
7–10 http://www.roffe.co.uk/articles/hereward.htm

Royal Irish Academy; Maguire, Cathal MacMaghnusa, O'Cassidy, Rory,
Hennessy, W. M. (William Maunsell), MacCarthy, Batholomew *Annala Uladh
= Annals of Ulster otherwise, Annala Senait, Annals of Senat : a chronicle
of Irish affairs* (DubliHM Stationery Office, 1897–1902) https://archive.org/
details/annalauladhannal01royauoft

Taylor, Edgar (trans) *Master Wace, his chronicle of the Norman conquest from
the Roman de Rou* (Toronto: University of Toronto, 1837) https://archive.
org/details/masterwacehischr00waceuoft

The Annals of Tigernach University College Cork Digitised Manuscripts https://
celt.ucc.ie//published/T100002A/index.html

The Ashmolean https://www.ashmolean.org/watlington-hoard

*The chronicle of Florence of Worcester with the two continuations; comprising
annals of English history, from the departure of the Romans to the reign of*

Edward I. Translated from the Latin with notes and illustrations (London: Bohn 1854) https://archive.org/details/chronicleofflore00flor

The Telegraph http://www.telegraph.co.uk/news/earth/environment/archaeology/12043749/British-Museum-unveils-unique-hoard-of-Viking-coins.htmlY Gododdin http://www.damowords.co.uk/pdf/Y_Gododdin.pdf

Thompson, Aaron, Giles, G.A. *Geoffrey of Monmouth's History of the Kings of Britain* York University http://www.yorku.ca/inpar/geoffrey_thompson.pdfNennius *Historia Brittonum* Transl Giles, G.A. York University http://www.yorku.ca/inpar/nennius_giles.pdf

Welsh Annals https://sourcebooks.fordham.edu/source/annalescambriae.asp

Wilkins, David (Sumptibus R. Gosling, 1737), '*Concilia Magnae Britanniae Et Hiberniae, a Synodo Verolamiensi A.D. CCCC XLVI. Ad Londinensem A.D. M DCCXVII. Accedunt*

Whitehead, Annie, *The Attack on Llangorse* https://englishhistoryauthors.blogspot.co.uk/2016/06/the-attack-on-llangorse-19th-june-ad916.html

Williams, John, Caradoc of Llancarvan, *Brut y Tywysogion: or, The chronicle of the Princes* https://archive.org/details/brutytywysogiono00cara

Index